THE POETRY OF MICHELANGELO

Other Volumes on the Renaissance by the Author

Critical Theory and Practice of the Pléiade
(Cambridge, Mass.: Harvard University Press, 1942
New York: Octagon Books, 1966)

Platonism in French Renaissance Poetry, with Robert V. Merrill
(New York: New York University Press, 1957)

The Peregrine Muse: Studies in Comparative Renaissance Literature
(Chapel Hill: University of North Carolina Press, 1959)

Picta Poesis: Humanistic and Literary Theory in Renaissance Emblem Books
(Rome: Edizioni di storia e letteratura, 1960)

Michelangelo's Theory of Art
(New York: New York University Press, 1961; New York: Gramercy Press, 1963;
London: Routledge and Kegan Paul, 1963; Milan: Mondadori [Il Saggiatore], 1964)

Michelangelo: A Self-Portrait
(New York: Prentice-Hall, 1963)

Michelangelo scultore, with others
(Rome: Curcio, 1964)

Michelangelo, editor
(New York: Braziller, 1966)

THE POETRY OF MICHELANGELO

ROBERT J. CLEMENTS

NEW YORK UNIVERSITY PRESS • 1965

Library of Congress Catalog Card Number: 65–19514

Manufactured in the United States of America

Designed by Sidney Feinberg

DEDICATED TO HER
OF THE PAULINE CHAPEL

PREFACE

After rejecting the plan to suspend a scaffold for the painting of the Sistine Ceiling, Michelangelo found himself with so much rope left that an assistant sold it and dowered two daughters. When I had completed two books of long gestation, *Michelangelo's Theory of Art* and *Michelangelo: A Self-Portrait*, I found that I might yet dower readers with some leftover reflections on the artist's poetry. It soon became obvious to me that despite the brilliant and erudite writing devoted to Michelangelo's art, no similar quantity or even quality of scholarship had been lavished on the *Rime*. There was, indeed, a great deal left to be said about this challenging corpus of poetry, abandoned by Rilke and other translators as too difficult —a great deal remaining to be said about this long-neglected poet, now hailed by many as the foremost madrigalist of the Italian Cinquecento.

Ideally, the excerpts from Michelangelo's poetry in the present volume should have been preserved and presented in the original Italian. Translations seem at best, in the intelligent metaphor of Cervantes, the reverse side of a tapestry. However, English seemed called for in this book, and as inclusion of both Italian and English texts would have made too bulky a volume, the verses are given as a rule in English. Many of these translations were undertaken by poets of distinction: Wordsworth, Southey, Longfellow, Emerson, Norton, Santayana, among others. Usually, attempts to retain Michelangelo's meter and rhyme have resulted in translations at one or more removes from the original thought. Sometimes translations by good poets were based upon faulty readings of early editions. For these two reasons, I have had to reject some translations which it would have been convenient to use. A third obstacle to honest and usable Englishings has been the desire of translators to give the English a finished quality lacking in many of Michelangelo's originals. The best corpus of English translations to date is that of Creighton Gilbert (see Bibliography), in which the translator has sagaciously abandoned the goal of rhyme for a freer rendering in assonance. The best corpus of the original *Rime* is that prepared by Enzo Noè Girardi (see Bibliography), in which the poems are presented in a carefully established chronological order.

For the readers who would like to refer to the original Italian versions, each excerpt will carry the number assigned to it in Girardi (= G). For them we add an index of Italian first lines. Indeed, such readers are reminded of the availability of the Italian edition of this present study (Mondadori, II Saggiatore, Milan, 1966), which gives throughout examples or excerpts in Italian. Quotations from the letters refer to the Milanesi edition of 1875, and are identified by capital Roman numerals. In the present volume discussion of style or vocabulary (alliteration, euphony, echo device, etc.) and of plagiarism will sometimes dictate that the original Italian verses be presented. In such cases it will be the Frey readings we shall present, as being truer to Michelangelo's own autographs. (Girardi supplies these only in his critical apparatus.) The names of the translators accompany the English versions; if no name is supplied, the version is my own. Whereas my own translations will hardly be hailed as lyric achievements, they will have the one merit, crucial for this study, of adhering closely to the original thought. Michelangelo's thought is the subject and the object of this book. As the critics and historians unanimously agree, Michelangelo the poet was less a stylist than a thinker.

The reader is asked to understand that certain verses of Michelangelo may be utilised two or three times throughout the book, as illustrative of different approaches to his thought. Cross-references will identify these inevitable repetitions, when the cross-reference affords translations or additional information. However, the reader might appreciate that occasional repetitions of a passage at least spare him the interruption of tracking down cross-references.

Progress on this volume was accelerated by a sabbatical year and a Fulbright research grant to Rome and Florence. In Italy I was able to use the magnificent libraries, study in hand the autographs of the poetry, and revisit the works of art with which I was correlating the poetry. The interrelationships of Michelangelo's art and poetry are such that no one ignorant of the latter can claim to understand well the artistic masterpieces. Especially, I was able to discuss the *Rime* with old friends and colleagues, even imposing critical readings of my pages on them. I am indebted to Professors Giacomo Debenedetti, Vittore Branca, Enzo Noè Girardi, Ulrich Middeldorf, Mario Praz, Natalino Sapegno, and especially Eugenio Battisti. I am grateful for the encouragement of the Litt. D. which the University of Rome conferred on me.

Closer at hand, I am appreciative of financial assistance from the Committee on Research of the Graduate School of New York University, and of editorial suggestions and continuing counsels by Mrs. Marcia Cobourn Wellwarth and Miss Kathleen McHugh. The editors of the *Publications of the Modern Language Association of America*, of *Italica*, of *Studies in Philology*, and of the *Acta* of the 400th Anniversary Convegno of Michelangelo Studies have consented to the reproduction of materials in Chapters III, XI, and XV.

Permission has been granted to reprint translated materials from the following works: Ralph Waldo Emerson, *Journals* (Boston: Houghton Mifflin, 1914); S. Elizabeth Hall, *Sonnets of Michelangelo* (London: Routledge and Kegan Paul, 1905); John Edward Taylor, *Michelangelo Considered as a Philosophic Poet* (London: John Murray, 1852); Nesca Robb, *Neoplatonism in the Italian Renaissance* (London: George Allen and Unwin, 1935); George Santayana, *Interpretations of Poetry and Religion* (New York: Charles Scribner's Sons, 1927). All other printed translations used are now in the public domain under existing copyright laws of the United States and the United Kingdom.

In his *Lirica del Cinquecento* Benedetto Croce writes of Michelangelo's *Rime* that "occasionally, in some of his comparisons, there is a reflection of the art he exercised." It is my hope that this volume will show to what extent the eminent historian with whom I once was privileged to spend an afternoon discussing these matters underestimated the interplay of Michelangelo's poetry and art.

R.J.C.

CONTENTS

PREFACE vii

PART I. Apollo-Apelles

1. THE ARTIST AND THE POETIC VOCATION 3

Origins of Michelangelo's fame as poet, 3. Periods of activity as poet, 7. Motivations for Michelangelo's turning to poetry, 10. Variety of theme and tone, 12. Editions of the *Rime*, 15.

2. STYLE AND LANGUAGE 22

Ut pictura poesis, 22. Form vs. content, 23. Poetic styles, 27. Language and spelling, 29. Metrics and rhyme, 32. Labor of the file, 33. Elements of style, 35.

3. MICHELANGELO AS A BAROQUE POET 38

Baroque values in Michelangelo's art, 38. Counter-Reformational elements, 40. Mystical and confessional character, 44. Irreality, tensions, abulia, conflicting polarities, *desengaño*, 46. Baroque stylistic devices, 54. The proto-baroque poet, 57.

4. ART AS THEMATIC IN THE POETRY 60

Michelangelo himself as a work of art, 60. Pride and modesty as artist, 61. God as source of art, 62. Theory of the *concetto*, 63. Sculpture, 66. Painting, drawing, casting, 70. Art *vs.* nature, 72. Portraiture, 73. Persuasions as artist: nudity, clothing, 74. Color, 76. Beauty, 77. Renunciation of art, 84.

5. POEMS AS EXEGESES OF SPECIFIC WORKS OF ART 89

1. The bronze statue of Julius II, 90. 2. The Sistine Ceiling, 91. 3. *The Creation of the Sun and Moon, Separation of Darkness and*

Light, The Four Times (Allegories) of Day, Day and Night, 93. 4. *The Night,* 98. 5. *Jeremiah,* 104. 6. *The Slaves,* 106. 7. *Resurrection of Lazarus,* 108. 8. *The Victory,* 109. 9. *Venus, Mars, and Cupid, Venus and Cupid,* 110. 10. *The Archers,* 112. 11. *Tityus,* 118. 12. *Phaeton,* 119. 13. *The Last Judgement,* 120. 14. *Christus Iudex,* 124. 15. *The Deposition,* 131.

6. THE FIFTY POEMS FOR THE TRUFFLES, TURTLE, AND TROUT 134

Cecchino Bracci, 134. Dominant themes of the epitaphs, 138. Michelangelo's relations with Cecchino, 144. Bowdlerising the poems and the relationship, 149.

7. THE LOST POEM ON THE BRONZE *DAVID* AND THE SCHOLIUM ON THE *DAVIDS* 154

The bronze *David,* 154. Translation of the "lost" poem, 155. The scholium on the Louvre drawings, 158.

8. ICONOGRAPHY AND ALLEGORY IN THE *RIME* 161

Allegory in the art, 161. Allegory in the poetry, 162. Giants, 166. Other figures, 169.

PART II. The Self-Portrait

9. PHYSICAL AND MORAL SELF-PORTRAIT 177

Self-portraiture in art, 177. In poetry, 178. Spiritual self-portraiture, 179.

10. MICHELANGELO INNAMORATO 184

Generalities about love, 185. Vittoria Colonna, 195. The conjectured young lady from Bologna, 202. Other alleged mistresses, 205. Love for males, with disclaimers in the *Rime,* 206. Tommaso Cavalieri, 209. Gherardo Perini and Febo di Poggio, 211. Love and death, 215. Old age and the renunciation of love, 216.

11. POETRY AS PRAYER AND CONFESSION 221

Prayers Michelangelo composed, 221. Fear for salvation, 223. Fear of Day of Wrath expressed in *Rime* while painting the *Last Judgement,* 226.

12. PLATONISM 228

Platonic education, 228. Platonic idealism, 229. Vision, 230. The winged soul, 232. Eros and Anteros, 234. Metempsychosis and reminiscence, 235.

13. POLITICAL, SOCIAL, AND SCIENTIFIC IDEAS 238

Politics, 238. Brutus, 243. Campanilism for Florence and Rome, 244. Scientific beliefs, 246. Finances and usury, 247.

14. EPISTOLARIO POETICO 251

Poems as letters, 251. Giovanni da Pistoia, 252. Julius II, 253. Gandolfo Porrino, 253. Luigi del Riccio, 254. Vasari, 254. Lodovico Beccadelli, 256.

15. BERNI AND MICHELANGELO'S BERNESQUE VERSE 259

The Bernesque vein, 259. Berni's capitolo to Michelangelo, 260. Michelangelo's capitolo in reply, 263. Other Bernesque pieces, 266. Influences of Berni on the *Rime*, 267.

16. MINOR THEMES AND MOTIFS 271

Fire, 271. The phoenix, 275. The mirror, 278. Fame, 279. External nature, 281.

17. OLD AGE, APPROACHING DEATH, AND RENUNCIATION 287

Thoughts of death, 287. Ballad of the dead, 289. Death of friends and family, 290. The "trembling hand sonnets," 293. Renunciation of life, 295.

18. APHORISMS 298

Philosophical maxims, 298. Optimistic and pessimistic aphorisms, 300. Those of greatest merit suffer most, 301. Causality, 303. Maxims on love, 304. On death, 306. Natural pessimism, 307. Jeremiads, 308. Balance sheet, 309.

PART III. Evaluations

19. SOURCES AND ORIGINALITY 313

Michelangelo's autonomy and ideas on imitation, 313. Dante, 315. Petrarch, 319. Boccaccio, 325. Poliziano, 325. Lorenzo il Magnifico, 326. Berni, 327. Accolti, 327. Vittoria Colonna, 328.

20. VALUES AND FAME AS POET 332

Michelangelo's posthumous fame, 333. Translations of the *Rime*, 334. Critical fortunes of the *Rime*: Germany, 335. England and America, 336. France, 338. Spain, 338. Elsewhere, 339. Schools of critical thought devoted to the *Rime*, 339. The *Rime* without Michelangelo are not the *Iliad* without Homer, 341.

BIBLIOGRAPHY 343
INDEX OF NAMES 349
INDEX OF WORKS OF ART 355
INDEX OF *RIME* 359

Ho visto qualche sua compositione;
Sono ignorante, e pur direi havelle
Lette tutte nel mezzo di Platone;
Sì ch'egli è nuovo Apollo e nuovo Apelle . . .

—Francesco Berni, *Capitolo a Sebastiano del Piombo*

Ne fu miracolo che egli riuscisse così grande
e quanto alla gravità delle sentenzie e quanto alla proprietà
delle parole; e fusse, come disse chi sapea che dirsi,
nuovo Apollo e nuovo Apelle.

—Benedetto Varchi, *Oratione funerale nell'essequie di Michelangelo*

Egli è nuovo Apelle e nuovo Apollo

—Pietro Bembo, *Rime*

PART I

Apollo-Apelles

1

THE ARTIST AND THE POETIC VOCATION

WHEREAS Michelangelo Buonarroti's painting, sculpture, and architectural monuments have been the objects of universal admiration since the moment of their completion—and even before completion, as in the case of the Sistine Vault—his poems have emerged into prominence only after years of relative obscurity.

The irony of this tardy fame is that Michelangelo was hailed as a major poet by his contemporaries. Just as he started to carve marble in a period lacking great sculpture, so did his poetry stand out more easily because of the paucity of great lyric verse in his lifetime. His *Rime* began to circulate early in the humanistic circles of Rome and Florence. Again ironically, it was the musical composers who first discovered Michelangelo as a poet. His conventional little madrigal, "Com' arò dunche ardire," complaining of the martyrdom of unrequited love, appeared in Naples as early as 1518 with *frottola* setting by Bartolomeo Tromboncino (whose own unrequited love led him to kill his wife and her lover). This appeared in the second book of *Fioretti di frottole, barzelletti, capitoli, strambotti* e *sonetti*. Even if Alfred Einstein and Leto Puliti are not impressed with the setting, it must have uplifted the artist then engaged in the unhappy task of getting marbles for the Façade of San Lorenzo. By 1533 his friend Luigi del Riccio, who pushed him in the direction of poetry, had given copies of Michelangelo's *Rime* to Constanzo Festa, first composer of *a cappella* madrigals and member of the Cappella Pontificia, and to the Parisian Jean de Conseil, composer attached to the pope. These musicians set two or more of Michelangelo's pieces to music, to his immense satisfaction and his outspoken modesty. He wrote to Sebastiano del Piombo from Florence in July (or August, according to Ramsden), 1533: "I've received the two madrigals, and Ser Giovan Francesco has had them sung several times; according to what I'm told, they're considered something marvelous for singing; surely the words weren't worth so much" (Letter CDXV).

It was about this time (1531–34) that the witty Francesco Berni hailed him in a *capitolo* as an "Apollo-Apelle," noting that Sebastiano del Piombo wrote words, while Michelangelo wrote "things." The fourth composer to help establish Michelangelo's fame as a poet was the illustrious Dutchman Jacob Archadelt, who wrote a four-voice setting of "Spargendo il senso il troppo ardor cocente," "Deh dimmi, Amor, se l'alma di costei," and its companion strophe "Io dico che fra noi potenti dei," including them in 1543 within his *Primo libro de' madrigali a quatro voci* (Venezia: appresso Francesco Rampazetto). The success of these madrigals in musical circles of the time is attested by the complimentary question of Donato Giannotti in his *Dialogi* (when Michelangelo was almost seventy), "Don't we hear sung by the most excellent musicians, among others, that madrigaletto of yours: 'Deh dimmi, Amor?' " (The setting given these eight lines, by the way, is a melancholy one.) During 1542 Michelangelo wrote a note of appreciation to the intermediary Del Riccio, who had approached Archadelt. The note is too brief for him to indulge in humble clichés and modest disclaimers: "Arcadente's [*sic*] song is considered very fine; and since, according to him, he intends to give no less pleasure to me than to you who requested it, I should not like to be ungrateful to him for such a favor." He suggests hurriedly that Del Riccio make some gift of textiles or money in his name.

Thus, from Tromboncino down to Hugo Wolf, Richard Strauss, Benjamin Britten, and others (see Chapter XIX), musicians have found lyrical qualities in the *Rime*. Although Enrico Bevilacqua has grumbled that it was not Michelangelo's talent as poet, but fame as artist, which drew the composers to him ("The poet's renown was already a half-guarantee of success for the musician"),[1] that talent is now widely recognised.

Luigi del Riccio was not the only friend circulating manuscripts of Michelangelo's verses. All the intimates with whom the artist shared his sonnets and madrigals—Vittoria Colonna, Francesco Berni, Giovanni Strozzi, Tommaso Cavalieri, Giorgio Vasari, Donato Giannotti, Lodovico Beccadelli, and others—were prominent in literary, ecclesiastical, and artistic circles, thus assuring that the poems would have wider hand-to-hand circulation. One can imagine the illustrious Vittoria Colonna, before the vicissitudes of her later life, exhibiting to her many friends her sonnets from Michelangelo, just as she had earlier passed around the manuscript of Castiglione's *Libro del Cortegiano* to the discomfiture of that worthy Mantuan. Michelangelo reciprocated by having the Marchioness's manuscript sonnets bound and by "lending them to many persons" (Letter CCXLIII).

In Florence, the counterpart of Luigi del Riccio as publicist of the poetry was Benedetto Varchi. On the second Lenten Sunday of 1546 Varchi read to the Florentine Academy a learned textual explication demonstrating the density of meaning contained in Michelangelo's most famous sonnet, "Non ha l'ottimo artista alcun concetto." Whatever moderns may think of it, Michelangelo's generation was impressed by this lecture. (Papini comments: "The commentary of Varchi, prolix and pedantic, with *arzigogolature* sometimes rhetorical and sometimes philosophical, larded with citations from Dante and Petrarch, drowned in a turbid sea of conceits the clear and lofty ideas of Michelangelo.")[2] In any case, when Luca Martini sent the published Libretto (Florence: Lorenzo Torrentino, 1549) to Michelangelo on behalf of Varchi, the artist indulged in unwonted hyperbole: "The sonnet comes from me all right, but the Commentary comes from heaven; it is truly a marvelous thing, I don't say in my judgement, but in that of worthy men, and especially Messer Donato Giannotti, who never tires of reading it."[3] (Michelangelo's disclaimer of being a literary critic will also be found in the footnote to his madrigal, "S'è ver, com'è, che dopo il corpo viva," where he again defers to Donato's judgement.) "As for the sonnet, I recognise it for what it is; but whatever it is, I cannot help taking a little pride in it, since it was the reason for such a fine and learned Commentary. But because I sense in the words and praises of the author of this Commentary that I am what I'm really not, I beg you to speak to him on my behalf, such as love, affection, and courtesy require. I request you to do this because I feel of little worth; and he who is held in good repute should not tempt fate; it is better to keep silent than to fall from high." The Libretto he is acknowledging was entitled *Due Lezzioni* and included a second lecture to the Academy which Varchi had delivered the following Sabbath on the rivalry of the arts: ("la maggioranza dell' arti, e quale sia più nobile, la Scultura o la Pittura"). The volume included as well Michelangelo's letter responding to Varchi's questionnaire on this contest of the arts.

The following year Giorgio Vasari published his life of Michelangelo as artist. He acknowledged Michelangelo's poetic status by including the quatrain composed in response to Giovanni Strozzi, "Caro m'è 'l sonno."

To complete the picture of appearances of Michelangelo's *Rime* during or close upon his lifetime, one must mention the publishing of two highly religious sonnets, "Scarco d'una importuna e greve salma" and "Mentre m'attrista e duol, parte m'è caro," in that Counter-Reformational Venice which found Michelangelo's reputation so impregnable that the Inquisitioners justified to Veronese the nudities in the Sistine Chapel. These two sonnets appeared in *De le rime di diversi nobili poeti toscani,* edited by Dionigi Atanagi in the year following Michelangelo's death. Finally, Donato Giannotti, like Varchi and Vasari, printed a few of Michelangelo's poems in his own published works.

The same Luigi del Riccio who distributed Michelangelo's poems to friends and composers also planned to publish a corpus of some 105 of them. Preparing the edition with Giannotti, Del Riccio encouraged Michelangelo to select the poems to be included. This florilegium of verses, printed together in Frey and subsequent editions (until Girardi's), constitutes the most finished of the poems, but not necessarily the most interesting or varied. Missing are poems revealing relations with his art, as are the Bernesque and most confessional pieces. Of course, the striking mystic effusions of the 1550s (up till 1560) are also missing. Copies were prepared for Michelangelo's revision, and probably at no other time did the artist work so consciously at the *labor limae*. (The story of the preparation of this intended edition is best reconstructed by Enzo Noè Girardi in the "Nota filologica" to his definitive edition of the *Rime*.)

Due in part to the sudden death of Del Riccio, the edition never went to press, even though final corrections were inserted and numbers affixed. The strain on the relations between Michelangelo and Del Riccio which had developed was in part due to the latter's insistence that the artist write fifty epitaphs for Cecchino de' Bracci (see below, p. 134–38), that he execute a bust of this boy, and perhaps even to Del Riccio's plan to publish some of these epitaphs. In any case, we have a letter and a poem in which Michelangelo expresses anger and disappointment to Del Riccio and demands that several *stampe* be destroyed. For example, the piece "Pietosa e dolce aita" bore the oblique line which indicated that it was chosen by Del Riccio for publication.[4]

Even though many of Michelangelo's poems were undiscovered by the year of his death, his contemporaries acclaimed him in burial ceremonies as poet no less than as artist and architect. Ginori's canvas of Michelangelo composing verses is a visual record of this recognition. Even Michelangelo's formidable opponent Aretino wished "to have every word of them enclosed in an emerald urn," an ambiguously worded remark probably intended as a compliment. The chief orator at the obsequies was none other than Michelangelo the poet's nonmusical "discoverer" Varchi. Varchi declaimed the eulogy quoted briefly in the front matter of this book and added that this Apollo-Apelles "surpassed by far whichever poets of the past, whether Tuscan, Latin, or Greek."[5]

Yet substantiation of any such claims was to come slowly. It was not until 1623 (see below) that this heralded poet was to be published in entirety.

What did poetry mean to Michelangelo?

Michelangelo's early schooling with the usually deprecated Francesco da Urbino did not bestir him to an interest in literature. Like Shakespeare, Michelangelo learned little Latin, no Greek. Indeed, when he was seventy, he reasoned to the *cenacolo* of Donato Giannotti that since Cato the Censor began to study Greek at eighty, he, Michelangelo, should start to learn Latin from Priscianese's grammar. Michelangelo's father and uncle had little patience with his wasting time on literature, no more than on painting and sculpture. They would have preferred that he enter commerce, the wool trade, or money changing. His apprenticeship to Bertoldo and to Ghirlandaio as well as his initiation into the works of earlier painters and sculptors made him aware that art was dependent on and inseparable from history and literature. He was exposed to the new credo of the artists that art was "una cosa mentale." He may have begun poetising even this early. Writes Insinga, "one must suppose, nevertheless, that the great man from his first years was clamping melodies within the iron pincers of a line of poetry."[6] Aside from these earliest apprentice days, there were four major periods in Michelangelo's long life when he was drawn to the study and practice of poetry.

His first consequential exposure to poetry was during his residence with Lorenzo il Magnifico, poet and literary historian. Under the Medicean roof the young man was able to eavesdrop on the brilliant literary discussions of Pico, Politian, Ficino, and other luminaries in attendance. We have every reason to suppose that Politian inspired Michelangelo's *Centauromachia* as he inspired Botticelli's *Primavera* and *Nascita di Venere*. We shall observe in Chapter XIX that the poet from Montepulciano also inspired two or three of Michelangelo's *Rime*. Michelangelo may well have done some tentative versifying at this time, only to destroy these efforts as, through dissatisfaction, he was to burn (1518) sketches and drawings. Too, since he habitually jotted poetry on work sheets, every burned *schizzo* or *pensiero* may have borne alongside it a poem or partial poem.

His second major exposure to poetry was during his first sojourn at Bologna (1494–95) in the house of Giovan Francesco Aldovrandi. This Maecenas of letters could hardly have failed to direct his young protégé's attention to poetry, since he himself frequented poets, wrote poetry (such as the *Magno torneamento*), and joined in the contemporary defense of poetry by writing an *Ars poetica*. We know of the older man's pleasure at having Michelangelo read to him in Tuscan accents the verses of Dante and Petrarch "finchè si dormentasse" ("till he fell asleep").[7]

His first two patrons, then, being practising and successful poets, were able to repair a fundamental weakness in Michelangelo's modest formal education. In certain Renaissance circles it was just as possible to learn through the salon as through the schoolroom. As someone said of Marguerite d'Angoulême, "Elle n'était pas instruite, mais elle avait dîné dans la bonne compagnie."

The third period of Michelangelo's addiction to poetry, one of study, lasted from 1503 to 1506. Indeed, two poems of his are dated by Girardi from this period: "Molti anni fassi qual felice, in una" and "Sol io ardendo all'ombra mi rimango," both being mere fragments of sonnets. The quality of his writing was more than compensated by his zeal for learning poetry. It was after the *Battle of Cascina*, according to Condivi, that he immersed himself in poetry. "He stayed for some time doing almost nothing in the fine arts, having given himself over to the reading of the vernacular poets and orators and to the writing of sonnets for his own delight."[8] Condivi's phrase tells that poetry held a therapeutic value for Michelangelo as had art itself for this man who would carve stone merely "per mio piacere" ("for my pleasure").[9]

The intensity of his desire to know poetry was such that he shunted aside two very important commissions for such a young man, eleven statuettes for Siena and eleven statues (excluding the *San Matteo*) for Santa Maria del Fiore. As Papini wrote: "After so much battling against stone, after such effort at anatomy, he felt nostalgia for the word, for the language of the soul."[10] In view of Michelangelo's total dedication to art, we can only assume that he was now totally aware of the unending *intrecciature* between literature and art. Of these interrelations he would be increasingly aware as he heard and read the discussions of *ut pictura poesis* during his lifetime. He found more and more humanists like Varchi, Zappi, and Strozzi penning poetry on his own statuary. He found that the creative processes and demands of poetry were not unlike those of the arts.

We can imagine the poets that he read most at this time were (in addition to Dante and Petrarch) Homer, perhaps Sappho, the *Planudean Anthology* in translation, Vergil, Ovid, Horace, Sannazaro, Lorenzo, Politian, Cardinal Bembo, Antonio Camelli, and the numerous Petrarchists. The German scholar E. Grisebach found a copy of Ovid's *Amores, De arte amandi*, and *De remediis amoris* apparently from Michelangelo's library and signed by him.[11] As for orators, historians, theologians, and philosophers, one assumes that he read Plato, Pliny, Plotinus, Pythagoras, Lucretius, Plutarch, Cicero, Villani, Alberti, and Ficino. Traces of all the foregoing authors may be found within the corpus of Michelangelo's writing. For example, Cicero's canon of living statues (*Divinatione*, I) and his notions on tyranny (*De Officiis*, III) find echo in Michelangelo. Later in his life he would read the following established authors: Ariosto, Bernardo Accolti, Aretino, Berni, Annibal Caro (father-in-law of his devoted Condivi), Giannotti, Machiavelli, Pulci (whose grandson had a voice pleasing to Michelangelo), Sadoletus, Varchi, and the writers on art and architecture from Vitruvius to Palladio.

The bulk of Michelangelo's poetry was written during a fourth period between 1530 and 1560.

During these four periods Michelangelo insisted that his poems were of little value. He expressed his scorn for them in a variety of ways. He laughed them off respectively as *zanbele*, *novelle* (novelties), *goffagini*, and *berlinghozzi* on four occasions. He inserted confusing letters into the first quatrains of his early "Grato e felice" (G 3) "as if he intended to make the reading of it more bewildering" (Girardi). To one poem he appended, "At carnival time it seems legitimate to those not masked to commit some folly." On the following folio he penned: "This is no carnival fireworks, so I'll just send it to you for Lent."[12] On the autograph to the right of his madrigal "Se costei gode e tu solo, Amor, vivi," he wrote, "This is for the curd cheese; this second one is for the olives, if it's worth that much."[13] In Chapter VI we enumerate the many deprecating notes which Michelangelo will add to the abundance of poetry he is cajoled into writing for the deceased Cecchino de' Bracci, all of these notes demeaning the poetry as *nugae* to pay off debts for fish, produce, and delicatessen items received. Compare also, following his intensely personal sonnet "Se da' primi anni aperto un lento e poco," the ridiculous and disenchanting jotting. "For one of the *buctagre* (mullets)," or, after his sonnet lamenting the passing of his hammer to heaven (G 46), the confused and even possibly Bernesque message to "Lionardo."

When Michelangelo feels obliged to respond to Berni's compliment on his writing "things" rather than words, he pretends that he is Sebastiano del Piombo and disallows with a blush:

> While I write it verse by verse,
> I blush crimson, thinking to whom I send it,
> This clumsy and crude effort, not my profession. (G 85)

He wrote in a note (19 September, 1554) accompanying a sonnet to Vasari that his poetising proved his arrival at second childhood: "You will say that I'm old and mad trying to make sonnets; but since many say I'm in my second babyhood, I've wished to play my part" (CDLXXIII). Three years later, in May, 1557, he will make the same disarming admission to Vasari that he elsewhere applies to each of the fine arts: "writing is a great nuisance to me, for it isn't my art" (CDLXXXII).

Michelangelo suspected words of being too often inadequate to communicate thoughts. In a religious outpouring he cried out to God:

> whence the pen
> Will not correspond to my acts, and makes the page a lie. (G 87)

This same concern he expressed wonderfully in an appeal at the end of a letter to his beloved Tommaso Cavalieri: "Read the heart and not the letter, because the pen cannot approach right intent" (CDXI).

Just as other artists asked him to correct their conceptions, so he too would occasionally submit a poem to Del Riccio, Vasari, or Giannotti, assuming that they could improve it. "Messer Luigi, you who have the spirit of poesy, I beg you to shorten and revise one of these madrigals, the one which seems to you the less wretched."[14] Like Molière's Oronte, Michelangelo had neither the self-confidence nor the interest to exhibit his *Rime* to this tiny circle of intimates or, sometimes, to the dedicatees.

Michelangelo was insufficiently interested in his *Rime* to copy or preserve them in a more permanent form, even when pressed to do so by friends like Del Riccio. This apathy allows us to conclude that his vocal modesty about rhyming was not empty protest, as were so many of his disclaimers about his abilities as artist. He jotted his poems down on the nearest sheet of paper or even vellum whenever the Muse seized him or whenever, as he once phrased it, the fountain was not dry. Thus, the poems were akin to the *pensieri* or preliminary sketches which he dashed off so frequently. Three sonnets, for example, were found on the verso of a letter to Michelangelo from Giuliano Bugiardini; another on the back of a letter from Figiovanni. The important fragment, "In me la morte, in te la vita mia," was also discovered scrawled on an epistle.

Fortunately, these letters, dated or datable, allow us to know more or less when many of the poems were composed. Thus we know that the piece "Quanto si gode, lieta e ben contesta" and the fragment "Là m'arde e lega et emmi e parmi un zucchero" may have been composed in Bologna at Christmastide, 1507, for they were penned on a letter of 24 December from his brother Buonarroto in Florence. The dating of poems penned on folios of sketches or architectural projections is equally valuable in establishing chronologies. The sonnet "Al zucchero, a la mula, e le candele" was written on a drawing for the stair of the Laurentian Library and bears two actual dates: "addì l gennaio 1554" and "26 settembre 1555," the second date being preferred. A sestina recently reproduced for the first time by Girardi passed unnoticed for centuries on a sketch in the British Museum. The mysterious distich "Davicte cholla fromba ed io choll'arco," penned alongside the Louvre sketch of the bronze *David* (see Chapter VII), challenges speculation on the collocation. At times the challenge is an empty one, for some verses will have nothing to do with the accompanying drawing. In any case, exploiting every possible clue of this sort, Enzo Noè Girardi has done a magnificent job of establishing the chronology of Michelangelo's entire poetic production.

Thus, out of disparate and often unexpected sources has been gathered the corpus of 343 poems and poetic fragments which now appear in ever-increasing editions the world over.

We have not yet come to grips with the basic question. Why did Michelangelo feel the necessity of setting his thoughts to verse?

A facile answer is that the Renaissance gentleman practiced poetry as one of the inevitable obligations to *cortegiania*. The courtesy books so stipulated. In Michelangelo's world many of his associates exercised in poetry as a *violon d'Ingres*—just as they tried their hand at collections of letters or at comedy. The indulgence in poetry of his first two patrons was to be continued by the closest friends of his later years, including Giannotti, Del Riccio, and Vittoria Colonna, courtly and prolific poetess. We have already observed that poetry had a therapeutic value for Michelangelo. It fulfilled two basic needs. First, he who found it difficult to reveal himself *viva voce* to even his dearest friends found in verse a medium to communicate to them, to express his affection and admiration or even, as with Del Riccio or Julius II, his anger and resentment. The second great need was a confessional one. Farinelli has explained: "Setting thoughts to rhyme was not for him a fashionable caprice, but an impulse from the heart, at the same time relief and torment."[15] Not only did Michelangelo feel the need of examining his own conscience by poetising an intimate journal, but he also turned directly to Christ in his later poetry, as he had earlier frequented the confessional. He appeals to Christ to strengthen his faith and tear away the icy veil of doubt, he prays to be spared from the Saviour's upraised and wrathful arm at the Last Judgement, to receive assurance of salvation—these appeals constitute some of the finest pages of religious verse ever written.

Another theory as to Michelangelo's versifying—applicable especially to the great quantity of verses composed after 1530—is that verse was a less exhausting channel for his creative impulse than were painting and sculpture. To Bevilacqua his riming was "a manifestation of his decline, a more restful exercise of his inexhaustible instinct for creation."[16] It would be well not to exaggerate the probabilities of this facile, logical theory.

A few of the poems were simply inspired or dictated by dreams, and the poet felt a need to record these. Indeed, two which he judged worthy of publication by Del Riccio and Donato originated this way. The curious allegory "Costei pur si delibra" (see Chapter IV) bears the notation of the artist: "I don't attribute this one to our I.O.U.'s, but to a dream." The madrigal "S' i' fossi stato ne' primi anni accorto" bears the note: "Song born at night in the middle of bed. To straighten out tomorrow evening. It would be sweet as Adam's apple [preserved fruit], but I have no apples [*mele* also means honey] in my body." We know that twice in his life Michelangelo had compulsive dreams which triggered flights to Florence and to Venice. Small wonder that his racing mind would leave him upon awakening in possession of a formed or half-formed poem to set down.

Some poems were written to give articulation to certain of his fixed ideas, to experiment with imagery which haunted him and which infiltrated his verse to the extent of producing recognisable motifs. Typical are the five poems probing the several meanings of night, a fecund, seminal obsession which accounts for the multiple symbols with which his sculptured *Notte* is laden. Other repeated concepts or images include fire, mirrors, skin, fame, and the phoenix. Indeed, it is the coincidence of such themes both in Michelangelo's poetry and art which enhances the interest and importance of the *Rime*.

Michelangelo has been described in the *Jambes* of Barbier as the man who apparently never laughed. A more authoritative scholar, Adolfo Venturi, concurred that in Michelangelo's works "the smile was unknown."[17] This humorlessness is at least untrue of the *Rime*; some of Michelangelo's poetry was pure divertissement, the sport of a man not addicted to sports. Typical are the playful pieces addressed to Giovanni da Pistoia and Francesco Berni, reminiscent of the satirical pieces by Aretino, Mauro, Bini, or Berni himself.

Despite Michelangelo's disinclination to see his poetry in print, a final motivation for his becoming a poet was the desire for Fame itself, "the nurse of the arts" (Cicero). Michelangelo, who thirsted for glory in several arts, knew that *scripta manent* and that written monuments outlast bronze. Though he had an inordinate admiration for a few artists, such as Apollonius of Athens, sculptor of his adored Belvedere Torso, one of his sonnets tells us that his greatest hero of all was a poet, Dante ("Simil uom nè maggior non nacque mai"). If he spoke often against artists, he never spoke against men of letters, with the exception of Aretino, who had attacked him. Indeed, he spoke hyperbolically of Dante, Giannotti, Berni, Varchi, and Vasari (as biographer). He was proud of his association with the literati in Florence, Rome, and Bologna. Late in life he reminisced, "If you will remember well, in Florence there was not a literary man who wasn't my friend."[18] His knowledge that Vasari's *Vite* could bring "eternal life" to his subjects, that the "sacri inchiostri" of Vittoria Colonna and "carmi divini" of Berni would bring them everlasting fame, no doubt explains why he gave in to the urging of Del Riccio and Giannotti and agreed, at least temporarily, to the printing of his *Rime*. It may explain why he wrote them in the first place.

These poems, their many variants included, are an important inventory of Michelangelo's thought. Sometimes the variants' indication of changed purpose or emphasis tells much about Michelangelo. These variant readings are carefully examined in the editions of Frey and Girardi. In Girardi's one finds 343 complete, incomplete, and fragmentary poems, with several times as many variants. What themes dominate this deluge of poetry? Pierre de Bouchaud saw them as "l'art, la patrie, l'amour, la mort, et Dieu."[19] Vincenzo Italo Pascale found them to be, similarly, "amore, patria, arte, e religione."[20] As we have suggested, the *Rime* vary both in subject and tone. The major concerns of the poetry are, in order of importance:

I. Poems celebrating his love for Vittoria Colonna or regretting her death. This autumnal love of the artist for the distinguished poetess and widow of the Marquis of Pescara stirred some of his most noble feelings. Never having had the time or inclination required for the sustained love of a woman, the artist felt—apparently for the first time—the impact and katharsis of a heterosexual if chaste love (see below, Chapter X).

II. Poems informed with a love of Christ, frequently confessional in character. Firmly convinced that mankind was saved through the blood of Christ, having during his youth considered becoming a Dominican monk under Savonarola, having dedicated himself entirely to Christian art (excepting the *Bruto*) once employed by the Church, Michelangelo was drawn inevitably to religious expression through the additional medium of poetry.

III. Poems of consuming affection for Tommaso Cavalieri. Scion of a humble family with thin connections through blood and marriage to more noble dynasties, Michelangelo found in this aristocratic Roman the epitome of a grace and *cortegiania* even more pronounced than his early rival Raphael's. Michelangelo's love for Cavalieri, also Platonic in nature, derived not merely from a need for affection but expressed the inevitable admiration of an antisocial individual who was surly in polite company and capable of such barbarous practices as sleeping in his boots, going about on a mule, and keeping his hat on in the presence of popes.

IV. A large body of the poetry attacks unpredictable themes in so far as one is not prepared for them by a reading of his letters or by a hasty inspection of his works of art. Thus, one hardly expects to find poems dealing with fire. The five pieces which return to the subject of Night we have already mentioned. The dominant theme of death is less surprising, for Michelangelo was already referring to "la mia propinqua morte" forty-eight years before his demise. Individual cities (Florence, Rome, Pistoia) are evoked in his *canzoniere*, as they had been in Dante's. Fleeting themes occupy a line or two in the poems: such motifs as the phoenix, the salamander, and so on. These disparate themes which cannot easily be fitted into the mosaic of the total production challenge one who would find the integral unity in Michelangelo's artistic, literary, and human creativeness.

V. A few poems are missives to individuals within Michelangelo's circle of friends. Julius II is informed (with such bluntness that the pontiff probably never saw this outburst by the incensed artist) that he is treating his protégé shabbily. Luigi del Riccio is given a bitter lecture (the provocation of which is not explicit) on ingratitude. Vasari is hailed as an immortaliser of artists, as we have seen. The deaths of his father, gruff old Lodovico, of his brother Buonarroto, of his devoted assistant Urbino, of the aristocratic Faustina Lucia Mancini Attavanti, all prompt poems of regret addressed to friends or to the deceased themselves. Most moving are those pieces which express the artist's desire to rejoin in heaven his father and his assistant.

VI. The sequence of poems to Cecchino Bracci constitute one of the most puzzling problems in Michelangelo scholarship. Why the artist, at one of the busiest periods of his career, should take time to write fifty or fifty-one pieces on the death of a fifteen-year-old *mignon* has never been satisfactorily explained. They are supposed to have been composed at the insistence of the lad's uncle, Luigi del Riccio. No more preposterous than the request was Michelangelo's acquiescence. There is a scabrous and possibly homosexual undertone to the entire matter, which is to be studied below in Chapter VI.

VII. A number of poems refer to art in general, and several to specific works of art by Michelangelo. Two of the most interesting and revelatory of the latter category are the Greek-chorus threnody chanted by the *Night* and *Day* of the Tomb of Duke Giuliano, who speculate on what might have been the future of the young nobleman had he not died so young, and the quatrain in which the sleeping *Notte* asks not to be awakened, lest she see the tyranny and injustices of the Medici Restoration. The extended sonnet in which Michelangelo describes his physical discomforts while painting the Sistine Ceiling is sheer comic delight and could of course be classified below among his Bernesque pieces. Various sonnets draw upon the processes and imagery of the fine arts; imagery and metaphor derived from the artistry of the goldsmith, sculptor, and painter filter into his verses. In one memorable burst of genius Michelangelo succeeded in reducing his entire theory of art into four lines (the first quatrain of "Non ha l'ottimo artista alcun concetto"). (See below, p. 64.)

VIII. Never a political hero or activist, Michelangelo nevertheless found that his self-chosen exile in Rome threw him into frequent contact with such political *fuorusciti* as Giannotti, Riccio, the Strozzi, and Jacopo Galli. Whereas he worried about the repercussions of these meetings on his family back in Florence, in a few poems he wrote as a *poète engagé*, albeit with varying degrees of circumspection. The dialogue "Per molti, Donna, anzi per mille amanti" is a bold allegory attacking the brutal Medici ravisher of Florence. Cautious and indirect *engagement* is illustrated by his two sonnets on Dante Alighieri, forced into political exile. In his life Michelangelo avoided the embroilments of politics; similarly, politics plays only a minuscule role in his poetry.

IX. The poems most obviously composed as pastimes grew out of Michelangelo's satirical or ironical vein (of which we have so many anecdotal evidences) and his talent for burlesque. We have mentioned the poem rich in description of the physical discomforts he endured while executing the vast fresco of the Sistine Vault. In a satirical spirit is the mock love song, "Tu ha' 'l viso più dolce che la sapa" (G 20), apparently modelled on another by Lorenzo the Magnificent. Completely Bernesque in tone is Michelangelo's curious self-portrait, with its humorous if clinical details (G 267), which distantly recalls the "faccia di spavento" self-portrait accompanying San Bartolommeo's pelt. In the *stanze* of "Io crederrei, se tu fussi di sasso" (G 54) Michelangelo's expansive declaration of love moves from the mocking tone of Berni to heightened metaphorical expression.

X. The pastoral stances "in praise of rustic life" as well as a few other poems and fragments are reminiscent of the eclogue vein which Michelangelo for the most part rejected. There is no more sentiment for external nature in Michelangelo's poems than in his painting, which contains only four trees, one of necessity being the Tree of the Knowledge of Good and Evil in the Garden of Eden. Michelangelo's grudging exploitation of nature motifs will be treated below in Chapter XVI.

These are the major thematic classifications of Michelangelo's *Rime*. They are by no means equal in importance; there are only a handful of Bernesque poems and even fewer nature poems in contrast to the abundance of poems in the other groups.

The story of the successive collections and editions of Michelangelo's poetry can now be fully traced.

We have already listed the scattered appearance of Michelangelo's poetry in other collections, those of 1518, 1543, 1549, 1550, and 1565.

Thanks largely to the insistence of Luigi del Riccio, the isolated pieces were collected together around 1546, and these in their various versions still exist in several collections. The basic corpus, Codice Vaticano Latino 3211, was copied by four hands, including those of Riccio and Giannotti, and carries corrections by Michelangelo. It was the basis for the projected edition of his works. This group of poems was gathered and bound in vellum by the Canonico of San Giovanni in Laterano, Fulvio Orsini. It is described in Codice Vaticano 7205 as "Michelangelo Buonaroti, le poesie, scritto di mano sua con alcune lettere in papiro in foglio et ligate in velluto verde."

The second most important collection, in Florence, is that of the Archivio Buonarroti: Codice XIII o Autografo. This group, containing autographs of Michelangelo, but of others as well, was divided by its curator Gherardi into six poetic areas: "Epigrafi ed Epitaffi, Madrigali, Sonetti e frammenti di Sonetti, Capitoli, Stanze e Canzoni ecc. separata l'una dall'altra da un foglio di carta azzurra recante, a stampa, il titolo del genere, e, a penna, il numero de' pezzi contenuti in ciascuna parte." This group is officially housed in the Casa Buonarroti on Via Ghibellina; though a less orderly and coherent collection, it complements and extends the collection in the Vatican. It was these copies which were in the possession of Michelangelo's nephew Lionardo and which passed thence to his grandnephew Michelangelo the Younger.

A third group in the Archivio Buonarroti (Codice XIV o Miscellaneo) contains several parts, prepared by Giannotti, Riccio, or the sculptor Accursio Baldi.

The fourth collection mentioned by Girardi is also from the Archivio Buonarroti: Codice XV o Buonarroti. These are the copies prepared by the grandnephew Michelangelo the Younger, for his edition of 1623 (see below). The folios are interesting for the marginal comments of the cautious grandnephew, such as, "It occurs to me that in speaking of the compositions of Michelangelo one could say that since they are grave and not lascivious, and not ornate; they would not be expelled from good republics" (fol. 18b). Or, on the poems to Cecchino Bracci, the very troubled remarks which we record in Chapter VI.

These and two other codices, the Magliabechiano, cl. VIII, n. 38, and the Beccadelli, containing versions of the poems on the death of Cecchino and of Urbino respectively, constitute the manuscript sources of Michelangelo's poetry (see also Chapter VI, note 2). Thus, like that of classical writers, Michelangelo's poetry was transmitted through copyists and variants—which must be studied. Like Ronsard and other self-conscious Renaissance poets, however, Michelangelo was able to revise his works or oversee revisions and thus to establish a definitive text for the poems written up to 1546.

As for the editions of his poetry, there have been many. Four, however, are important and each is successively an improvement over the preceding one.

The devotion of Michelangelo's nephew Lionardo was maintained by Lionardo's son, Michelangelo il Giovane. An active member of the Florentine Academy at seventeen, an even more active one of the Crusca later, the *pronipote* inherited the artist's taste for poetry, his love of nobility and the Medici, and his thirst for fame. Moved by the same sentiments which led him to compose a history of the Buonarroti family (which Michelangelo would have applauded), he decided to collect and edit the artist's poetry which was lying in manuscript in the Vatican and in the family archives. The history of this enterprise is thoroughly chronicled in Girardi's *Studi sulle Rime di Michelangiolo.* A poet whose interests lay in writing "Lodi dei fagioli" ("praises of beans") and such *nugae,* he was not the man to come to grips with the powerful verse of the artist. Yet he was a careful student of language, a scholar and editor on the first three editions of the *Vocabolario della Crusca.* His dramatic writings, *La tancia, La fiera,* and *Mascherate* were written at least partly to exhibit the languages of various social classes.

His academic experience and scholarly methods however did not triumph over his desire to present a great-uncle above reproach both as poetic craftsman and as moral human being. He tampered with the texts in his possession and altered those from the Vatican. He especially suppressed and revised texts of poetry addressed to men, changing masculine to feminine pronouns. (It was a prudence practiced by Michelangelo himself in several revisions, as noted by Girardi in *Studi,* p. 117.) He seemed to leave nothing which might offend the polite society for whom he wrote his *Mascherate,* or which would have the artist "scacciato dalle buone repubbliche." In the preface he expressed worry to Cardinal Barberini about allegations by commentators: "Soviemmi che chi commentasse queste composizioni di queste imperfette si potrebbe servire per allegazioni, e luoghi per provare delle perfette e così non andrebbe male niente." The fifty epitaphs to Cecchino Bracci, which bothered him particularly, were reduced to five; his further comments on them will be quoted below in Chapter VI. This edition, which has irritated modern scholars, was the only available one until 1863, and was to serve as proof of the grandnephew's claim: "It seems to me that, as Dante vanquished Petrarch, Michelangelo surpassed the other modern poets through a certain ancient gravity and grave ancientness." Michelangelo suffered after death the same humiliation with respect to his poetry that he had endured in life when Piero Urbano retouched his *Cristo risorto* and the public deemed it the product of a baker of *zanbele,* or when *il Braghettone* (breeches-maker) Volterra retouched the figures of the *Giudizio.* Michelangelo might well have repeated his ironical remark about an architect, "I don't know what will happen to that storey on Judgement Day, when all bodies will take back their members, for nothing will remain left of it."[21]

By 1863, long after Sainte-Beuve and other scholars had started to revive interest in re-editing mediaeval and Renaissance texts, another academician of La Crusca, Cesare Guasti, prepared a more faithful edition of Michelangelo's *Rime.* Foscolo had complained that the Italians praised Michelangelo's poetry without actually studying it. Guasti's edition helped to remedy this situation. This basic edition was inspired by the printing in Rome of the accurate versions of the poetry in the Vatican, a printing prepared by the academician Alessandro Maggiori, who realised that the grandnephew had not transcribed the Vatican versions but who assumed that the 1623 edition was an honest reproduction of texts in the hands of Michelangelo il Giovane. The German biographer Grimm discerned the truth, working on his *Leben Michelangelos* (1860–63). If Guasti's edition did not always present optimum texts or fix an orderly chronology, it nevertheless brought almost all the poetry together for the first time. Guasti's grouping of the poems by poetic form very possibly induced the first translators of Michelangelo to take blocks of sonnets and leave other forms. Guasti's aim, and this his modern critics underestimate, was not only to make all the poetry available but also to make it understandable. He added under each piece a prose paraphrase in a simpler Italian, which has often been appreciated by Italians and foreign readers alike. With the exception of the Viau edition in Buenos Aires, modern editions, following suit, have added such paraphrasing in marginal or appendix position and have patently leaned on Guasti's interpretations. Moreover, the Guasti edition was beautifully printed on an excellent paper, in sufficient numbers for copies to be acquired by libraries the world over.

Toward the end of the nineteenth century German scholarship and *Grundlichkeit*, which were to dominate not only Europe but America as well, turned to the poetry. The distinguished professor of art in Berlin, Carl Frey, produced an equally large edition, which appeared in 1897, soon after his *Sammlung* of letters to Michelangelo and his editions of Vasari's and Condivi's biographies of Michelangelo. This magnificent monument of method was not entirely appreciated in an Italy already questioning the rigors of German methodology. In his *Come si pubblicano i nostri classici*, Barbi wrote to Ugo Ojetti a long denunciation of the Frey edition, including a censure of the Italian editors who were following Frey's numberings and readings: "Have a look at the Amendola edition and that of Papini, and you will find repeated this very *materialità* which is repugnant to good critical sense, as if in withdrawing from the learned German they were afraid to appear less precise and scientific than he." How the anti-pedant Papini must have bolted upon reading that charge! A more moderate criticism is expressed by Enzo Girardi, the recent editor of the *Rime*: "The fact is that if the grandnephew sought perfection, in a certain sense, beyond the poetry of Michelangelo, Frey sought it just this side of the poetry, identifying the object of his edition not so much with the poetry as with the material instruments of poetry: manuscript pages, lines, words, and letters."[22] The reaction against German method was just as typical of the *Zeitgeist* as was the addiction to it. However, without Grimm, Thode, Wittkower, Redig de Campos, and the German-trained De Tolnay, Michelangelo studies would have made little progress up to the present. Frey's numbering and chronology of the poems, his inclusion together of the block prepared for the Riccio edition of 1546, even his counting of them, his inclusion of fragments with completed pieces have all been criticised. It has been alleged that by making no concession toward modernising spellings, Frey has sacrificed intelligibility to method. Actually, as we shall point out in Chapter II, Michelangelo's curious spellings are less unintelligible than his ideas themselves and, indeed, tell us much about the man.

It is not necessary to level picayune criticisms at the magnificent edition of Frey as the Italians have done in order to recognise the superiority of the most recent edition in the Scrittori d'Italia series. "When will a new edition come out—an Italian edition, God willing!—which will be prepared with the autographs accurately studied and with a literary interpretation adhering to the text which will perfect and complete the meritorious work of Guasti? It will be a new proof that really critical editions do not render an author illegible, as people think today, but rather free him from whatever makes him embroiled and confusing, and clarify him and equip him with whatever is strictly necessary for a perfect understanding and a just evaluation." This hope of Barbi has been largely fulfilled by the current edition of Enzo Noè Girardi (Bari: Laterza, 1960), which avails itself of the best scholarship to date. Though he emphasizes clarified and slightly modernised versions of the poetry, Girardi presents in an appendix the Frey versions and other variants from the various manuscripts, a prose reworking for greater understanding, and incidental notations on and information about the autographs. His history of the various manuscripts is authoritative and he has checked them all himself. He states clearly all of the philological problems and explains his disposition of them.

The greatest problem presented by the autographs, that of dating, was never solved before Girardi's edition was to establish the chronology of the poems. To accomplish this almost impossible task Girardi gathered evidences of both external and internal nature. External evidence is of six classes:

1. Explicit testimonies
2. Letters, addresses, records, and various annotations found on the manuscripts
3. Designs and drawings
4. The evolving character of Michelangelo's handwriting
5. Type of paper and of ink; filigranes
6. Position of the autographs in the manuscripts

External evidence could also include appearances of poems by others which influenced him (see below, p. 330). The internal evidences, which Girardi claims to have used at a minimum, are of course relationships to the poet's biography, evolution of a literary style, and so on. In any case,

Girardi's prudent establishing of a chronology is typical of the thorough and objective editing done throughout. It is certain that he has, in Buonarrotian terms, broken the basic problem of form, and that his order will prevail with few modifications hereafter. The importance of Girardi's particular contribution for all future scholarship on Michelangelo can scarcely be exaggerated, whether it be to clarify Michelangelo's state of mind when he is executing a given work or to clarify that work itself. For example, we have leaned on Girardi's chronology below to demonstrate that Michelangelo's angry sonnet "Qui si fa elmi di chalici e spade" was penned soon after he learned that his hard-accomplished bronze statue of Julius II had been melted down and recast into a cannon.

A final contribution of the Girardi edition is a definitive renumbering of the poetry, totaling 302 poems and 41 fragments. Unfortunately, Girardi appends no corpus of footnotes clarifying the meaning of individual verses or even poems.

In spite of all this brilliant philological work—or perhaps because of it —certain mysteries present themselves to be solved. What became of the six poems from which Varchi quoted in his *Lezzioni?* Where did the two extra verses come from in Tromboncino's version of "Com' arò dunque ardire?" Is the madrigal "Costei pur si delibra" really an allegory on art? How many more of the poems were actually written to Febo other than the two which pun on his name? Is there a fifty-first poem, as we suggest, written to Cecchino Bracci (see Chapter VI, note 2)? Was there really a "donna aspera e fiera," a highly-conjectural woman mentioned by many scholars of Michelangelo's life and poetry? Were any of the poems actually written to a woman (excluding those obviously to Vittoria Colonna), or does Michelangelo merely make male loves into female ones, just as male models originated many of his female figures—just as in a mystical effusion to God he makes himself feminine (*sposa*)? We shall hazard some answers in the following pages.

NOTES

[1] Enrico Bevilacqua, "Michelangelo scrittore" (fasc.), (Milan-Rome, 1926), p. 642.
[2] Giovanni Papini, *La vita di Michelangiolo nella vita del suo tempo* (Milan, 1949), p. 437.
[3] *Le lettere di Michelangelo Buonarroti*, ed. Gaetano Milanesi (Florence, 1875), p. 524.
[4] Michelangelo, *Rime*, ed. Enzo Noè Girardi (Bari, 1960), p. 340.
[5] Benedetto Varchi, *Orazione funerale* (Florence, 1564), p. 10.
[6] Arture Insinga, *Michelangelo poeta* (Palermo, 1919), p. 14.
[7] Ascanio Condivi, *La vita di Michelangelo*, xvi.
[8] *Ibid.*, xxiii.

[9] *Le lettere di Michelangelo Buonarroti* (Florence, 1875), p. 4.
[10] Papini, *La vita, ed. cit.*, p. 109.
[11] E. Grisebach, "Ein Buch aus Michelangelos Bibliothek," *Zeitschrift für Bücherfreunde*, I (1897–98).
[12] *Rime*, ed. Girardi, p. 217.
[13] *Ibid.*, p. 325.
[14] *Le lettere, ed. cit.*, p. 478.
[15] Arturo Farinelli, "Michelangelo poeta," in *Raccolta di studi critici dedicata ad A. D'Ancona* (Florence, 1901), pp. 20–21.
[16] Bevilacqua, *op. cit.*, p. 638.
[17] Adolfo Venturi, "Michelangelo e Raffaello," in *Il messaggero della Domenica* (Rome, 15 December, 1915).
[18] Donato Giannotti, *Dialogi de' giorni che Dante consumò nel cercare l'Inferno e 'l Purgatorio* (Florence, 1939), p. 66.
[19] Pierre de Bouchaud, *Les poésies de Michel-Ange et de Vittoria Colonna* (Paris, 1912), p. 43.
[20] Vincenzo Italo Pascale, *Michelangelo Buonarroti poeta* (Naples, 1902), p. 40.
[21] Giorgio Vasari, *Le vite* (Florence, 1878–85), VII, 280.
[22] Enzo Noè Girardi, in *Rime* di Michelangiolo Buonarroti, *ed. cit.*, p. 517.

2

STYLE AND LANGUAGE

SOMETIME BEFORE OR DURING 1534 Michelangelo, a "Sunday poet" of some increasing stature, wrote to Tommaso Cavalieri:

> Just as in pen and ink
> There is high or low or intermediate style,
> There are in marbles rich or base images,
> So far as our genius can draw them out. (G 84)

This surprising quatrain, his contribution to the discussions of the *ut pictura poesis* in his time, is important in several ways. He seems to allege that just as marbles hold *in potentia* the *concetti* to be executed by the sculptor, such *concetti* are contained equally in ink itself. To be truthful, the parallel is carried one step further, for his inference here is that ink will produce high or low (or Horace's "median") style according to the writer's genius, or possibly even that ink carries the varying levels of style which the Renaissance judged appropriate respectively to epic or romance, to Pindaric or Anacreontic poetry, to tragedy or comedy and farce. Whichever meaning is accepted, the artist gives us to understand that his poetic burden is a kind of *concetto*, which must have a close correspondence to the material, the *hyle*. In poetry, the *hyle* was the mass contained within several prescribed poetic forms: madrigal, canzone, *capitolo*, quatrain, ballad, or epitaph. One may anticipate then that Michelangelo will attempt to fill in this preordained form as densely and completely as possible. This is precisely his aim in his poetry. It is to this objective that Francesco Berni referred in writing his famous comment to Sebastiano del Piombo, "E' dice cose e voi dite parole." Some of Michelangelo's sonnets, like the three-planed "Non fur men lieti che turbati e tristi," were so crammed with ideas, with *cose*, that the crowded thoughts expand even as we are reading them, like the "immago che crescie" while the spectator contemplates one of Michelangelo's works of art.

Yet there is a difference between traditional art and poetry in this respect. The sculptor Michelangelo walked through Serravezza, Carrara, or Pietra Santa and saw blocks of many varying sizes and shapes. He perceived the latent form within them—that form *in potentia* to which the Aristotelians referred—and ordered the stones to be marked with his "M" and interlacing circles, as several drawings of his testify. As a poet, however, he saw only a half-dozen prescribed and homogeneous formal patterns. His thought must be contained within these fixed, traditional molds, whether it be a speculation on the death of his father, an explosion of a consuming anger toward a patron, or a tribute to a beloved friend.

In many cases the correspondence between the poetic mold and the dense thought is almost exact. Pierre de Bouchaud, so often mistaken in his assessments of Michelangelo's poetry, was correct in observing, "A part quelques rares défaillances, sa pensée remplit justement le cadre de la composition."[1]

To match Michelangelo's powerful ideas to the same poetic forms utilised by the Petrarchists and court poets was not an easy task. His wedding of form and content in the fine arts was not always successful; marble or paint did not always embody the correspondence desired, even though "la mano ubbediva all'intelletto." There are *non finiti* or incomplete works in his art. This lack of correspondence accounted, as well, for many *non finiti* and fragments in his poetry. As Farinelli wrote many years ago, "He hammers verse like marble, but the tyrannical form, more indocile than stone, stifles, mutilates, and shatters the idea."[2] A conspicuous example of poem in which Michelangelo could not bring his *concetto* and *materia* together is the madrigal "Te sola del mio mal contenta veggio." Even more obvious examples are the abandoned attempts and the fragments which Frey grouped under CLXVI. There were also occasions when more materials, more verses—like more clay or more applications of oil paint—were required, accounting for the many *sonetti caudati* in his *Rime*. Writing extended sonnets was parallel to working in the oil painting or modeling he scorned (rather than in fresco or stone). Both sonnets apparently to Giovanni da Pistoia are *caudati*.

Sometimes the thought does not entirely fill out the mold. His poem on old Lodovico Buonarroti's death ends when there seems nothing more to say, even though the *terza rima* is left suspended. Indeed, Michelangelo il Giovane felt compelled to add two verses to fill out the rime, two jubilant lines on inevitable salvation. This technical fault has served as pretext for various disturbed comments by editors and translators. One translator into English has explained the abrupt ending by the fact that Michelangelo broke into tears and silence. Saviotti finds Michelangelo at this point "beaten down by furious waves of sentiment," and Papini also speculated on the point.[3] So also a poem deliberating suicide ends when the poet seems to have nothing more to say:

If it is licit in this world for one to kill himself
In the belief that through death he doth go to heaven,
Then none would have a greater right than he
Who lives serving so loyally though wretched and unhappy.
But since man is not like the phoenix
Who arises and returns in the light of the sun,
My hand doth tarry and my foot slows its pace. (G 52)

This thought, which Petrarch expressed in eight lines ("S' io credessi per morte essere scarco") is handled by Michelangelo in seven. The rime is left incomplete, but the thought is totally expressed and satisfying. Here we have an excellent example of a "conceit not circumscribed exactly."

Similarly, in a few cases quatrains which seem fragments of sonnets turn out to be finished products in themselves. Most of the epitaphs to Cecchino de' Bracci are quatrains. In fact, Michelangelo seemed to have accepted the quatrain with embracing rime (*abba*) as a unit of expression. Thus the quatrain:

Love, thy beauty is not mortal;
No face is there among us which doth equal
The image in the heart, which inflames and governs
With another fire and moves with other wings. (G 49)

with its rhyme scheme (*mortale/pareggi/reggi/ale*). The most autonomous quatrain of all is the celebrated reply to Giovanni Strozzi, "Caro m'è 'l sonno e l'esser di sasso," which we discuss below in Chapter V.

When preparing his duly criticised edition of 1623 and confronted with variant forms of the same poem, Michelangelo il Giovane was true to his great-uncle's aims in one respect: he accepted the principle that the version to choose for publication was the one "più ricca di concetti."[4]

Only once did Michelangelo abandon completely the challenge of attaining an exact correspondence of thought and form in poetry, as only once did he practice that painting in oil which he deprecated as for lazy and minor talents.[5] This was the *poème en prose* wherein the statues of the *Notte* and the *Dì* speculate on the interrupted career of Duke Giuliano de' Medici (see p. 96). Michelangelo not only resorts to prose, but for once he indulges in a Greek choral recital about fate, just as though he were composing a recitative for one of the new operas of the Camerata dei Bardi. The editor Piccoli says of this chorus: "One cannot state that this is a rhythmic prose, deliberately written as such, nor rather a first draft to be versified later; it is certain that there rises out of it a creation singularly akin to our present-day sensitivity. The prose has an intense and powerful rhythm, with a solemn and calm pace which renders even more tragic this dialogue on life and death."[6] To Piccoli, moreover, it seems an echo of Aeschylus.

It is obvious that Michelangelo in seeking the most challenging media of expression with which to match his material would resort to *terza rima*. Dante's victory over this meter endeared that hero "without peer" all the more to Michelangelo. The sonnet, in its traditional form, offered a similar challenge. If some writers in the Renaissance made the madrigal, like the elegy, more elastic in form, Michelangelo, knowing that musical settings required an exactitude of "beat," allowed himself varying numbers of lines, but regular lines, in his madrigals. Like Ronsard and the other lyricists whose poems were set to music by Lassus, Jannequin, Costeley, or Archadelt, he did not have to accommodate his words to music. Rather, the conventional sequence was true: settings were composed for his completed poems.

In general, then, it may be stated that in poetry as in art Michelangelo illustrated the Parnassian ideal so well expressed in Théophile Gautier's *L'Art:* a work emerges the finer when executed in a more difficult medium. χαλεπὰ τὰ καλά.

From the foregoing exposition, it is clear that any discussion of Michelangelo's poetry—content, form, or style—will lead to inevitable confrontations with his art. We shall see below (Chapters IV, V, and *passim*) how similar themes and thoughts are reflected in Michelangelo's poetry and art. Others have confronted the two ever since Berni claimed to see the same Platonism in both types of creativity of this Apollo-Apelles. In his unusually lengthy lecture on the many disciplines governed by Dame Painting, which he delivered to Francisco de Hollanda and their friends, Michelangelo himself asserted that painting was the sovereign of "writing and the writing of histories."[7] In these same conversations, during a discussion of poetic and pictorial license, Michelangelo quoted the famous lines of Horace which attribute similar powers and techniques to the sister arts: "Pictoribus atque poetis aequa potestas," lines taken from the very treatise in verse which bequeathed to later generations the seminal phrase: "ut pictura poesis."

Many commentators in recent times—ever since Ugo Foscolo's two essays on Michelangelo's poetry appeared in England (1826)—have paused over the resemblance between Michelangelo as poet and as artist. Sir Joshua Reynolds claimed that Michelangelo was great as a poet precisely because he was a great artist. "I will not say Michael Angelo was eminently poetical only because he was greatly mechanical: but I am sure that mechanic excellence invigorated and emboldened his mind to carry painting into the regions of poetry, and to emulate that art in its most adventurous flights: Michael Angelo equally possessed both qualifications."[8] The most unrestrained comment on this coincidence is the oft-quoted claim of Farinelli: "To Michelangelo there was apparently granted an art never conceded to men, an art halfway between poetry and sculpture which brought out his thought and gave it poetic figuration without the need of creating style, language, meter, or versification."[9] (To this claim Bevilacqua responded ironically "Grazie tanto!" and observed that this made of Michelangelo a hybrid.)

Numerous other scholars have commented more soberly on this identity of technique and procedure. Nesca Robb, returning to that Platonism which was observed by Berni in both arts, comments: "It was left for Michelangelo to inform the Petrarchan-Neoplatonic lyric with something of the fire and vigor which distinguishes his art."[10]

Several commentators have insisted that Michelangelo's poetry partakes of his sculpture. In his edition of the poetry, Professor Amendola viewed the poetic corpus of Michelangelo as "the laboratory of a sculptor who has only partially extracted from the marbles the phantasms of his art."[11] In *Nuova antologia*, Isidoro del Lungo wrote back in 1909: "In the rough verse of Michelangelo you can hear the repercussion and hammering of the mallet with which he has hitherto fought to liberate the *concetto* in the marble."[12] More recently, Valerio Mariani has insisted on this point, seeing in Michelangelo's poetry the hand of the stonecutter: "His poetic expression becomes a keen chiseling in hard material, and the roughness of certain words is quite close to so many parts of his sculpture left scarcely indicated on purpose, so that there may result a sharper contrast with those verses which he turns and elaborates so tirelessly."[13]

As we have written elsewhere, Michelangelo's painting and sculpture not only parallel and elucidate his own writings, but reflect other literary sources: Plato, the Bible, Ovid, Tommaso di Celano, St. Ambrosius, Dante, Petrarch, Villani, Guicciardini, Poliziano, Ficino, Sannazaro, and Savonarola. Thus, the Paragone between the arts is further intensified.

As committed to both arts as he was, Michelangelo never became involved in the Cinquecento's disputes on the relative values of painting and poetry. Had he done so, he would have stressed resemblances rather than distinctions between art and poetry (as in his letter to Varchi on the Paragone). Art to Michelangelo was not a mere manual craft, but an intellectual pursuit. He wrote to a prelate at the court of Paul III: "I reply that one paints with the brain and not with the hands."[14] He wrote in another context to Giovan Francesco Fattucci, "you can't work on one thing with your hands and on another with your brain."[15] Even his famous quatrain "Non ha l'ottimo artista alcun concetto" stresses that the hand is merely the agent of the intellect. Thus, Michelangelo agreed for once with Leonardo da Vinci, who decreed painting "una cosa mentale." It was easy for him to equate the power and intentions of poetry and sculpture, as he did in the passage with which we began this chapter.

One always speaks of "the style" of Michelangelo. Actually, he had several, both in his art and his poetry. He was not unaware of this himself. On a Louvre sketch of a group including the Madonna, the Christ Child, and Saint Anne he penned, "Chi dire' mai che sie di mia mano?" ("Who could ever tell that it was by my hand?") For most of the varied styles of Michelangelo there are convenient labels. There are tentative attempts at pastoral, not sustained for long, the most conspicuous being his *Stanze in lode della vita rusticale* ("Nuovo piacere e di maggiore stima") and his sonnet "Rendete agli occhi miei, o fonte o fiume." Since his art is so lacking in bucolic themes and settings, it comes as no surprise that the *Rime* devote little attention to external nature. The most common style is the "troubled confessional," emotional style of Petrarchism, which influenced Michelangelo's early lyrics and was never completely displaced until the disturbed soul searchings of the 1540s and 1550s. There seem to be evidences of the *dolce stil nuovo* in his verse, especially in such pieces as "Perchè pur d'ora in ora mi lusinga" and "Passa per gli occhi al core in un momento." A Gothic piece, "Chiunque nascie a morte arriua," (see Chapter XV) has a mediaeval refrain worthy of Villon's *Ballade des pendus:*

Like you we were men,
Like you happy and sad;
And now we are, as you see,
Sun-warmed clay deprived of life.
Everything ends in death, etc.

This ballad is unique, akin to the rare macabre notes in his painting. He achieves this somber mediaeval tone elsewhere only in a stray verse, as in his image of a scythe-bearing Father Time "come falce e noi sian come fieno."

Gothic realism, however, was no more dissonant than was the Bernesque trend of the times. There are moments in the *Rime* which shock one more abruptly than do any of the nudities or pudenda of his painting. Thus, such a confessional *capitolo* as "I' sto rinchiuso come la midolla," with its brutal portrait of an aging, sickly man:

D'intorn a l'uscio ho mete di giganti,
Chè chi mangi uua o ha presa medicina
Non uann' altrou' a cacar tutti quanti.
I' ho 'mparato a conoscer l'orina
E la cannell' ond'esce, per quei fessi

Che nanzi dì mi chiaman la mattina.
Gatti, carogne, canterelli o cessi
Chi n'ha per masseriti' o men uiaggio
Non uien a mutarmi mai senz' essi. (G 267)

(For translation see p. 266.)

Vincenzo Pascale calls all this the work of a "student of anatomy."[16] Certainly the function of poet as well as artist was preceded by that of surgeon when Michelangelo was performing illicit anatomies on the corpses from the morgue of the Church of Santo Spirito in Florence. There are Bernesque traits in many of the poems, particularly in "Tu hai il viso più dolce che la sapa" and in "Io ho gia fatto un gozzo in questo stento" (see Chapter XV).

There are touches of preciosity which seem to look forward to the age of Voiture, such alembications as:

Vorrei uoler, Signior, quel ch'io non uoglio (G 87)

Tu sai ch' i' so, Signor mio, che tu sai . . .
E sai ch' io so che tu sa' ch' i' son desso. (G 60)

However, since preciosity is so alien to Michelangelo's character, such verses might better be attributed to baroque disorder or to that mediaeval attitude which allowed even the greatest poets to view poetry as learned trickery (cf. Dante: *Inf.* xiii, 25: "Io credo ch' ei credette ch' i' credesse").

After Michelangelo's Petrarchism and Platonism, the most striking style in his poetry is the baroque. Since baroque is more than a style—indeed an orientation of the personality and a special temperament in itself, I shall reserve for the following chapter a full discussion of Michelangelo as an early baroque poet and stylist.

If Michelangelo's poetic styles are several, his poetic moods are even more variable. To Pope Julius and to Luigi del Riccio he writes with bitterness. To his dead father Lodovico he displays tenderness and reassurance. To the godless who profane the capitol of Christianity and those who hanged and burned Savonarola he writes in righteous wrath, the wrath of the *Christus Iudex*. To Febo di Poggio he rhymes in abjection and regret. To Tommaso Cavalieri he expresses exaltation and an almost religious passion. In the notes to his poems to Cecchino de' Bracci he attains vulgarity. To his God he writes with humiliation and even terror. If color makes for a great work of art, a premise which the artist never accepted, the emotional coloration of Michelangelo's poems makes them even more worthy of universal attention.

Michelangelo was not so original in his choice and exploitation of genres as he was in other respects. His manipulation of the sonnet was orthodox, in so far as its external form was concerned. He gave considerable variety to the madrigal. He seized on the quatrain as the easiest and most economical way to write *epitaffi*. He was only rarely a practitioner of the "ottava d'oro" of his time. He tried his hand at the *ballade* in "Chiunche nasce a morte arriva" but he could not carry it through to its mediaeval length. He found the *capitolo* a delightful, free form to work in, despite the extra discipline of *terza rima*. He did not consciously write epigrams, that genre so popular with the neo-Latin group, but his own ironic nature led him in many of his pieces to work up to a *pointe* in the very last verse, in the best tradition of Marot, Scaliger, and the rest. Thus one might classify as epigrams those poems which led up to last lines phrased as aphorisms and frequently introduced by *che* or *chi:*

> He who grows up wanting, 'tis good that he die. (G 204)
> For a little wind will bring down a winter flower. (G 218)
> He cures all ills who takes life. (G 137)

There are many of these epigrammatic *pointes*, as will be shown in Chapter XVIII.

It should be noted that Michelangelo seemed little concerned with the nomenclature or even traditional strictures of these various forms, calling a madrigal a "canzone" and finding even vaguer words ("novelle," etc.) for his poems. These categories, as we have noted, seemed important enough to Guasti for him to present the poetry by poetic forms rather than by chronology. Fortunately Frey, Girardi, and the other editors decided that an accurate chronology is a better way than loose generic distribution to dispose these poems.

Michelangelo's language and spelling may be considered together. Michelangelo's vocabulary, by the standards of the better Renaissance poets, is simple enough. He uses very few proper nouns requiring a knowledge of history or mythology, nouns so frequent in the work of the Renaissance *doctus poeta*. Daedalus, Medusa—fewer than a half-dozen of these are named. Missing are the names of Tityus, Phaëton, and Ganymede, celebrated in the drawings. The vocabulary of the love poetry was no more complicated than that collected in McKenzie's *Petrarch Concordance*. There are none of the invented words and neologisms which Sperone Speroni, Du Bellay, and others were urging poets to introduce into the vernacular. Nevertheless, Michelangelo managed to be one of the most obscure of poets. As one of his editors (Ceriello) writes: "Rough poetry, then, carved in grey stone, scarcely articulated, dark as a December vespers, and yet intimate and suggestive . . . In Michelangelo the strength of the poetry is enclosed in the hermetic form itself, etc."

Ever since the edition of Guasti, the Italian editions of the *Rime* have included in marginal position or in an appendix a complete translation or paraphrase of the poems, set as prose. Despite the simplicity of vocabulary (forms like "istienti" and "ammezzami" are rare), the poems have required "translation" even for Michelangelo's compatriots. Translators into English and French have often "explained" the poems rather than rendered exact equivalents. The learned Grimm gave up his translation project, and Rilke abandoned a complete translation. Just as Alberti, Lomazzo, and Pino were claiming that art must "veil" truths, so Michelangelo casts a slight veil over his meanings in the *Rime*. Aretino, admirer of Michelangelo's poetry even more than of his art, claimed in Dolce's *Dialogo della Pittura* that Michelangelo imitated the Philosophers who veiled truths.[17] It is probably paying Michelangelo an excessive compliment as a poet to assume that his obscuration was a conscious, planned thing. Michelangelo, so eager to force ideas into a given poetic form, did not always achieve clarity and polish. Nor was he usually interested, as we shall see in a moment, in the labor of the file. Criticism of Michelangelo's habit of forcing thoughts into his molds—jotting thoughts quickly into poetic expression on the back of letters, plans, and sketches just as he would jot down artistic *pensieri*—is in a sense well taken by Enrico Bevilacqua. On evaluating Berni's comment that Michelangelo said things and not words, Bevilacqua demurred that the poet's mission is to deal in words and to make them an important objective.[18] To other critics, however, the very roughness of Michelangelo's verse has won praise as a distinguishing feature.

Certainly the modernising of Michelangelo's spellings do not achieve a greater clarity, as some editors seem to believe. The Italians have attacked Carl Frey unjustifiably for keeping the archaic spellings of the autographs, holding that modernisation makes for intelligibility. Modernisation hardly seems justified, for even in more familiar orthographical dress, Michelangelo still requires the same accompanying paraphrasing. As already suggested, the autograph readings tell us much about the man himself, notably that this honorary citizen of Rome, whose loyalties were so often divided between Rome and Florence, continued to write and pronounce in the Tuscan manner.

Michelangelo seems to have had a particular disregard for spelling, just as for grammar. However, if the modern reader has no trouble with such forms as "l 'opre suo" and "il mie lauoro," he need not flinch before Michelangelo's peculiarities of spelling, which may be divided into several distinct categories.

First were the spellings showing that throughout his life he remained faithful to Tuscan pronunciations. We remember that it was for precisely this marked Tuscan accent that Aldovrandi in Bologna had the young sculptor read him to sleep with passages from the Florentine poets. Tuscan phonetics is responsible especially for the softened palatal forms:

chape', chome, chontemplare, chor, chui, pastinacha, chol, fuocho, locho, piangho, inchredibile, Christo, berlinghozzi

archo, apicha, tocha, pechato, richo, secho

After 1527–28, according to Miss Lucilla Cuilich (see below), this *ch* becomes c. His Tuscan habits allow him to work toward suppression of the palatal plosive:

giaccio, giaccia, giande, viscio, sciecto, pregiere, ciusi, ciaro, ciave

until he finally eliminates the palatal completely:

iaccia / stiavi

The soft palatal x which infiltrated Spanish and Portuguese is found:

confuxa, uxo, uxur, bixognio, dexio

Indeed, Michelangelo's most common misspellings deal precisely with the palatals or sibilants:

bracca, piacco, gusto, gunto, gumelle, giacco, cucho, vagi, lusingi, luogi, pagi, priegi

Ciuco has two elements of misspelling, both palatal:

cucho

Even Roman phonetics seem to infiltrate, however, such forms as:

obrigi

Then there were the special spellings which revealed the artist's pretensions to learning and etymology. Some of these would seem to betray what little Latin he did know:

rocta, cicta, ecterno, gacti, secte (from septem), socto, tucto

Although Miss Cuilich suggests that the phonosyntactic doublings *acte* (for *a te*) and *sectu* (se *tu*) prove this *-ct* a mere graphic convention with the artist, without connections with etymology. In this regard it is interesting that Riccio and Giannotti, those fervent humanists, tried to Latinise his spellings with such revisions as "ha, havete, huom, honor, hor," and the like. (In his own writings Giannotti habitually used *et* for e, and closed letters to Michelangelo with *vale!*) That they succeeded only in embarrassing the artist is revealed in the *Dialogi* of Donato, where Michelangelo admits to precisely these two editors: "You almost awaken a desire in me to study this book of his [the Grammar of Priscianese] to learn Latin letters."[19] This same lack of Latin is apparent from such spurious forms as *sine peccata* in his footnote to Riccio after G 192. The constant use of *u* for *v* (uiuo, uuol, etc.) was common among the humanists and might well be expected from an officer of the Florentine Academy, as might also such retarded forms as:

gratia, satio, iuditio, iustitia, penitentia

The curious "rocta" is distorted from Petrarch's verse "rotta è l'alta colonna" and is found on the sketch of the bronze *David* in the Louvre. A final type of Latinist or "grammarian" spelling were such forms as "inmago, inmortale, and inmagine."

Miss Cuilich's paper "La grafia di Michelangelo" read to the Florentine sessions of the 1964 Convegno di Studi Michelangioleschi states that the period 1527–28 marks a simplification of Michelangelo's spelling, while the period 1540–46 is characterised by disappearance of the diacritical *i* (*nascier* to *nascer*) and phonosyntactic doublings (*arroma, annoi,* etc.).

For the rest, Michelangelo's spelling habits grew out of haste, carelessness, or inability. Many of them seem to show an inclination toward phonetic spelling, a movement of language reform which was taking root among such linguists as Jacques Peletier during the Cinquecento. Thus,

im parte, impietra, com pari
da mme, a ddio, a sse

were forms which might have proceeded more quickly had not the sixteenth and seventeenth centuries created academies in Western Europe precisely to retard such reforms.

Michelangelo, born at the very end of that long and complex period which invented rhyme, used conventional rhyme and metrical patterns and almost never indulged in blank or free verse. Rhyme was not one of his obvious talents. Sometimes he makes compromises to syntax, even meaning, to achieve rhyme. Sometimes he leaves the perfecting of rhyme till last, and never attaining it, leaves lines suspended without a rhyming line. There are many of these cases, two such orphaned lines being "Per poco spazio dentro par che cresca" in the madrigal "Come può esser ch'io non sia più mia" and "Sì di raro e' mie' veggon gli occhi vostri" in the madrigal "Se 'l commodo degli occhi alcun costringi." His rhyming can be careless in other ways. Often he will match a word with itself (*antico* with *antico*; *volse* with *volse*; *propitio* with *propitio*). His insouciance about rhyming a word twice with itself, without changed meaning, is most apparent in the first two quatrains of the following sonnet:

Quand'el ministro de' sospir mie' tanti
al mondo, agli ochi mei, a sè si *tolse*,
Natura, che fra noi degnar lo uolse,
restò in uergogna, e chi lo uide in pianti.

Ma non come degli altri oggi si uanti
del sol del sol, ch'allor ci spense e *tolse,*
morte, ch'amor ne uinse, a farlo il *tolse*
in terra uiuo e 'n ciel fra gli altri santi. (G 47)

(For translation see pp. 200–201.)

Variant forms of this sonnet show the artist struggling further with this problem of form and content.

The famous *enjambement* which was to become such an issue between the neoclassics and romantics is practiced without question by Michelangelo:

Non uolse morte non ancider senza
l'arme degli anni e de' souerchi giorni
la beltà, che qui giace, acciò ch'or torni
al ciel con la non persa sua presenza.

La carne terra e qui l'ossa mie, priue
de' lor begli occhi . . .

These overflows did not bother Michelangelo, any more than did his painting across the guide lines plotted out in advance on the Sistine Ceiling.

Nor was he concerned when a verse either lacked a syllable or provided a superfluous one. Enzo Girardi has provided in his edition a list of the following *ipermetrie:*

e 'l sangue di Cristo si vend'a giumelle (10, v. 2)
d'ora in or manca ogni mortal bellezza (22, v. 48)
negli occhi di quest'angel lieto e solo (61, v. 10)
ben provvide natura, ne conviene (69, v. 1)
luci l'ore del fin fian men moleste (98, v. 7)

Girardi has observed the verses which seem to lack a syllable:

S'e' giudizi temerari e sciocchi (164, v. 7)
l'anima e 'l corpo e lo spirto 'nsieme (110, v. 2)

In these and other cases Girardi has resorted to synaloephe, elision, hiatus, diphthongisation, and other licenses to make the verses scan properly.[20]

Study of Michelangelo's metrics and rhyming confirms our impression that he viewed the basic challenge of poetry, as he did that of art, to be the capture of essential form, the *concetto.* The terminal process was of lesser interest to him. As an artist he had assistants to whom he might entrust the finishing. Michelangelo's relegation of a poem to Luigi del Riccio, Donato Giannotti, or Vittoria Colonna for their retouches paralleled his entrusting the final details of a statue to Cristoforo Solari or Francesco Urbino.

This lack of concern for the polishing process accounted for the Homeric nods mentioned in the previous section. There are others. In a long poem on the effects of love, as Girardi also has noticed, he shifts the pronoun from *tu* to *voi.*

He knew withal that experimentation and *labor limae* were a recognised necessity in both art and poetry. He accepted them in painting as a normal phase:

> No different is it with rustic papers;
> Before the ready hand takes the brush,
> It tries out and reviews the most perceptive and fine
> Of the learned first drafts; and forms its subject. (G 236)

The labor of the file interested him less as a poet since he felt he had no reputation at stake. However, when it became a question of publishing a florilegium of poems, he chose the most finished of his productions and showed a willingness to polish them further. In a letter (CDXXIV) to Del Riccio in 1542 he wrote:

> I further beg your Lordship to send me my draft and that of Perino or Pierino, and also that sonnet I sent you, so that I can have a glance at it and straighten it out, as you said.

In a note to Riccio, appended to the sonnet "Appena prima i begli ochi uid' io," he asks that Riccio make any necessary revisions:

> Messer Luigi, the last four verses of the eight at the head of the sonnet which I sent you yesterday contradict themselves; therefore I beg you to send it back to me and fit in these instead of those, so that it will be less clumsy; or else you straighten it out for me.

The madrigal "A l'alta tuo lucente diadema" bears the simple penned notation: "A rachonciar questo dì (to be revised today)."

It is not possible, of course, to divide Michelangelo's creative activity in poetry into an "art" (planning) phase and a "nature" (rapid execution) phase, as we have done elsewhere for his artistic production. Some of the poetry was dashed off with preliminary planning, certainly, even though Michelangelo paid lip service to the classical doctrine of inspiration. The gift of poetry "rains" down on the elect, as he knew grace rained, and thus feeds the Pierian pool. When his inspiration fails him, he cries to Riccio: "Silly things! The spring is dry. We must wait till it rains, and you are in too great a hurry" (Letter XXXIII). Another time the *furor poeticus,* in which his Neo-Platonist friends believed (as in the other three furies of the *Phaedrus*), fails to stir him. To Riccio he complains; "Because poesy has been tonight in the doldrums, I send you four crude ring cakes for the three honey cakes of the economiser" (Letter XLV).

Sometimes, in his revision, Michelangelo essayed an entirely different form. We find two redactions of "Le gratie tue e la fortuna mia"; one is a madrigal and the other is an incomplete sonnet, "La tuo bellezza e la fortuna mia." To this piece Michelangelo il Giovane appended the note: "He tried to write a sonnet and didn't finish, so he made a madrigal." However, Girardi claims that the contrary was true. Sometimes the existing variant forms of a piece show that several phases of elaboration have been undertaken. Many intermediate steps accompanied the evolution of the incomplete sonnet "D' un foco con i be' uostri' ochi accesi" to the complete "Sento d'un foco un freddo aspetto acceso." The inclusion of variant readings in the Frey and especially the Girardi editions affords an idea of the extent to which Michelangelo revised his *Rime*. He revised less than do professional poets, but at the suggestion of friends, of musicians, or in preparation of the edition planned by Riccio and Giannotti, he revised more than is usually supposed. Some 55 poems out of his total of 302 have variant readings of importance, and many have more than two variant readings. Indeed, "Per ritornar là donde venne fora" and "Non so se s'è la desiata luce" have seven readings, "Ogni cosa che io veggio mi consiglia" has twelve. Many have six variant versions, including "Per quel che di uoi, Donna, di fuor veggio," "S' alcuna parte in donna è che sie bella," "Amor, se tu se' dio," and "S'avvien che spesso il gran desir prometta."

The extent of this revision allows one to suppose that Michelangelo, despite all his disclaimers, occasionally felt the vocation of poet and accepted the consequent responsibilities.

The scholars mentioned in our Bibliography have varied considerably in their assessments of Michelangelo's worth as a stylist. Almost all have conceded him the status of poet for his force, self-revelation, and originality, rather than for his "style." In a sense, critical opinion has praised Michelangelo for the content rather than the form of his poetry. Croce was one of the first to deny him status as a poetic craftsman, saying of the *Rime*: "Those verses, if one observes them well, are expressive rather than poetically expressive, strong prose rather than song."[21] Amico-Mantia held the same general view: "If the *Rime* have a defect, this is to be found in the outer austerity of form, arising in him mainly from a lack of art and aptitude for versifying. He was a Petrarchist in form because the century's taste demanded it and because, lacking totally in classical culture, he could not attempt new ways. Nevertheless, in a style formally condensed, in forms not always beautiful and often disordered, he had originality of conceit, he had deep thoughts."[22]

Another who feels that the style is defective is Giuseppe Guido Ferrero, in his brief volume *Il Petrarchismo del Bembo e le Rime di Michelangelo*: "In conclusion, even of Michelangelo as rimer, one may say more or less what has been said of Gaspara Stampa: His poetic work is deficient in *style*;

whether by style one intends, in its deepest meaning, unity and coherence of fanciful vision, in which a personality is completely expressed, or whether the word is to have a more superficial sense: clarity and finished quality of form . . . there is in Michelangelo material, albeit partly raw (*grezzo*), for a poetic world; his work in verse has remained, not in this or that composition but in the whole, a preliminary sketch."[23]

The writers of the principal manuals of Italian literature have been extremely cautious in praising Michelangelo as a stylist, even while finding other compensating qualities in the *Rime*. Attilio Momigliano finds that Michelangelo has usually lost the struggle to enclose his thought in poetic form. Mario Sansone agrees that Michelangelo, "rarely a poet," was not quite successful in his effort to dominate his material and translate it into lyrical expression. While finding more to praise than do the other historians, Natalino Sapegno also finds contortions and harshnesses and improprieties characteristic of writers whose thought struggles laboriously with form.

A small group of vocal enthusiasts, descending from Farinelli, finds Michelangelo great even as a stylist. In concluding his readable monograph, *Michelangelo Buonarroti poeta*, Pascale displays the growing attachment or "crystallization" which a biographer or scholar usually develops for the subject of his study: "The style is noble and grave, it takes from poesy the vivacity of colors, from eloquence its movement and strength; for this reason it gives that vigor to his poetic language, which the Petrarchists were debilitating more and more."[24] Following in this vein, other critics have congratulated Michelangelo for achieving frequently the poetic style of Dante rather than of Petrarch. Still others, like Flamini, minimise any and all affinities with other writers and assert of Michelangelo: "in poetry, also, he has the virtue of resembling no one."[25]

The outstanding criticism of these and other scholars is that Michelangelo lacked polish and finish as a poet. But he lacked polish and finish as a man and often as an artist. Furthermore, he was disinterested in the finishing process, in poetry or art, viewing it as a laborious dedication. Only the matching of *concetto* and *materia* held his interest. That he did not retouch five out of six poems shows this. Michelangelo wished to display a quality discussed by the art theorists variously as "prontezza di mano" (Paolo Pino) or "prestezza senza fatica" (Armenini). He even states in the *Diálogos em Roma* that he should prefer an artist who works more rapidly and less well to one who is slower and slightly better. This conviction he applied to himself as a poet. He wrote rapidly, even carelessly. He did not always win his hasty struggle with form. Raphael, his artistic antagonist, wrote poetry more slowly and with certain style. But no one reads Raphael today, whereas Michelangelo increases in stature. In any case, recognising Michelangelo's stylistic defects, we agree in principle with a comment about him cast in the eloquent rhetoric of 1831: "The errors and vices of those who are outstanding in heart and genius are worth more than insipid virtues and timid, pusillanimous beauties."[26]

NOTES

[1] Pierre de Bouchaud, *Les poésies de Michel-Ange et de Vittoria Colonna* (Paris, 1912), pp. 98–99.

[2] Arturo Farinelli, "Michelangelo poeta," in *Raccolta di studi critici dedicata ad A. D'Ancona* (Florence, 1901), pp. 306, 331.

[3] Gino Saviotti, *La vita e le Rime di Michelangelo Buonarroti* (Livorno, 1916), p. 48; G. Papini, *La vita, ed. cit.*, p. 9.

[4] See Girardi edition, p. 400.

[5] R. J. Clements, *Michelangelo's Theory of Art* (New York, 1961), p. 306.

[6] Valentino Piccoli, *Le Rime* (Turin, 1930), note to no. XVII.

[7] Francisco de Hollanda, *Diálogos em Roma* (Porto, 1930), pp. 206 ff.

[8] Sir Joshua Reynolds, *Discourses*, IV.

[9] Arturo Farinelli, *Michelangelo e Dante* (Turin, 1918), p. 5. See also Enrico Bevilacqua, *op. cit.*, p. 645.

[10] Nesca Robb, *Neoplatonism of the Italian Renaissance* (London, 1935), p. 240.

[11] *Poesie di Michelangelo*, with preface by Giovanni Amendola (Lanciano, 1911 and 1931), p. 240.

[12] Isidoro del Lungo, *Nuova antologia*, I (Sept. 1909), 4.

[13] Valerio Mariani, *La poesia di Michelangelo* (Rome, 1941), p. 135.

[14] *Lettere*, ed. Milanesi, p. 489.

[15] *Ibid.*, p. 450.

[16] Vincenzo Pascale, *Michelangelo Buonarroti poeta* (Naples, 1902), p. 62.

[17] Lodovico Dolce, *Dialogo della Pittura* (Florence, 1734), p. 242. On the hermeticism of Michelangelo's *Rime*, see Girardi, "Michelangelo Buonarroti," in *Letteratura italiana* (Milan, 1961), pp. 864–66.

[18] Bevilacqua, *op. cit.*, p. 643.

[19] Donato Giannotti, *Dialogi, ed. cit.*, p. 65.

[20] Girardi, ed., pp. 536–37.

[21] Benedetto Croce, *Poesia popolare e poesia d'arte* (Bari, 1933), pp. 392 ff.

[22] Antonio Amico-Mantia, *L'amore e le Rime di Michelangelo* (Trapani, 1899), p. 32.

[23] Giuseppe Guido Ferrero, *Il Petrarchismo del Bembo e le Rime di Michelangelo* (Turin, 1935), p. 93.

[24] Vincenzo Pascale, *op. cit.*, p. 163.

[25] F. Flamini, *Il Cinquecento* (Milan, 1900), p. 201.

[26] G. B. Niccolini, "Del sublime in Michelangelo," in *Opere in prosa* (Florence, 1831), p. 163.

3

MICHELANGELO AS A BAROQUE POET

Michelangelo Buonarroti's influence upon baroque sculpture is now widely recognised by historians. Ever since that morning in 1506 when he and the Sangalli, father and son, watched the white Pentelic marble of the *Laokoön* emerge from the farmland of Felice de Freddis near the Baths of Titus, Michelangelo's restless mind found authority in antiquity for a revision of his aesthetic canons. In this agonising group Michelangelo found justification for moving beyond the symmetry, restraint, and *proportione divina* of the Donatellian mode of sculpture, the static scientism of Da Vinci's painting, and the Vitruvian rules of architecture—even though he paid lip service to those rules and even recited them to popes. Whereas Michelangelo did not acknowledge this influence in writing, or apparently in speaking, his contorted and anguished *Haman* (1511–12) on the spandrel of the Sistine Vault was an admission of the influence of this Rhodian group—just as El Greco's newly restored *Laokoön* in Washington acknowledges it as the one work of art which initiated European baroque. Moreover, the anguishes of the Vatican *Laokoön* and the expressions thereof were to parallel those tensions—visible even in his death mask—of Michelangelo's own soul and to leave an imprint upon his poetry. Laokoön, it should be remembered in view of his impact upon European baroque, was a militant, ritualistic priest.

The assessment of the baroque values in Michelangelo's painting and sculpture—and in the drawings, where almost every figure reveals Michelangelo's addiction to the serpentine line and accentuated *contrapposto*—has been undertaken by various studies recorded in the Steinmann-Wittkower bibliography.[1] Many of the catch phrases of the historians of aesthetics find immediate application in Michelangelo's art. The *visión lejana* of Ortega or the "emancipation from the earth" of Eugenio d'Ors describing the celestial plane of baroque representation finds magnificent articulation in the histories of the Sistine Ceiling ("là . . . fra i rari e demidei")[2] or in the *Giudizio universale.* In fact, to some observers this latter piece of "pessimistic art" initiates the baroque period in painting.[3] The Sistine "loft" antedates such conspicuous baroque "faraway visions" as Andrea Pozzi's vault in Saint Ignatius, Rome, or the shining heavenly visions of El Greco, Tintoretto, Murillo, the Carracci, and other artists of the Counter-Reformation. The uncertainties and polarities of the human spirit appear as clearly on the face of Michelangelo's figure *Il Sogno* as they do on the perplexed visage of that other baroque dreamer for whom life is illusion, shadow, fiction, and dream: Segismundo in Calderón's *La vida es sueño.* Life, especially to those who look back on it, like the recently deceased Cecchino, seems a dream:

> . . . and if anyone remembers me,
> He seems to dream; so quick and greedy is death.
> That what has been seems never to have been. (G 200)

The violent martyrdom and metamorphoses of Michelangelo's flayed St. Bartholomew exceed in kathartic horror the sufferings of St. Matthew, St. Sebastian, St. Ursula, or other holy men and women portrayed by the baroque Spanish painters at the urging of Luis Vives and the Church.

It would not be difficult to find further examples in Michelangelo's art of elements identifiable as baroque, whether baroque in form, content, or expression. It is a more challenging task to establish the baroque character of his outpouring of sonnets, madrigals, *canzoni, stanze,* and fragments (*non finiti,* as in his art). I say baroque, and not merely manneristic, a more superficial term which can hardly be applied to the intense Michelangelo. Two authors have dedicated monographs to Michelangelo's poetry without undertaking this particular task.[4] Tentative suggestions have been voiced, however, that Michelangelo's poetry was at least partially baroque.[5] The first problem to be faced is that baroque is above all else a spirit which transcends individual genres, and secondly, a grouping of characteristics which may be valid for one art form but not transferable to another. The radiant or ruddy gleams which transfuse or highlight a baroque canvas may be adapted to poetry, but not to sculpture, where the lighting is (as Michelangelo told Cellini) "il lume della piazza."[6] The puns which are a paradoxical device of literary baroque are hard to achieve in painting, even though Michelangelo will pun with his Cumaean Sibyl, holding her book at arm's length to show that she is "farsighted." Even sculpture will have its own baroque elements (contrasts of planes and recessions, for example) which poetry and music would find hard to duplicate.

In measuring the baroque spirit and characteristics of Michelangelo's

Rime, this chapter will be limited, then, to elements which may or may not be carried over to his works of figurative art. When a transposition is useful to the understanding or enrichment of a poem, it will be established. Slowly, after the pioneering of Wölfflin, more and more unanimity has been achieved in the definition of baroque style, language, or expression. Dominant characteristics will be selected from among those proposed, not without controversy, by Weisbach, Praz, Wellek, Hatzfeld, Raymond, Rousset, Odette de Morgues, Friedrich, Buffum, and Warren.[7] However, before dealing with the commonly accepted elements of baroque, I shall seek to establish that Michelangelo exemplified the spirit, as well as the letter, of baroque.

The baroque nature of Michelangelo's *Rime* resulted from the historical moment of the composition of the bulk of the verses, that is, during the latter half of the almost nine decades of his life (1475–1564). It resulted, further, from the intensely mystical nature of the man, particularly as he aged. It derived from his increasing uncertainty about the values he had adopted for his life and his career—an increasing and ego-shattering awareness of life's instability and irreality. Finally, it represented the sum of stylistic devices recognised as typical of baroque, and occasionally also manneristic expression, some of these abundantly present in Michelangelo's poetry.

It becomes, therefore, the aim of these pages to show that Michelangelo's verse is baroque because it is Counter-Reformational, because it is mystical and confessional, because it is riddled with doubt, contradiction, and *desengaño*, and lastly, because it utilises modes of expression now generally conceded to be typical of this religious and aesthetic movement.

Baroque has been viewed, especially since Werner Weisbach's *Der Barock als Kunst der Gegenreformation*, as an outgrowth of Counter-Reformational feeling. It is symptomatic that Ignatius Loyola, who launched the countermovement, hailed Michelangelo as the kindred spirit to undertake construction of his mother church, the Gesù, often cited as a model of baroque architecture after its completion by Vignola and Giovanni della Porta. Loyola's exaltation over Michelangelo's willingness to do the work, expressed in a circular letter (1554) to members of the Order, is a tribute not only to Michelangelo's stature as superintendent of the *fabbrica* in St. Peter's but also to his Counter-Reformational spiritual formation. In the militant language of the Counter-Reformation Michelangelo says that he knows not under what other standard (*insegna*) he is to combat (G 66). This spirit informs his late poems just as it affected his choice of artistic themes, his channeling of energies entirely to Christian subjects once he had settled in Rome (with the single exception of the bust of Brutus, nevertheless involved in Michelangelo's mind in a curious equation: Brutus: Caesar = Judas: Christ).[8]

Several of the key issues disputed by Protestants and Catholics are treated in the *Rime*. The Counter-Reformational line is upheld throughout.

On the issue of grace and the elect, Michelangelo hoped ardently that he was to be one of the chosen. The entire *Giudizio universale*, echoing the plea of Thomas of Celano in the *Dies Irae*, is a personal appeal for grace, paralleling the many similar pleas during the last period of the *Rime*. Grace "rains," but varies according to the worth and readiness of the recipient (G 273). Michelangelo's concern over grace was often expressed during his late years, at the nones and vespers of his life ("ma nona e vespro, e prossima la sera"). In one of his most disturbed sonnets, "Vorrei uoler, Signior, quel ch' io non uoglio," the old poet begs for grace and, fearing his own inadequacy, wonders how he may be so blessed:

> Now do I know well
> How I may open the door of my heart to grace,
> That it may enter there and cast out prideful resistance. (G 87)

His piece "Per qual mordace lima" (G 161) works up to a final plea: "Lord, in the final hours, stretch out to me thy merciful arms, take me from myself, and make of me someone thou mayest care for!" In a late sonnet the old man who has striven so hard to keep the faith pleads for grace:

> Oh, extend to me, My Lord, that chain
> Which is attached to every heavenly gift:
> Faith, I mean, toward which I strain and press,
> For, mea culpa, I have not entire and full grace. (G 289)

The effort to be worthy of grace must be constant and unbending: "Nel cor, ch'è piu capace, piu s'appiglia" (G 273). However, he later sympathised with the conviction of Juan de Valdés that grace depended more on faith than on works. Grace is more difficult to obtain for one who lives on into old age, when the demands of ascetic Christianity are harder to meet: "Non gioua senza gratia l'esser uechio," he wrote (G 263). The belief that one endangers salvation by longevity troubled this artist who almost completed his ninetieth year:

> I am grieved that one seldom finds grace and mercy
> In one's late years after so many sins . . . (G 294)

> And I see clearly, that grace and good fortune
> In this life are of brief and short duration . . . (G 234)

The belief proved a consolation, however, when the four babies of his nephew Lionardo died, for the great-uncle knew that these infants were assumed to a state of grace in their original innocence, and not in original sin as Calvin would have had it. This "gift of heaven" reappears in Michelangelo's love poetry and "rains" from the divine Vittoria Colonna (G 159). It was also in the context of a love poem that he expressed his desire to "ascender uiuo fra gli spirti electi/per gratia tal c'ogni altra par men buona" (G 279). Rare indeed is the word "elect" in his writings, but it is sometimes found—even if his belief in predestination was not Reformational, but Platonic. Indeed, he believed that man had a free will ("sciolto uoler"), and that only through sinning could man forfeit it (G 32). Nevertheless, his grandnephew found it necessary to revise two verses of "Vivo al pechato" as follows: from

> mie ben dal ciel, mie mal da me m'è dato,
> dal mie sciolto uoler, di ch'io son privo

to

> dalla cui fosca nebbia traviato,
> cieco cammino, e son di ragion privo.

Michelangelo sided with the Counter-Reformation on the mass. We have several references in letters and elsewhere to his attendance at mass, the last mention just preceding his death, when F. Miniato Pitti told Vasari in a letter (10 October, 1563) of meeting Michelangelo at mass. There is no reference to mass in the poems, however, nor to the selling of indulgences. Papini went so far as to theorise that Michelangelo's genius was the initial cause for the Reformation, since the Tomb of Julius II, entrusted to the artist, required huge sums of money and the consequent intensified sale of indulgences which spurred Luther to his schism.[9]

In general, the poetry complements Michelangelo's letters and quoted statements in which he condemns apostasy, upholds orthodoxy, and has little use for the critics of the Church, within and without. On the three grounds of authority, orthodoxy, and decency he will not stray from the Church's position. His scorn for Calvinists, Lutherans, and Zwinglians is revealed by his comment that heretical monks had "spoiled the world." At the bottom of the *Giudizio universale* lurks a monk held by many to be Luther. Michelangelo could criticise popes as men but not as successors to Peter. He could write a sonnet (G 6) chiding Julius II for being a fallible patron and a "withered tree" (see Chapter V), but he would never question the infallibility of a pope as Vicar of Christ. Savonarola's treatment by Alexander VI, it is true, brought him to the verge of such condemnation. Papini claimed that Michelangelo was unorthodox in his belief that man was redeemed through Christ's blood, yet this chapter will suggest that his preoccupation with Christ's blood in the *Rime* was not schismatic, but merely betrayed an emphasis shared in common with many baroque mystics. As for decency, only one poem depends upon offensive language and imagery (the *capitolo:* "I' sto rinchiuso come la midolla") with its clinical and cloacal details. The other 342 poems and fragments are usually as inoffensive (see Chapter XV) as the Venetian Inquisitioners held his *Last Judgement* to be, even when those censors were indicting Veronese for painting soldiers and dogs in the *Feast at the House of Simon.*

Most of Michelangelo's deeply religious and Counter-Reformational convictions shine through the poetry. His belief in the efficacy of prayer is exemplified by his three poetic orisons.[10] His poems expressing fears about his own unworthiness illustrate his belief, expressed elsewhere to his friend Francisco de Hollanda (and probably heard much earlier from the lips of Savonarola) that only the most worthy artists deserve to paint church images.[11] On the matter of images and iconolatry, Michelangelo in practice and even by implication in one poem (G 20) believed in art's function as *Biblia laicorum.* Even though he never sculpted a Crucifixion, except the adolescent wooden *Crocifisso di Santo Spirito,* he composed a powerful sonnet to the Redeemer rising from the Cross: "Non fur men lieti che turbati e tristi" (G 298). The baroque structure of this piece is pointed out by Ceriello: "With the powerful imagination that intuited the tragic terribility of the *Giudizio universale,* Michelangelo in this sonnet unfolds the mystery of the Redemption. On a stage of three superimposed planes, hell, earth, and heaven, there towers over all a rearisen Christ, liberator of man from original sin."[12] Obviously, Michelangelo disapproved of the Protestant rejection of Purgatory, first established graphically by his idol Dante ("Che uisto ebbe l'inferno giusto e 'l pio") (G 248). Michelangelo's belief in confession stands revealed by the "mia colpas" of his poetry, even though his confiteors do not require priestly intercession. He did not spurn the saints in heaven, as did the Protestants, and they are mentioned in a general way in his poetry ("Che 'n ciel non nuoce l'esser men beato") (G 140). None is pointed out individually, like his sculptured Matthew or his painted Bartholomew. His alleged self-portraits, incidentally, are of saintly men —Bartholomew, Nicodemus, Proculus, and John the Baptist. His attitudes on other issues disputed between Northern and Southern Christians—free examination, miracles, relics, and the rest, are known to us from other sources than his *Rime.* Finally, the artist's belief in the efficacy of penance is only too clear from the poems.

Michelangelo's bulwark of belief concerning Church and theological matters then was that professed by the majority of baroque writers. If there was an occasional baroque poet among the Protestant schismatics (D'Aubigné, Du Bartas, Milton), baroque was so essentially a Catholic canon that Crashaw, son of an Anglican minister, went to live and work in Rome, as had Michelangelo himself, and Johann Scheffler likewise became converted.

The greatest baroque poets were Catholics who made of poetry a vehicle for the propagation of the faith; these poets were, moreover, mystics who spoke directly to God, Christ, the Virgin, or even the martyred saints. Michelangelo, who could make of verse a kind of anxious prayer, imprecation, or monologue to God or the Saviour, belongs firmly in their ranks. Like Saint Teresa, Crashaw, Southwell, Quevedo in his ascetic phase, and Marguerite de Navarre of the *Prisons*, Michelangelo voiced an increasingly mystic and anguished outpouring in his *Rime*. Sometimes the Signore he addresses is God, sometimes the baroque Christ whose blood purges mankind. The blood which drips from the Christ of the more baroque Crucifixions in Spain and Italy is not overlooked in Michelangelo's poetry:

I speak to thee, Lord, for every trial of mine
Outside of thy blood cannot make man blessed. (G 280)

Since Thou wast not avaricious with thy blood,
Will the gift of thy clemency be as great,
Since heaven will not be opened for us by any other key? (G 289)

May thy blood alone lave and heal my guilt,
And more abound as I grow older. (G 290)

To many Thou openest with thy blood the closed portals of heaven (G 298)
And with thy blood dost purge and heal souls (G 302)
Yet it seems that one gains understanding in thy blood (G 294)

As with other baroque imagery in these poems, this image of blood-sacrifice is mirrored in the verses on profane love: "And pound by pound she draws the blood from my fibers and veins" (G 172).

Mystic poetry is above all an expression of the *amor bueno*, love of God. This God of love and charity may be seen in the upper lofts of baroque paintings in anthropomorphic majesty, like the benign God of El Greco's *Baptism of Christ*. Michelangelo thus incarnates God in the Creations of the Sistine Ceiling. To Michelangelo the arm of God creates and the arm of Christ judges. He is almost as concerned with the arms of Christ as with Christ's blood. As a mystic he recalls and longs, as did Dante, for those arms:

Who opened his arms on the Cross to enfold us (G 285)

Lord, in the last hours,
Stretch out to me thy merciful arms. (G 161)

whose possible gesture of rejection, like that of the Christus Iudex of the *Last Judgement* fills his soul with foreboding:

> Non mirin con iustitia i tuo sant' ochi
> Il mie passato, e 'l gastigato orechio
> Non tenda a quello il tuo braccio seuero. (G 290)

(For translation see p. 125.)

Even that curious practice of the male mystics, calling themselves brides of God, is found in Michelangelo's troubled sonnet in which he calls upon God to brush away the veil of ice which separates the heats of their love—a fine baroque conceit:

> Send thy announced gleam of light, ordained to us,
> To thy beautiful bride, that I may burn. (G 87)

The whole question of the expression of mystical love in Michelangelo's *Rime* is complicated by the fact that he was in addition a Petrarchist and Platonist. Petrarchism in his poems parallels and even apes the religiosity in them, as the reader will observe. Platonism in his poetry vacillates between serving Michelangelo's God and the men he loved (or that spiritual companion, Vittoria Colonna, "un uomo in una donna," as he called her). The preponderance of Michelangelo's love poems being to men, he would seem to illustrate Constandse's theory that antifeminism and homosexuality were baroque traits. Michelangelo is martyrised by Christian anguish in "Penso e ben so, c'alcuna colpa preme" (G 291) and by earthly love in his madrigal, "Se 'l uolto di ch' i' parlo, di costei (G 245)." Love in the poems will be now sacred, now profane. The torments of Petrarchan love mirror, but are not confused with, the erotic ecstasy of the mystic longing to be joined to God. And one must sometimes read well into a poem before understanding whether the Signore addressed is God or one of those men on whom Michelangelo bestowed affection: Febo di Poggio, Gherardo Perini, or Tommaso Cavalieri. Even as we identify the baroque elements in the religious verse of Michelangelo, we find them paralleled in the stanzas of love. Take, for example, the traditional image of the Flaming Heart, originating with a vision of Teresa of Ávila and given concrete form in Bernini's *Saint Teresa in Ecstasy*, in Santa Maria della Vittoria. This image, rightly viewed by Mario Praz and Austin Warren as the epitome of baroque conceits, becomes a commonplace in Michelangelo's verse (G 121, 93, 138, 143, and *passim*). His heart flames in his mystical poetry:

> For it still burns and has burned these many years (G 92)

and is kindled by profane love:

> I cannot think how my heart burns (G 54)
> No longer a heart, but cinder and coals (G 92)

The image, found in other baroque and manneristic poets, of a flood of tears putting out the flames in the heart reappears in the *Rime* (G 231 and 170).

The legitimate concepts and vocabulary of baroque (suffering, uncertainty, *desengaño*, ecstasy, contrast, metamorphosis, imbalance) have spilled over into love poems where they become mere Petrarchistic or manneristic devices. Even martyrdom, as we have suggested: Michelangelo's eagerness for self-immolation "Nor do I shrink from martyrdom/Rather do I fear I may not have the chance of it" (G 138) is addressed to a woman to whom he offers his flaming heart, and not to God. Perhaps it would be more accurate to say that these conceits were restored by Michelangelo to the Petrarchan love poetry where they evidently originated. Indeed, I have sometimes felt that if any one man were the *capostipite* of European baroque as he was of mannerism, it was Petrarch. Michelangelo's familiarity with Petrarch's *canzoniere*, of which we have so many evidences, guided his steps, then, along the path to baroque. Perhaps no passage in literature was so seminal for the development of baroque love poetry, mystical as well as earthly, as Reason's definition of love in Petrarch's dialogue *De remediis utriusque fortunae* (i. 49): "Bene ais: uror. Est enim amor latens ignis, gratus vulnus, sapidum venenum, dulcis amaritudo, delectabilis morbus, iucundum supplicium, blanda mors." These words, so important a legacy to the baroque and metaphysical poets fond of paradox, oxymora, and metaphorical antithesis, find echoes in many of their works, including Quevedo's.

Since the mystic longs to be rejoined to God, the enforced stay on this earth becomes intolerable. Saint Teresa cried, "muero que no muero." Life on earth becomes a sentence in prison. Fray Luis looks up to the "innumerable lights" adorning heaven, his heart aflame and his eyes a fountain, and commiserates with his soul: "Qué desventura la tiene en esta cárcel baja, escura?" In his sonnet, "Como de entre mis manos te resbalas," Quevedo laments that every instant of life in this earthly duress is a "new execution." On several occasions Michelangelo assents that life is a prison from which he awaits deliverance:

> For it will be a happy moment
> To set down the burden once out of this earthly prison (G 264)
>
> In which prison here on earth the soul doth dwell (G 197)
>
> To return up there whence came forth
> Immortal form to thy earthly prison (G 106)

The prayer in Michelangelo's papers attributed to him by Guasti is a mystical appeal for such release: "Give me grace, that for so long a time as I shall stay in this prison inimical to my soul, in which thou alone holdest me, I may praise thee."[13] (For full text see p. 222.) This longing to return soon to God is expressed in the *Rime* in a variety of ways:

For I am envious of the dead (G 161)

For I am undone, if I die not soon. (G 267)

Sometimes the death of a loved one intensifies this desire for death. It was the demise of his assistant Urbino, for example, which pinpointed this new desire for death (Letter CDLXXVII): "In dying he taught me how to die, not with displeasure, but with desire for death." The letter is dated 23 February, 1556. Even when he wrote to his departed father, old Lodovico, he admitted:

> Thou art through dying made divine,
> Thou fearest no longer changing life or will,
> Scarce can I write thee this without a touch of envy. (G 86)

To the deceased Vittoria Colonna, he anticipates: "death and grief that I long for and seek" (G 45). To his perplexed query why death will not come sooner, he voices his resentment in a line with two oxymora:

> Cruel pity and pitiless mercy
> Left me alive . . . (Frey XCIX)

On several occasions Michelangelo had the experience of watching men die. In their eyes he saw God revealed, and wished for death himself:

> Now I cannot fail to see within a dying man
> Thy eternal light without a great desire. (Frey XXX)

A Christian longing for death may well convince himself that death is near. This motif finds curious expression in Michelangelo's verse. He is "eating on credit at the hostel of death" (G 267), for example. (One recalls here Petrarch's "Di mia morte mi pasco" [CCVII].) He is "already numbered among the dead" (G 62), "weary and near his last word" (G 268).

> With death at hand
> I lose the present and the future is taken from me. (G 144)

> Arrived at last at this the term of my life (G 285)

> What now remains to me of the day
> Of this short and brief life is fleeing. (G 143)

> I make my peace with death,
> Weary and near my last word. (G 268)

Death continues to haunt his poetry. He is "so close to death and so far from God" (G 66). He must "repent, make ready, and take counsel with himself with death near" (G 51). He feels death "right now" (G 130). He has reached his "final hours" (G 133 and 158). His very birth was already toying with death (G 263). Suddenly the glimpse of his white head reminds him that he "has already in hand the plow of the other life"

(G 263). Death is so near, but still the decline of his body is slow (G 232). Yet this imminence of death was more imagined than real—though he speaks as early as 1513–18 in a madrigal (G 12) of his forthcoming death ("propinqua morte"), he was to die in 1564, a half-century later!

One of the common themes of the baroque mystics is the nothingness of the body in which the soul is imprisoned. The instability of human life is nowhere better illustrated than by the threat of the "double death" which hangs over us, a death of body and soul from which the worthy among us will, however, be spared through God's encompassing love: "A la terra la terra e l'alma al cielo" (G 215). Man will rise from this body like a phoenix soaring forth from its own ashes:

> Nor does the unique phoenix take on new life
> If not first burned, whence I, if I die burning,
> Hope to rise up again more bright . . . (G 62)

The notion of a Christian phoenix is the basis of Michelangelo's other references to the body as ashes (G 239). His image of the body as a leather pelt was not a mere conceit. As with the mystic poets, it reflected a profound belief and it recurs constantly in his poetry. Michelangelo's awareness of the increasing debility of his own body obsessed him and he complained in letters and poems of some eleven maladies, including blindness, deafness, gallstones, dizziness, rheumatism, headaches, cramps, gout, arthritis, dysuria, and colic. His awareness that he was shrinking away toward death, captive within his pelt, reached its graphic culmination in his self-portrait as the dried skin of Saint Bartholomew in the *Giudizio universale*. However, there is graphic wording in his *Rime*; a great variety of usually perjorative nouns denote his body. The following sampling of verses will give an adequate idea:

> Dinanzi mi s'allunga la *chorteccia* (G 5)

> Or che 'l tempo la *scorza* cangia e muda,
> La morte e l'alma insieme ognior fan pruoue (G 51)

> Non posso altra figura immaginarmi
> O di nud' onbra o di terrestre *spoglia* (G 82)

> L'anima, della *carne* ancor uestita
> Con esso è gia piu uolte asciesa a Dio. (G 83)

Man's body is little more than that dried epidermis of the serpent which is rubbed against rock and so dissolved:

> Thus I should like my fate to clothe
> My lord's living body with my dead pelt,
> For, as a serpent sheds its skin against a rock,
> I should like to change my condition through death. (G 94)

Even that most beautiful of adolescents, Cecchino de' Bracci, is clothed in nothing more than "la carne terra" (G 197). Elsewhere (G 199) Michelangelo has the youth cry out in death that man is but a withered tree (a favorite image of our poet) and that "uom morto non risurge a primauera"! The image of death as a withering is repeated in (G 158), "Fallen is the fruit and dry already is the husk." The poet as prisoner of his encompassing flesh is comically described in the autobiographical *capitolo* already referred to:

> I' sto rinchiuso come la midolla
> Da la suo scorza, qua pouer' et solo,
> Come spirto legat' in un' ampolla. (G 267)
> (For translation see p. 266.)

The soul is imprisoned in the body much as the art form is hidden within the mass of marble:

> So some worthy actions
> For the yet trembling soul
> Are concealed by the surface of the flesh
> And its crude and coarse and hard husk. (G 152)

> Through what acid lime
> Does thy weary carcass now decrease and come apart,
> Infirm soul? (G 161)

Other references to the body as withered fill the poetry. Obsessed by the thought of the Last Judgement, Michelangelo could not forget that on the Day of Wrath God would reclothe these souls: "Se l'alma al fin ritorna/ Nella suo dolce e desiata spoglia" (G 140). Michelangelo returns to this "baroque theme"[14] several times in his poetry (G 186, note 227).

Michelangelo's mystical attachment to Christ is once again evident when he charges that Rome after Alexander VI violates the teachings of Jesus and when he adopts baroque expression to accuse Rome of "selling the pelt" of Christ and "vending the blood of Christ by the bucketful" (G 10).

One of the inherent functions of baroque poetry or art is to express the unstable, tentative, contradictory nature of life. Life is irreality, transition, paradox, even *desengaño*, "y los sueños sueños son." Similarly, Michelangelo has Cecchino conjecture that life was the real death:

> Che l'alma uiua, i' che qui morto sono
> Or ne son certo e che uiuo, ero morto. (G 226)

Nothing in life is to be taken for granted. Values are difficult to establish. "The truth does not surge forth," complains Michelangelo (G 295) to his God. More specifically, "What used to be festival and sport to me is now death" (G 281). Even Michelangelo's dedication to the fine arts, which led him to the highest artistic post offered by Christendom, may have consumed time better spent on other pursuits and brought him to *desengaño,* disenchantment. Antitheses find no easy synthesis in the baroque mind, even if the word "baroque" itself may have come out of mediaeval syllogistic logic. It is symptomatic that no fewer than forty-six of Michelangelo's poems begin with se (if), stressing uncertainty, hypothesis, or mutability of condition. This astonishing statistic does not include *incipits* within the body of poems, of which there are great numbers (G 6, 10, 28, and *passim*). Indeed, "S' un casto amor, s' una pieta superna" (G 59) contains ten se conditions. Even verses which should be outright affirmations come veiled as grammatical concessions:

Se 'l foco il sasso rompe e 'l ferro squaglia (G 64)

Se qui son chiusj i begli ochj e sepoltj (G 179)

Se dalla morte è uinta la natura (G 188)

Se 'l mie rozzo martello i duri sassi (G 46)

This same note of mutability and the provisional is attested by twenty-seven poems which begin with negatives. The uncertainty is not only implicit, but sometimes explicit: "Nè so," "non so" ("Nor do I know," "I don't know"), and the like.

The vacillating character of the baroque poet caught between contrasting polarities leaves him in a moral dilemma or even abulia:

Between vice and virtue
My confused heart travails and wearies me (G 162)

In twain it holds me confused (G 168)

What is to become of me? What guide or what escort
May there be of value and use to me against thee,
If thou burnest me by staying and killest me by leaving? (G 80)

My happiness is melancholy (G 267)

Sometimes his will is left subjected to the slightest tip of the scales:

. . . a yes or a no moves me (G 76)

What more can I do? What am I to do? (G 22)

The uncertainties of love are akin to those of mystic passion in that the poet is caught "between two perils, whence I sleep and am wakeful" (G 232). Love and cruelty create a dilemma in him:

One is armed with mercy, the other with death;
The latter kills us and the other keeps us living. (G 112)

My free will has been made slavery, my God
Has become mortal. Oh unhappy state! (G 32)

The baroque mentality viewed suffering and pain as an erotic-ecstatic experience, memorably phrased in Crashaw's "delicious Wounds." The divine or profane loves of Michelangelo thus motivate the following paradoxical thoughts:

O wondrous thing!
If the evil of the fire often heals the fire. (G 54)

The more one kills me the more one defends me (G 57)

Life grows as the malady grows (G 39)

And does me good when most harming me (G 57)

And harms me most when most delighting (G 296)

Even now as she kills me she defends and saves me (G 127, 128)

Compare Michelangelo's statement in a letter: "I don't know which is better, evil which helps or good that harms."

A common device of the baroque poet is the paradox which transcends sense and logic. There are several isolated lines exploiting this device. One of Michelangelo's early pieces is unusual in combining three such lines:

Bound tight, am I yet loose and free?
If thou chainest people without chains
And without hands or arms dost enfold me (G 7)

Many of these paradoxes arise from the life-death duality and are reminiscent of Robert Southwell's and Richard Crashaw's "living death" and "dying life," or even Saint Teresa's "Vivo sin vivir en mí." Writes Michelangelo, "And thus, within my soul for a brief moment together contrary life and death do I feel" (G 124). Other prominent examples are the lines evocative of Loyola's self-flagellation: "Viuo al pechato, a me morendo uiuo" (G 32), "E quel riposo c' anzi al nascer muore" (G 133), and "per morte uiue" (G 118 var.).

A device of baroque expression which challenges logic and juxtaposes polarities and contradictory ideas, such as the "living death" just mentioned, is the oxymoron. Michelangelo lifted one of the most common, the "dolce amaro" (bitter sweet) (G 76 and 158) from Petrarch. It appears again in "Vestito di dolceza e d'amar pieno" (G 17). However, the concept of bittersweet became so common that the French and English poets made a compound adjective of it. One notable verse with two oxymora has already been quoted, "Crudel pietate e spietata mercede." However, Michelangelo did not use this particular device of rhetoric and baroque expression too commonly; Marino was to be the champion Italian practitioner of oxymora.

The burning-freezing states which informed Petrarch's verses are frequent in Michelangelo's, applied to both sacred and profane love:

For today at one time my heart burns and freezes (G 19)

One freezes my heart and the other inflames me (G 257)

Which burns people from afar and turns them to ice (Frey CVIII)

A veil of ice hides between the fire and the heart (G 87)

Cold in the sun, warm in the coldest mists (G 89)

In this passage, recording the poet's need for God to manifest himself more fully, Michelangelo comes closest to becoming an "oxymoron incarnate," as Spitzer called Phèdre.[15] These flames which flicker in the baroque poetry and art of others are found everywhere in Michelangelo's *Rime*. They are, of course, harbingers of the all-consuming flames of the Day of Judgement ("solvet saeclum in favilla"), even more destructive than love's burnings. Flames and fire purify "to the highest degree," just as the goldsmith's fire makes a "perfect work" (G 153 and 62). Thus, Michelangelo writes of his soul, "like gold purged in fire to God it doth return" (G 243). And again, "we are made smoke and dust/I shall truly be eternal, if I endure the fire" (G 63). Flames are agents, also, of metamorphosis, reducing the heart to cinders or the body to ashes. The flaming heart dominates the entire series of poems grouped by Frey under CIX. Fire, that "calcinates hard rock," burns the heart to a crisp (G 170). A sonnet centers on the point that if love's fire can destroy a "green heart," how much more quickly does an old, dry heart go up in smoke (G 233 and 143).

Before leaving these engrossing paradoxes and contrasts in the artist's mind, we should attend to several remarkably baroque lines of varying categories, verses more or less self-explanatory:

I should be deadly except for my death (G 118)
From a fount of mercy gushes my evil (G 16)
The harder I try, the less I please thee (G 6)

This last complaint was addressed to Pope Julius II, who had been listening to unkind rumors about the artist, and whose slights and harshness had left Michelangelo in an agitated state.

The more time passes, the less good will lasts (G 269)

states Michelangelo's belief that grace is more difficult to achieve the longer one lives.

For he never dies who never gets well (G 120)

The forthright paradox, "best would be worst" (G 145), is followed immediately by

> Contrary foods have such contrary effects,
> They would take enjoyment from her, but life from us. (G 145)

Another paradox is the contrary pull of the Platonic Eros and Anteros: "The one pulls toward heaven and the other pulls to earth, the one lodges in the soul and the other in the senses" (G 260).

Mention should be made of the baroque element of chiaroscuro. The light-shade contrast in Michelangelo's painting is not striking. In the poetry there are no word pictures of a "cierto claroescuro," such as Hatzfeld has found in Cervantes, Góngora, Tasso, and Racine.[16] If Michelangelo contrasts Night and Day on the Tomb of Giuliano de' Medici, there are few lighting effects in the six poems in which night figures (G 98, 102, 257, 103, 104, and 129). I cannot agree with my friend Hatzfeld's enthusiastic statement that "Michelangelo, like Rembrandt, is permeated by this motif." In all these works there is only the briefest mention that a torch or a lightning bug can "vanquish" night and a poetic reminder that at night the sun still lights the stars from afar.

The inability of the baroque mind to view life as a positive or even a reality led him to the Calderónian premise that life is a dream. Michelangelo, capable of panic dreams,[17] capable of composing poetry in his dreams,[18] and even capable of viewing life as fleet and transitory as a dream, uses the word "dream" in the Calderónian sense once in the *Rime*. In one of his epitaphs, partially translated above on page 39, the dead Cecchino reflects:

> . . . e s'alcun mi ricorda,
> Gli par sognar: sì morte è presta e 'ngorda,
> Che quel ch'è stato non par fussi mai. (G 200)

Such a dream is furthermore conveyed in his curious drawing *Il Sogno della vita umana.*

Since Michelangelo's increasing mysticism led him to question the values by which he had lived his long life, we can only take satisfaction that doubts about art so evident in the late poetry did not reduce his production earlier in his career. Late in life he wondered whether he should not have become a Dominican friar, as had his brother, the better to serve God. As Calderón put it, without God "las humanas glorias son polvo, humo, ceniza, y viento."[19] Read the unhappy renunciation of the fine arts in the following lines:

> Love, the muses, and the flowery grottoes,
> My scribblings on these matters and my crude drawings
> Have been put to use by innkeepers for wrapping

Have served for privies and for brothels.
What does it avail me to create such childish things
If they have but brought me to this pass, like the man
Who voyaged over the sea only to drown in the slime of the shore? (G 267)

or the magnificent complaint, where early pride is crowded out by the senescent's terror:

> With such servitude, with such tedium,
> And with false concepts and great peril
> To the soul, sculpturing here things divine. (G 282)

In discussing the paradoxes and ambivalences of the baroque mind, we have actually intruded upon the subject of this fourth section, devoted to the stylistic devices of baroque. For paradox is not only a state of the spirit; it is as well a habit of verbal expression. Therefore, in the course of probing Michelangelo's baroque mentality we have shown how often he returned to stylistic effects which betrayed a dichotomy of the spirit: antithesis, oxymoron, and contrast.

If we turn now to other stylistic elements of baroque, we shall find many of these in Michelangelo. A vocabulary and repertory of images vibrant with energy and emotion is present. One means of achieving heightened emotional effect is repetition or echo effect:

> Oilme, oilme, oilme! (G 7)
> O Dio, o Dio, o Dio! (G 8)
> Vorrei uoler, Signior, quel ch' io non uoglio. (G 87)
> Non muor, morendo, anzi per morte vive (G 118 var.)
> Se l'amo e bramo e chiamo a tutte l' ore (G 117)

Occasionally a series is compounded for the same purpose:

> My peace, my repose, my salvation (G 61)
> Those sobs and weepings and sighs (G 12)
> The anguishes, plaints, and sorrows (G 19)
> Oh flesh, oh blood, oh Cross, oh searing pain! (G 66)

The set of values changing as one grows older is fourfold:

> To change life, love, habit, and fate (G 293)
> One changes taste, love, desire, and thoughts (G 283)

One has the impression that these scattered examples of echo devices and repetitions are significant precisely because they were not consciously introduced for literary effect, as in the baroque poetry of a D'Aubigné, and thus they indicate an unconscious tendency rather than studied art.

Alliteration is not usually practiced by Michelangelo, although there are a few noteworthy examples:

Lezi, uezzi, carezze o feste e perle (G 115)
Mi sprona, sfrena e sferza (G 263)
Se la miseria medica la morte (G 269)

Concomitant with the transitory nature of life is metamorphosis, a concept to which the baroque poets gave the most elastic meaning. These transmutations are found also in Michelangelo's poetry. Over and over the loved one's eyes set fire to the lover and reduce him to burnt wood (G 176 and 171). Indeed, three such changes (fire > ice, laughter > weeping, body > charred wood) occur in the stanza "Nella memoria delle cose belle." In the sequence to Cecchino de' Bracci, the beauty of the dead adolescent leaves Michelangelo in a mood to ponder rebirth. The thought of the boy's regaining his beauty keeps coming back. The boy's beauty has been reborn in the headstone. The boy will recapture his beauty ("il suo bel uelo") even before souls are reclothed on Judgement Day (G 227). Or can the lad's beauty ever be regained, like a withered tree blooming again in springtime? No, for as we have seen, "a dead man rearises not in the spring" (G 199).

The changes in Michelangelo's own body during the lengthy aging process are a constant, gnawing theme:

Fallen is the fruit, and dried now the rind,
I now seem to taste as bitter what once was sweet. (G 158)

Although I am changing my skin
During these last, short years,
I cannot change my old and former habits. (G 161)

Another common theme of metamorphosis is that of the phoenix (see Chapter XVI), which Michelangelo employed five times (G 61, 217, 266, 108, 62), applying it to himself; "il ciel m'inuola,/Un carbon resto acceso e ricoperto" (G 266). (For translation see p. 277.)

Lists of baroque elements in literature often include the pun, not so much as an evidence of humor as of the instability and mutability of words themselves. Crashaw's Latin and English puns are a variant of his epigrammatic "points," expressing paradox and antithesis, according to Warren.[20] By quoting the example of the Cumaean Sibyl holding her book at arm's length (see above, p. 39) we have alleged that Michelangelo sometimes punned in his art. He also punned by replacing the word Corvi in his address (Macel dei Corvi) with the sketch of a crow, and by placing horns on his Moses.[21] Yet there are many puns in his *Rime*, all based on names. The reader may decide whether these derive from a baroque mind or imitation of Petrarch, whose double-punning verse "Rott' è l'alta colonna e 'l uerde lauro" (G App. 3) he copied onto the Louvre sketch of his bronze *David*. Or, whether they are both baroque and Petrarchan since this would not be inconsistent, to repeat a point made earlier. The line is reproduced after the name punned upon:

Tommaso Cavalieri	Resto prigion d'un Caualier armato	(G 98)
Febo di Poggio	Mentre che Febo il poggio tucto ardea	(G 99)
Pope Julius II	A prender fructo d'un arbor, ch'è secho (i.e., "a tree that is withered" or "a Della Rovere [oak] one is with")	(G 6)
Clement VII [de' Medici]	Al Medico maggior de nostri mali	(G 85)
Monsignor Pietro Carnesecchi	La Carne, che nel sal si purg' e stenta	(G 85)
Faustina Lucia Mancini	Se con la drieta man face', difesa, Campaua; onde nol fe', ch'era Mancina.	(G 177)
Cecchino de' Bracci	Meglio era esser de Piedi per fuggire Che de Bracci e non fare da lei difesa.	(G 184)
Cecchino de' Bracci	Qui stese il Braccio e colse acerbo il fructo	(G 222)

The habit of incarnation or personification associated with baroque extended to the allegorical figures in Michelangelo's *Rime*. The allegories of Night and Day have the power of speech (G 247 and 14). In the stanzas in praise of rustic life, allegorical figures of Doubt, Truth, Fraud, Hypocrisy, and Adulation are depicted in detail (see Chapter VII). Thus, Truth is a poor and lonely wanderer, with body of gold, heart of diamond, and one gleaming eye. Elsewhere the two gigantic figures representing Fury and Pride (according to Michelangelo the Younger, who edited the poetry), parents of the Seven Deadly Sins, are portrayed fully (G 68). A final personification is that of the city of Florence, an attractive young woman ravished by the Medici tyrant (G 249).

The occasional surrealistic visions or dreams of baroque were not unfamiliar to Michelangelo. Magnificent visions they were: Saint Teresa seeing Christ play with her soul as with a tennis ball, Richard Crashaw viewing the wounds of Christ as mouths and eyes, Théophile witnessing a serpent on a tower tearing apart a vulture, John Davies of Hereford contemplating "frozen hearts floating in sulphred streams." Michelangelo was capable of such visions, such "brainwork of a perverted intelligence," as Eliot puts it.[22] After the martyrdom of Savonarola he saw a flaming sky over the city of Florence.[23] If he did not see through the special vision of a Brueghel or a Bosch, he had such various moral visions as the Day of Wrath, the *Baccanalia dei putti*, and the *Saettatori* (albeit patterned on a Roman model). Touches of surrealism are notably few, however, in the *Rime*. He had a curious conception of divine arms which can move weights without motion:

> I feel the fire of a cold face inflamed
> Which burns me from afar even as it freezes.
> I feel the force in two graceful arms
> Which move every other weight without motion. (G 88)

Indeed, this baroque quatrain reminds us that the fire-that-freezes and the ice-that-burns are concepts of precisely this curious "brainwork." A touch of surrealism is found in his apocalyptic vision:

> Heaven extends the keys;
> Love twists and turns them
> And opens milady's breast to the worthy. (G 254)

This image of a heavenly arm proffering keys to its kingdom, which love takes and turns to open the heart is reminiscent of Petrarch, XVII:

> Largata al fin con l'amorose chiavi
> L'anima esce del cor per seguir voi.

The veil of ice separating the artist from his God: "Between the fire and the heart a veil of ice is hidden" (G 87) would also fall into this category, as would the curious transformation: "it makes of my entire body a single eye" (G 166).

Of the four categories of baroque here explored, the Counter-Reformational spirit and the mysticism of Michelangelo's poetry inform his art as well. His intimate relationship with Christ, based now on pity and affection and now on fear, becomes autobiographical in the Nicodemus-Michelangelo commiserating with Christ in the *Deposizione* of Santa Maria del Fiore or in the Bartholomew-Michelangelo left despoiled by the Christus Iudex in the *Giudizio universale*. The lack of will, abulia, ambivalence conveyed by his poetry can be read on the features of such figures as Adam of the *Creazione di Adamo*, the *Sogno*, or even the *Bacco*. Of the devices utilised by baroque poetry, spectacle and theatricality reach a high point on the Sistine Vault. In general, the emotionalism and tensions which characterise baroque are more consistently observable in Michelangelo's *Rime* than in his art. Late in his life, when this genius set down his mallet and chisel and neglected his brush in that "season which cracks the bow and wings" (G 131), his pen became more active than ever and his style more predictably baroque.

Michelangelo's *Rime* thus assure him a place in the recently expanding family of baroque poets. True, he does not illustrate evenly the various characteristics of baroque. Some are abundant, some are barely represented, and, indeed, some (asyndeta, etc.) are absent from his *canzoniere*. But then many of these characteristics now recognised as baroque are absent in Crashaw himself, and Douglas Bush could no longer define baroque as the way Richard Crashaw wrote poetry, any more than we could define it as the way Michelangelo wrote his sonnets and madrigals. Even Corneille does not illustrate evenly all the elements of neoclassicism. Scott and Byron, so unlike, are indisputably English Romantics. Sooner or later it will be acknowledged that a similar variation is permissible to the baroque writers. Nor should the rich and complex baroque be confused with such narrower stylistic movements as manneristic, "Bartasian," or metaphysical.[24] Considering the fact that Michelangelo was born in 1475, forty years before Teresa Sánchez de Cepeda y Ahumada de Ávila, one hundred and thirty-seven years before Richard Crashaw, he was not only one of the most versatile baroque poets, but also one of the earliest. Thanks to his longevity, however, his death preceded by only sixteen years the date (1580) most usually assigned to the beginnings of literary baroque.

NOTES

[1] Ernst Steinmann and Rudolf Wittkower, *Michelangelo Bibliographie* (Leipzig, 1927). See also Steinmann-Wittkower, *Michelangelo im Spiegel seiner Zeit* (Leipzig, 1930).

[2] Carl Frey, *Die Dichtungen des Michelagniolo Buonarroti* (Berlin, 1897), p. 181.

[3] Helmut Hatzfeld, "Baroque Style: Ideology and the Arts," *Bucknell Review*, VII, 2 (Dec., 1957), p. 71.

[4] Valerio Mariani and N. Façon (see Bibliography); the other, generally less important studies in our Bibliography do not even see the problem of baroque as existing.

[5] Hatzfeld, "L'Italia, la Spagna, e la Francia dello sviluppo del barocco letterario," in *La critica stilistica e il barocco letterario* (Florence, 1957).

[6] Giorgio Vasari, *Le vite, et. cit.*, VII, 280.

[7] Still most useful is René Wellek, "The Concept of Baroque in Literary Scholarship," *Journal of Aesthetics*, V (1946), 77–109, with its bibliography.

[8] For Michelangelo's fascination with Brutus, see Chapter XIII.

[9] Giovanni Papini, *La vita, ed. cit.*, pp. 126–27.

[10] Michelangelo's three prayers are quoted in Chapter XI.

[11] Francisco de Hollanda, *op. cit.*, pp. 235–36.

[12] Ceriello edition of the *Rime*, p. 276.

[13] Guasti edition of the *Rime*, p. xl.

[14] So called by Odette de Mourgues, *Metaphysical, Baroque and Précieux Poetry* (Oxford, 1953), p. 85, where other baroque treatments of the theme are discussed.

[15] Hatzfeld, "A Clarification of the Baroque Problem in the Romance Literatures," *Comparative Literature* (Spring, 1949), pp. 128–29.

[16] *Ibid.*, p. 128.

[17] Flights to Venice (1529) and Bologna (1494) resulted from such panic; in the latter case, two dreams of Andrea Cardiere set Michelangelo off. Condivi, XIV, and *Lettere*, ed. Milanesi, p. 457.

[18] These admissions by Michelangelo are reproduced in the Ceriello edition of the *Rime*, pp. 250–51.
[19] Calderón, *El mágico prodigioso*, III, 21–24.
[20] Austin Warren, *Richard Crashaw* (Ann Arbor, 1957), pp. 81–90.
[21] Margaret MacLean, "The Horns on Michelangelo's Moses," *Art and Archeology*, VI (August, 1917), 97–99.
[22] Quoted in De Mourgues, *op. cit.*, p. 84.
[23] "Una visione del Buonarroti," *Il Buonarroti*, IV (April, 1866), 103.
[24] Is it not valid to generalise that mannerism is generated in the intellect and baroque in the viscera?

4

ART AS THEMATIC IN THE POETRY

MICHELANGELO'S MAJOR WORK OF ART was himself. Living in an age when man, as Burckhardt reminds us, tried to make a work of art of everything, including the state itself, our artist tried to shape himself with the same care and discipline he used in giving form to the *hyle* of art. None of his works is more magnificent than his own head, translated into bronze from the death mask by the worthy and faithful Daniele da Volterra. God, as Michelangelo declared, was the master sculptor behind him, guiding his hammer. Buonarroti was aware that the materials present in his own poor body were defective, making it less adaptable to a great work of art. He complained (see above, p. 48) of at least eleven illnesses.[1] Recent scholarship has found him the victim of the "mal francese,"[2] which the French called "la maladie italienne." As he admitted in a letter to Bartolommeo Angiolini as early as 1523, Michelangelo was "in bad shape, for if I work one day I have to rest four days" (CCCLXXVIII). Sometimes he felt that his talents were meager and that he was indeed a poor specimen of art. Berni's *capitolo* serves as *praetextum* for his admission:

> So I am yet in the number of those
> Whom some worthless and clumsy painter
> Has eked out with his brushes and paintpots. (G 85)

Thus, when he refers to his own *turpissime* paintings (G 79) which he offers to Vittoria Colonna, he could perforce be including himself.

> He will try, however, to make a better creation of himself:
> To make an actual man into a good painting

This concept of Michelangelo himself as a work of art is brilliantly exploited in Rilke's tale "Von Einem der die Steine belaüscht,"[3] as well as in

Meyer's "In der Sistina," where Michelangelo cries, "Bildhauer Gott, schlag zu! Ich bin der Stein."

The notion that one depicts himself in one's art is occasionally found in the *Rime*. (See p. 178.) It was an idea which Michelangelo may have heard or read from Savonarola, or even Leonardo: "It is in one's nature to paint oneself/and in every work make one's mood manifest." His madrigal (G 173) to the Marchioness of Pescara bears the thesis that an artist paints himself—his subjective self—even into his portraits of others. If the artist is happy or sad, his subject will share this mood:

> Thus each would benefit thereby,
> To paint her with light heart and dry eyes,
> She would be made beautiful, nor should I be made ugly. (G 168)

Attempting a synthesis of his two greatest current loves, sculpture and Vittoria Colonna, Michelangelo compares himself to a *concetto*, an art form, which is brought into full realisation through the working of love. The manner in which the lady purges him of his baser nature is analogous to the paring away of the excess of a figure lodged in marble.

> As when, O lady mine,
> With chisell'd touch
> The stone unhewn and cold
> Becomes a living mold,
> The more the marble wastes,
> The more the statue grows;
> So, if the working of my soul be such
> That good is but evolved
> By Time's dread blows,
> The vile shell, day by day,
> Falls like superfluous flesh away.
> Oh! take whatever bonds my spirit knows,
> For will and power inert within me stay. (G 152)
> (Mrs. Henry Roscoe)

Thus, as Panofsky has also observed, the katharsis accomplished by a noble love is similar to the creative process of sculpture, in which the inner *sensus visivus* recognises only the ideal and authorises only ideal creation.

In the *Rime* there are evidences of the struggle between pride and modesty which stirred ceaselessly in Michelangelo.[4] In his moments of assurance he could indulge in a burst of vanity:

> To the great peril of my soul
> Sculpting here things divine. (G 282)

At other times he would reveal a modesty and even pose a philosophic and Christian basis for his humility. In his *Stanze in lode della vita rusticale* he writes as a principle:

Pride devours itself (Frey CLXIII)

Even the poems to Febo and Cavalieri show a tremendous self-abasement, akin to his later appeals to Christ.

Michelangelo's letters and recorded conversations bear out this struggle between *hybris* and modesty. He was capable of writing to the King of France that he would turn out for that patron "una cosa di marmo, una di bronzo, una di pittura" to rival the best of the ancients.[5] He is confident that his Façade of San Lorenzo will be "the mirror of architecture and sculpture for all Italy."[6] His claims and boasts of competence in his three major arts would make a long list. There is at the same time a curious humility to counterbalance them. In Letter CDXXII he admits "I am a poor man and of little worth, going about striving in that art that God has given me," a humble admission which nevertheless reminds his correspondent Martelli that he is one of God's elect! When people praised him he was uncomfortable and asked them to desist: "Leave me alone wrapped in my shroud."[7] He disclaimed the talents people attributed to him, not wishing to be like the "crow in Aesop": "so that if the legitimate owners of the ornaments with which you have clothed me will come for them, I remaining naked shall be the laughing-stock of everyone."[8]

In the contrary pulls of pride and modesty there was always as a deterrent his knowledge that artists were mere executors for God, the *sommo artefice*. True, this knowledge could contribute to his confidence, since he was given an *intelletto* by God to bring out the divinely implanted beauties in the materials. But even more, it contributed to his modesty, since the greatest works of the artist could be viewed as the eventual creations of the "divine hammer" rather than of his own mallet. The *principium et fons* of art, as the *Rime* insist over and over, is God himself. In a sonnet which Frey and Girardi assign to the Cavalieri group, shortly after 1534, Michelangelo acknowledges his debt to heaven:

> In that fine art with which one may defeat nature,
> If he bears it down from heaven with him,
> Even though nature exert herself at every point. (G 97)

Nature is viewed equally as an ally or agent in the productions of heaven:

> Nor does it happen otherwise with lofty and novel things,
> That nature produces with effort;
> At the birth of these heaven is liberal with its gifts. (G 106)

God is not only the master creator who empowers a select few artists to complete his task for him. He also supplies the lofty subject matter of art, the most noble being the human body itself.

> He who made the whole made every part,
> And then from the whole chose the most beautiful part,
> To exhibit here below his most lofty creations,
> As he has now done with his divine art. (G 9)

In examining below several of the *Rime* dedicated to the art of sculpture, we shall find confirmation in Michelangelo's allegedly Platonic piece on the divine hammer of the *Cratylus:* "Se 'l mie rozzo martello i duri sassi" (G 46).

The artist's view of God as the fountainhead of art is amply chronicled in the *Diálogos em Roma* of Francisco de Hollanda. Francisco quotes Michelangelo as saying, "This sublime science comes not from any single land, but from heaven."[9] Or again, art is a gift "received from the immortal God."[10] When, in the *Diálogos,* Michelangelo is asked to define great painting, he replies, "That painting which I celebrate and praise will be merely the imitation of some of the creations of immortal God, done with great care and wisdom."[11]

Yet the *Rime* give evidence that Michelangelo cannot remain content with his modest role as apprentice to God. Just as he suddenly changes character and writes at one point that, like Christ's, his sputum can cure blindness,[12] so does he pridefully arrogate to himself powers he usually attributed only to God, such as the power to create life:

> Thus I can give to both of us long life
> Whether in color or in stone. (G 239)

He can give beauty:

> Portray her with light heart and dry eyes:
> She would be made beautiful and I not ugly. (G 173)

Finally, he even sees himself placing *concetti* within the marble:

> As I do in stone or on candid paper,
> Which had naught within, and now has what I wish. (Frey CVII)

Since Christian doctrine held that only God actually creates, this thought is so untypical of Michelangelo that he could have expressed it only in an exalted moment when feeling like unto God himself.

Michelangelo's theory of the *concetto,* the art form contained within marble or other materials, is by now familiar to students of his life. Although it is implicit in his works of art themselves, especially in the *San*

Matteo and the *Schiavo detto "Atlante,"* it is explicit only in his poetry. The theory has of course Platonic origins, with the Neo-Platonists believing that every Idea of the Higher Soul has a reflection here on earth, an image actually guarded within the *hyle*. There are, in the words of Vincenzo Danti, three elements in the creation of a work of art: the *intelletto* which conceived of the work originally and implanted it in nature; the *mano* which obeys the *intelletto* and "discovers" the implanted forms; and the *materia* which is the custodian of the form, "gardien du contour pur," as Gautier phrased it.[13] Plato's three categories of divine form—Ideas, Concepts, and Seeds—are all lodged in this material. As Ficino notes: "Eodem ordine a natura in materiam formae descendunt."[14] The most succinct statement of this belief is in one of the love poems, which we have quoted above (p. 61), "Sì come per leuar, Donna, si pone." As this poem illustrates, the work grows out of the rock, the *concetto* is disengaged from its *soverchio*, as the artist's *intelletto* guides his hand. All three of these italicised words are found *passim* in Michelangelo's poems based on the theme of the fine arts.

No poem explains more clearly this basic process of art than the following quatrain, "Non ha l'ottimo artista," of 1538–44.

> Nothing the greatest artist can conceive
> That every marble block doth not confine
> Within itself; and only its design
> The hand that follows intellect achieve. (G 151)
> (H. W. Longfellow)

No four lines of Michelangelo's were more famous, not even the quatrain on the *Notte*, written in reply to Strozzi's epigram. Indeed, his contemporaries were quick to seize the seminal importance of these verses. Benedetto Varchi launched Michelangelo's fame as a poet in the Florentine Academy by giving an explication of them in 1546 and calling the full piece "a most lofty sonnet full of that ancient purity and Dantean gravity." (The sonnet was received with greater enthusiasm than Varchi's commentary, which was to be called by Foscolo, in one of his two essays in English on Michelangelo's poetry, "an elaborate dissertation of an alarming length.")[15] Later in the century this had become the only poem of Michelangelo's known to Renaissance France, hungry for theories on art and saturated with plagiarisms of Italian poetry. Although the *Rime* of Michelangelo were not translated into French until 1860, Philippe Desportes (1546–1606) lost no time in recognising the importance of this sonnet (see below, p. 338).[16] Danti, Bellori, Lomazzo, and even Galileo knew this quatrain and commented on its underlying theory. In Spain it was known early to Saavedra Faxardo (see Chapter XX). Bellori redefined Michelangelo's *concetto* as a "perfection of nature, miracle of art, prefiguration of the Intelletto, example of the mind, light of the imagination."[17]

Although the notion corresponds exactly to the Platonic view of art, it reflects also the notion held by some Aristotelians of the Renaissance that (in the words of a contemporary Latin version of the *Metaphysics*): "In lapide est forma Mercurii in potentia." Or, "Actio agentis nihil aliud est quam extrahere rem de potentia ad actum" and "agens extrahens rem de potentia ad actum, non largitur multitudinem sed perfectionem."[18]

Several incidental features of this theory of Michelangelo appear in different poems. The *concetto* within the rock, metal, or pigment is living, a fact which explains the recurrence of the expression *pietra viva* in his writings:

> After many years and many attempts
> The wise man in his quest arrives at the right concept
> Of a living image,
> In Alpine and hard stone—only as he nears death. (G 241)

> The living image
> Lasts longer in the hard Alpine stone. (G 239)

> When godlike art has, with superior thought,
> The limbs and motions in idea conceived,
> A simple form, in humble clay achieved,
> Is the first offering into being brought:
> Then stroke on stroke from out the living rock,
> Its promised work the practised chisel brings,
> And into life a form so graceful springs,
> That none can fear for it time's rudest shock. (G 236 var.)
> (Fanny Elizabeth Bunnett)

This latter sonnet to Vittoria Colonna is important in explaining the role of preliminary models in the Platonic theory of the artist. The presence of the *concetto* waiting in the rock does not obviate the necessity of practice and training, and indeed the necessity of possessing a God-given *intelletto*. *Intelletto* (the νουσ of Plato and Platonism) is mentioned as a perceptive power, given sparingly as grace, in a number of poems (G 164, 166, 273) and in the *Diálogos* of Francisco de Hollanda.

It was easy for Michelangelo, who mused over swords in sheathes (G 54) and spirits in bottles (G 267), to mull over figures in stone. Once the artist conceives of the *concetto* living in marble or paint, it is a slight step to suppose that this hidden form has the powers of movement and speech: "if rocks . . . could speak like us" (Letter XXXVI). As we have noted in the sequence of epitaphs to Cecchino de' Bracci (G 212, 216, 195), the headpiece of stone speaks to lament the boy's death and even to regret that it was brought down ("against my will") from its lofty mountaintop (G

275). In some pieces of the Bracci series it is hard to distinguish whether Cecchino or his living headstone or bust is speaking, for now the lad has become a living *concetto* within the stone.

The dating of the poems attesting to Michelangelo's belief in pre-existing art forms shows it to be a basic tenet of his philosophy of art until not only 1547, but even 1550. We cannot accept James Ackerman's view that it was a conviction limited to Michelangelo's "Florentine period," whatever is meant by this latter expression. Michelangelo was so haunted by the theory of potential form that he applied it to the art of writing, in the surprising incomplete sonnet already referred to (see above, p. 22), "Siccome nella penna e nell'inchiostro." The theory is applied in an unusual way even to the art of the silversmith or the goldsmith. Just as the rocks in the quarry wait for the sculptor to come and liberate their inner form, so does the mold wait expectantly for the smith:

> Not only does the mold, empty of a completed work,
> Wait to be refilled with gold
> And silver melted down by fire,
> Which only in breaking can then yield forth . . . (G 153)

The tremendous importance of Michelangelo's *Rime* in providing an avenue of understanding to his art is never more clearly demonstrated than here. For this basic belief of his, without the documentation of his poetry, would have passed into his grave with him.

Sculpture, as Michelangelo's preferred art, figures largely in the poetry. Although Michelangelo eventually evolved a conviction that he had achieved excellence in all three major arts, his feelings about sculpture were entrenched during youth, when he had left Ghirlandaio's studio to work with Bertoldo. He admired Ghiberti and Donatello greatly and when he went to Rome he signed his letters "Michelangiolo scultore" consistently until 1526. Indeed, one example of Michelangelo's irony was his *ricordo* of 10 May, 1508, when he acknowledged, "I, Michelangelo Buonarroti *sculptor,* have received 500 ducats on account, for the *paintings* of the Sistine Chapel [italics mine]."[19] He would have been willing to call himself exclusively a sculptor in those late years when he still struggled with the Palestrina and Rondinini Pietàs, except that the world's voice was louder than his own and he now held the coveted post of artist-architect laureate of Christendom.

Let us consider his poems involving sculpture in chronological sequence. One sonnet, written at some time between 1528 and 1546, hails God himself as the master sculptor. A curious mixture of Platonic and Christian sentiments inspired this piece in which he acknowledges God as the force behind his hammer.

If my rude hammer the unwilling stone
To human form and attitude doth mold,
It moves with him, who doth it guide and hold,
His will and impulse taking for its own.
But one diviner doth in heaven abide,
Which shapeth beauty with no hand to aid;
No hammer is, save by another, made,
Then doth th' eternal one make all beside. (G 46)
(Elizabeth Hall)

The poet then states that whereas the blow which falls from highest is most forceful, his own inspiration has gone up to heaven. Whether this deceased person is his brother Buonarroto or a friend is not certain. His hammer will falter, unless God, the divine smithy (*divina fabbrica*) will grant that his beloved friend, unique in this world, help him to perfect his instrument. After this sonnet Michelangelo penned the name "Lionardo." In any case, after the sonnet he wrote a rough (and if the friend was Vittoria Colonna, possibly Bernesque) comment: "He/she was alone in exalting virtues in the world with great virtue; nor had he/she anyone to handle the bellows. Now in heaven he/she will have many companions for there are found none but those whom virtues pleased; when I hope that here below my m[allet] will end up up there . . . He/she will have in heaven at least someone to handle the bellows, whereas down here there was no companion at the forge where virtues are exalted." This last phrase could refer to the convent seclusion in which Vittoria passed her last years.

Girardi, after examining the handwriting, conjectures that the sonnet may have been written on the death of Michelangelo's brother Buonarroto in 1528, the prose being a reminder to the nine-year-old Lionardo, his nephew, of Buonarroto's virtues. Not only is the Platonic *Cratylus* vaguely remembered in the reference to the heavenly instrument which has its earthly counterpart, but also, as Girardi reminds us, the Dantean passage:

Lo moto e la virtu de' santi giri,
come dal fabbro l'arte del martello,
da' beati motor convien che spiri, etc. (*Para.* II, 127–29)

Around 1545–50 Michelangelo leaned on sculpture as a theme for several poems. A sonnet (1545–46) pays tribute to the durability of art, and especially sculpture, hailed as the "prim' arte."

With deep delight may sound, sane taste behold
That work of highest art, complete and rare,
Which shows the face with movements apt and fair,
With wax, or clay, or stone, in human mold.

But if injurious time too rough or bold,
Shall shatter or distort those limbs, or tear,
Then not in vain the beauty lingering there
Recalls in thought what was so fair of old.

So does thy own great loveliness allow
To see His work who did the Heavens adorn,
Th' Eternal Artist unto whom we bow.

Time passes, comes old age, and still more thou
Comest as each thought of that fair past is born
Unchanged, unchilled by passing winter now. (G 237)
(G. Grinnell-Milne)

These lines are most typical of Michelangelo's theory of art, except for the assumption that works in wax or clay could stand as equals with works of stone. The only worker in terra cotta whom Michelangelo is known to have praised was Antonio Begarelli, and Michelangelo could only wish that he had worked in stone: "If this earth were to become marble, woe to the statues of old."[20]

Perhaps contemplating a bust he had just executed of Vittoria Colonna, as some conjecture, Michelangelo acknowledges that God is after all the greatest sculptor.

In this mere living stone
Art would have milady's face
Go on living here throughout the years:
How should heaven feel about her,
She being its handiwork, but this being mine,
Not mortal now, but divine,
And not merely so in my eyes?
Yet she must depart, sojourning here a short time.
Her fortune is crippled on its stronger side,
If a stone remains while death hustles her away. (G 240)

(One is reminded of Berni's indignant observation that great artists like Michelangelo must die "like asses.")

Who will exact vengeance therefrom?

That a death must be "avenged" is apparent also from the threnody of the Night and Day (G 14); that time and death are traitors we know from the allegory on art (G 172).

Nature alone, if only her children's works
Abide here below, while her own time steals away. (G 240)

Nature must carry out the revenge, since her creation (the model) decays and man's work (the bust) remains.

Michelangelo, who had spent so many years perfecting himself in the disciplines of his profession, writes a madrigal stating his belief that mastery comes late, so late as to be "near death." Certainly sculpture, which had required so many types of study, including those years at anatomy which "ruined his stomach," is the best medium to illustrate his point. Indeed, on his deathbed Michelangelo complained that he was dying before having mastered the "alphabet" of his profession.

> That wise man, who through labors manifold
> And length of years, toils at the rebel stone
> Shall see one form alone
> Perfect, in living grace, before he die;
> Since to high things untold
> Late we attain, and soon must bid goodby.
> If nature equally
> From age to age devising many a face
> Have beauty's absolute created here
> In yours most fair, she's old and must decay;
> And therefore does your grace
> Combine with potent fear
> With strangest food my soul to stay
> Nor can I deem or say
> Beholding you, which most shall harm or bless
> Creation's end, or so great happiness. (G 241)
> (Nesca Robb)

Underneath is appended a bizarre postscript of Michelangelo to Riccio: "Since you wish some installments, I can send you only what I have on hand. It's your bad luck, and your Michelangelo encloses his respects."

His severe belief that mastery in the arts comes almost on the threshold of death is confirmed by a fragment of the *Rime:*

> No one attains full mastery
> Before the extreme term
> Of art and of life. (G App. 35)

Since Michelangelo believed this conviction he expressed twice in the *Rime,* it not only furnished him the appetite to work on into his last years but also explained his bitterness at the relatively young craftsmen who gave him so much trouble in the workshop of St. Peter's during the winter of his life.

The notion that the poet paints or sculpts his own moods into the subjects he portrays has been discussed earlier in this chapter. When the artist is picturing someone he loves, the model inevitably provokes the moods which are subsequently placed back into the finished work.

If it is true that one working in hard stone
Makes others' images in his own likeness,
So do I often make it pale and weak
Just as milady makes me.
And it seems that I keep taking myself as model
When my intention is to make her.
I might well add that the stone,
Being so harsh and hard,
Resembles her all the more, and thus me, the model.
In any case, I'd be unable,
While she destroys and shatters me,
To carve aught else but my afflicted limbs.
But if my art commemorates her beauty
Over the years, and makes her endure,
This will cheer me up and I shall make her fair. (G 242)

Under this madrigal Michelangelo wrote "Da scultori," an unusual admission that for once he is writing as a sculptor for sculptors.

If painting in general is never the central theme of a poem by Michelangelo (individual paintings will be discussed in the following chapter), there are a few poems which speculate on painting and sculpture together. One of these ("I' mi son caro assai piu ch'i' non soglio") will be mentioned below in our brief discussion of poetic treatments of the rivalry between art and nature.

An interesting sonnet clarifies the role of the sketch or model in the art process. Michelangelo, whose dynamic brush and chisel strokes so often led him to disregard the carefully elaborated *pensiero* (draft) or model, pays lip service (1545–46) to this preparatory phase of art:

Da che concecto à l'arte intera e diua
Le membra e gli acti di alcun, poi di quello
D'umil materia un semplice modello
È il primo parto che da quel deriua.
Poi nel secondo im pietra alpestra e uiua
S'arrogie le promesse del martello,
E si rinascie tal concecto bello,
Che 'l suo ecterno non è chi 'l preschriua. (G 236, var.)

(For translation of this variant see page 65.)

Michelangelo, as this poem and its variant testify, insisted then on not merely single sketches or models but on a plurality of them from which the artist might choose the most perfect. This implied advice is also apparent from other counsels, one to the painter Antonio Mini ("Draw, Antonio, draw, Antonio, don't waste time") and one to the young sculptor Giovanni Bologna whose clay model he criticised with the sharp comment: "First learn to sketch out, and then to finish."[21]

The art of the goldsmith or silversmith, if we are to believe Benvenuto

Cellini (whom Michelangelo flattered as "il maggior orefice che mai ci sia stato notizia")[22] was a craft "totally unknown" to Michelangelo.[23] Yet, as in the verse of Gasparo Visconti, Tebaldeo, Cei, and Serafino d'Aquila (as Girardi shows), fire was an important theme in Michelangelo's poetry, fire that inflames the heart, fire that calcinates rock, and fire that purifies metal and man alike. Fire refines and cleanses man, just as does a noble love. The image of the phoenix renewed by fire also intrudes several times upon the poet's imagination, since love may be viewed as a rebirth. This is the burden of "Sol pur col foco il fabbro il ferro stende" (G 62, see p. 272 below). The tremendous heat achieved by the founder's furnace is no more intense than that of the poet's passion, which kindles him until he fairly sparkles:

> Never did a furnace or stove burn so hot
> That my sighs might not have made it more roaring;
> And when it happens that I have (him/her) about for a while,
> I give off sparks like iron in ardent fire. (G 54)

The intensity and durability of the fire which bespeaks a great love are as rare as are those of the fire which was needed to cast his *Giulio II,* and just as difficult to achieve.

Michelangelo's *Rime* reflect the debate among the humanistic writers on art and on poetry as to whether nature or art was the greater formative factor of genius. Usually this rivalry was viewed as a competition between native genius and the disciplines of training and practice. In Michelangelo's aesthetics this was an important issue, and his own conclusion was the compromise effected by preceding theorists all the way back to Horace: One might as well renounce art unless one's gifts were God-given ("quell'arte che Dio m' à data"), for even then one had to study and practice for long years.[24]

There are several reflections of this conflict in the *Rime,* some in excerpts already quoted in other contexts. A majority entertain the hopeful thought that art can triumph over nature:

> . . . and still it is a great boon to me
> If I vanquish nature in making her beautiful (G 172)

> Cause bows and gives in to effect,
> Whence by art is nature vanquished. (G 239)

For nature is made better by art:

> As a stone enriched by carving,
> Is of more value than its original rock,
> Or as a paper with writing or painting
> Is regarded more highly than a torn or cut sheet. (G 90)

The inclusion of the words "scritta carta" in this context of the fine arts shows how Michelangelo the poet like a Procrustes tried to fit his art theories (as he did in the sonnet "Siccome nella penna e nell'inchiostro") into tentative literary theory.

However, looming over the rivalry of art and nature are two forces even more powerful. The first is fear of death in the face of which both competing forces can avail naught:

> If in thy name I've conceived some image
> It is not without conceiving death at the same time,
> At which thought art and genius take flight. (G 284)

The second force is God himself. God surpasses the normal creative processes of nature and artist alike. The sepulcher of Cecchino Bracci was to carry the legend:

> Buried here is that Braccio, by whose face
> God wished to correct nature. (G 213)

The contest between art and nature makes an interesting appearance in the curious madrigal "Costei pur si delibra," which we shall examine in Chapter VIII, in which the artist exults that he can defeat nature.

One final time he shows his pleasure that art can outdo nature. The ability of art to award immortality—Michelangelo cautiously uses sculpture as his first example but then includes painting as well—assures eternity to artist and subject alike. Like Pindar, he might have claimed as much for poetry, as he was elsewhere to hail the immortal "inchiostri" of Vittoria Colonna and Giorgio Vasari. Yet the following poem (1545–46) was in its own way to win the artist eventual immortality, for it was sent not only to the Marchioness of Pescara but also to Giannotti for inclusion in the printed florilegium being prepared.

> Lady, how can that be, which each discerns,
> As slowly passing years the truth make known
> That longer lives the image carved in stone,
> Than he, the maker, who to dust returns?
> To the effect doth yield, surpassed, the cause,
> And art of man doth nature's self subdue;
> I know, who in fair sculpture prove it true,
> Which still of time and death defies the laws.
> Thus I to both us twain long life can give,
> In paint or marble, as my wish may be
> The semblance of thy face and mine to show.
> A thousand years hence after we have lived,
> How fair thou wert, and I how sad, they'll see;
> And that I was no fool to love thee so. (G 239)
>
> (Elizabeth Hall)

This poem has been called "one of the most singular that the prodigious artist wrote, interpreting the omnipotence of his genius."[25] It is interesting that to Michelangelo immortality meant a thousand years, not even the Great Year of Plato. Similarly, when the likenesses of his Giuliano, and Lorenzo in the Sagrestia Nuova were challenged, he countered by asking who would care a thousand years hence.

There are three versions of this sonnet. In his effort to match *concetto* and *materia* Michelangelo's first version filled the form more densely. With the same number of syllables, the variants of the first draft included new attributes: "in una pietra dura" is enriched to "in pietra alpestra e dura" and the "quante uo' bella fusti" is added at the expense of only the adjective "destructo." This sonnet seems to explain the willingness of Michelangelo to do a portrait of Vittoria Colonna, despite his intense dislike of portraiture.

This distaste for portraiture, so evident from an examination of his artistic production, had solid grounding in his Christian and personal, as well as aesthetic, convictions. Portraits were denials of the humility which Christ preached to even the mighty. They were an imposition of the Renaissance Maecenate system, often offensive to the dignity and inventive license of the artist. Part of Michelangelo's troubles with patrons may well have resulted from his unwillingness to indulge in portraiture; conversely, this would be a reason why Titian, Raphael, and Velásquez ate high on the hog at princely tables. It is symptomatic that Michelangelo's most famous rupture with Giulio II was healed only by his accepting "a noose around his neck" to execute a bronze statue-portrait of that pontiff. The final major objection was of course Michelangelo's admitted habit of viewing subjects with his "inner eye" rather than outer vision. His Medici dukes were *typoi,* Platonic ideals which troubled those older Florentines who remembered them as bearded men looking different from the conceptions of Michelangelo. Michelangelo declined to do portraits, but it was not easy to resist pressures from the wealthy and powerful patrons who assumed that portraiture was a fixture of the social system or from friends who expected it as a natural concomitant of affection.

Here again the poetry exhibits Michelangelo's position on this dilemma of the ethical artist. There are two pieces which display his reticence and indeed his ability to extract himself gracefully from such pressures. Both come from the early 1540s, when he was sufficiently established to speak out.

The first pressure was exerted in two sonnets by Gandolfo Porrino of Modena praising Michelangelo and requesting that the artist do a commemorative portrait of Faustina Lucia Mancini Attavanti, who died in 1543 and whose tomb existed until recent times in a chapel of Santa Maria Aracoeli, Rome. This young matron was greatly admired by Porrino, Molza, Annibal Caro, and her prestige among the humanists might have swayed a younger artist. Yet Michelangelo's sonnet responds to the request with courtesy and firmness:

> That new transcendant fair who seems to be
> Peerless in heaven as in this world of woe
> (The common folk, too blind her worth to know
> And worship, called her Left Arm wantonly),
> Was made, full well I know, for only thee:
> Nor could I carve or paint the glorious show
> Of that fair face; to life thou needs must go,
> To gain the favour thou dost crave of me. (G 178)
> (J. A. Symonds)

In eight verses Michelangelo has praised the young lady, protected her name from vulgar gossip which led Guasti and Frey to assume her a courtesan, indulged in one of his Petrarchan puns (Mancina = left-handed), and turned down the request. Now, a sonnet written for his own amusement or escapism could end here as a *non finito*. But a sonnet for circulation requires six more lines. Michelangelo accordingly fills six more verses with further praise and a second refusal.

As we shall learn in Chapter VI, Michelangelo declined to undertake a portrait for the sepulcher of young Cecchino Bracci, who was more intimately associated with him than was La Mancina. More intimate, moreover, was Luigi del Riccio, who exerted an even greater pressure than Porrino. Michelangelo again insisted that the dead youth was closer to the petitioner than to himself. Having suggested in the first case that Porrino do a word portrait of La Mancina instead, Michelangelo here objects that Riccio and Cecchino had become one, and thus:

> It is fitting that to do him one portray you. (G 193)

It was the egotistical and wealthy men who wished effigies of themselves who could set up the most irresistible pressures. Michelangelo's belief that an artist cannot work well under pressure, so vividly expressed in his *Lettere*, is adumbrated in a brief note to his quatrain: "His splendor was your life" (G 214). This note also supports his belief that quality is often at odds with quantity. Apologising for the quality of his stanzas, he adds: "Clumsy things, but since you want me to do a thousand of them, there are perforce all sorts."

Other persuasions on the fine arts make less sustained appearances in Michelangelo's *Rime*. This practitioner of the arts who disliked shop talk to the point of avoiding any company where he might have to "lecture" and who never got around to writing a treatise on the arts, as he once expressed the intention of doing, could not help letting his convictions and prejudices about art infiltrate his poetry. We have seen above how images and processes of the fine arts inform the *Rime*. Sometimes the artist stands blatantly before us, as in the *sonetto caudato* on the painting of the Sistine Vault, with its outright disclaimer that painting for him is the wrong endeavor (see p. 92). Even when Michelangelo is writing exclusively in his capacity as poet, his ideas on art intrude incidentally or accidentally. Sometimes he plunders the fine arts' natural propensities for metaphor. For example, he makes memory itself into a fine art. Writing on the death of old Lodovico, his father, he sighs:

> Yet memory paints my brother for me,
> And sculpts thee living within my heart,
> While filial piety then stains my face even more. (G 86)

The impression seems to remain that sculpture, his "alma scultura" and his "prim'arte," leaves a deeper impression than painting.

Michelangelo's interest in the nude figure, even to the extent of using it for decoration where other artists would use foliage, emerges at several points, sometimes subtly and even unconsciously.

> Nor does God in his grace show himself to me elsewhere
> More clearly than in a graceful and mortal veil:
> And that alone do I love because in this he is mirrored. (G 106)

> Here it is fitting that I pause and sleep for a while,
> So that I may return my terrestrial veil in all its beauty. (G 209)

> So that I may make eternal in stone my terrestrial veil. (G 215)

Complementary to Michelangelo's love of the nude figure was his dislike of the clothing so exploited by Venetian, Flemish, and French painters. In a penned annotation to a poem on Cecchino's death he cannot refrain from a sarcasm against "the usual clothes of silk and gold which would beautify a tailor's mannequin" (G 192). This scorn for clothes dummies breaks out again in G 54, "Thou art not made like a mannequin at a tailor's." He admits his disinterest in rich raiment in G 267, noting that his own clothes are of the sort draped on a scarecrow. When he wishes to depict Dame Poverty, so much more worthy than overdressed and overbejeweled Wealth, he dresses this excellent woman "in rough and dull-colored clothing" (G 67). One recalls Michelangelo's scornful answer to Pope Giulio II, who had complained that the apostles intended for the first version of the Sistine Ceiling were not sumptuously dressed. Finally, in the stanzas in praise of rustic life, the allegorical figure of Truth goes about as naked as any of Michelangelo's *Ignudi* or *Dannati* or *Noè* and his sons.

> Poor and nude Truth goes about alone.

Whereas Fraud is dressed like a Venetian portrait:

> Clad in gold and variegated embroideries
> Fraud goes about . . . (G 67)

If the sonnet "Veggio nel tuo bel uiso, Signior mio" embodies Michelangelo's belief that the body is infused with divinity and light and is thus a reflection of God, this is a thought he had probably read in the commentary of his early friend Ficino: "Non enim corpus hoc uel illud desiderat: sed superni luminis splendorem per corpora refulgentem admiratur, affectat, et stupet."[26] Not as a Platonist, but simply as a *membrificatore* who had studied anatomy for years, Michelangelo asks his listeners in the *Diálogos em Roma:* "What judgement will be so barbarous as not to understand that a man's foot is more noble than his shoe? That his flesh is more noble than that of the sheep from which his clothing is made?"[27]

A corollary to Michelangelo's dislike of rich clothing and draperies was his disregard for high colors. He had greater esteem for line than color, as is well known. Vasari records Michelangelo's complaint that poor artists cloak the poverty of their techniques with "the variety of tints and shades of colors."[28] Armenini recalls Michelangelo's scorn for a public which looks at the high colors in a painting rather than the figures which show spirit and movement.[29] Even in this Michelangelo was Platonic, for Ficino had held color to be a minor element in art: "Eadem nos ratio admonet ne formam suspicemur esse colorum suavitatem."[30] In his *capitolo* on Michelangelo supposedly addressed to Sebastiano del Piombo, the discerning Francesco Berni wrote that those who would follow Michelangelo must reject color:

> Whoever wishes to practice your trade,
> Let him quickly sell his colors to the ladies.

An amusing indictment of color is contained in the curious *contr' amour* "Tu ha' 'l uiso piu dolce che la sapa," derived from the amusing praise of Lorenzo's *Nencia* by her country-bumpkin admirer. In this satirical piece, of which two variant versions remain, white seems to be the target of laughter: the white of the maligned lady's hair, teeth ("white as a parsnip"), and even cheeks. The high color of the lady's face is better set off by this white background:

> Thy cheeks are red and white as when thou siftest flour,
> Like poppies against fresh white cheese. (G 20)

In his note to this piece Ceriello also notes the "whimsical violence of the colors."

Perhaps the most curious marriage of poetry and art in the *Rime* are the *terzine* from the mid-twenties, seemingly an instruction on the painting of the eye. Since two or more lines are missing, it may be that these are part of a longer didactic piece:

> The eyelid, with its shading, does not prevent my seeing
> When it contracts, but the eye is free
> From one end to the other in the socket in which it moves.

The eye, underneath the lid, moves slowly.
The lid uncovers a small part of the large eyeball,
Revealing only a small part of its serene gaze.
The eye, being under the lid which covers it, moves up and down less.
Thus, when not raised up the lids have a shorter arc;
They wrinkle less when extended more over the eye.
The whites of the eyes are white and the black more so than funeral drapes,
If that is possible, and more than leonine
The yellow which crosses from one fiber to the next.
But even if you touch its upper and lower edges,
You'll not surround the yellow and black and white. (G 35)

Nothing is known of the intent, extent, or even content of this poem. Michelangelo's didactic moments, like the one which provoked his disputed letter to Pope Paul III on the Vitruvian principles, were few. Frequently love poems open as disguised observations on art and even on technique, but of course never with such long or incompatible *exordia* as this. The poem seems to be an exercise on a passage from the work on optics by Leonardo or Leon Battista Alberti. Typically, Michelangelo is disinterested in the color of the eye and when he reaches this point in his lesson, he halts abruptly. Indeed, *color* in the first line merely means *ombra* (shade).

In Michelangelo's time painting, sculpture, and the kindred arts were not yet known as the "belle arti," this etiquette attaining currency by the eighteenth century, alleged incubator of the "science" of aesthetics, when the Abbé Du Bos and others spoke and wrote of the "beaux-arts." Certainly the current Cinquecento term of *arti del disegno* was one more compatible to Michelangelo, who steadfastly maintained that design was the common denominator of all arts, who counseled, as we observed, to Antonio Mini, "Disegnia, disegnia, disegnia," and who in the dialogues of De Holanda went so far as to claim that design was the binding principle of all arts, trades, and many disciplines. This is not to conclude that Michelangelo would have denied to art the term "belle arti" through a denial of beauty, nor that he did not speak of "la bell'arte" (G 97), but rather to assume that he and his colleagues preferred a term (*disegno*) explaining *what* art is rather than *how* it is.

Beauty, never easy to define in any age, was no more easily formulated in the Cinquecento. The two competing definitions were the Aristotelian and the Platonic, distinguished without impartiality by Benedetto Varchi in his *Libro della Beltà e Grazia:* "We should then know that beauty is taken in two ways, one according to Aristotle and the rest, who claim that it consists in the proportion of the members, this being called corporeal beauty known and consequently loved only by the crowd and plebeian men—and, as is known, enjoyed with all five senses; those who love this beauty principally are little or no different from brutish beasts. The other beauty consists in the virtue and customs of the soul, whence is born the grace we are discussing; this is called spiritual beauty, which is consequently known by good and speculative men only; so declared Plotinus, the great Platonist, inferring from this beauty that no beautiful person was evil."[31]

Despite the Platonic theorising on beauty at the time, especially in Pico and Bembo, the definition of beauty as physical proportion enjoyed wide circulation, partly resulting from Vitruvius's treatise and such other works as Agnolo Firenzuola's *Dialogo delle bellezze delle donne*, Dürer's *Proportionslehre*, and Luca Pacioli's treatise on "divine" proportions. Even Vasari, whose aesthetics so often coincided with Michelangelo's, departed from him in declaring that "beauty is a rational quality dependent on rules, whereas grace is an indefinable quality dependent upon judgement and therefore on the eye."[32]

Michelangelo, who talked little of grace but much of beauty, followed rather the Platonic tradition in his thinking. Beauty is not an agreeable concordance of lines and proportions. What Vasari called grace just above would serve as a Buonarrotian definition of beauty. He knew very well the Ficinian chapters on beauty in the *Commentarium in Convivium*, such chapters as "Pulchritudo est splendor divini vultus" and "Pulchritudo est aliquid incorporeum." The emphasis on "typical" rather than rational or geometric beauty Michelangelo knew from Plotinus, with whom he was acquainted, as was Varchi. If, as Varchi suggests, Plotinus held that good men perceived beauty more easily, Michelangelo would rather state that those possessed of the *intelletto* recognised beauty. Here, however, Michelangelo did not depart from Plotinus, for Plotinus assumed that the beholder of beauty must be endowed with *nous*, or Intellect Principle, before perceiving beauty. As Michelangelo explicitly simplifies his theory, this perceptive gift is necessary: "Every beauty visible here on earth/Resembles that merciful fount whence we all derive/More than anything else, to men with perception" (G 83). Savonarola, Michelangelo's early idol and a Dominican versed in the Platonism of his antagonists, could express the same view of beauty attributed by Varchi to Platonists. "You won't say that a lady is beautiful just because she has a beautiful nose or beautiful hands, but only when all the proportions are present . . . This beauty then comes from the soul." Compare Savonarola's archenemy Ficino, "Proportio, illa cuncta includit corporis composita membra, neque est in singulis, sed in cunctis, etc."[33] In a sermon based on Ezekiel, Savonarola, almost like a Platonist, distinguishes Higher beauty and beauty of the senses: "The beauty of man and woman is greater and more perfect in so far as it is similar to the primary beauty."

The true nature of beauty as something transcending the five senses is very clearly set forth in a poetic dialogue in which the poet Michelangelo asks Love to define the exact nature of the beauty to which he aspires:

> Tell me please, Love, if my eyes
> See the true nature of the beauty for which I long
> Or if I possess it within me when, gazing on the face
> Of my lady, I see it sculptured.

Love explains that the true *concetto* progresses from outer to inner vision where it is converted to beauty itself, something divine.

> The beauty which you see comes truly from your lady;
> But this beauty grows, since it ascends to a better place
> When through mortal eyes it passes on to the soul.
> There it is made into something divine, worthy, and fine,
> Since any immortal thing wishes other things similarly
> immortal.
> This divine beauty, and not the other, guides your eyes
> onward. (G 42)

This sonnet, according to Michelangelo the Younger, dates from *ca.* 6 January, 1529. It accompanies the sonnet "Spirto ben nato, in cu' si spechia e uede" (G 41), infused with the theme of beauty (*belle membra, bell'-opera, in belta, la belta, bell'opera*) and details the interplay of love and beauty. This transfer of the *concetto* through the visual sense to something divine is even more economically expressed in the quatrain (1524–29):

> As I draw my soul, which sees through the eyes,
> Closer to beauty as I first saw it,
> The image grows therein, and the first image
> Recedes as though unworthy and without value. (G 44)

Michelangelo found a similar conversion of the image of the soul in Ficino's *Commentarium*; "Nam procedente tempore amatum non in mera eius imagine per sensus accepta perspiciunt, sed in simulacro iam ab anima ad ideæ suæ similitudinem reformato, quod ipso corpore pulchrius est, intuentur."[34]

In his *Rime* Michelangelo returns several times to two constants of his theory of beauty. First, the source of beauty is God or Nature. Second, God grants to only a certain elect the power to discern divine beauty. The divine process of creating beauty is endless, if one is to believe the curious sonnet "Sol perche tuo' bellezze al mondo sieno" (Frey CIX, 46 var.). Here Michelangelo states that nature bestows beauties on certain individuals, only to take them back when that person declines, and use them to form again another "angelic and serene" beauty. Still another poem posits God as the source of all beauty:

He who made the whole, created every part
And then from all selected the most beautiful,
To exhibit here on earth his lofty creations,
As he has done just now with his divine art. (G 9)

This early poem (1511–12), which does not correspond closely to any theory of invention of the artist, while vaguely reminiscent of the compounding of the plurimodellistic Crotonian Venus, was abandoned by the artist. It is not one of those autonomous *non finiti* of his poetry, but seems rather an effort abandoned.

Michelangelo, to whose art posterity has denied the term of grace and allotted stintingly any acknowledgement of beauty, definitely felt that beauty was an objective he was achieving. Describing his art, in a passage partially quoted above, he slips unconsciously into the phrase "bell'arte." Such art was, moreover, a goal to which he was predestined:

If I was born neither deaf nor blind to beautiful art,
Destined to one who burns and steals my heart,
The fault is his who predestined me to fire. (G 97)

Or even more simply:

As a faithful augury of my vocation
Beauty was given to me at birth,
Which is the lantern and mirror of both the arts. (G 164)

Here the term "both arts" is usually accepted as meaning painting and sculpture. It could even be construed to mean both categories of art, pictorial and literary. Mariani, in his *Michelangelo,* finds this an echo of the delicate admission of Sappho in a recently discovered fragment: "I cherish elegant beauty; destiny has allotted to me since childhood the love of all beauty." A third passage finds Michelangelo claiming to discern beauty through predestination:

Since by my clear star
My eyes were made capable
Of distinguishing easily one beauty from another. (G 173)

Granted Michelangelo's special perception for beauty, what are the particular beauties he will seek to render as an artist? Condivi listed the types of natural beauties which attracted the artist: "Not only did he love all human beauty, but universally every beautiful thing, a beautiful horse, a beautiful dog, a beautiful countryside, a beautiful plant, a beautiful mountain, a beautiful wood, and every site and thing beautiful of its kind."[35] Curiously, the natural subjects listed by Condivi offered little interest to Michelangelo. He did not exercise his craft in *lontani.* He felt that the artist's first duty was to capture beauty, terribility, and mansuetude in religious painting and sculpture. In grasping for an example of extreme beauty, Michelangelo almost spontaneously makes an analogy with church art:

> Thy beauty appears much more beautiful
> Than that of a man painted in church. (G 20)

As has been suggested, to Michelangelo the finest beauty for an artist is that of the nude male, for it is in the noble human body that divine beauty is most manifest (G 106). The beauty of Tommaso Cavalieri and of Cecchino Bracci is the theme of many of his greatest paeans. True to his dislike for descriptive portraiture, he avoids telling the color of their eyes or hair, the shape of their face, and the like. To Cavalieri he expressed his assurance (*ca.* 1534) that in contemplation of the friend's physical beauty he transcended to something above the senses, something which brought him rather feelings of peace:

> No mortal object did these eyes behold
> When first they met the placid light of thine,
> And my Soul felt her destiny divine. . . .
> And hope of endless peace in me grew bold:
> Heaven-born, the soul a heavenward course must hold;
> Beyond the visible world she soars to seek
> (For what delights the sense in false and weak)
> Ideal Form, the universal mould.
> The wise man, I affirm, can find no rest
> In that which perishes; nor will he lend
> His heart to aught which doth on time depend.
> 'Tis sense, unbridled will, and not true love,
> That kills the soul; love betters what is best,
> Even here below, but more in heaven above. (G 105)
> (William Wordsworth)

Similarly, even a beautiful (*leggiadra*) body can be a mere *spoglia* (corpse) (G 139) when love is impossible.

When the comely young Cecchino Bracci died, Michelangelo found himself in a position requiring him to compose a block of funereal verse. He discovered beauty the most dependable theme and he exploited it in a number of ways. Indeed, the theme (*begli*) occurs in the very first verse of the initial poem in the series and in the last line (*beltà*) of the final poem. To judge from the gentle, regular face probably designed by Michelangelo and carved by Urbino (Francesco Amadori) in the Church of Aracoeli the boy deserved the overworked epithet.

Naturally, the poems on Cecchino return again and again to the struggle of beauty and death:

Death wished to strike, without the heavier blow
Of weary years or overweight of days,
The beauty that lies here, that seen in heavenly rays
We still his earthly countenance might know. (G 182)
(Ednah Dow Cheney)

The beauty which lies here, on earth did win
By far over every other beautiful creature,
That death, ever resentful of nature,
To become friends with her, did kill and extinguish it. (G 183)

He who controls me cannot through death
Return the beauty . . . (G 186)

This insistent theme of beauty eventually tires the reader and proves a thinning vein. In any case, the unfairness of a youth dying just at his *Blütezeit* disturbed Michelangelo deeply, for whom Cecchino

Remains creditor of so many years and beauty. (Frey LXIII, 50)

As we have seen, the sonnet "Sol perche tuo bellezze al mondo sieno" held that beauty is deathless, being taken by God from one individual to be reborn in another. Another familiar piece (see p. 68) stresses the deathlessness of beauty, which will outlast even the work of art which has given it long existence:

The beauty, which existed at first, is remembered
And keeps vain pleasure for a better place. (G 237)

The purport is that even if sculpture has its term (certainly the suggested media of wax and terra cotta will reach that term before stone) the work of art still affords a glimpse to be remembered of the God-ideated *concetto*.

There are a few generalities about the power of beauty, as there were about the power of love. For example, beauty scatters a burning fire (G 170). Many are the poems deploring the fact that beauty keeps an old man at war with himself.

Most of the remarks on beauty occur in the context of love. Indeed, love itself can be defined as beauty. Beauty perceived through the eyes becomes converted into love:

Love is a concept of beauty
Imagined or seen within the heart,
Friend to virtue and gentility. (G 38)

However, if beauty is converted into love, true love survives the passing of external beauty. Of this Michelangelo was ever more certain as he aged. Thus, in 1546 he wrote:

Only fallacious hope is offered by that love that dies
As beauty dies, fading continually from hour to hour,
And subject to the changing of a beautiful face . . . (G 259)

The love that outlasts the changes of the flesh attains paradise on earth: "e qui caparra il paradiso."

Dealing with the theme of unrequited love, Michelangelo asserts that the more the lover's face is distorted with anguish, the more beautiful does the beloved's face appear (G 123), but he does not mind. How much more beautiful her face would then seem if he were to die, but then her beauty and the analogy would die.

On the relation of beauty to love, the poet asks Love itself to arbitrate his question.

> If there is one part in women which is beautiful
> Whereas the other parts are ugly,
> Must I love them all,
> Because of the pleasure I take from the one alone?
> The part that appeals,
> While the enjoyment saddens us,
> To our reason, yet would have us
> Excuse and even love our innocent mistake.

The answer is given in indirect discourse:

> Love, which recounts to me
> The annoying vision,
> Says in its wonted angry voice
> That its heaven expects or claims none such.
> And yet the heaven which I seek
> Wishes that kindness toward what displeases be not vain.
> For in the eyes habit makes every unsightly feature whole. (G 256)

Girardi feels that these verses from 1545–46 are not addressed to Vittoria, although that lady's limited beauty might have inspired them. The idea that in the realm of love reason has no place foreshadows the debates on reason versus passion in the following century. The thought that habit eventually blinds the lover to the faults of his mistress or lover anticipates the Stendhalian phenomenon of *crystallisation.*

The madrigal "Ben uinci ogni durezza" (G 114) is an ecstatic outpouring of appreciation for beauty combined with infinite grace and kindness, a combination which leaves an old scarred veteran like himself, inured to the fire-ordeals of love, half dead with joy and blinded from the contemplation of it.

Michelangelo, like his master Petrarch, knew that beauty and cruelty often came hand in hand. Nature in her wisdom provided that beauty be accompanied by an equal amount of asperity: "Che l'un contrario l'altro ha temperato" (G 69). However, the beauty more than compensates for the cruelty.

Other minor improvisations on the theme of beauty show a tremendous preoccupation with it on the part of a man who rationalised that his own ugliness served the useful function of accentuating the beauty of his friends and even his art ("Costei pur si delibra"). Yet the inability of the beauties surrounding him to bring him peace is interestingly conjectured by Amendola, in the preface to his edition of the *Rime*: "This superb creator of spirituality and beauty wanders through the world like a chilly Eros; he loves more than he is loved, he produces beauty rather than enjoys it; he enriches the world of others, but remains poor and sad in his own soul, which is turned elsewhere."[36]

If the constant stream of poetry composed up until 1560 is a revealing *journal intime* acquainting us with Michelangelo's final relations with his art, so also are the letters a lifelong record of the tribulations brought on by the fine arts. They contain a complete repertory of the hardships of the artist's life: financial distress, dissatisfaction with the Maecenate system, troubles brought on by assistants, technical problems seemingly insoluble, pressures, humiliations, and even enmities. Many times the dissatisfaction boils over, as in the following two letters. The first, to Luigi del Riccio, complains that thirty-six years of loyal service to his profession have left him wondering if he should not have followed a trade:

Painting and sculpture, fatigue and loyalty have ruined me, and things are still going from bad to worse. It would have been better if in my youth I had hired myself out to make sulphur matches. I should not now be in such a passion.[37]

No glowing picture of the artist's life is drawn for his unappreciative brother Giovan Simone:

I've knocked about all over Italy leading a wretched life for these twelve years. I've endured every shame, suffered every hardship, racked my body in every task, exposed my very life to a thousand perils . . .[38] (For full statement see p. 95.)

Throughout, Michelangelo was sustained by the knowledge that he was serving God through his art, perhaps even more fully than was his brother Lionardo in a Dominican cowl. However, late in life, when Michelangelo was turning ever more longingly toward Christ and nursing a very real concern for his salvation, he went through moments when his entire life seemed a *vanitas vanitatum* (see pp. 296–97). At such moments he set down renunciations of the arts which bespeak crises rather than momentary vexations.

There are visible in the *Rime* periods of renunciation and dissatisfaction with the arts, times when his patience simply ran out. Obviously no religious scruples lie behind the outburst in his *capitolo:* "I' sto rinchiuso come la midolla" of 1546–50.

Love, the muses, and the flowery grottoes—
My scribblings and drawings now are used
For inns and privies and for brothels.
What avails it to try to create so many childish things
If they've but brought me to this end, like one
Who crosses o'er the sea and then drowns on the strand.
Precious art, in which for a while I enjoyed such renown,
Has left me in this state:
Poor, old, and a slave in others' power.
I am undone if I do not die soon. (G 267)

Two sonnets composed several years later show that grave concern for his salvation was leading Michelangelo to renounce the fine arts. In 1554 Michelangelo knew that the death he had considered imminent for almost five decades would not now be long in coming. Accordingly, he penned his magnificent sonnet of renunciation:

The course of my long life hath reached at last,
In fragile bark o'er a tempestuous sea,
The common harbor where must rendered be
Account of all the actions of the past.
The impassioned fantasy, that, vague and vast,
Made art an idol and a king to me,
Was an illusion, and but vanity
Were the dreams that lured me and harassed.
The dreams of love, that were so sweet of yore—
What are they now, when two deaths may be mine,
One sure, and one forecasting its alarms?
Painting and sculpture satisfy no more
The soul now turning to the Love Divine,
That oped, to embrace us, on the cross its arms. (G 285)
(H. W. Longfellow)

This sonnet was sent on 19 September, 1554 to Vasari, precisely the biographer who had done so much to bring glory and satisfaction to Michelangelo. It forms a curious contrast with the self-confident and assured sonnet which Michelangelo had sent to Giorgio on the first appearance of the *Vite* (1550). The change of tone was so marked that Giorgio sent him a letter pressing him to come back to Florence, even urging him in the name of Duke Cosimo.

On his autograph manuscript of this poem Michelangelo, as if to reaffirm his renunciation, added the variant verse: "Or ueggio ben com' era d'error carca" ("Now I see clearly how [this fantasy] was laden with error").

Another sonnet (1555) directed to Vasari and to his friend Beccadelli echoes this turning away. Indeed, it strikes the sternly religious and ascetic note which characterised some of Beccadelli's verses:

Earth's work and toys have occupied, amused
Years granted me on God to meditate;
Not only I forgot Him in that state,
But e'en His favors I for sinning used.
And what made others wise in me infused
But folly, making me perceive it late . . .
Grant me to spurn all here of greatest worth,
Those beauties that I honor most and prize;
Ere death give earnest of eternal day. (G 288)
(Warburton Pike)

The sincerity of these verses is incontestable. Angiolo Orvieto has shown the dismay which lay behind them. "Particularly dramatic in these lines is the new aspect, almost of vanity, in which art appears to him . . . Art is vain, no less than love; only death remains. Or what is worse, death with its menace of a thousand punishments."[39] As he so often did on catching himself being "serious," Michelangelo toned down the mood of the poem with a bantering footnote or commentary. To Vasari he wrote, "I send you two sonnets. Although they are silly things, I'm doing it so that you may see where I'm keeping my thoughts. And when you are eighty-one years old, as I am, you'll believe me." Both recipients were, however, sobered by the message of the verses. Beccadelli, off to Austria on one of his missions, took time to reply with a pious sonnet, equally humble, but making no reference to Michelangelo's turning his back on the values which had sustained him during his brilliant career.

There are earlier hints—from the 1530s—which forecast abdication:

False hopes and vain desire (G 51)

Oh false world, I recognise clearly
The error and damnation of humankind. (G 132)

Led through many years to the last hours,
Late I recognise, oh world, thy empty pleasures. (G 133)

These doubts and dissatisfactions eventually focus upon painting, sculpture, and architecture. Yet, even as he was torn by this psychomachy, the old artist resolutely plied his profession, almost to the last day of his life.

Sometimes the fine arts seem to fade in importance as they are set against deep human or ethical values. The "natural man" in the stanzas praising rustic life knows the trivial value of the "crowning achievements of art." This is not to say that Michelangelo's Platonism ever led him to an ethical condemnation of art, comparable to the belittling of art in the *Republic*. Imitative art, however, like genius and memory, gives way before virtue:

And now I well see the error of those who would believe
That grace divine which rains from you
Might correspond in worth to my weak and waning works of art.

Genius and art and memory give way:
For even in a thousand attempts a gift of heaven
Can never be paid for by mere assets of mortal man. (G 159)

Whereas mere poetry, the "sister art" of painting (Lomazzo), cannot make art pale in comparison, the deeply spiritual sonnets of Vittoria Colonna are something greater than words and succeed in making Michelangelo's paintings and drawings *turpissime* (G 79). We have seen painting and sculpture cast in the shadow by love of God, fear of death, and the rest, but here it is the *cortesia* of a great lady, raining from her like grace, which invalidates the fine arts.

It is understandable that Michelangelo, beset by failing health, unrequited loves, professional pressures, religious crises, should make dismissal of the arts part of a more general renunciation of life itself (see Chapter XVII). Less understandable is that Michelangelo should revise his basic definition of art, so abundantly characterised in his spoken and written words as "a gift of God," "art from heaven," and so on. It seems in his despair to have become a mere worldly activity. Could this old man, who spent a few of his last hours half-blind, running his hand over the smooth surfaces of the Belvedere Torso, actually have lost his faith in the divinity of art?

NOTES

[1] Cf. R. J. Clements, *Michelangelo's Theory, ed. cit.*, pp. 360–64.
[2] Giovanni Papini, *La vita, ed. cit.*, pp. 497–98.
[3] See R. J. Clements, *The Peregrine Muse* (University of North Carolina, 1959), pp. 37–39.
[4] Cf. R. J. Clements, *Michelangelo's Theory, ed. cit.*, pp. 410–13.
[5] *Lettere*, ed. Milanesi, p. 519.
[6] *Ibid.*, p. 383.
[7] See Valerio Mariani, *La poesia, ed. cit.*, p. 87.
[8] Donato Giannotti, *Dialogi*, ed. cit., p. 43.
[9] Francisco de Hollanda, *Diálogos em Roma, ed. cit.*, p. 191.
[10] *Ibid.*, p. 241.
[11] *Ibid.*, p. 239.
[12] *Rime*, ed. Girardi, p. 53.
[13] Vincenzo Danti, *Prime libro delle perfette proportioni* (Perugia, 1830), p. 87.
[14] Marsilio Ficino, *Commentarium in Convitum*, II, iv.
[15] Ugo Foscolo, *Opere*, Edizione Nazionale (Florence, 1953), X, 450.
[16] Philippe Desportes, *Oeuvres* (Paris, 1858), p. 186.
[17] Giovanni Battista Bellori, *Vite dei pittori, scultori ed architettori* (Rome, 1672), p. 13.
[18] J. E. Taylor, *Michelangelo Considered as a Philosophic Poet* (London, 1852), pp. 83–85.
[19] From Michelangelo's *Ricordi*, 10 May, 1508.
[20] Vasari, *Vite, ed. cit.*, VII, p. 281.
[21] *Ibid.*, VII, 219; also F. Baldinucci, *Notizie dei professori del disegno* (Florence, 1846), II, 556.

[22] *Lettere*, ed. Milanesi, p. 532; Thode, *Michelangelo*, I, 83 ff.
[23] Benvenuto Cellini, *Vita*, viii, 41.
[24] See R. J. Clements, *Michelangelo's Theory, ed. cit.*, pp. 43–48.
[25] *Rime*, ed. Ceriello, p. 256.
[26] Ficino, *Commentarium in Convitum*, II, vi.
[27] Francisco de Hollanda, *Dialoghi* (Rome, 1953), pp. 141–42.
[28] Vasari, *Vite, ed. cit.*, VII, 210.
[29] Giovan Battista Armenini, *De' veri precetti della Pittura* (Ravenna, 1586), pp. 226–27.
[30] Ficino, *Commentarium in Convitum*, V, iii.
[31] *Trattati d'arte del Cinquecento*, ed. P. Barocchi (Bari: Laterza, 1960), p. 89.
[32] A. Blunt, *Artistic Theory in Italy, 1450–1600* (Oxford, 1940), p. 93.
[34] *Ibid.*, VI, vi.
[35] Condivi, *Vita*, lxv.
[36] G. Amendola, *Le poesie di Michelangelo* (Lanciano, 1911), p. 19.
[37] *Lettere*, ed. Milanesi, p. 488.
[38] *Ibid.*, p. 151.
[39] Angiolo Orvieto, in *Il marzocco* (17 May, 1931), p. 1.

5

POEMS AS EXEGESES OF SPECIFIC WORKS OF ART

In a deep sense every one of Michelangelo's 343 poems and fragments is a comment on his production as artist. To state the relationship in another way, there is almost no work of his painting or sculpture which may not be better understood through a knowledge of his poetry. Among the rare exceptions would be the *Bacco,* and one is tempted to conjecture that among his *juvenilia* which Michelangelo destroyed around 1518 there may have been some exercise in the popular form of the Bacchic ode. The varying moods of his art reappear in his poetry. The Bernesque verses among the *Rime* (see Chapter XV) reveal an ironic temperament capable of drawing a self-portrait mocking a sad, aging woman by a vulgar *fica.* As we saw in Chapter II, his mood of *desengaño* and desire to mortify his flesh prepare us far in advance for the self-portrait as the pelt of St. Bartholomew. The poems composed during painting of the *Giudizio universale* betray a heightened concern over grace and redemption. The "trembling-hand sonnets" of old age explain the drive which impelled him to carve the Rondanini and Palestrina Pietàs long after his ebbing strength could easily handle the hammer. Such *rapprochements* between the art and the *canzoniere* are continuous and meaningful.

Many poems are direct commentaries on individual works of art, whether or not there exists a close chronological correspondence. The task of correlation sustained throughout this volume will become intensified in this chapter. The commentaries on art via the *Rime* are of two types: obvious parallels, pointed out more or less in passing, and poetic exegeses lending themselves to a more extended analysis. Rather than separate these two types, we shall group together in chronological order the seventeen works under consideration. In a few cases, where works of different periods are being discussed together, the date of the more important example will determine their order in this chapter. Thus the meaning of the *Notte* and *Allegories of the Times of Day* must be examined along with that of the *Creazione del sole* and *Dio separa la luce dalle tenebre.*

1. *The Statue of Pope Julius II* (1506–08). Michelangelo's disappointment over patrons never exceeded his first painful disillusionment with Julius II, whose ill-treatment of the artist was the more keenly felt since it alternated with encouragement and high hopes. There were several stages of this early disenchantment: the physical expulsion from the papal chambers culminating in the flight arrested at Poggibonsi (1506), the periods when the pope listened willingly to the detractors among Raphael's clique, the trips to Carrara embittered by rumors of Michelangelo's mismanagement and financial swindling. Each of these trials incited the artist to plaintive letters and exculpations addressed to family and to friends at the *curia*. None of these recitals of grievances was more resentful than the economical sonnet composed probably in 1506, venting his rancor and sense of humiliation. It is a sonnet ennobling personal feelings by proverb and aphorism. Further dignity is achieved by apostrophising the pope with a classical or Biblical *tu:*

> If truth in any ancient saw there be,
> 'Tis here, "Who can, he never hath the will":
> To tales and foolish talk thou listenest still,
> Rewarding him who is truth's enemy.
> I am of old thy faithful servitor,
> To thee belong as to the sun its rays:
> But thou, unrecking of my wasted days,
> Art more displeased, as I toil the more.
> I trusted thy greatness to ascend:
> Need is of sword and scales to shield the weak,
> Not empty words by Echo uttered.
> In scorn it is that heaven doth virtue send
> To dwell on earth, who mocking bids it seek
> Fruit of its labor from a tree that's dead. (G 6)
> (Elizabeth Hall)

To the aforementioned dignity of proverb and aphorism is added allegory: justice with its sword, Echo replacing rumor. These elegances would indicate that the artist fully intended to send the sonnet to the pope. It is unlikely that he did so. For a young man just turned thirty to preach a moral lesson to the aged pontiff might have provoked irreparable hostility.

It has been questioned whether this sonnet dates from 1506, the date assigned to it by Guasti. Michelangelo the Younger thought it addressed "perhaps" to Julius II. Guasti noted the pun on Della Rovere (oak) and "arbor secho" (dry tree). Frey wondered whether Michelangelo in 1506 would have called himself a "servo antico," since he had served the pope only since the first months of 1505. Frey sees as more possible the date 1511, when Bramante wished to have Raphael substituted for Michelangelo in the Sistine Chapel, a situation recorded by Condivi. Indeed, once at this stage the pope actually struck Michelangelo with a *mazza* (Vasari) when the artist could not give him a completion date for the Sistine Ceiling. Girardi, whose work on the chronology of the *Rime* is the most reliable, accepts the date of 1511. The resentment these verses express was nurtured in the artist's breast even as he was executing the bronze statue of the pontiff, to whom he had been forced to genuflect and apologise publicly "with a halter around his neck," as he wrote in a letter. The failure of the initial casting of this statue did not mollify the artist, certainly, nor did his realisation that he who opposed portraiture was being forced to execute a bronze portrait. The reference to the just sword of the pontiff refers probably to the days when Michelangelo was planning the bronze statue and wondered if Julius wished to be carrying a book in his left hand while the right hand gave a benediction. He was then told by the pope: "Give me a sword in it, I am no scholar."

This is not the only sonnet charging the recipient with ingratitude. Such is the burden also of the bitter sermonising on ingratitude ("Nel dolce d'una immensa cortesia" [G 251]) delivered to Luigi del Riccio. Michelangelo, who condemns the seven deadly sins in the *Rime*, must have applauded the protest against papal ingratitude by Andrea Mantegna, who had painted as a papal commission the seven mortal sins, and then portrayed an eighth—Ingratitude—alongside them.

2. *The Sistine Ceiling* (1508–12). The earliest of the *Rime* to provide an insight into the creation of one of Michelangelo's masterpieces is the sonnet doubly *caudato* on the painting of the Sistine Vault. It corroborates passages in Vasari, Condivi, and Bernini on these hardships, and especially Vasari's statement that Michelangelo's neck became so arched and his vision so impaired that he had to read books by holding them over his head. The sonnet adopts the coarse, physiological vocabulary of the artist's other Bernesque verse:

> In this hard toil I've such a goiter grown,
> Like cats that water drink in Lombardy,
> (Or wheresoever else the place may be)
> That chin and belly meet perforce in one.
> My beard doth point to heaven, my scalp its place
> Upon my shoulder finds; my chest, you'll say,
> A harpy's is, my paint-brush all the day
> Doth drop a rich mosaic on my face.
> My loins have entered my paunch within,

My nether end my balance doth supply,
My feet unseen move to and fro in vain.
In front to utmost length is stretched my skin
And wrinkled up in folds behind, while I
Am bent as bowmen bend a bow in [Spain].

The theme of the Syrian bow (not as Elizabeth Hall here has interpreted, bow of Soria, Spain) is found in Berni and occurs later in another of the artist's Bernesque pieces, "Tu ha' 'l uiso" (G 20), to express the exaggerated "twist" of a woman's eyebrows. The poet now (*ca.* 1510) turns from his physical disabilities to the mental derangement which is in his view linked with them. (The idea that mental disturbance complements physical maladjustment will be repeated in "I' sto rinchiuso come la midolla.")

No longer true or sane,
The judgment now doth from the mind proceed,
For 'tis ill shooting through a twisted reed.
Then thou, my picture dead,
Defend it, Giovan, and my honor—why?
The place is wrong, and no painter am I. (G 5)
(Elizabeth Hall)

This final verse is the first of a long series of disclaimers found in his letters and poems, denials that Michelangelo is a painter, architect, or a poet, but also disclaimers of competence in making daggers (XLVIII), writing business letters (XCVIII), other letters (CDLXXXII), and shopkeeping (CLXXXII and CXCV). The evidence here of injured feelings at having to work in fresco was amusingly repeated on the earlier-mentioned receipt: "I, Michelangelo Buonarroti, sculptor, have received five hundred ducats on account, for the paintings in the Sistine Chapel." Condivi, Vasari, and Piero Rosselli all noted that Michelangelo worked unwillingly "in terra."

Since *vivo* was the highest accolade paid to Michelangelo's art, and a consummate compliment when he himself applied it to works of Sebastiano del Piombo, Tommaso Guidi, Antonio Begarelli, and others, the most damning adjective would thus be *morto*, the quality of art undertaken against one's will. Even the adjective *turpissime* he applied to his own paintings (in "Felice spirto, che con zelo ardente") (G 79) is less devastating.

The recipient of this sonnet and of another *capitolo* equally Bernesque, Giovanni da Pistoia, will be identified and discussed on pages 252–53. This extended sonnet of 1510, describing the discomforts which were to be endured another two years, is an amusing commentary on such facile compliments as Vasari's well-intended observation that the *Giudizio universale* looked like a work accomplished in a single day.

3. *La creazione del sole; Dio separa la luce dalle tenebre; Le allegorie del tempo; il Dì e la Notte* (1508–12, 1525–34).

Among the many anguishes of Michelangelo as man and artist was his awareness of the flight of time: "Che 'l tempo è breue, e 'l necessario poco." Few artists of his generation were so subjected to pressures of time. To meet these challenges, Michelangelo invented a curious headgear bearing a candle, allowing him to work nights as well as days in his studio, where he could carve on twenty figures at once. Seven popes and the great princes of his era pressed him with commissions. He cried out desperately, "I am solicited so much that I cannot find time to eat." Finally he was even pressured as a poet. When Luigi del Riccio demanded fifty poems within a short space of time, at length Michelangelo objected: "You're in too much of a hurry" ("Uoi auete troppa fretta"). Thus, as artist and poet he was all too aware of the onrush of time, bringing deadlines, marking delays, and exhausting him. He wrote that "no wrong is equal to the wasting of time" (G 51).

Yet time had a curious, further meaning for Michelangelo as a man. It signaled approaching death. Aware of his "imminent death" (G 12) even before the Fates had spun out half his life, he felt like a mystic that death was all too slow in coming (see Chapter III). He had a Gothic or Piagnone fear of the passing of days and nights. If he did not paint us a Gothic Father Tempus, with hourglass and scythe, he did leave behind a poetic reminder of the *memento mori*, viewing Death as a reaper:

> Time moves on, and like a loathsome poison
> Metes out the hours of our days.
> Time is like a scythe and we are like hay. (G 17)

This somber word picture dates from about April, 1521.

Michelangelo was aware as a lover that time passes, that (as Ausonins wrote and Shakespeare and the Renaissance poets echoed) youth and beauty do not endure. Indeed, later in this same piece he adds, "Trust is brief and beauty endureth not." The notion of the fragile flower lasting only "l'espace d'un matin" is found twice in Michelangelo's *Rime*, by the way (G 17 and 218). It is a theme Michelangelo found while reading Poliziano's "I' mi trovai, fanciullo, un bel mattino," or his *Serenata, ovvero Lettera in Istrambotti:*

> Che 'l tempo vola, e non s'arreston l'ore,
> E la rosa sfiorita non s'apprezza; . . .
> El tempo fugge, e tu fuggir lo lassi . . .

or again, in the same poet's *Rime varie* (*incerte*), he sighs that "Il tempo passa in men che non balena."

An artist who found time so precious that he would sleep fully clothed to save it could easily reflect that he has been wasting time in love:

> With death at hand
> I lose the present and the future is taken from me. (G 144)

Is it any wonder that this harassed genius should have chosen to initiate the nine histories of the Sistine Ceiling with not one, but two paintings commemorating the passage of time: *La creazione del sole e della luna* and *Dio separa la luce dalle tenebre*? As a poet Michelangelo pondered the creation of these planets and the separation of light and darkness, that initial moment in the void of history. The following commentary on the first two histories dates, however, from the period when the artist was painting the *Giudizio universale:*

> He who from nothing, and ere all things were,
> Did time create, divided it in twain:
> To one, he made the lofty sun a share;
> And to the other, moonlight's dusky train. (G 104)

Certainly the poet working for five years on the *Giudizio* must have often meditated on the message of his frescoes of 1508–09 which he saw every day.

Michelangelo makes these creations precede the formation of man, not merely to correspond to Genesis, but because man must be born into a world governed by these two Times of Day. Although we cannot see the face of God in the first history, the Creator's face as he makes the sun and moon shows the well-known gravity and *terribilità* acclaimed by popes, critics, and friends of the artist. God is aware that these Times of Day will be a reminder and a burden to man, whom He is about to create. If Michelangelo on one occasion viewed the creation of the sun and moon as a charitable act of God providing a temperature balance to protect man from freezing or burning,

> Thus in turn our eternal orbs,
> The one hot and the other cold restore us,
> That the world will no longer be consumed, (G 45)

he is certain at other times that God intentionally imposed these circumscribing units of time from which man will be delivered only by death. As he wrote almost enviously to his deceased father and brother:

> The different hours do not pressure you. (G 86)

"Fortuna" and "tempo" lose their authority only when man is exempt from them in death. Only on the Day of Judgement will the planets cease their relentless marking of time:

> Oh that happy day if this be true!
> Let time and its hours halt in a moment,
> And the day and the sun in its ancient track. (G 72)

As a lover Michelangelo also finds both day and night fearful:

> Night is the interval, and day the light;
> The one chills my heart, the other enflames me
> With love, faith, and a celestial fire. (G 257)

However, when all goes well, love may lend unity to those two separate Times of Day:

> Whence I divide time:
> The day is for eyes, night for the heart,
> Without any interval is my yearning for heaven. (G 258)

This is the miracle worked by Vittoria Colonna, his autumn love. He no longer experiences the dual attrition represented by day and night.

Michelangelo's concern over the perilous interworking of day and night first translated into the Sistine Vault (1508–09) became even more pronounced by the period of the Sagrestia Nuova of San Lorenzo (1526–33). Here the Times of Day became four, just as they had been in Dosso Dossi's *Aurora, Meriggio, Vespero,* and *Notte* at Ferrara, a work which Michelangelo apparently recalled to his friend Francisco de Hollanda. Yet he remains interested principally in Dì/*sole* and Notte/*luna*. The two themes which dominate the tomb of Duke Giuliano are that of premature death, or—phrased in another way—the brutality of day and night.

The injuries which the Times of Day may dispense are decried in an angry letter of the artist to his brother Giovan Simone (CXXVII). The ever-swift course of time has brought disaster. "I've gone knocking about through all Italy for these twelve years, endured every shame, suffered every hardship, lacerated my body in every tiring task, exposed my very life to a thousand perils, only to help my family; and now that I've begun to raise it up a bit, you want to be the one to undermine and ruin in one hour what I have done in many years at so much cost."

Michelangelo had witnessed many such reversals of fortune, as abrupt as those peripeteias demanded by his fellow academicians of Florence, the "Aristotelian" writers of tragedy: the sudden trial by fire of Savonarola, the precipitous death throes of Lorenzo il Magnifico, the overnight disgrace of the Maréchal de Gié, for whom he had intended his bronze *David*. This sudden strike of ill fortune weighed on his mind as he contemplated his two effigies of Day and Night, as we must forthwith explain.

One of Michelangelo's dilemmas while living in Rome at the time of the Medicean Restoration in Florence resulted from his allegiance to the Medici of earlier years. He smoothed his daily relations with such Florentine exiles as the Strozzi, Luigi del Riccio, Donato Giannotti, and Antonio Petreo by composing his anti-Medicean quatrain on the statue of the *Notte* (see below) and his pathetic dialogue between a *fuoruscito* and the allegorical figure of Florence: "Per molti, Donna, anzi per mille amanti" (G 249). Yet he could not forget that it was Lorenzo il Magnifico who had taken him into his home and directed him toward sculpture. Just as Michelangelo carved the young Giuliano de' Medici, victim of a premature death, so did he pay tribute to this victim in his *Rime*.

The poet imagines an unusual free-verse recital in which the "living" figures of Night and Day conjecture what might have been the illustrious career of this young man, had he lived out a normal span. The piece is not a verbal exchange, but rather a Greek choral recitative of two, since the figures speak in unison as they conjecture on the vicissitudes of fate. The poem was probably composed after November, 1523, at the beginning of the Medicean Clement VII's pontificate, when Michelangelo was under heavy pressure to intensify his efforts on the Medici Tombs and would thus have been most sensitive to the passing of time. Night and Day represent the swift flight of time, responsible for the death of every living thing.

> Day and Night speak and say:
> In our rapid course
> We have led Duke Giuliano to his death.
> It is meet that he should take vengeance upon us as he does.
> And the vengeance is this:
> We having killed him, he thus dead has stolen our light from us
> And with his closed eyes has sealed our own, which no longer shine
> over the earth.
> What might he have done with us, then, had he lived? (G 14)

In view of the indignation at premature death which Michelangelo attributed to his two statues, one wonders what he felt on hearing that after Duke Alessandro was murdered by Lorenzino, the body was secretly deposited in the sarcophagus under the reclining figures of *Dawn* and *Dusk*.

This same concern over a young man deprived by death of a bright future overwhelmed Michelangelo when he was apprised of the death of the fifteen-year-old nephew of Riccio. On Cecchino's tomb there are no symbols of fleeting time. Michelangelo comforted himself rather with the thought that the adolescent Bracci had indeed lived much in his brief life. The poet addressed the youth:

> If two hours here have stolen from thee a hundred years,
> A luster must perforce deceive eternity. (G 195)

Reflecting still on the velocity of time, Michelangelo regrets that two short hours (interpreted variously as Cecchino's lifetime or his death agony) have cheated him of a long life. Five years then must of necessity defraud

Cecchino of eternity. The poet consoles Cecchino with the thought that his limited lifespan has deprived him of hours on earth, but not of eternal salvation, which would have been more difficult to achieve with longevity, which is relatively but a luster. The basis for this consolation is Michelangelo's belief, expressed several times (see Chapter XVIII), that the longer one lives the more impossible are grace and salvation to achieve:

> For he has least grace who sojourneth here longest:
> And he who lives least returneth lightest to heaven. (G 132)

Cecchino speaks like a sage rather than the mundane *mignon* he must have been. He counters that his life has been a rich one and fraught with experience:

> —No, for in one day he has lived a hundred years
> Who in that day has acquired all knowledge and dies. (G 195)

The lad's reply that he has lived most fully in his "daytime" of life would seem to be as well as a contradiction of Michelangelo's belief a reminder that grace does not depend on the length, but on the intense activity, of life.

Three verses of 1520–23 throw further light on Michelangelo's thoughts about his allegories of the Times of Day. In fact, they accompanied sketches of the tombs in the Sagrestia Nuova:

> Fame holds the epitaphs lying still:
> Fame goes neither forward nor backward.
> For they are dead and their activities stayed. (G 13)

We shall comment at length on this lesson in Chapter XVI, in connection with Michelangelo's ideas on fame. Let us merely reproduce here De Tolnay's summary of it: "This would signify that by death the instability of terrestrial life is overcome and eternity is thereby attained."[1] These curious lines—and by extension the allegory of the tomb itself—are a restatement of the already-quoted thought which Michelangelo penned to his dead father and brother: "The different hours no longer exert force on you" (G 86). Indeed, the epitaph on Fame may be further clarified by a tercet in that pious poem to old Lodovico, the more so if *epitaffi* could signify the *Dì* and *Notte*. Michelangelo reminds his father that his reputation is now beyond change or harm:

> Your splendor is not toned down by night
> Nor is it ever increased by day, however bright,
> Even though among us the sun intensifies the heat. (G 86)

Again the truism on Day and Night is valid: "e è 'l 'loro operare fermo," (G 13) whether one's reputation was illustrious, as was Giuliano's, or as humble as was Lodovico Buonarroti's.

4. *La Notte* (1525–31). Apparently the first friend of Michelangelo to attribute speech to the figures in the Sagrestia Nuova was the communicative Anton Francesco Doni. In a letter of 12 January, 1543, from Piacenza, Doni alleges to Michelangelo that he has often been tempted to try waking the figure of Night. "Even though I made an effort to wake her a thousand times, as though she were a goddess formed in paradise sleeping there, and went back on three or four occasions, I still have this illusion in my breast: that if I went there once in your company she would rise suddenly to bow reverently to you."[2] Later, in his *Marmi* of 1552–53, the "Dialogo tra il Pellegrino e il Fiorentino" has the *Aurora* relate how the *Notte* woke, raised her head, and spoke to Michelangelo and a friend.

More famous is a quatrain on this subject by Giovanni di Carlo Strozzi (1517–70) of the anti-Medicean family which housed Michelangelo during an illness in Rome. Young Strozzi, consul of the Academy of the Umidi, wrote the now familiar lines on the *Notte:*

> The Night thou seest lie here so gracefully
> Asleep, was by an Angel wrought in stone,
> And that she lives is by her sleeping shown;
> Wake her, if thou hast doubts, she'll speak to thee.
> (Warburton Pike)

The traditional quality of this quatrain is noted by James Hutton, in his *Greek Anthology in Italy*. He concurs with Grimm that Strozzi may have borrowed the conceit from the *Planudean Anthology:* "The satyr was put to sleep, not sculptured by Diodorus. If you prod him you will wake him. The silver is asleep."[3] This was only one of hundreds of compliments on the lifelike qualities of Michelangelo's figures; indeed, Michelangelo occasionally paid the same compliment (see p. 92). Because of their quality of nascent action, his own figures particularly inspired this praise, but Michelangelo would have paid little attention to the quatrain had not the author been a Strozzi. His rejoinder of 1545–46 has become one of his most quoted poems:

> Sweet is sleep—Ah, sweeter, to be stone,
> Whilst wrong and shame exist and grow;
> Not to see, not to feel, is boon,
> Then not to wake me, pray speak low! (G 247)
> (Ralph Waldo Emerson)

To Bevilacqua the epigram does not hark back to the *Greek Anthology*, but anticipates the conceptual literature of the following century. "Everything hangs on a witty conceit [*argutezza*]. Night which is of stone and yet is not; which sleeps and yet does not; which hears not, yet hears . . . Quick-witted inventing, delightful hair-splitting (*cavillare*), 'urbane enthymemes,' Count Emmanuele Tesauro would say a century later."[4]

Whatever affinities this simple conceit may display, Michelangelo's well-known irony feeds itself upon history. A figure honoring one generation of the Medici speaks scathingly of a later generation odious not only to the Strozzi, but to most Italians. Perhaps only once before, in 1512, Michelangelo had spoken against the Medici, for their responsibility in the Sack of Prato (Letter XXXV).

The background is easily constructed. As early as April, 1521, Michelangelo ordered marble for the *Notte* and he had been able to start work upon the figure by the spring of 1524. It was completed a decade after its conception, by August or September of 1531. Thus, it was after 1531 that Strozzi paid his compliment and the artist responded with his epigram. Accordingly, Michelangelo was deploring conditions in Florence after the Medici restoration of 1530, when Duke Alessandro took over the town weakened by its siege of 1529. If Michelangelo wrote his bitter reply around 1531, he was no doubt reflecting on his own vicissitudes during that siege and the futility of his efforts at fortification as well as on the unworthy hands into which Florence fell.

Yet there is good reason to conclude that the two epigrams were written about 1545, a date supported by Frey and Girardi. First, young Strozzi would have been only fourteen in 1531; Michelangelo's relations with Strozzi were closer in the 1540s; this later dating would make the quatrain contemporaneous with Michelangelo's anti-Medicean, "Per molti, Donna, anzi per mille amanti." It is clear that Michelangelo did not ideate the *Notte* as a civic protest, as the nineteenth-century historians supposed, for it was conceived and planned from six to nine years before the loss of Florentine freedom. If the epigram was written about 1545, when Michelangelo was in close contact with the Florentine *fuorusciti* in Rome, it aims rather at the iron rule of Duke Cosimo, and such events (*danno e uergogna*) as followed the stabbing of Duke Alessandro by Lorenzino (12 January, 1539).

Although Duke Cosimo was urging Michelangelo to return and promising him honors, the usually passive Michelangelo (who agreed with a report that he was not "un uomo di stato") shared the indignation of the Florentine exiles and executed his bust of Brutus (see p. 243). Furthermore, as we have observed elsewhere, "if Michelangelo's reply does date from as late as 1545 or 1546, then the 'harm and shame' may refer also to the artistic conditions in Florence, where Bandinelli is coddled and Cellini plays a lackey's role."[5] It should be noted that Michelangelo's intended editors, the anti-Medicean Del Riccio and Giannotti, planned to include "Caro m'è 'l sonno" and "Per molti, Donna," in the florilegium to be published under their care. When the Florentine exiles gathered for their discussion of Dante and politics, recorded in Giannotti's *Dialogi*, Messer Donato asks graciously of "Caro m'è 'l sonno": "That epigram which you made recently about your Night . . . could it have been better woven, more sententious, more delightful?" Antonio Petreo adds his admiration: "Surely beautiful, and very appropriate to our times, when, being unable to see or hear anything from which to derive reasonable pleasure, one is most fortunate to be deprived of one and the other sense."[6] These high praises of his modest epigram make Michelangelo uncomfortable, and he protests that they are embarrassing him. The four lines of poetry, however, continued to win similar praises in Italy and elsewhere, partly because of their inherent political protest and partly because of their peripheral or exegetical relationship to one of the world's great statues. Giorgio Melchiori has shown that this was the first poem of Michelangelo's to be translated into English, appearing in Christopher Hervey's *Letters from Portugal, Spain, Italy, and Germany*. Hervey felt that it deserved a place alongside Vincenzo da Filicaia's "Italia, Italia, o tu."[7]

If the interplay of Day and Night ceaselessly dwelt in Michelangelo's thoughts, the individual allegory of the four Times of Day which most fascinated him was the Night. Certainly this figure, heavily laden with symbols, interested him most as a poet, too: Night is a recurring theme in the *canzoniere*. In view of the abundance of these expressive symbols, a spectator reflecting on this work might well feel that he understands the fullest meaning which the statue held for Michelangelo. Night was the comforting time when moon and stars invited the soul to sink into welcome lethargy, the body to give way to drowsiness (the poppy), unmindful of sinister activities going on outside the circle of one's life (the owl). These sinister doings which proceeded under the veil of night can occur even in the precincts of the Vatican itself. One remembers the curious passage in Michelangelo's letter complaining of Sangallo's plan for the rebuilt St. Peter's which explains that under cover of darkness much mischief will be done, including the impregnating of nuns and the counterfeiting of money.[8]

To the weary artist who complained constantly of his exhaustion and insufficient energies, who cried that for every day he worked he must rest several days, who plied his craft until he fell exhausted, dressed and shod, onto his bed, the restoration of body and spirit remained the foremost property of night. This is the meaning which he celebrated in his grateful paean:

> O Night! O season fair, though black thou be,
> All strife in thee doth find its peaceful end;
> Clear eyes, pure hearts, take thee to be their friend,
> And wholesome are his thoughts who honors thee.
> Thou lopp'st away all weary cares from me;
> While dewy shades unbroken quiet lend,
> In dreams thou leadest me where I would wend,
> And high exalt'st me, from low passion free.

Michelangelo verges on self-description in the fourth line, himself having honored Night so well. The tone of this poem has won universal praise. Saviotti calls it "studioso e prezioso" but goes on to state that "in the emphatic and ample swing of the periodic expression there is something which renders well the gravity and solemnity of night."[9] Amendola does not qualify his praise: "Then the habitual form of the cry and invocation is attenuated into the unhabitual one of melancholic elegy, in which desire breaks forth and finds accents no longer merely Michelangelesque, but sweet, humble, and as vast as human life itself."[10]

Having sung of the peace which nighttime brings, the poet exalts the healing, therapeutic power of night like that of Dante's *aer bruno* (*Inf.* II, 1–3). The succeeding tercets (1535–41) have been compared to Foscolo's initial lines to evening, "Forse perche della fatal quiete/Tu sei l'imago."

> Shadow of death! on thee the deathless soul
> Stays every sorrow fatal to life's peace.
> Irksome no more the good man's moments flow:
> His flesh and sense infirm thou makest whole,
> His tears thou driest, his weary labors cease,
> Latest and best release from haunting woe. (G 102)
> (Franklin B. Sanborn)

Bevilacqua shares the general satisfaction with Michelangelo's sonnet. He finds it "profound and solemn as the nocturnal silence of the stars," and "the best of the entire canzoniere," while adding the reservation, "even though a certain studied and precious quality noticed by others does not escape me."[11] The theme was far from new. Lorenzo's "O brevi e chiare notti" hailed Night's "healing power over blind and bitter thoughts" even while seeing this Time of Day as "immagine del morir." Philip Sidney was already hailing sleep as "the certain knot of peace" and Shakespeare was to commemorate slumber:

> Sleep that knits up the ravelled sleeve of care,
> The death of each day's life. . . .
> (*Macbeth* II, ii, 36–37)

Yet Michelangelo succeeded all the more because of the familiarity of the theme; as Horace said, it is more difficult to state commonplaces well. Mindful as always of the duality of body and soul, the poet views the healing and restoring of spirit as important as the resting of the senses and body. In this sonnet that horrid marble incubus which threatens the repose of the *Notte* (we have a record of at least four panic nightmares of Michelangelo himself) is replaced by lofty dreams. In view of Michelangelo's selection of the *Notte* and the *Giorno* to decorate the Medici Tombs, it is noteworthy that he penned a curious sonnet (1535–41) to demonstrate that night is superior to day, for while day generates the earth's living matter, night regenerates man himself. This thought is a sequitur of the final verses of the sonnet just discussed. Again, on nighttime:

> Each hollow space, that closed or covered lies,
> Whate'er by matter dense is screened from light,
> Preserving darkness in the sun's despite,
> To day her radiant privilege denies.
> And if or flame or fire dark night assail,
> The sun thereby, with meaner agents, may
> Her holy image blur and chase away;
> Yea, a poor worm to mar it doth avail.

One thinks inevitably of Michelangelo's invention of the candle-headgear which he wore to penetrate nocturnal blackness of his studio. Although he stresses the fragility of night, which can be dispelled by a mere candle or firefly, one recalls how, lest Vasari observe that he had injured the *Madonna della Febbre,* Michelangelo dropped the single candle and plunged the studio into darkness. The sonnet concludes:

> Beneath the shining sun lies bare the earth,
> And with a thousand herds and seeds she teems,
> While o'er her the rude farmer ploughs his way
> But darkness only doth to man give birth,
> Who than all other fruit more precious seems;
> Then is the night more holy than the day. (G 103)
> (Elizabeth Hall)

This sonnet is sometimes contrasted to its disadvantage with "O nott', o dolce tempo" (G 102). Saviotti finds it "quite the contrary: a bill of particulars, slightly jocular, against night, such a wretched thing that the slightest gleam of light kills it, etc."[12] Bevilacqua finds in it "an excessive studied and precious quality to the point of verging on Marinism."[13] This theme of night which regenerates man is dismissed in other poems. Night could become a torment, as it had for Petrarch, who often found his empty bed a battlefield. There were nights when the artist was wracked with passion and worry, such as the evening when he wrote that work was impossible in Gherardo's absence. He was, he feared, fated to be a "night man," and an unhappy one:

> Then in a moment came, in dread array,
> Chance, fortune, fate: by which, alas, I see.
> Predestined when I in the cradle lay,
> The time of darkness was assigned to me.

This sonnet (1535–46) is evocative of the second history of the Sistine Ceiling, as we have noted. If the papal censor chided Montaigne for using the word "fortune" instead of providence, if Machiavelli dissociated fortune from providence, Michelangelo lumps together *caso, sorte,* and *fortuna* and considers them all the direct maneuvering of God. The poet concludes:

> So, struggling with my own more darkened doom,
> Since where most night is, there is greatest gloom,
> My labors dark are pain and grief to me:
> Yet I console myself: for this my night
> Aids by its contrast to set forth thy light,—
> That sun which, at thy birth, was given to thee. (G 104)
> (Fanny Elizabeth Bunnett)

The sunlight evidently refers to the Apollinic radiance and beauty of Cavalieri, the same luminosity which furnished the pun-tribute in the former poems to Febo (Phoebus). In fact, the despondency of the poem might relate more easily to Michelangelo's unhappiness over Febo di Poggio than to his happiness in possessing his lifelong friend Tommaso Cavalieri. The editor Ceriello writes of these last two *terzine:* "They go beyond fantasy and express quite openly the infinite sadness of the poet, who makes an effort to console himself over his nocturnal destiny."[14]

Similar in spirit to the preceding sonnet is the fragment (G 257) written apparently to Vittoria Colonna, and quoted above: "La notte è l'intervallo, e 'l dì la luce." Michelangelo regrets that the moments of exaltation over lofty and eternal things come to him now more rarely. Perhaps a thing which comes to a man at rare intervals is all the more desirable. Intervals which in a sense are like the nights which separate the days. Night thoughts, like that incubus on the *Notte,* give him the shivers. Michelangelo never composed the third tercet, nor was there really anything more to add. Here was one of those cases where the *concetto* was awkwardly matched to the poetic materials at hand.

One further sonnet (1535–41) is dedicated to Night, daughter of the sun and earth, Phoebus and Cybele. Here again Michelangelo plays with the thought that night is an all-encompassing darkness which may be shattered by the merest glow:

> When Phoebus doth no more encircling fold
> Within his shining arms the earth's cold frame,
> The multitude do night the season name,
> Since now no longer they the sun behold.
> And she doth seem so weak, a candle may,
> A little candle, where it sheds its light,
> The life of night destroy; and eke so slight
> That steel and tinder do her rend and slay.
> And if perchance she's anything at all,
> Of earth and sun she doth the daughter seem,
> Since one creates her, and she dwells in one.

Howbeit who praises her, his wit is small;
Unmated she, and of such poor esteem,
With her a glow-worm wageth war alone. (G 101)
(Elizabeth Hall)

This sonnet, with its saltations from macrocosmic to microcosmic, was considered by Frey one of Michelangelo's most successful. The personification of the sun as having arms, the contrast of brightness and blackness, the repeated progressions from the vast to the minuscule, the instability of such huge forces as the sun and the night, all these make this sonnet a versatile exercise in the baroque. The unflattering conception of night as a widow is amusing in view of Michelangelo's misogynistic bent.

But night continues to fascinate Michelangelo in still another poem:

With a greater light and by a greater star
Heaven kindles its night-stars from afar;
Just as thou dost render still more beautiful
Everything less beautiful which approacheth thee. (G 129)

This madrigal with echoes of Petrarch, however, loses its interest after the momentary speculation about night.

5. *Geremia* (1508–12). Michelangelo frequently identified himself with one of the saintly figures of his art. At least nine *autoritratti* have been pointed out in his works. No one, however, has demonstrated fully how Michelangelo grew to resemble his *Geremia* in mood if not in physical aspect (see also pp. 308–309). Mariani sagaciously observes; "It seems that Michelangelo was particularly fond of this spirited and dolorous image as if intending to project through Jeremiah his own soul."[15] The artist may well have heard Savonarola's sermons on Jeremiah in 1493–94.

Michelangelo had moments of extreme pessimism about mankind. As Charles Morgan says of the painted prophet, "Jeremiah has heard too clearly. The revelation has overwhelmed him with the realisation of man's unworthiness, and he hunches forward in his throne, plunged in despair."[16] Of all the Biblical prophets who graced the Sistine Ceiling after the decision had been made to substitute prophets and sibyls for the disciples of Christ, none had a voice more closely resembling Michelangelo's. The jeremiads are especially frequent in the letters, complaints about the world in general, about patrons, critics, rivals, workers, materials, finances, health, and mankind itself. The phrase "il mondo è cieco" was more than once written by Michelangelo, as in the complaint:

The world is blind, and bad examples still
Prevail and swallow up every best usage. (G 295)

Mariani cites four of the lamentations of Jeremiah which have generally Buonarrotian sound. I should like contrariwise to present a number of passages from the *Rime* which have the authentic note of the jeremiad. Perhaps most typical is the very late (1560):

My eyes are saddened at many things
And my heart by as many things as the world encloses. (G 301)

As Michelangelo observed humanity for almost ninety years, he reached certain cynical or plaintive conclusions concerning man's ceaseless struggle against fate, other men, and even God Himself. Often these jeremiads took on the succinct character of maxims, and most will therefore be found again in Chapter XVIII. We find them in great numbers in the letters:

Man must not laugh when the whole world weeps. (CDLXXII)

It is said that he who does good to the good man makes him become better, but makes the evil man worse. (CXXVII)

It seems to me that things which have a bad beginning cannot come to a good end. (CCLVII)

Many maxims which echo the *Lamentations* are couched unobtrusively in the *Rime*. These may frequently be found at the end of a poem, like the *pointe* of an epigram, and introduced by *che*. Michelangelo's complaints about man's condition do not grow out of a conviction that man is weak and self-centered, but rather out of the fact that forces operate against man:

And I see well that in life the hours
Of felicity and grace are brief and short. (G 269)

Michelangelo had already remarked on seeing careers broken in his day, like the tragic fall of the Maréchal de Gié, that nature and providence seem most intent upon holding down men of greatest merit. Yet it was Dante's misfortune which stirred him most deeply:

For only worthy men lack salvation. (G 248)

Writing his second sonnet on Dante, he was again struck by the fact that the Trecento poet was singled out for persecution:

. . . Whence it is a clear sign
That the most perfect men abound in the most troubles. (G 250)

The two allegorical giants in his *Stanze* and their offspring the seven deadly sins also prey upon only the worthiest men,

And make intrigue and war only upon worthy men (G 68)

Still another unfortunate example of this truism was Michelangelo himself. After recording his loyalty and services to Julius II and his legitimate expectations of better treatment, the poet sets down a bitter conclusion, here more literally rendered than above:

Heaven scorns to grant any good thing
In this world when from a withered tree
One seeks to gather fruit. (G 6)

A few final examples of these jeremiads may be set down without comment or explanation:

He who seeks disaster, God will grant it to him. (G 267)

Less favor and less bounty last longer,
For to the ill-starred death is lazy and late. (G 208)

For he who believeth not doth remain better off. (G 85)

For evil can harm much more than good can help. (G 124)

One of the most cynical definitions of life seems to be contained in a jotting of Michelangelo's, "dolce stanza nell'inferno" ("sweet chamber in hell") (G App. 7).

Even Michelangelo's renunciation of the arts, which we discussed in the preceding chapter, seems an authentic jeremiad. Take for example one of the earlier quoted condemnations of the fine arts as vanities:

Whence the indulgent fantasy
Which made of art my idol and monarch,
Now I know well how laden it was with error. (G 285)

For Jeremiah himself cried out against the vanity of graven images:

Confusus est omnis conflator in sculptili, quia mendax est conflatio eorum, nec est spiritus in eis. Vana sunt opera et risa digna, in tempora visitationis suae peribunt.

(*Geremia*, li, 17–18)

6. *Gli Schiavi* (1513–19). The question of servitude had both a theoretical and a personal meaning to Michelangelo. Philosophical discussions of freedom and servitude were intensified by treatises discussing Machiavelli's political theories in Italy, France, and elsewhere. That Michelangelo was a participant in such discussions we know from the ample testimony provided in Donato Giannotti's *Dialogi*, where the artist, the humanist Luigi del Riccio, Antonio Petreo, and Francesco Priscianese ponder political bondage. On several occasions—especially during and after the siege of Florence—Michelangelo had reason to fear for his civil freedom. However, this concern is not apparent in his poetry.

His *canzoniere* remind us that he was a slave to his arts and the Maecenate system during his entire adult life. Back in 1911 Boyer d'Agen called Michelangelo "un esclave enchaîné sur les marbres."[17] Michelangelo's feeling of servitude began in his early days in the service of Julius II. After their most important rupture, Michelangelo had to seek the pontiff's pardon at Bologna, as he said, "con la correggia al collo." In a sonnet (already quoted in this chapter) prompted by his troubles with Julius II, Michelangelo indignantly writes:

I am and have long been thy ancient slave. (G 6)

Indeed, his early menial position prompted him to complain to Vasari that those who begin early to be asses of princes assume a lifetime burden.[18] Much later, after the death of Vittoria Colonna, Michelangelo wrote an unhappy *capitolo* complaining of his health and living habits:

Precious art, at which for a time
I was held in some esteem, reduces me to this:
Poor, old, and slave in others' power. (G 267)

Yet his greatest servitude was to passion itself. Sometimes he could not throw off the yoke of sinful passion, as his fearful complaint in "Viuo al pechato, a me morendo uiuo" bears witness:

Servile my free will, mortal my God—
Such have I become. Oh unhappy state! (G 32)

In this incomplete poem Michelangelo regrets that he has lost his free will (*sciolto uoler*). At other times he regretted the servitude of love, beyond morality:

That my loyal servitude become forgotten. (G 12)
That my great servitude be not dear to thee. (G 54)

. . . he who with such loyalty
Lives serving wretched and unhappy. (G 52)
By a look alone I became prisoner and prey. (G 176)

In view of Michelangelo's ever-present sense of bondage, it is interesting that his first great sculptural commission, the Tomb of Julius II, was to include figures of slaves, the *Schiavi* or *Stiavi*. Condivi assumed these to be the arts which died along with the pope or the arts held in subjection by the magnificence of Julius II. Such assumptions as Condivi's are weakened by the further presence of four gigantic prophets (Moses, Saint Paul, St. John, and perhaps David), spokesmen for subjected peoples. These figures of slaves, now in Florence and Paris, represented to Vasari those provinces which the pope had subjugated and incorporated into the Papal States.

If the slaves were symbols of man struggling with his destiny or with the material values of life represented by the *soverchio* of the marble still present, this struggle meant a great deal to Michelangelo. The great danger was in giving up the contest. A poem (1524) is devoted to the sad truth that man is too willing to accept bondage, too quick to accustom himself to his fetters, "so that he could scarcely ask for liberty."

When some poor slave, bound by a cruel chain,
Doth many days a hopeless prisoner lie,
Use doth so mate him with his misery,
He scarce desireth to be free again. (G 25)
(Elizabeth Hall)

This *sonetto caudato* proceeds to a discussion of the psychology of love, and particularly love after youth. The poem accompanies the beginning of a letter to Giovambattista Figiovanni, with the initial words only: "la fantasia del papa." If the letter is from the summer of 1524, Girardi believes that it refers to the pope's decision to place six rather than four tombs in the Sagrestia Nuova. Whatever the pope's "fantasia" was, this project or the 1525 plan to erect a colossus in the Piazza San Lorenzo, it would be imposed on the artist and impinge upon his freedom. When one reads the bitter burden of "Quand' il seruo il signior d'aspra catena," one thinks of the pessimistic and "realistic" comment of Valerio Mariani on Michelangelo's bondage to the Tomb of Julius II; ". . . he created by himself that 'slavery' of which, as the years passed, beyond the pain, he seemed to feel the necessity."[19] Could even this sententious poem be another example of Michelangelo's unremitting self-projection as an artist?

The tragic burden of the poem, that a man learns to live with servitude, is carried over into one of Michelangelo's "flaming-heart" madrigals, the one with the docile *incipit:* "Porgo umilmente all'aspro giogo il collo" ("I place my neck meekly under the harsh yoke"). The lover, like the political slave, not only becomes accustomed to his yoke but also fears lest it come to an end:

Nor do I draw back from martyrdom,
But rather fear lest I be without it. (G 138)

These lines were written for the so-called "donna altera, bella, e crudele," adjectives which befit a love tyrant.

Carving the slaves early in his career and after such episodes as the Canossa-like surrender at Bologna, Michelangelo could be discontented working for such popes as Julius and Clement. Even at that period the magnificent lines of "Quand' il seruo" could not have so full a meaning—in the civic, professional, or amatory sense—as they were to have for him later. Their deepest meaning to him became political, perhaps around the period when the full political meaning of the *Notte* crystallized in his mind.

7. *La Risurrezione di Lazaro* (1516). Michelangelo gave evidence of his friendship with Sebastiano del Piombo by sketching several studies of the *Risurrezione di Lazaro* for that beloved "compare," as the master called him (see Chapter XV). When he saw the finished painting, he commented

in a letter to Sebastiano: "Keep your peace and reflect that you will be more famous for resurrecting the dead than for painting pictures which appear alive." In the *Diálogos em Roma* Michelangelo mentions that this painting, then at Narbonne, was well worth seeing.

Whereas the raising of Lazarus is not mentioned in the poetry, there is a striking reminiscence in a love poem of Christ's miraculous powers. The last tercet of his sonnet, "I' mi son caro assai piu ch'i' non soglio" reads:

> I have powers against the waters and against fire,
> Under thy sign I give light to every blind man,
> And with my spit I heal every wound. (G 90)

Michelangelo, who so often projected himself in the holy figures of his art, indulges for a moment in an identification with Christ. The lines recall *Marcus* vii, where the Christ spat and healed a deaf-mute, and *Marcus* viii, where the Saviour spat on the eyes of a blind man and gave him sight:

Marcus vii, 33–35: Et apprehendens eum de turba seorsum misit digitos suos in auriculas eius et exspuens tetigit linguam eius et suspiciens in caelum ingemuit et ait illi: Ephphetha, quod est adaperire. Et statim apertae sunt aures eius, et solutum est vinculum linguae eius, et loquebatur recte.

Marcus viii, 22–23: . . . et adducunt ei caecum et rogabant eum ut illum tangeret. Et apprehensa manu caeci, educit eum extra vicum et exspuens in oculos eius, impositis manibus suis, interrogavit eum si quid videret.

Finally, Michelangelo was mindful of the similar healing in *Johannis* ix, 6–7, where Christ spat on the ground, made clay of the spittle, and anointed the eyes of a blind man with the clay.

It becomes clear that Michelangelo prepared himself for the drawing of poignant scenes of Christ's passion by rereading the four evangelist-biographers and that their retelling of Christ's miracles provided him with a vocabulary for the depiction of the miraculous powers of love.

8. *La Vittoria* (1519). No work of Michelangelo's other than the *Leda* is more frankly erotic than the statue of the *Victor* which dates from around 1519. It has been variously viewed as an allegory of the Platonic Eros (Brinckmann) or oversimplified into the overthrow of tyranny (Justi). It cannot predate 1518, for that was the date of the first quarrying of the Seravezza marble of which it was carved. Conjecture assigns Tommaso Cavalieri as the model.[20] Whether or not Tommaso posed for it, he was the *typos* illustrated. For the theme of the total victory of Tommaso over Michelangelo is a theme of the *Rime* and is revealed on several occasions in the *Lettere* (see Chapter X). Indeed, it is hard to decide whether the letters or

the poems express more fully the artist's complete and willing subjection to this noble Roman.

The pseudoclassical cape which the young Victor drapes over his back reminds us that the portrait which Michelangelo executed of Tommaso Cavalieri showed the young man "dressed in the ancient manner."

The poem which seems closest in spirit to this statue and which puns on the name of Tommaso Cavalieri is a sonnet from the early 1540s:

> Why should I seek to ease intense desire
> With still more tears and windy words of grief,
> When heaven, or late or soon, sends no relief
> To souls whom love has robed around with fire?
> Why need my aching heart to death aspire,
> When all must die? Nay, death beyond belief
> Unto these eyes would be more sweet and brief,
> Since in my sum of woes all joys expire?
> Therefore because I cannot shun the blow
> I rather seek, say who must rule my breast,
> Gliding between his gladness and his woe?
> If only chains and bands can make me blest,
> No marvel if alone and bare I go
> An armed Cavaliere's captive and slave confessed. (G 98)
> (J. A. Symonds)

9. *Venere, Marte e Cupido* and *Venere con Cupido che la bacia* (*ca.* 1522). The black chalk drawing of the heartless and militant Venus accompanied by Cupid and Mars was drawn for, or at least presented to, Gherardo Perini. These figures are three scourges of man, represented as implacable. Over the stern face of Venus rises a helmet, and her armed appearance has reminded scholars that Venus was so represented in Sparta. Her costume is also Petrarchan, since she sports her "guisa di guerra" mentioned by the Trecento poet. Michelangelo, caught in his passion for Gherardo, had reason to fear and resent the onslaughts of Venus and Cupid. Indeed, in the *Rime*, he addresses complaints and questions to Love as a neophyte troubled by love's power and intentions. In his edition of the drawings, Goldscheider finds the *disegno* alive with meaning. "The drawings of the 'Furia' and 'Venus and Mars' which Michelangelo presented to Gherardo Perini thus seem to me to contain a confession, the language of which is even clearer than his most dolorous love poems."[21]

Another drawing of Michelangelo's represented the same mistrust of love's militant power. This is his *Venere con Cupido che la bacia*, a *cartone* executed for Bartolommeo Bettini, according to Vasari, which he had Pontormo execute in color along with the *Noli me tangere*. (Against

Michelangelo's wishes, the painting was turned over to Duke Alessandro.) In this sketch of Michelangelo's, Venus is repelling the affectionate approaches of Cupid.

These two drawings have many echoes in Michelangelo's *Rime*. His unhappy experiences in love (one-sided infatuations for Gherardo and Febo, a cryptically expressed passion for Cecchino de' Bracci, [regretfully] sublimated affections for Tommaso Cavalieri and Vittoria Colonna) led him to appreciate advice to shun love and to understand complaints about the bondage of love. Petrarch had preached caution, warning lovers to avoid his own unhappy fate:

> Poiche mia speme è lunga a venir troppo
> E de la vita il trapassar sì corto,
> Vorreimi a miglior tempo esser accorto
> Per fuggir dietro piu che di galoppo
> E fuggo . . .
>
> Ond' io consiglio voi che siete in via
> Volgete i passi; e voi ch'Amore avampa,
> Non v'indugiate su l'estremo ardore . . .

The refrain was picked up by several contemporaries of Michelangelo, including Boiardo, in his sonnet "Alma felice, che di nostra sorte" and Aquilano in his *Rime*. Indeed, two *strambotti* of Aquilano begin "Fuggite, amore, o voi miseri amanti" and "Fuggite, amanti, el seguitar Amore." Still a third piece reads:

> Venite innamorati al mio lamento . . .
> E pigli esempio dal mio gran tormento.[22]

Finally, the analogy with Pamfilo Sasso's "Gridate tutti, amanti" (Girardi, *Studi*, p. 148) seems relatively remote. It is my belief that Michelangelo was most likely influenced by a stanza of Poliziano, his early friend and adviser on literary and artistic matters. Poliziano's plaint reads:

> Pigliate esempio, voi ch'Amor seguite,
> Dalla mia morte tanto acerba e dura
> Che 'l traditor con suo' crudel ferite
> M'ha fatto diventare un' ombra oscura;
> E ben che l'ossa mie sien seppellite,
> Non è ancor l'alma del martir secura.
> Fuggite Amor, per dio, miseri amanti;
> Che dopo morte ancor restate in pianti.

Apparently we are the first to point out this octave as the source of Michelangelo's pained outcry, wounded by the arrow of Love and similarly urging others to profit by his example:

Fugite, Amanti, amor, fugite 'l foco;
L'incendio è aspro, e la piaga è mortale,
Ch' oltr' a l'impeto primo piu non uale
Ne forza ne ragion ne mutar locho.
Fugite, or che l'esemplo non è pocho
D'un fiero braccio e d'un acuto strale;
Legiete in me, qual sara 'l vostro male,
Qual sara l'impio e dispietato giocho.
Fugite e non tardate al primo sguardo:
Ch' i' pensa' d'ogni tempo auere achordo;
Or sento, e uoi uedete, com' io ardo. (G 27)

(For translation see p. 325.)

If Frey was correct in assigning this poem to 1524 (it was written on the verso of an architectural design for the Medici Tombs), then it very possibly does depict the unhappy passion of Michelangelo for Gherardo Perini, initiated in 1522. The drawing of *Venere, Marte e Cupido* thus dates roughly from the same period as the incomplete sonnet. We know from a notation of the artist on a work-sheet that during at least one evening or night he found it impossible to accomplish anything in the absence of Perini. De Tolnay also notices the similarity of Michelangelo's poem with the first *pensiero* of Michelangelo's *Venere e Cupido.*

Michelangelo, who so seldom plagiarised from other writers, seems to have eased his conscience by hinting that other poets have issued the same warning: "Or che l'esemplo non e pocho." Whereas the immediate source of Michelangelo seems to be Poliziano, both Michelangelo and Petrarch, as Mr. Donald Remstein reminds me, urge that delay will be fatal ("non tardate al primo sguardo"/"Non u'indugiate su l'estremo ardore"). If Michelangelo would normally have been more likely to borrow from his idol Petrarch—several such borrowings are known—Poliziano was also an important influence upon him. It is our belief that Michelangelo plagiarised from Poliziano elsewhere, particularly in his tribute to a supposed Bolognese girl ("Quanto si gode, lieta e ben contesta") (G 4) which derives from Poliziano's second *Stanze* ("Candida è ella, e candida la vesta").

10. *I Saettatori* (1530). One of Michelangelo's sketches that has puzzled many generations of scholars is the red-chalk *Saettatori,* or *Arcieri.* The drawing represents six male and two female figures in the act of shooting arrows at a herm. Five *putti* are intermingled with the running archers, as is a faun, the only figure which actually holds a bow in his hand. None of the arrows fired from the invisible arms has succeeded in striking the herm, but a few of them are lightly embedded in the socle, in the mantel, or in a shield scarcely visible. Seeing a copy of this work, Goethe assumed naturally that it was a "mysterious, allegorical picture, probably depicting the power of fleshly

lusts."[23] The herm then could mean man in general or Michelangelo in particular. If the resemblance of the bust to the artist is not so striking here as in other cases (the *Nicodemo* in the Florentine Duomo, the St. Bartholomew pelt in the *Giudizio universale*), neither is it in his little sketch of himself accompanying the autograph of his *sonetto caudato* on the difficulties of painting the Sistine Ceiling. As Michelangelo replied when chided for not making the effigies of the Medici Dukes resemble their real-life counterparts, "A thousand years from now who could recognise that they were different?"[24] Moreover, the fact that there are more men than women assailing the herm strengthens the belief that it is his own moral and sexual problems he is recording here.

As in so many other cases, the artist's *Rime* offer not merely a clue but a solution to the meaning of the allegory. If the drawing was done in early 1530 and illustrates how defenseless he felt against the stings of love provoked by Tommaso Cavalieri, the theme of the arrows of love is found *passim* in his *canzioniere*. It is exploited in poems on at least three of his other passions.

The first appearance in the *Rime* of attacks by the love-archer occurs in poems penned as early as 1504–11. The archer is either Eros specifically or love in general, aiming at the lover *saette, frecce, ale, dardi, strali*, or *penne*.

The *strali* of love are a recurring theme in the poems. They are pointed darts with a "medicine" which passes straight to the heart (G 39).[25] Love knows that a gentle heart is always hit by his bow (G 142). The poet boasts that for a long time "no damaging arrows ever before attained my heart," but they have at last found their target (G 3). This poem dates from 1504–11. A curious *plainte* (G 137) suggests that the fatal wounds produced by love's arrows end in a merciful death, bringing to a halt the poet's sufferings: "m'è piu caro ogni strale."

A long complaint (G 22) addressed directly to love laments the abulia of the lover and asks for surcease from a new infatuation:

> The years of my career have reached their goal,
> Like an arrow arrived at its target,
> At which time the ardent fire should slake.
> For thy past wrongs to me I pardon thee,
> Since now my heart resists and shatters thy weapons,
> And love has no more power to put me to its tests.
> And if thy blows were some novel game
> For my eyes, as for my soft and tender heart,
> Could it still want what it used to want?
> At this age death alone is my defence
> Against fierce arms and piercing arrows,
> The cause of so many evils,

That on no condition do I pardon them,
Because of place or time or fortune. (G 22)

The herm would seem therefore to be the idealised, impersonal symbol of this victim of an aggressor who cares naught for time, place, or rank. Composed early though it was, this madrigal is part of a sequence expressing resignation, a farewell to love anticipating Metastasio's "Addio a Nice." The arrows of love shatter and imbed themselves in his shielded heart, just as in the drawing. According to a rejected variant of G 296, the evil ways of the world also imbed themselves in the bewildered soul like arrows.

A sonnet in this series, although written in the early 1520s, portrays an exhausted and worldly-wise victim whose hair is greying like Anacreon's in the service of love. Once again the verses are a complaint voiced directly to love:

I've been now these many years a thousand times
Vanquished and wearied if not wounded and killed
By thee, *mea culpa*, and now, with head of white,
Shall I be taken in again by thy foolish promises? . . .
Of thee I complain, Love, with thee I speak,
Unleashed from thy wiles, why dost thou then
Take up thy cruel bow to shoot in vain? (G 23)

The poet feels it as useless for love to waste further arrows on him as it would be for a saw or a moth to attack burnt wood, or for a runner to challenge a rival already retired from the race.

An incomplete sonnet from about this same time helps equally well to explicate the *Saettatori*. Here, the arrows which demand a shield are the shafts from a woman's or a man's eyes:

I made of my eyes my poison's gate,
When they gave free passage to thy fierce arrows:
Of my memory which will never fade
I made a nest and niche for tender glances.
Of my heart an anvil, of my breast a bellows
For the making of sighs with which thou kindlest me. (G 24)

In the early 1530s the passion for Tommaso Cavalieri had incubated. The cruel archer Eros made of life a living death—Eros, who can alleviate or prolong our torment, so that the lover living on death does not perish:

I weep, I burn, I consume myself; of this
My heart is nurtured. What a sweet lot!
Who is there who lives on his death alone
As I live on troubles and sorrow?
Alas, cruel archer, thou knowest well the hours
For tranquillizing our anxieties and brief miseries

With that strong hand of thine.
For he who lives on death doth never die. (G 74)

This particular suffering was long to endure, for Tommaso Cavalieri was destined to outlive the master.

The searing rays of Michelangelo's affair with Febo di Poggio also left their scar. The wings with which he hoped to scale the heights of Phoebus (G 99) were little more than the feathered arrows which wound, "fiero dardo, con che s'arma amore" (Frey XL).

The love of Vittoria Colonna (see Chapter X), precisely because it was so sublimated, brought pain with its great pleasure. In a madrigal addressed apparently to the marchioness, the poet states that although it is high time for him to withdraw from love's martyrdom, his blind and deaf soul cannot survive without affection. Nor without beauty, one supposes, for in another poem he claims that he was born neither blind nor deaf to beauty. Even if his cruel mistress should shatter or cut the cord, it is better to continue enduring love's torments; for so long as one senses pain he is keenly alive:

And if it should come about that thou
The bow and the string shouldst cut away
And shatter into thousands of pieces,
It begs thee not to miss even one of its inflictions,
For he never dies who is never cured. (G 120)

The lesson, that even if arrows are not to meet their target the archers' attack will continue, is clear also in the drawing.

During the mid-1540s Michelangelo is still fascinated with this theme. He observes that whereas stone and paper are improved by their contact with artists, so is he better after being made the herm for Tommaso Cavalieri:

So have I become, since I became the target
Marked out by thy sweet face; I grieve not thereat. (G 90)

The idea that archers when love partners cast their destructive shafts from their eyes rather than from weapons would explain the absence of the bows in the hands of the saettatori. From this same period (*ca.* 1546) dates the madrigal purportedly to a "donna bella e crudele" in which the aging poet calls for an armistice from this love which always pierces his defenses:

Not yet recovered, Love, from thy golden shafts,
Not even from the smallest of my wounds of old,
My prophetic mind thou dost transport
From evil endured in the past to even worse present.
If thou art less harsh with the aged,

And makest not war upon the dead, then let me be.
If thou aimest the shafts of thy bow
At me limping and nude,
Under the banner of those eyes
Which kill even more than thy fierce darts,
What solace is left to me?
Neither helmet nor shield,
But only what honor I can save in defeat
And the blame thou wilt gain if thou dost me burn.
A weak old man, for me it is late
And flight is slow to where protection may be found.
For he who wins by fleeing, let him not stay on the field. (G 175)

Once more Michelangelo summarises his stanza with a moral aphorism, one even more ironic than the familiar saying, "Soldato che fugge è buono per un' altra volta." Again he pictures the many loves of his past assailing him; he is without helmet or shield, as is the herm. Like the history of the *Expulsion* on the Sistine Vault, the drawing of the *Saettatori* brings together past and the "worse" present.

The final major piece to exploit the archer theme dates from around 1547; it is probably a tribute to Vittoria Colonna, who died on 25 February of that year. The poet addresses Love a last time, but his is no longer a beseeching voice. He states merely that if Love wishes the old tribute of heat and tears, Love must bring back the object of his recent affection. As it is, Love can scarce take pleasure in the soul-state of an old man:

My soul almost arrived at the other shore
Shields itself from thy shafts with others more merciful:
Fire makes a poor test on a log already burned. (G 272)

The theme, we see, is identical with that of "I' fu', gia son molt'anni, mille uolte" (G 23). However, near 1547 the message rings truer, for by this time Michelangelo had apparently grudgingly renounced love; he claimed that thoughts of love were "laden with error" (G 285).

The nonobjective elements in the *Saettatori* drawing—the lack of bows, the paucity of arrows, the lack of wounds—all draw one's attention and imbue the sketch with a curious, puzzling charm. We should not dwell at length over the "mysterious" character of the work, however: when Michelangelo paints the crucifixion of Haman, there are no nails, no wounds. This arresting quality of the drawing is merely an oxymoron transferred to art. One thinks of Michelangelo's complaint about love:

If thou enchainest one without chains,
And dost enfold me without hands or arms . . . (G 7)

In the poem "Mestier non era al'alma tuo beltate" Michelangelo again explains that damage may be inflicted without physical lesion:

It was not necessary for thy dear beauty
To bind me vanquished with any cord;
For, if I remember well,
By but a single look was I made prisoner and prey. (G 176)

As early as his "Come puo esser ch'io non sia piu mio?" Michelangelo marvels that love can pierce his heart without touching his skin:

Oh God, oh God, oh God!
How can he reach my very heart
Who seems to touch me not? (G 8)

Perhaps the best verse-commentary on this aspect of the *Saettatori* is Michelangelo's madrigal explaining that death chases away the archer, Love, who used to triumph over him both armed and unarmed ("nude"):

Now Death, Love, doth from the very place
Where thou starkly didst ever triumph,
Even without bow and piercing shafts,
Expel and shatter thee . . . (G 167)

The love-archers in the drawing who cast their arrows at Michelangelo are as unarmed yet as effective as love itself, "con esse mi gugniesti."

There is an autonomous line attached to a quatrain on the verso of a letter from Michelangelo to Andrea Quaratesi, dating from 1532, which could also serve as a perfect caption for this curious invention:

But what shields have I from all of them? (G 65)

Frey and others place a question mark at the end of this line, but Girardi does not. As a question, the exclamation expresses the helplessness of the poet-herm faced with his new loves of this period.

The sequence of poems recorded in these pages allows us to understand several of the most curious elements of the *Saettatori:* the impersonality of the herm, representing at the same time a Michelangelo of various ages and an Everyman of varying "loco, tempo, e fortuna"; the presence of both men and women archers; the thickly outlined and transparent shield which is of little or no protection against arrows; and the intent look on the countenances of the archers. The little winged *putto*-Cupid who lies asleep through this attack shows that love as a symbol is less to be feared than the flesh-and-blood individuals who have come into Michelangelo's life to replace the mere Petrarchan symbols, the objects of his first love lyrics. He is also a reminder that the frightful force of real love is not that of a *putto.*

Scholars have sought the meaning of this sketch in Lucian, Cristoforo Landino, Mario Equicola, and Pico della Mirandola. One need not go so far afield from Michelangelo's habitual and restricted literary diet, especially if the major theme is assumed to be that the defenseless lover cannot see the weapon which is destined to wound him. This thought Michelangelo read in Petrarch. It occurs as early as the third sonnet of this poet whom he idolised and often plagiarised—indeed, whose verses he copied literally, just as he copied lines by Masaccio or Giotto as a fledgling painter:

> Trovommi Amor del tutto disarmato
> et aperta la via per gli occhi al core,
> che di lagrime son fatti uscio e varco.
> Pero al mio parer, non li fu onore
> fer me di saetta in quello stato,
> e voi armata non mostrar pur l'arco.

Precisely as in Petrarch, the shot arrows in Michelangelo's drawing are indistinctly seen, whereas the bows of the assailants are invisible. We have hoped to show, however, that the theme of the attack of the love-archer was a most common one in the *Rime*, that it was a common literary motif by the year the artist executed the *Saettatori*; that most of the "mysterious" elements in the allegory originate in Michelangelo's *canzoniere*, that one need not seek alien sources.

11. *Tizio* (1532). In speaking of Michelangelo's affection for Tommaso de' Cavalieri, Vasari enumerates the drawings and *teste divine* offered to the young nobleman. "The latter was still young and loved art. Therefore, in order to instruct him in drawing, Michelangelo presented him with a number of most magnificent pages, among them divinely beautiful heads done in black and red chalk. He gave him also a *Ganymede*, whom the bird carries away to Zeus, a *Tityus*, whose heart the vulture is tearing out, and furthermore, a *Fall of Phaeton* with his sun chariot into the Po, and a *Baccanalia dei putti* . . ."[26]

The sad plight of Tityus, felled by a monstrous vulture, was told in antiquity by Vergil, Ovid, and Hyginus. For having tried to seduce Latona, mother of Apollo, Apollo condemned him to eternal torture in Tartarus. As has been noted, Lucretius, in the third canto of the *De rerum natura*, interprets the figure of Tityus as a man whose heart is gnawed by pangs of love and "a shameful amorous desire." Goldscheider comments that "this drawing represents not only the tortures of the lover, but sin and its penalty, the punishment for a wanton desire that leads to the greater sin of defection from God."[27]

Thus Tityus becomes the symbol of eternal pains, condemned by sense, or "la voglia sfrenata," as Michelangelo put it. He represents the anguish or *Schuldcomplex* of the artist, enamored of Febo di Poggio, of Gherardo Perini, and captured by ambivalent sentiments for Cavalieri. This guilt feeling is expressed in the *Rime* from the early 1520s.

Unbridled desire is sense, not love,
Which deadens the soul . . . (G 105)

Nor do I have the power itself which needed is
To change my life, love, habits, and destiny. (G 293)

I live in sin, I live a living death,
My life is no longer mine, but sin's! (G 32)

The drawing of *Ganymede* which accompanied the *Tizio* has been lost, although a copy by Giulio Clovio exists in Windsor Castle. Goldscheider notes that "the counterpart to the mental anguish of Tizio is Ganymede's flight to Heaven" and recalls the lines on spiritual union from the sonnet to Cavalieri: "S'un spirto, s'un uoler duo cor gouerna,/S'un'anima in duo corpi è facta ecterna,/Ambo leuando al cielo e con pari ale . . ." (G 59). (For translation, see p. 186.)

12. *Fetonte* (1533). Michelangelo's deep concern in his late poetry over obtaining grace parallels his early confessional poems about falling from grace. The experience with Febo di Poggio shook him considerably, and when it was over he referred to it in at least three different pieces of poetry. Indeed, the fall from grace through too close a contact with Phoebus describes both the fall of Phaeton, unable to govern the chariot of Phoebus Apollo, and the fall of Icarus, who sought to rise to new heights and attain perilous proximity to Phoebus, only to be struck down by a thunderbolt. Michelangelo, unable to control the Platonic steeds representing the passions and drawing too close to Febo, fell from grace like Phaeton and Icarus —and even Daedalus.

Michelangelo's three black-chalk drawings of Phaeton's fall, complete with hurtling horses and chariot, follow the text of Ovid's *Metamorphoses* (I, 750; II, 400), as has been stated. In 1533 Michelangelo executed these drawings, now in the British Museum, the Academy of Vienna, and Windsor Castle. They were sent to Tommaso Cavalieri, who acknowledged them in a letter of 5 September, 1533. The letter, which is grateful and full of praise, gives no sign of his having understood the intimate message contained in their allegory.

It is curious that a theme associated with Febo di Poggio should dominate drawings being sent to Cavalieri. However, this very period (1533–34) was the season of Michelangelo's flame for Febo di Poggio. He did not consider his love for Tommaso a fall from grace—and the love apparently never descended to a homosexual relationship—but no doubt he felt a continuous desire to convert it into a passion, a desire which he had to restrain and even hide from the younger man.

The Lucifer-like fall to the pit occasioned by his love for Febo is amply admitted in his verses of 1534–41:

When first the heavens forged thy living ray,
Alone to eyes not mine unveiled devotion,
Racing o'er their course with timeless motion,
Yielded us thy light, thee the journey's way.
Blithe bird, excelling us by fortune's sway,
Of Phoebus thine the prize of lucent notion,
Sweeter yet the boon of winged promotion
To the hill [*poggio*], whence I topple and decay! (G 100)
(Donald Remstein)

With Febo even the fall and death were sweet:

Easily could I soar, with such a happy fate,
When Phoebus brightened up the heights [*poggio*],
Up from the earth I rose with his wings,
And death itself I could have found sweet.
Now he has disappeared from me . . .
His feathers were wings to me and the hill the stair.
Phoebus was a lantern to my feet; nor would death then
Have seemed to me less than a marvelous salvation. . . . (G 99)

The theme of Daedalus's misadventures with Phoebus makes a dim, uncertain, but autobiographical appearance among Michelangelo's fragments:

Not otherwise was Daedalus unhinged,
Not otherwise doth the sun dispel shadow. (G App. 24)

Buscaroli's interpretation of these three gift drawings would make them parallels to Michelangelo's apologetic letter to Tommaso Cavalieri in which he excuses himself for having presumed too much and taken liberties with the younger man. To Buscaroli, they are emblematic of "the punishment for pride, for the *hybris* of a man who has dared or dares to substitute his own law for that decreed by nature or divinity."[28]

We might conclude, however, that if Michelangelo drew the three falls of Phaeton as symbols of his recent love for Febo di Poggio, from which he plunged humiliated like Phaeton, his offering of these drawings to his new friend Tommaso Cavalieri constituted a katharsis, a purgation of an old passion to accommodate a new love. The distinction between his respective feelings for the two younger men is set forth in the verse: "Voglia sfrenata amore non è."

13. *Il Giudizio Universale* (1536–41). In our chapter on the baroque qualities of Michelangelo's poetry we noted how constantly death preyed on the artist's mind. As a mystic he even anticipated death as a release from this earthly prison. Yet he was equally aware that death did not necessarily mean a return to him "who opened his arms on the Cross to embrace us" (G 285). Death was a time for accounting: "ou' a render si uarca/Conto e

ragion d'ogni opra trista e pia" (*ibid.*). On this terrible day of reckoning the number of the damned will be great: in Michelangelo's fresco of the *Giudizio universale* the Book of the Damned is thicker by far than the Book of the Saved. The number of poems begging for understanding, grace, forgiveness—in a word, salvation—is great. In the same spirit as Thomas of Celano, who wrote the *Dies Irae* to obtain intercession from Christ, Michelangelo wrote such imprecations and also painted his *Giudizio*. Some of the *Rime* petition for forgiveness and charity, plead for God to tear away the veil of doubt which separates them, and express outright dread that grace might not be forthcoming on the Day of Wrath: "Nor have I, *mea culpa*, entire and full grace" (G 289).

If no entire poem is dedicated to this momentous day when souls regain their bodies, there are echoes of the event in the poetry. In one early lament "Oilme, Oilme, ch'i' son tradito" the poet fears that his misuse of free will will win him only eternal damnation:

> I see, O Lord, the eternal damnation for my sins,
> Committed knowingly with free will,
> And know not what hope there is for me. (G 51)

There are other poems in which he fears that after his death he will suffer the "double death" of body and soul (see Chapter III).

As he reflected on the death of the adolescent Cecchino Bracci, who had admittedly had many lovers, Michelangelo found himself wondering about Cecchino's surviving the day of rendering "conto e ragione." He seems to have been most impressed by the possibility that when souls reassume their bodies, Cecchino would regain his beauty. He claims that divine pity has removed Cecchino from the earth before the day of final reckoning, since if his body were still in the tomb on that day, he would be the only one worthy of going to heaven:

> Divine Braccio has assumed again his beautiful veil.
> He is no longer here, for ere the Day of Judgement
> Pity has taken him from earth; were he even yet buried,
> He still would be alone worthy of paradise. (G 227)

Michelangelo uses the word "velo" here as elsewhere in the sense of the nude figure of the youth.

Another epitaph to Cecchino mentions the Day of Wrath. Again Michelangelo consoles himself that Cecchino's beauty is not lost forever, as he will reassume it when all are recalled from their graves. In a footnote to G 186 the boy Cecchino, like Dante clarifying a sonnet of the *Vita Nuova*, explicates: "If heaven took every beauty from all other men in the world just to make me beautiful—as it did—and if by divine law I am to return on the Day of Judgement the same as I was when alive, it follows that I cannot restore the beauty given me to those from whom it was taken, but that I must remain more beautiful than they throughout eternity, and they ugly." Strange, un-Christian words to put in the mouth of a pampered young man who might well be thinking more ominous thoughts about the Day of Wrath!

Writing to another loved man or woman, Michelangelo pays his beloved the compliment of anticipating that after the Day of Judgement, after the reclothing of his love's soul, either heaven or hell will benefit by the beauty which it will gain:

> If the soul at length returns
> Into its sweet and desired flesh,
> And heaven damns or saves, as is believed,
> There would be less pain in hell
> If thy beauty did adorn it,
> And one could see and contemplate thee there.
> If the soul rises and returns to heaven,
> As I wish to rise with it,
> And with such care and so warm affection,
> It will be less to enjoy God,
> For every other pleasure pleases less
> Than doth thy divine and gentle aspect down here. (G 140)

The insistence here again is on the reclothing rather than on the terrible moment of judgement.

Whenever the artist reflects on his own hopes for that terrible day, his emphasis is strictly on the judgement. After all, his own poor body and "faccia di spavento" will make a poor showing, the grotesque body he attributes to himself in the sonnet on the painting of the Sistine Vault. As Michelangelo grew more mystically devout with the years, the final judging loomed up as a terrible ordeal for his soul. The intolerable prolongation of man's period of trial made him come to believe that it was better to die young in life; thus one might have greater expectations of innocence and salvation: "Tristo m'è ch'a trouar gratia e mercede/Negli ultimi anni a molte colpe è raro" (G 294). Out of the same feeling he could write those aforementioned words to his nephew Lionardo on the death of a child: "One must have patience and conclude that it is better than if death came in old age." Old age is a torment if grace is uncertain: "Non gioua senza gratia, l'esser uechio" (G 263). (See also below, p. 306.)

Grace, the theological issue debated by Catholics and Protestants and groups within these two churches, was a simple product of charity to Michelangelo's thinking. His preoccupation with grace is revealed by the many mentions of this boon in his poetry. His pleas for it, as we have stated, were numerous, as if he believed the verse he composed for Tommaso Cavalieri; "as grace abounds to him who requests well" (G 72). One sonnet, albeit incomplete, is devoted to the variety of ways in which God rains grace upon the Christian:

If always alone and unified is he
Who moves everything high and wide,
Never will he reveal himself to us for an instant
Except through the greater or lesser amount of his grace that rains.
  One way to me and other ways elsewhere:
More or less clear and shining or dark
According to our merits, when exposed
To God's intellect and to the divine tests. (G 273)

Despite his claim that God reveals his disposition toward the artist, Michelangelo never felt assured that grace would "rain" on him. For example, he expresses his concern with much this same vocabulary, in a sonnet to God:

nor do I know where
That door opens to grace, which saturates
The heart . . . (G 87)

Christ's sufferings were necessary that his blood bring men salvation:

They promise to the unhappy soul
Grace for real repentance and hope for salvation. (G 290)

The ever-present thought of imminent death was of course a theme of the *prediche* of Savonarola, so familiar to Michelangelo. The Day of Judgement even intruded upon his sense of irony. Vasari records Michelangelo's harsh comment on an artist who plagiarised to excess: "On Judgement Day, when all bodies take their members back, what will become of this storey, for nothing will remain of it?"[29] Certain it is that his thoughts of death were immediately involved with thoughts of salvation. When his brothers Gismondo and Giovan Simone died, Michelangelo's instant reaction was to ask whether they had died *confessi* and *communicati*, to ensure further their salvation. When he himself was at the point of death, the final judgement was paramount in his thoughts. Bernini tells that the moribund Michelangelo was asked if he had any last regrets. He replied that he had two; that he was dying just as he had begun to learn the alphabet of his craft, that he had not done enough for the salvation of his soul.[30] This last-minute concern showed a weakened allegiance to Juan de Valdés's doctrine that faith and not works was the surest guarantee of winning grace and salvation.

His poetry itself is indicative of this final concern. The last extant poems which he wrote, and which may be dated as post 1560 since they were written on the verso of a letter to Cardinal Rodolfo Pio de' Carpi of that year, express the artist's hope for "aíta" and "perdono" (G 301) and "amore" (G 302) from Christ. Indeed, the controversial word *electi* appears in a variant reading of this latter poem, only to be rejected, perhaps because it might seem not to refer to the selection on the Day of Judgement but to the Calvinist and Lutheran views on predestination. Michelangelo, who made a point of being extremely cautious in his politics, was aware of the sufferings borne by his beloved Vittoria Colonna for her slight departures from orthodoxy and aware of the condemnation of Juan de Valdés's book.

14. *Christus Iudex* (1536–41). Michelangelo's concern for his own salvation on the crucial Day of Judgement led him to utter direct appeals to Christ, appeals which closed the magnificent range of his *canzoniere*. Indeed, these pleas begin in his earlier writing and constitute one of the great recurring themes of his poetry. The Christ of that Day will not be the charitable and clement Redeemer, but rather an angry judge. What relation exists between the *Rime* and this *terribile* Saviour, so removed from the calm and rational *Cristo risorto* and the pathetic Redeemer of the Florentine *Deposizione?*

The *Rime* contribute to an explanation of the wrath of Christ, an anger about which there has been much speculation in print. It has been analysed by McGreeby as the Saviour's fury at the destruction of Italian liberty by Charles V and other invaders.[31] This and other such interpretations based on contemporary politics and society are surely gratuitous. The Day of Judgement is a Day of Wrath; heavenly anger is directed toward each and every sinner who offended God. The poetry would lead us to suppose that in pondering Christ's impatient and bitter emotion the artist was thinking principally of himself as its target. Yet there were other moments when he knew that Christ's greatest wrath was directed toward those who were making a mockery of the Church of Rome.

Let us examine the poetry for evidences of these two viewpoints.

Certainly as Michelangelo was executing the *Christus Iudex* the words of the *Dies Irae*, that great mediaeval imprecation of Thomas of Celano, rang in his ears:

> Recordare, Jesu pie,
> Quod sum causa tuae viae:
> Ne me perdas ille die.

Michelangelo communicated his own *terribilità* into that central figure of Christ. Nothing would remain concealed from that exacting judge, as the mediaeval hymnographer sang:

> Judex ergo cum censebit
> Quicquid latet apparebit.

Michelangelo's mind cannot help running over the sins in his life, which led him to admit that he was "living a living death" and prey to sin (G 32). Contemplating that upright arm, eternalised in his great fresco—an arm perhaps raised to bless, but staying to condemn—he cries out (in 1555):

> With justice mark not Thou, O Light Divine,
> My fault, nor hear it with Thy chastened ear:
> Neither put forth that way Thy arm severe. (G 290)
> (William Wordsworth)

The arms of Christ are elsewhere on his mind, as we noted in Chapter III. In the very years he was painting this Christ (1538–41) he ejaculated a prayer against the occasion of his death:

> Lord, in the last hours
> Stretch toward me thy merciful arms,
> Withdraw me from myself and make me one who may please thee. (G 161)

Indeed Michelangelo, like Dante, hopes to be accepted in the mystical embrace of Christ and to experience on Judgement Day the greatest love of his life:

> Oh happy that day, if this is to come to pass!
> Let time and its hours at some point give pause
> And the day, with its sun in its ancient circuit,
> That I may possess through no merit of mine
> My desired sweet lord
> In my unworthy but ready arms.

This particularly effusive sonnet (early 1530s) draws a curious analogy between the divine love he can feel for a fellow man on that day of decision when the winds and sun will stop and he will grow to require that love from Christ. A variant of the last tercet describes even better the weary sinner:

> That I may forever embrace, though not for merit of mine,
> The breast and throat of my lord
> With my unworthy and weary if ready arms. (G 72)

However, Michelangelo will eventually recognise as a sin even this attempt to sublimate a great earthly love into one divine. It will be numbered among his transgressions, perhaps to be pardoned, as the Franciscan monk had begged:

> Juste Judex ultionis
> Donum fac remissionis
> Ante diem rationis . . .
> Supplicanti parce, Deus.

Michelangelo prays that not *ratio* but *caritas* will win him salvation. *Ratio* cannot soften the judgement of an ireful Christ. It will require many appeals to achieve this charity, and so his poetry is filled with pleas for intercession in order that he may eschew the terrible double death of body and soul:

> Heavy with years, and vexed sore by sin,
> Rooted in uses of iniquity,
> The first and second death at hand I see,
> Yet cherish evil thoughts my heart within.
> Not mine, Oh Lord, the power that I need,
> To change my life, my passions, and my fate,
> Unless Thy light my path illuminate,
> And Thou, not I, my steps control and lead.
> 'Tis not enough the deep desire to give
> For that pure world where, grown divine, the soul
> No more from nothingness shall be created.
> Ere thou of mortal garb do her deprive,
> Make short the steep path to that heavenly goal,
> That brighter hope may on my footsteps wait. (G 293)
> (Elizabeth Hall)

The attempt to dissipate the wrath of Christ and win his intervention continues to the ultimate poems, as suggested above. The second-last poem extant is the jeremiad in which he worries about the fate of mankind in addition to his own:

> By many things are my eyes saddened,
> Saddened my heart by all things in this world;
> Were it not for thy courteous and dear gift
> Of thine own self, what should I do with life?
> Despite my evil habits and the bad examples
> In this shadowy thicket where I am found,
> Succour I hope to find as well as pardon;
> For to whomever thy showest thyself this much thou must promise. (G 301)

The last poem, written on the letter of 1560, reads:

> In no other way now canst thou rid me of love,
> Of the perilous and vain emotions
> Than through adverse fortune or strange happenings,
> Whereby thou dost release thy friends from this world.
> Dear my lord, thou alone who dost clad and strip away
> And with thy blood alone dost heal and purge
> Man's actions and his immense sins . . . (G 302)

These last two stanzas were composed in the "trembling hand" of the final autographs, just before the time when Michelangelo adopted his policy of not writing letters but merely dictating and signing them. The hand shakes with emotion and fatigue, for hand and arm are weary ("coll' indegne mie pronte e stanche braccia") (G 72 var.). The praying to, the beseeching of the Christus Iudex have gone on for years (see Chapter XI). The sonnet breaks off without the usual sestet. His last poetic *non finito* has served its purpose. The plea is transverbalised. Christ's anger has fled. Christ understands. The veil of ice will be broken. The Christ of *ratio* of 1514–18 and the Christ of *iracundia* of 1536–41 will soften into the Christ of *caritas* (1550–53).

This, then, is the deep personal meaning of the *Christus Iudex* to Michelangelo. There is, however, a secondary and localised provocation inciting Christ to anger. Indeed, it aroused anger in Michelangelo himself, an anger which may have welled up in him again two decades later as he executed the vast fresco on the weighing of mankind. One of the most bitter sonnets from Michelangelo's pen is a verbal prefiguration of the Christ of *iracundia* which he eventually painted in the Sistine Chapel. This piece is one of the few "signed" poetic creations of Michelangelo.

> Here swords are wrought from cups of sacrament,
> The holy blood of Christ is sold for gold,
> For lance and buckler, cross and thorns are sold:
> The patience of the very Christ is spent!
> Let Him within our borders come no more,
> Since Rome, who in her Saviour's blood doth trade,
> Will sell His flesh for any price that's paid:
> And hath to every virtue closed the door.
> If by my work, the offspring of my mind,
> I too with treasure would my coffers fill,
> I see in Peter's chair Medusa throned.
> Though poverty in Heaven do favor find,
> What recompense shall be of earthly ill,
> If earth's defeat undo the life beyond? (G 10)
> Your Michelangelo in Turkey
> (Elizabeth Hall)

There are two distinct questions raised by these lines: the sense of the sonnet itself and the sense of the appended signature line.

The meaning of the sonnet can, of course, depend on its date. Like other poems ("Caro m'è 'l sonno" [G 247], etc.), the lines may be rich in contemporary reference.

Let us suppose for a moment that the lines are absolute and timeless. Then they may be considered one of the criticisms, voiced in every century, of a Rome which is the depository of the sacred patrimony of Christianity and fails to live up to its trust. In this sense, the lines are a reminiscence of Dante's condemnation of Rome as "là dove Cristo tutto dì si merca" ("there where Christ is bartered all day long") (*Par.* xvii, 51). Similarly, the artist recalls Petrarch's condemnation of Rome and Avignon-Babylon ("Fontana di dolore") which also warns of Christ's eventual anger: ('Se Cristo teco al fin non s'adira").

When Michelangelo il Giovane edited this sonnet in his defective edition, he annotated the autograph copy "sonetto da Roma." He noted further on his own manuscript edition, "I believe for the siege of Rome" and hazarded the guess that the poem was addressed to Giovanni da Pistoia (see Chapter XIV). In his more careful edition, Guasti doubted that the sonnet referred to the besieged Rome of 1527, since Michelangelo was not in the city ("qua") at that time. He felt rather that it was aimed at the bellicose Julius II and assigned it to April, 1512, after the Battle of Ravenna; at this date Michelangelo could have composed the poem in Rome. This hypothesis has been accepted by Girardi and others. Certainly Michelangelo was disturbed by the military ambitions of Julius II. He wrote from Bologna on 2 May, 1507: "Know now that here everything is wallowing in armor, and the region is up in arms, with great uproar and danger, especially to the Church's partisans."

If Rizzi, Dobelli, Cicognani, and Girardi interpret the sense of verse 4 as "Christ's patience continues to prevail," the meaning "loses patience" is consonant with both context and sources. Religion is giving place to war and the idea of a Christ of Wrath is shaping in Michelangelo's mind. As the Italian paraphrasts and commentators have agreed, the last two tercets mean: "If ever I desired not to earn anything, this is the right moment, for here I have no more work, and the Pope can turn me to stone as did Medusa with Atlas, but if poverty pleases up there in heaven, how can we then attain rewards for our pains, if the sign of war takes away our hope of the other life?" The paraphrase is Girardi's.

Michelangelo's principal complaint here is that war is harmful to the fine arts. He will develop this theme in the *Diálogos em Roma*, stating that kings should close the gates of war and devote their monies to the arts.[32] Indeed, as early as October, 1509, Michelangelo wrote in a letter concerning times of war: "Sons molto contrari all'arte nostra." Actually, the summer of 1512 was to make this point more tragically with the destruction of Prato, which he personally deplored, and with other architectural ravages in Tuscany.

No one has pointed out, however, what probably provided the initial provocation for this emotional sonnet also decrying the dangers which befall works of art. Granted that the sonnet dates from *circa* April, 1512, the year after Giulio II formed the Lega Santa, what provided Michelangelo with the precise image of works of art (chalices and crucifixes) being reduced to swords, lances, and helmets? It was precisely some bad news he had just heard. Shortly before, on 30 December, 1511, the angry citizenry of Bologna destroyed his bronze statue *Giulio II*, unveiled not quite four years earlier, having decided to melt it into a cannon. Indeed, this cannon was nicknamed "La Giulia." Legend has it that Michelangelo was to see it on a trip of inspection at Ferrara in 1529.

The statue was his first successful bronze (the bronze *David* was to come a year later) and had cost him not only physical but spiritual travail. Thus, this conversion of a holy figure (giving a benediction and holding the Keys to the Kingdom) into a cannon is at the basis of the sonnet. (Had Michelangelo waited until later in the year, during the turbulence of the Medici Restoration in Florence, he would have had another *praetextum* to embitter him further in the destruction of his wall painting *La Battaglia di Cascina.*) The anger of the poet is not directed against the Bolognesi, but at the pope who had said to Michelangelo with the cynicism of a modern dictator that the left hand of the statue ought not to hold a book but a sword (see p. 91). A further evidence for our theory is provided by the first tercet, which might well be translated, or rather understood as: "But if I had ever wished to lose a treasure of mine, this is it, for a work of mine has disappeared [from earth], and the pope [whose actions have caused my effigy to be destroyed] has frozen me like the Medusa in Mauritania." This rephrasing allows for absolutely literal meanings to be given to *tesauro* and *opera*. The last tercet contains the meaning elucidated above.

The seventh and eighth verses are more general in nature, not limited to warlike conduct, but to the general misconduct in the papal capital which disillusioned many a Renaissance poet, Catholic or Reformist, and inspired neo-Latin (Michel de l'Hospital, Pontanus) and vernacular (Du Bellay, Antonio Camelli, Francesco Berni) censure in verse.

The signature line is not so mysterious as some editors and commentators have assumed. Nor does it hark back to Michelangelo's apparently projected transfer to Constantinople in the late spring of 1506 at the invitation of Sultan Bayazid. In Florence Michelangelo had attended the services of Savonarola in Santa Maria del Fiore and heard such condemnations of Rome as the following: "It is the clergy that keeps alive every sort of wickedness. All this starts in Rome itself, where they mock Christ and His saints; they are worse than Turks, worse than Moors. Not only do they refuse to suffer for God, but they actually sell the sacraments. Today brokers sell benefices and these go to whoever pays the highest!"[33] The signature line may be further explained by a sonnet against churchmen ("Contra li preti") by Berni, another associate of Michelangelo. Like Michelangelo, Francesco knows that divine patience is running out with the water of the clepsydra.

> The time will come when your entire heritage,
> Which you are today wasting in such ugly ways,
> Will be taken from you; for God intends to strike you
> With such a thunderous blow as never heard or seen.

Michelangelo surely knew this sonnet by the satirical poet with whom he exchanged *capitoli.* Even before they appeared in collected form, Michelangelo predicted that the "carmi divini" of Berni would make that poet's name eternal. Indeed, Michelangelo's curious mention of Turchia after the ominous "finis" can be explained by this same sonnet of Berni. For Berni's sonnet views Rome as a city which would be overrun by Turks if the sorely taxed patience of Christ ran out: "più da Turchi e concilii vi difende."

It is generally believed that Michelangelo's sonnet was written to the same Giovanni da Pistoia to whom Michelangelo dedicated the seriocomic *sonetto caudato* on the painting of the Sistine Vault. If Michelangelo il Giovane believed this Giovanni to be Antonio Camelli (1430–1502) who used the pseudonym of Giovanni da Pistoia, his was an understandable error. For Camelli composed five satirical sonnets on "La vita di Roma," purporting to be a dialogue between the poet and the ill-starred Prince Djem, "brother of the Grand Turk." At one point Camelli seems to have inspired Michelangelo directly, for after Djem enumerates the items of Christian privilege which are sold in Rome (sacred offices, justice, benefices, indulgences), he expresses fear at the exhaustion of Christ's patience:

> Voi fate ognor paura a vostro Cristo,
> ch'ogni dì perdera la signoria.

Apparently composed in 1512, Michelangelo's sonnet could not have been written to Camelli, except as a posthumous tribute. Whether or not Michelangelo addressed a poem to him, he certainly could have had the satirical "Vita di Roma" in mind. However, it is more likely that the recipient of this sonnet was Giovanni di Benedetto da Pistoia, as Frey proposed. Frey reproduces five light sonnets written to the artist by this chancellor of the Florentine Academy. These sonnets set the stage for comic signature-salutations like the artist's ("Your Giovanni da Pistoia/Always with you except . . ." "Your more or less Giovanni da Pistoia, at six P.M. with the French Malady," etc.). There are light and passing criticisms of the times in these sonnets, not sustained or developed:

> Ognidì mille volte e 'l cielo assalto;
> E se non fussi la churial micha,
> Ancor faria far loro piu magior salto. (Sonnet II)
>
> Sagio è chi in questi tempi vive acorto
> E stassi lieto al suo povero speco. (Sonnet IV)

But the moderate tone of the Florentine Giovanni da Pistoia was not the one which prevailed over Michelangelo the poet and painter when he reflected on the offenses to Christ. It was the more violent censure of the Giovanni da Pistoia (Camelli) who had died in Ferrara in 1502.

15. *La Deposizione* (1550–56). To many admirers of Michelangelo's works there is none more moving than the *Deposition from the Cross* in Florence. All the themes of Christ's Passion are present in the drawings, sculpture, and painting, and yet if there is one reason why this statuary should appeal to us more than the others, it is precisely that Michelangelo himself is so dominant in this group. Years ago when I was studying in Florence, we foreign students were inevitably led to see the self-portraits of Cellini on the rear of *Perseo*'s head in the Loggia dei Lanzi and of Michelangelo in the features of *Nicodemus* in this group of the Duomo. It was thrilling to contemplate the magnificent expression of sorrow and mansuetude on Michelangelo's lithic face, looking down in contrition upon Christ's mask of death and helping the two Marys support the Saviour. If the *Giudizio universale*, Michelangelo's vast personal imprecation for grace, was greatly inspired by the *Dies Irae* of the Franciscan friar Thomas of Celano, this statuary representing Michelangelo's desire to share the sufferings of Christ seems inspired by the Franciscan Jacopone da Todi's *Stabat Mater*, that other magnificent piece of mediaeval hymnody:

> Fac, ut portem Christi mortem
> Passionis eius sortem
> Et plagas recolere.
> Fac me plagis vulnerari,
> Cruce hac inebriari
> Ob amorem filii.
> Inflammatus et accensus,
> Per te, virgo, sim defensus
> In die iudicii.
> Fac me cruce custodiri,
> Morte Christi praemuniri,
> Confoveri gratia.

Certainly Michelangelo's preoccupation with Christ's wounds and blood, with salvation and grace, and with the Day of Judgement, are consonant with this hymn; moreover, pleas for Christ's intercession are found in the *Rime* even if the misogynistic poet never petitions the Virgin in the same way. Michelangelo and Christ dominate this group, as they do the artist's poetry during this period of his life (1550–60).

The empathy which Michelangelo felt for Christ when executing the piece can be gathered from the fury of its creation. Blaise de Vigenère watched him working on it and commented: "He had passed his sixtieth [seventieth] year, and although he was not very strong, yet in a quarter hour he caused more splinters to fall from a hard block of marble than three young masons in twice or thrice the time. . . . He attacked the work with such energy and fire that I thought it would fly into pieces." Vasari, who first stated that Michelangelo lent his features to the *Nicodemus*, claimed further that the artist began it with the intention of erecting it above his own tomb.[34]

Michelangelo's appeals to God and Christ for grace are made on several occasions in the *Rime* (see Chapter XI). Just as the Michelangelo-Nicodemus looks down on the Christ's face and seems to be murmuring to him, so does Michelangelo address Christ directly in the poetry. We have already mentioned, in connection with the *Giudizio universale,* Michelangelo's direct petitions for remission of his sins.

Although no poem mentions the act of the *Deposition,* one powerful sonnet-hymn to the Redeemer probably dating from this stage of Michelangelo's life seems to reveal the feelings of the artist looking down with consummate commiseration upon the Saviour's august face. Of all the poetry which directly expresses Michelangelo's concern for Christ's shedding his blood for man (G 280, 289, 290, 294, 302), none is a finer translation of the statue's visible *sympatheia* than the following piece (1555–60), three-planed in vision like a baroque composition:

The blessed spirits were no less happy than disturbed and sad
On seeing that not they, but thou wast condemned to death.
Thou didst with thy blood open the closed portals of heaven to man.
They were happy, since, thou having created man,
Thou didst redeem him from original sin
Which had made his fate so miserable.
They were sad, since they felt that with harsh and cruel pain
Thou hadst become on the cross like a slave of slaves.
But whence thou camest and who thou wast
Heaven showed by a certain sign,
For the skies darkened, the earth opened,
The mountains trembled, and the waters became turbid.
The patriarchs were taken from the shadowy kingdom,
The fallen angels submerged in greater mourning;
Only man exulted, for at his baptism he was reborn. (G 298)

This poem parallels a sonnet to the Redeemer of Vittoria Colonna (see Chapter XIX). It also carries Dantean echoes, for when the Trecento poet reflects on the Crucifixion he recalls the Biblical convulsion of heaven and earth:

> Pero d'un atto uscir cose diverse;
> che a Dio ed ai Giudei piacque una morte:
> per lei tremò la terra e il ciel s'aperse. (*Par.* VII, 46–48)

Michelangelo's magnificent assurance to Christ that his sacrifice will not prove vain is closer to the spirit of Michelangelo-Nicodemo than are the many poems in which Michelangelo speaks of his own salvation to the divinity. More compelling than the thought of his own redemption at this pitiful moment is his realisation of the enormity of Christ's mortification and sacrifice to make that salvation possible.

> And yet the shedding of thy blood doth make us understand
> That if thy martyrdom for us was without equal,
> Thy dear gifts to us are likewise without measure. (G 294)

NOTES

1 Charles de Tolnay, *The Medici Chapel* (Princeton, 1948), p. 73.
2 G. Papini, *La vita, ed. cit.*, p. 426.
3 James Hutton, *The Greek Anthology in Italy* (Ithaca, 1935), p. 312.
4 Enrico Bevilacqua, *op. cit.*, pp. 649–50.
5 R. J. Clements, *Michelangelo's Theory, ed. cit.*, p. 224.
6 D. Giannotti, *Dialogi, ed. cit.*, pp. 44–45.
7 Giorgio Melchiori, *Michelangelo nel Settecento inglese* (Rome, 1950), p. 74.
8 *Lettere*, Milanesi ed., p. 535.
9 Gino Saviotti, *La vita e le Rime di Michelangelo* (Livorno, 1916), p. 49.
10 Giovanni Amendola, *Le poesie di Michelangelo* (Lanciano, 1911), preface.
11 Bevilacqua, *op. cit.*, p. 649.
12 Saviotti, *op. cit.*, p. 48.
13 Bevilacqua, *op. cit.*, pp. 649–50.
14 *Le Rime*, Ceriello ed., p. 233.
15 Valerio Mariani, *Michelangelo, ed. cit.*, p. 94.
16 Charles Morgan, *The Life of Michelangelo* (New York, 1960), p. 94.
17 Boyer d'Agen, *L'œuvre littéraire de Michel-Ange* (Paris, 1911), p. 1.
18 Quoted in a letter of Vasari to Bishop Minerbetti, 26 October, 1553.
19 V. Mariani, *Michelangelo, ed. cit.*, p. 66.
20 Ludwig Goldscheider, *The Sculptures of Michelangelo* (New York, n.d.), p. 15.
21 L. Goldscheider, *The Drawings of Michelangelo* (London, 1951), p. 38.
22 Quoted in Giuseppe Guido Ferrero, *Il Petrarchismo del Bembo e le Rime di Michelangelo* (Turin, 1935), p. 59.
23 Goethe, *Reisejournal*, under date of 14 March, 1788.
24 Quoted in De Tolnay, *The Medici Chapel, ed. cit.*, p. 68. From a letter (1544) of Niccolò Martelli.
25 Cf. Arnold von Salis, *Antike und Renaissance* (Zurich, 1947), p. 241.
26 Giorgio Vasari, *Le vite, ed. cit.*, VII, 271.
27 L. Goldscheider, *The Drawings, ed. cit.*, p. 44.
28 Rezio Buscaroli, *Michelangelo: La vita, la teorica dell'arte, le opere* (Bologna, 1959), pp. 161–62.
29 Vasari, *Le vite, ed. cit.*, VII, 281.
30 M. de Chantelou, *Journal de voyage du Cavalier Bernin* (Paris, 1885), p. 140.
31 Thomas McGreevy, "The Severe Bearing of Christ in the Last Judgement," *London Studio*, XX (1940), 202–03.
32 Francisco de Hollanda, *Diálogos em Roma, ed. cit.*, pp. 221 ff.
33 Erasmo Percopo, *Antonio Camelli e i suoi sonetti faceti* (Rome, 1913), p. 337.
34 See Vasari's "Life of Baccio Bandinelli." Also, the full discussion of this group in Paola Barocchi's edition of Vasari's *Vita di Michelangelo* (Milan, 1962) III, 1437–44.

6

THE FIFTY POEMS FOR THE TRUFFLES, TURTLE, AND TROUT

MICHELANGELO'S DISLIKE OF PORTRAITURE was deep-rooted, not only because he scorned literal representation, but because he could not be bothered devoting so much of himself to any individual. He found himself, as he affirmed in his dialogues with Donato Giannotti and the other Florentine *fuorusciti*,[1] avoiding commitment for long to any person, since absorption with that person would waste his time, would dissipate himself and his energies. Thus, if he was to devote much time to one individual, whether in his art, poetry, letters, or personal life, it was someone for whom he felt a strong attachment or one who occupied a major role in his life.

In his poems there are but a few individuals who played such a part: Dante, to him the genius without peer; Julius II, to whom he considered himself given "like the rays to the sun"; Luigi del Riccio, who looked after him in illness; Donato Giannotti, whose Latin and learning he envied; Vasari, who recorded his life; Vittoria Colonna and Tommaso Cavalieri, highborn objects of admiration and affection; and finally his beloved father Lodovico and assistant Urbino, whose passing intensified his mystical desire for a prompt death. As for the so-called "blackmailer" Febo di Poggio, his two or more appearances in the *Rime* are so diaphanous that most editors of the poetry refuse to perceive him (see below, p. 213). All the above save Cavalieri and the Marchioness of Pescara are honored in one or two poems apiece.

What, then, is one to conclude of the stream of fifty (or fifty-one)[2] poems, forty-eight or forty-nine of them quatrains, which Michelangelo poured out to the young Francesco (Cecchino) di Zanobi Bracci? Whereas Michelangelo's poetry has been the object of study ever since Benedetto

Varchi read "Non ha l'ottimo artista alcun concetto" (G 151) before the Florentine Academy in 1546, no one has taken a hard look at this sequence composed on the death, at age fifteen, of the favorite nephew of Luigi del Riccio. These poems praising the youth's beauty and improvising with varying success on necrological themes have been the subject of a conspiracy of silence and even, as we shall demonstrate, of misrepresentation. To the early biographers of the artist, from Condivi and Vasari to Hermann Grimm, the boy simply did not exist. Others, like Romain Rolland, mentioned Cecchino only in passing, noting vaguely that Michelangelo was a friend to the beautiful Cecchino Bracci. Only Giovanni Papini devotes as many as four pages to this lad (see below). The large block of poetry to Cecchino has been neglected even by translators, and until recently only Charles Eliot Norton had Englished as many as six of them. Their form itself has elicited some comment, and Vincenzo Pascale writes: "Through their content these epigraphs are true elegies, and only a few of the forty-eight quatrains have epigraphic form and style."[3]

Who was this adolescent boy whose beauties Michelangelo sang until he finally exploded, "the fount is dry"?

Cecchino Bracci (Michelangelo, who was partial to young aristocrats, adds the particule "de' " several times in the *Rime*) was from an ill-starred family. His grandfather, as Papini states, was the Giovan Battista who supplied Machiavelli with the purgative pills which hastened that historian's death.[4] Born in 1529, he came to Rome with his exiled Florentine father, but soon passed into the custody of his admiring uncle, Luigi del Riccio. Cecchino's father was arrested and imprisoned in 1530 because a brother had fled the besieged city of Florence (as had Michelangelo himself just prior to the siege) and passed over to the enemy.

There is little clue to the relations between Michelangelo and Cecchino before the latter's death, except for two letters we shall quote below. In a contract which Michelangelo drew up with two stonemasons for work on the Tomb of Julius II (10 May, 1542) Cecchino appears as a witness along with Del Riccio and Donato Giannotti. If Papini found it strange that a thirteen-year-old boy should be a witness to the contract, the incident is obviously one of the many attentions with which Luigi and Michelangelo humored a *mignon* who was becoming inseparable from them. Michelangelo was of an age to dote on the lad, being sixty-six at this date.

The intimate association came to sudden and tragic term two days after Epiphany, 1544, when Cecchino died in unknown circumstances. On the very day of his death Luigi del Riccio conceived the idea of gathering a florilegium of verses in honor of his nephew, an enterprise familiar to the Renaissance although customarily reserved for authors and humanists of conspicuous rank. The two men closest to Cecchino other than the uncle were Buonarroti and Giannotti. Michelangelo was informed immediately and apparently composed the first of his tide of verses by 8:30 P.M. ("a ore 20 e mezzo") on the very day of the death:

> If here his fair eyes are closed and buried
> Before their time, only this may comfort us:
> While they yet lived, that pity had died here
> Which now that they are dead, lives on in many others. (G 179)

This first expression of sorrow and perhaps bitterness, simple and sincere despite the baroque contrasts, was of a quality not always maintained by the forty-nine others written under pressure, real or feigned, from Del Riccio.

Donato Giannotti was apprised by a letter written four days later. On 12 January, 1544, Luigi sent a frantic appeal to the eminent humanist, then at Vicenza:

> Alas, Messer Donato mine—Our Cecchino has died! I impress upon you the memory of the love and reverence he bore us, and of his kind and rare qualities, which were infinitely multiplied since your leaving; so much so that the heavens, which always take away the best, took him from us. All Rome mourns him. Messer Michelangelo is designing for me a fitting marble tomb, and you are to do the epitaph and send it to me with a comforting letter; if only it gets here in time, for my heart is broken. Patience! I live thousands and thousands of deaths each hour. O God! How fortune keeps changing its way!
>
> Thy despairing Luigi del Riccio[5]

Donato obliged with a Latin epigraph, apparently composed in Rome and thus implying that he had returned with dispatch to the capital. Moreover, he composed three sonnets on the tragedy, filled with decorous regrets, which show touches of Petrarch, the master mourner. The line on Laura's death, "Non la conobbe il mondo mentre l'ebbe,"[6] is echoed in:

> Fuggito ha il mondo, che non conoscea
> Quanto di ben nel suo gran seno avea.

Other formulas of regret roughly parallel those in Michelangelo's poems: We must not weep over his death, but our own as we wander disconsolate and sad; the world is left without its sun; we remain eager to rejoin Cecchino in heaven. In a curious reminiscence of Catullus, the departed boy is urged to return to earth and kiss Del Riccio a thousand times. Donato's three sonnets are competent exercises in consolatory verse, somewhat rhetorical and weakened by commonplaces. There is nothing in them to suggest that pederasty lay behind the excessive grief of the uncle.

Luigi himself penned a sonnet, "Idol mio, che la tua leggiadra spoglia," in which he repeats that the light has gone from his life and that his soul and spirit are already longing to pursue his Cecchino. It is this sonnet (and so many others) in which the poet asks his soul why it lingers on earth rather than soars to heaven.[7] Other poets responded to Del Riccio's invitation. Giovanni Aldobrandini lent a classical elegiac note to his quatrain,

"Et lachrymas, Nymphae, ad tumulos et spargite flores." Fra Paolo del Rosso contributed a sonnet, "Poscia che sì per tempo a sdegno haveste," which portrayed Luigi del Riccio sighing and weeping at all hours, consumed by the pure and gentle fire which Cecchino had kindled. Anton Francesco Grazzini, "Il Lasca," wrote a madrigal and a sonnet describing a bereft Rome, left without the bright sun of Cecchino. Carlo Gondi sent from Ancona a sestet and two Latin couplets. He was the only one of these humanists to suggest that Michelangelo was suffering as deeply as Del Riccio:

> Death, stirred by such great beauty,
> Out of jealousy of Riccio, and to make war
> Upon Buonarroti, having found their souls
> In his breast, carried him from this earth.
> Thus at one stroke it was rapacious of all three:
> Now lie in death with his body the souls of these two.[8]

Unlike the other humanists, the sculptor-poet was called upon by Del Riccio to exercise both of his talents. Riccio's letter (recorded by Guasti) reads:

Most magnificent Messer Michelagnolo: I send your Lordship two Lunghezza melons and a bottle of San Gimigniano Greek; enjoy them for love of me. I beg you to look up a certain drawing which I gave you a while back for carving the head of Cecchino, for I am still of the same mind; you told me you would do one yourself, since mine didn't please you. Take your time about it, but send me that one back once you've found it. If not, it's not important. At your commands, Luigi Del Riccio

Entreated thus to design the boy's tomb and execute a bust of him, Michelangelo planned the tomb set up in the Church of Aracoeli. As for executing the bust, Michelangelo summoned up his well-tested talents of refusal and cast his reply in verse:

> Scarce had I seen the beautiful eyes open
> Of him who was paradise and life to you,
> Before he closed them that day when the last die was cast,
> And opened them in heaven to contemplate God.
>
> Too late I recognise, too late my heart mourns
> Their pleasing beauty. Nor was his passing my fault,
> But premature death's. His beauty, though ever-present to you,
> Has fled beyond my ardent desire.

The extrication from this commission is rationalised in the final two tercets:

> Then, Luigi, to portray the beauty, unique in this world,
> Of Cecchino, of whom I speak, and render it eternal
> In living stone, now that he is here returned to dust—

Art, not having this beauty before it, cannot picture it.
If it is true that one lover is transformed into the other,
Then to portray him I should picture you. (G 193)

Cecchino's bust was finally modeled by Michelangelo's assistant Urbino, no doubt in consultation with the master sculptor and possibly even Luigi, who had sent the master a suggested (and rejected) design.

Buonarroti did not similarly refuse to do the many poems requested by Del Riccio. Why did he comply? It has been conjectured and repeated that Michelangelo was constrained to compose them through gratitude to his benefactor Del Riccio, who looked after him during his illness of June–July, 1544. As we shall see below, however, half of them were written before that sickness. This conjecture is reminiscent of Michelangelo's reportedly having to make a snow man for young Piero de' Medici in return for Medicean generosities. Michelangelo penned petulant footnotes to many of the poems, leaving the impression that Luigi was pressuring him with bribes of trout, truffles, mushrooms, fennel, Lunghezza melons, turtle, fig bread, "Adam's-apple" conserves, and a bottle of San Gimigniano wine. Strictly speaking, the melons and *greco* were bribes to induce him to carve Cecchino's bust, but Michelangelo pretends to consider them bribes for poetry, so great was his disinclination to do the effigy. Yet Michelangelo was not a man to buckle under pressures and importunities. Would this strong personality who turned down commissions from Bayazid the Turk, Francis I of France, Cosimo de' Medici, and other princes of church and state feel obliged to keep churning out verses just to compensate for foodstuffs or satisfy an insistent friend?[9]

The question must be answered, then, whether Michelangelo was moved to write fifty poems through his love for Cecchino, through his love for Del Riccio, or through the latter's love for Cecchino. As Papini puts it, perhaps Michelangelo "admired Cecchino for his beauty or simply made a good deal of him out of love for his uncle." To arrive at the answer we must now examine respectively the poems themselves, the notes appended by Michelangelo to his poems, the circumstances of their composition, the letters of the artist, and finally the dubious manner in which the poems were edited and published.

Throughout these quatrains there are some two dozen identifiable motifs, some inventive, the majority familiar to the age. A few themes occur over and over. Some dominate the earlier pieces (the beauty of Cecchino's eyes); some are more common in the later quatrains (time is relative and life is brief, the dead youth lives on in his lover or lovers, the sepulcher is bereaved over the youth it contains). A few themes are scattered evenly throughout, the most prominent being the idea that the soul lives on forever whereas the body decays. When one encounters the same motif in quick succession, he concludes that Michelangelo was grasping for something new and falling back into the same pattern. Sometimes one senses an influence of Petrarch's poetry mourning the deaths of Colonna and Laura, but no doubt Christian poets singing threnodies to dead friends are bound to exploit familiar themes.

In order to get inside these poems, it might be well to list a few of the most prominent themes and quote an illustrative verse or two for each. One of the most obvious, of course, is that death after all is a blessing (18, 43, 45): "Gran uentura qui morto esser mi ueggio," "Di si bel cambio e di morte mi lodo." Death aims to destroy beauty (3, 4, 5, 8, 28, 32, 34, 47): "Non puo per morte gia chi qui mi serra/La belta, c'al mortal mie largir uolse." Death aims to destroy nature (5, 10): "Se dalla morte è uinta la natura." Whatever happens to the body, the soul continues unchanged and free (7, 9, 13, 14, 37, 42): ". . . sì che l'alma di me nuda/S'achorge a pena auer cangiato stato." Cecchino's death was unnatural and before his time (3, 15, 44, 46): ". . . colse acerbo il fructo/Morte, anz' il fior, c' a quindic' anni cede." Time is relative and yet life is brief (17, 22, 25, 29, 40, 50): "Ch'un fior di uerno picciol uento il fura." The deceased goes on living in the lover (15, 16, 25, 26, 33): "Resto in te uiuo, c'or mi uedi e piangi." Cecchino's eyes haunt the poet (1, 11, 15, 32): "Se gli ochi aperti mie fur uita e pace." Even in death Cecchino wins immortality through his portrait (24, 37): "D'entrar dipinto, ou'io non pote' uiuo." The sepulcher itself regrets the passing of the youth (34, 36, 37, 38, 40, 41): "Qui serro il Braccio e suo belta diuina."

The thought "all Rome mourns him" in Luigi del Riccio's letter to Donato Giannotti finds roundabout echo in Michelangelo's "Roma ne piange, e 'l ciel si gloria e ride" (42).

If these quatrains reveal as much admiration as affection, as much regret as grief, they present no clear evidence of a carnal passion between the old man and the boy. Is there any such evidence in the notes sent along with the poems to Luigi del Riccio?

These penned notes would indicate, as we stated initially, that Luigi kept prodding the poet with fruits, wine, and other gourmet's tidbits. Let us now examine those notes which elucidate the circumstances of the composition of the quatrains, that is, the understanding between Michelangelo and Del Riccio. Although there is a note appended to quatrain 8 (Frey's numbering here, above, and below) about Cecchino's being reclothed on Judgement Day, it is not until 12 that there is a mild comment on Luigi's prodding: "Quando voi non ne volete, non mi mandate piu niente," indicating that the flow of bribes had begun. After quatrain 16 comes specific naming of foodstuffs: "I didn't want to send this to you, but the trout and truffles would force heaven." By quatrain 18 the note has a mock, businesslike character, as befitted an artist addressing his business manager: "Now that the promise behind the 15 installments is carried out, I'm no longer indebted to you for them, if another doesn't show up from Heaven, where he [Cecchino] is." The note to 20 reads: "For the salted mushrooms, since you wish nothing else." After 21: "This clumsy piece, said a thousand times, for the fennel." After 23: "This piece is said by the trout, and not by me; so, if you don't like the verses, don't marinate them any more without pepper." After the solemn thoughts of quatrain 28, Riccio read: "I send you back the melons, but not yet with the I.O.U. and the drawing: but I'll do it in any case, since I can draw better now [after his illness]." After 29 Michelangelo adds: "For the turtle; for the fish Urbino will do [the honors], for he gobbled them down."

It is with 33 that the poet feigns creative exhaustion, just as Michelangelo the artist often complained of exhaustion. He admitted in a note: "Clumsy things. The fountain is dry. One must wait till it rains, and you're in too much of a hurry." The objection after 36 is equally strong: "Clumsy things, but in wishing me to make a thousand of them, there has to be a bit of everything." After 40 Michelangelo is succinct again: "For the fig bread." Again he reports a lack of poetic fury after 45: "Because poetry tonight has been in a calm, I send you four crude ring cakes for the three honey cakes of the economiser." After submitting the final poem agreed upon (50), the seemingly exhausted poet adds: "Per baia e non pel numero" ("For the fun of it and not to make up the total"). This note could actually mean that the poem sent was the fifty-first (see note 2)!

Biographers of Michelangelo have not always dissociated the spirit of the poems from the spirit of the accompanying comments, distinct in inspiration and sometimes set down long after the poem had been composed. The contrast of mood is often striking. Some of the best of the quatrains are followed by the most disclaiming and belittling notes. Thus, the piece (21) which contains the axiomatic line on the finality of death, already quoted:

> He who mourns my death here waits in vain,
> Drenching my bones and my sepulcher,
> As if he could make me return like fruit to a withered tree;
> For a dead man rearises not in spring. (G 199)

This, as Michelangelo adds, may have been said a thousand times, as have most thoughts about death, yet this poem is a successful one. Furthermore, it would be unreasonable to accept these penned afterthoughts to Del Riccio as indications of the value of the "crude cakes" (*berlingozzi*), since Michelangelo's public and sometimes private statements about the best of his works always denigrated them. After finishing the Sistine Ceiling, or rather the first phase, Michelangelo dismissed it as an afterthought to his father: "I've finished that chapel that I was painting" (Letter XV). Moreover, Michelangelo often disclaimed in his letters and poems any competence whatsoever in painting, sculpture, and architecture.[10] One of these disclaimers was addressed to none other than Luigi del Riccio (Letter CDLX) in 1546 (see below). It was only natural that Michelangelo should shrug off these quatrains or other of his poems, for as Vasari recorded, "He mistrusted his ability to express in writing what he would have liked, not being trained in discourse."[11] Condivi corroborated this.[12] We have quoted Michelangelo's own disclaimer in a letter to Tommaso Cavalieri, "The pen cannot even approach one's intent," (CDXI) and his admission, "Writing is a great annoyance to me, for it is not my art" (Letter CDLXXXII). It is significant that when Michelangelo sends Vasari one of his finest sonnets (G 288) it will again be talked down as a silly thing (*cosa sciocca*); he will dismiss another magnificent mystical sonnet (G 285) as the whim of a man in his second childhood (*rimbambito*).[13]

Thus, the deprecating tone of the notes should not affect our evaluation of the poetry, nor should the impatience discerned in those notes. It is possible that Michelangelo was already worried that Del Riccio might wish to publish these poems (see below). It is equally possible he was irritated that Luigi should be pressing him to publish them when he, Michelangelo, had loved the boy no less than had the uncle.

Nor should it be alleged, as it has been, that the hasty composition of fifty poems must of necessity diminish their quality. Michelangelo did not respond with such promptness as is commonly supposed to the exhortations of Del Riccio. Frey has established the over-all chronology of this sequence. The first four pieces were completed by 7 February, numbers 14 through 24 during February and March, numbers 25 through 27 apparently before Michelangelo's illness in June–July, number 28 after this sickness, numbers 29 through 40 during late August and early September, number 41 in November (Saint Martin's Day is mentioned), and numbers 42 through 50 during the closing weeks of 1544. It is seen from this chronology that Michelangelo took eleven months to write 220 lines of poetry! This is not an excessive assignment for the artist who took refuge in poetry while completing the frescoes of the Pauline Chapel. While Michelangelo rebelled against pressures and commitments lasting over a period of time, such as those attending his "calvary" of the Tomb of Julius II, his protestations have no bearing on the quality of his productions.

If any circumstance was to weaken the quality of these poems, it was simply the difficulty for a man of sixty-eight, who had been through so much, who had "been lapidated every day as if he had crucified Christ" (Letter CDXXV of 1542) to sustain long sorrow over a death and to continue verbalising it. Even the death of the Marchioness of Pescara did not inspire more poems than these. (Petrarch's one hundred pieces on the death of Laura remain a tour de force.) It is not surprising, then, that the madrigalist and sonneteer Michelangelo limited all but two of these poems to quatrains and that as early as the twelfth poem he began to comment on the great number of them he was to write. A secondary factor tending to reduce the quality of this quatrain-sequence is that Michelangelo exercised best in large-scale compositions, whether in the plastic arts or in poetry.

Insinga finds beauties in many of the epitaphs, but is troubled by the "almost joking and irreverent verses," as well as by the notes: "in place of Michelangelo the poet now comes instead Michelangelo the jokester."[14] The uneven quality of these poems has been considered a measure of his feelings for Cecchino. Papini claimed that Michelangelo could not have felt deep passion for Cecchino. "If Michelangelo, as it appears from the letters of 1542 [see below], were really a lover of Cecchino, one would expect here some accent of heartfelt grief and anguished lament. Here begins the mystery. These funereal epigrams are, contrary to what one might expect, cold and labored compositions, often based on trumped-up conceits and puns, which the rimer himself (here we do not dare call him poet) judges 'clumsy'."[15] Whatever one may think of this romantic premise that the greatest love dictates the greatest poetry—the fact that one quatrain contains three *enjambements* would thus demonstrate a lesser passion—the worth of the poems themselves has been the subject of two contrasting opinions.

In the judgement of Carl Frey, "Michelangelo's Gedankengang wie Sprache sind bisweilen unklar, gequält, ärmlich, und absonderlich, was der Dichter selbst zugestanden hat."[16] Frey then adduces Michelangelo's cynical obiter dicta to strengthen his opinion. If most scholars have accepted Frey's evaluation of this sequence there have been one or two recent dissenters. Thus, the editor Ceriello comments: "Yet this poetry has its own particular cachet and often succeeds in freeing itself from the commonplaces of Petrarchism, from baroque *arguzie* and hyperbole, representing death with sudden and powerful foreshortenings, with cries of rebellion and accents of infinite pity, and bears us to the pure atmosphere of the most genuine and dolorous humanity of the artist."[17]

Valerio Mariani, in his *Poesia di Michelangelo,* finds some of these efforts "authentic gems of poesy" and again, "a few most beautiful attempts at funereal poetry genuinely Michelangelesque."[18]

There need be no disagreement about the quality of these quatrains. That they were intended as potential inscriptions, any one of which might actually be placed on Cecchino's sepulcher, is attested by the brief quatrain form and by the fact that *qui* (or once *qua*) of the *hic iacet* formula occurs in 39 of the 48 quatrains. What values they possess are close to the surface. Only a few of them approach the magnificent heights of the mystical poems in which Michelangelo anticipates his own death. Nor do these poems reveal a katharsis comparable to the one discernible in the sonnets on the death of Vittoria Colonna. However, most of them compare favorably with the hyperbolic mortuary poetry of the Renaissance. It must be remembered that all recent literary historians in Italy are unanimous in their view that Michelangelo's poetry is not outstanding for its lyricism, its metaphor, its classical reference, or even its language, but rather for its thought content, its sincerity, its originality, and for the avenues it affords into the artist's mind. Limited to quatrain structure (with two exceptions) and to the single theme of the death of a beautiful boy, these pieces will of necessity supply fewer insights into Michelangelo's mind than will other poems of freer inspiration. Nevertheless, there are some intimate glimpses into the complex mind of the artist. Here for example (48) we first learn of Michelangelo's conviction that the aged have less chance for salvation than those who die young ("Chi manco uiue piu speri perdono"). Here alone (23) do we find his echo of a Petrarchan triumph over death:

> Beyond the pale of the years and hours
> Which enclosed me here, I should fear to return to life
> Were it possible, more than I feared leaving,
> Since I was really born where death itself dies.

or (35) the artist improvises on the theme of God transcending nature:

> Buried here is that Braccio with whose face
> God wished to correct Nature.
> But because that wealth is lost of which men take not care,
> He showed him to the world and quickly took him back to himself.

There are, moreover, interesting baroque touches in these quatrains, already noted in Chapter III. We have mentioned the two life-death polarities of the initial quatrain. Whenever confronted with death, whether that of Vittoria Colonna, Urbino, Cecchino, his father Lodovico, or his own, Michelangelo's poetry assumes baroque motifs and characteristics. Like the baroque mystics he meditates upon Cecchino's life and agrees with Calderón that life is a dream: ". . . e s'alcun mi ricorda,/Gli par sogniar: si morte èppresta e 'ngorda" (22). The adolescent reminds him that this life is a prison: "In che carcer quaggiu l'anima uiue" (19). The body is a mere leathery pelt subject to dissolution, like the pelt of Saint Bartholomew: "A la terra la terra e l'alma al cielo" (37, also 14). The baroque spectacle of the Last Judgement is very much on his mind at this period (8 note, 31, 39, 49): "c'anz'al al gran di l'a tolto/Pieta di terra . . ." The artist's fear of the Day of Wrath and concern for his salvation were accentuated by the belief quoted above that grace is more available to the young man than to the aged. Even puns, which point up the ambiguous and unstable value of words themselves, appear in the two plays on the name Bracci (6, 44).

The fact remains that the other humanists solicited by Del Riccio wrote from one to three poems apiece. Michelangelo wrote fifty or fifty-one. It is our belief that Michelangelo's relations with the boy were such that he could do no less.

Even in the liberal atmosphere of Rome on the eve of the Counter-Reformation sodomy was still a mortal sin and a legal crime. It would indeed be rare that any accusation or innuendo on the subject should be set down in writing. Yet Aretino in a letter of November 1545 referred to Gherardo Perini and Tommaso Cavalieri ("Tomai" is the form used) as homosexual partners of the artist, and wrote, "Even if you are divine, you don't disdain male consorts."[19] There is a veiled allusion to Michelangelo's deviated sexual practices in Annibal Caro's *Dicerie*.[20] Few of the biographers in our century face this issue. One book has been written to interpret Michelangelo's love of the male nude as homosexual narcissism.[21] A letter of Michelangelo to Niccolò Quaratesi (CCCLIII) tells of a father who wished his son to be an apprentice of the artist and praised his beauty: "Once you saw him, you'd chase him into bed the minute you got home." Michelangelo explained his refusal to take the lad in. "I tell you that I am giving up (*rinunzio*) this consolation, and I don't want to take it from him." Whether the letter contains a confession depends on the semantic value of *rinunziare*, which could imply abandoning a practice or a moral tergiversation.

Michelangelo's probable homosexual relations with Gherardo Perini and Febo di Poggio cannot be dismissed by a dispassionate student of his life, even though the Catholic and Victorian-Anglican biographers like Symonds (himself an admitted deviate) explain Michelangelo away as physically frigid. Symonds imputes everything to Platonism and accepts (or pretends to accept) Ammitari's claim that Michelangelo led an immaculate life. Nor are Febo and Gherardo mentioned in Mariani's essay on the *Rime* of the artist. Pierre de Bouchaud writes in indignant tones as he ignores the very presence of the poems to young men: "L'artiste aurait aussi, ajoute-t-on, composé des madrigaux en l'honneur de ce jeune homme. Mais je me demande quelle preuve on avance à cet égard. . . . Pour ma part, voici de longues années que j'étudie la question sans découvrir le moindre indice permettant de mettre sur le compte du noble artiste un pareil scandale."[22] More modern critics, however, are beginning to question the Victorian view. As Papini admits, the theory of pederasty has been accepted from Aretino to Grimm, Lombroso, Havelock Ellis, and others. Freud subscribed to it. Ludwig von Scheffler felt that Michelangelo could love only men.[23] After all, had he not declared in his sonnet "Non è sempre di colpa" that the love which aspires to lofty heights cannot be satisfied by a woman; that to waste oneself on love for a woman "is not worthy of a wise and virile heart" (G 260).

Like the tell-tale poems, there are the tell-tale letters. Michelangelo wrote the passionate declaration to Febo di Poggio: "and I would have you understand that so long as I live, wherever I may be, I shall always be at your service with loyalty and love, as much as any other friend you may have in the world" (Letter CDXX). There is a poetic reminiscence of this earlier subjection to Febo di Poggio: "Easily could I soar with such a happy fate" (see p. 213). The sonnet "Ben fu, temprando il ciel tuo uiuo raggio" (see p. 214) alludes to the beautiful face of Febo just as the quatrains sing of the beautiful face of Cecchino. Both of these sonnets regret the "happy days" at the memory of which "I collapse and fall." An admission written on a folio showing a *putto* urinating states that Michelangelo cannot work without the presence of Gherardo: "I beg you not to make me draw this evening since Perino's not here." Other veiled statements in the correspondence are equally conclusive, even though Papini thought that the pair's respective ages (Gherardo was in his early forties when Michelangelo was in his late forties) were hardly "ideal for a youth (*efebo*) and his paramour."[24]

Michelangelo's punning verse to Tommaso Cavalieri ("Prigion resto d'un Cavalier armato") has been viewed by even his uneasy great-nephew as indicating a homosexual capitulation. In his adulatory letters to Cavalieri the artist confessed that it was "your name which nourishes my body and soul" (CDXVI), sentiments echoed in the poetry ("Deh rendimi a me stesso, accio ch' i' mora") (G 91). It seems probable, however, that this younger married man and paterfamilias channeled the older man's passion into an idealised relationship. That there was gossip about it by others than Aretino is revealed in the sonnet (*ca.* 1534), "Veggio nel tuo bel uiso, Signior mio," when the artist protests:

> And though the throng, malign and brutish, free
> Its gibes and scoffs at what the few possess,
> There fails no joy from this warm eagerness,
> This chaste desire, this love, this fealty.
>
> (Nesca Robb)

To the evidence of homosexuality in the *Rime*, *Letters*, and on the folio should be added those in Michelangelo's art itself: the sensuous *ignudi* so out of place on the Sistine Ceiling, the robust nudes cavorting behind the Madonna Doni, the revealing *Saettatori*, the gift-drawings, the employment of male models for female figures, including *la Notte*—all these evidences of his preference for the male nude brought Vasari out quoting Michelangelo to the effect that the human body was a more suitable ornament than was foliage.[25] The artist himself felt called upon to clarify matters by asserting of the male nude:

> Nor doth God, in his grace, show himself to me otherwise
> Than in some graceful and mortal veil
> And that alone I love, for in it he is mirrored. (G 106)

Indeed, he even denies that his love for the male figure has anything strange about it (G 164) as the "arrogant and stupid judgements" are claiming:

> If one thinks otherwise, his opinion is wrong. (G 164)

No Aretino accused Michelangelo of improper relations with the boy Cecchino. However, even if there were no evidences of homosexual tendencies in Michelangelo's writings, art, or biography, the episode of Francesco di Zanori Bracci would of itself constitute a strong affirmation of them. There is first of all evidence in the letters to Luigi del Riccio. In 1542 Michelangelo had a Freudian dream about Cecchino. It was related in his letter (CDXXIII) sent to Del Riccio in the Strozzi Ulivieri Palace, which apparently accompanied a madrigal or sonnet:

I sent this [madrigal] a short while ago to Florence. Now that I have reworked it more fittingly, I send it to you, so that you may give it, if it please you, to the flame, that is, to the one who consumes me. I should like even another favor from you, and that is that you should clear up a certain perplexity which has laid hold of me since last night; when greeting our idol in a dream, it appeared to me that he was laughing and threatening me; and I not knowing which of the two things I am to believe in, I beg you to find out from him, and that when we see each other tomorrow, you may clear it up for me.

Yours with infinite obligations,
and as always . . .

To which Michelangelo added a curious postscriptum:

If it please you, have it copied clearly and give it to those bonds which unite men without discretion, and remember me to Messer Donato. (CDXXIII)

It was hardly a grandfatherly feeling that consumed Michelangelo like fire and which caused him to writhe in his sleep while the boy threatened and mocked his senile love. This letter gives us the important news that some of Michelangelo's love poetry of 1542–43 was addressed to Cecchino, a fact no editor has taken into account. Another curious missive (CDXXVI) from 1542 reads as follows:

Messer Luigi, dear my Lord—My love has ratified the agreement which I made of myself to him; but of the other ratification which you know, I don't know as yet what he thinks of me and of it. So I enclose my best wishes to you and to Messer Donato and to the third party, afterward or before as you wish.

Old things out of (or destined for) the fire without witness.

Your Michelangelo full of worries, Rome.

Editor Gaetano Milanesi states that the "other contract" concerns the agreement with the Duke of Urbino over the Tomb of Julius II. Since the first approval so obviously alludes to Michelangelo's feelings for Cecchino, the "other" most likely refers to Cecchino's reciprocating the artist's feelings. If Luigi called Cecchino "my idol" in the sonnet on the lad's death, the latter becomes "our idol" in the recounting of the dream. It would seem that Michelangelo's "fire without witness" which left him "full of anxieties" was shared by Luigi, making them both "men without discretion" "bound together."

The poems remind us more than once that this fifteen-year-old boy already had lovers:

> Here I am believed dead who for the comfort
> Of the world lived, and with a thousand souls in my breast
> Of true lovers . . . (G 190)

It is suggested in "Se l'un nell'altro amato si trasforma" (G 193).

There is, moreover, one conclusive evidence involving Michelangelo and Luigi in the poetry, one of those appended notes intended for the eyes of Luigi del Riccio alone and then "for the fire." It accompanies the epigram:

> The earthly flesh, and here my bones deprived
> Of their charming face and beautiful eyes,
> Do yet attest that grace and delight was I,
> In what a prison here the soul doth live. (G 197)

After rereading these verses on the physical charms of Francesco, Michelangelo, in an impatient mood (we are now at a moment when eight consecutive poems, 14 through 21, are accompanied by bantering notes), revises the last two verses to:

> Do yet attest for him how gracious I was in bed
> When he embraced, and in what the soul doth live.

To which he scribbles the final sarcasm: "Take these two verses below, for they're a moral thing; and this I send you for the fulfillment of the fifteen installments." Thus, on a quick impulse, Michelangelo reveals the secret of the "fire without witness." Little did he expect in that moment that these few words would reappear in future editions of his works—even though, we must add, no editor has as yet paid the slightest attention to them in commenting on the poems. (One translator, at our suggestion, has called attention to them in his notes.)

The story is not yet told. Michelangelo was recognised as a poet, we remember, ever since the public reading from his works by Varchi in 1546.[26] It was inevitable that his poetry should sooner or later be printed. Not that Michelangelo originally expected it to be. Indeed, he jotted down his stanzas on the backs of letters, on the margins or backs of drawings, so that even in the past decade, as previously noted, at least one poem was discovered on the back of a drawing in a British museum.[27] The artist made no attempt to keep together the corpus of poetry, even for eventual publication by someone else.

However, in view of the Renaissance custom of gathering and publishing encomiums, it was certainly on Luigi del Riccio's mind to do something with the distinguished humanists' tributes to his beloved nephew. We may suppose that this had been on his mind from the outset. So Carl Frey assumed from the careful copying and numbering of the poems by Del Riccio.[28]

Del Riccio's intention of publishing his poems on Cecchino may have stirred the cautious Michelangelo to anger. We possess both a letter and a sonnet to Del Riccio which Frey assigns to early 1546. The letter (CDLX) was published by Milanesi, who also dated it from that year. Miss Ramsden proposes rather January 1545. In Symonds's translation, it reads:

Messer Luigi, You seem to think that I shall reply according to your wishes, when the case is quite the contrary. You give me what I have already denied you, and refuse me what I begged. And it is not ignorance which makes you send it to me through Ercole, when you are ashamed to give it to me yourself.

One who saved my life has certainly the power to disgrace me. But I do not know which is the heavier to bear, disgrace or death. Therefore I beg and entreat you, by the true friendship which exists between us, to destroy that print and burn the copies which are already printed. And if you choose to buy and sell me, do not do so to others. If you hack me into a thousand pieces, I will do the same, not indeed to yourself, but to what belongs to you.

Not painter nor sculptor, nor architect, but what you will; but not as a drunkard, as I said to you at home.

The key to the meaning of this letter hinges on the word *stampa.* As Frey notes, Heath Wilson, like Symonds, translates: "destroy that print and burn the other impressions." Editing the letter, Milanesi believed that some print of one of Michelangelo's paintings was involved. Frey concurs, pointing out that technically the word *stampa* refers to a copper, stone, or woodblock print. It is, however, our belief that the printing of a book or pamphlet is involved here, an interpretation which occurred also to Frey's compatriot Scheffler.[29] The word *stampa* could easily have been used in the sense of bookprinting by Michelangelo, who by his own admission had never "examined closely" the art of printing (*stamperia*) until Priscianese explained it to him in 1546.[30] It seems most likely that such a phrase as "if you hack me into a thousand pieces" must allude to something more damaging than the mere selling of a print. (Michelangelo had twice had copies of his art works sold in quantity, without audible complaint.)[31] The phrase, "and if you wish to make commerce of me, don't make it of someone else" could easily refer to the dead Cecchino. The threat of retribution ("cose vostre") or exposure, clearly contained in the letter, also supports the thesis of publication of the quatrains. Finally, the sentence "you give me what I've already denied you" suggests the unauthorised printing of pages or proofs which Del Riccio had been copying, numbering, and preparing ever since they were submitted.

The sonnet (1544–46) to Del Riccio could also express this same indignation:

> Oft in the bosom of sweet courtesy
> There lurks a sword, that striketh unawares
> Honor and life: beside such hurt appears
> Less dear the gift of health thou gavest me.
> Who maketh swift the feet, and then doth spread,
> Straight in the path, a net concealed from sight,
> He quenches, when it fain would burn most bright,
> The flame of gratitude by love that's fed.
> Then, my Luigi, free from all alloy
> Keep thou that love to which my life I owe,
> That so the winds of wrath disturb it not,
> For wrath fair kindness' image doth destroy.
> If aught I know of friendship, this I know:
> A thousand joys are in one grief forgot.
>
> (G 251)
> (Elizabeth Hall)

Whether or not Luigi realised it, the final line is cribbed literally from Petrarch's sonnet "Io mi vivea di mia sorte contento." The reason for this outburst against Michelangelo's erstwhile benefactor and host during his illness is not known, but again the intensity of wording in the final verse could signify that a thousand pleasures enjoyed with Cecchino were not at this late date worth the torment of having these "indiscreet" verses in print.

In any case, whatever the stage of preparation reached by Del Riccio in his project of bringing out these poems before his death in 1546, any such edition was indeed destroyed.

However, the telltale sequence was destined to come out sooner or later. *Habent sua fata libelli.* When in 1623 Michelangelo il Giovane finally brought out with Giunti the collected *Rime,* it was a bowdlerised version. In fact, nothing could have cast greater suspicion on the relations existing between the artist and Cecchino than this timid doctoring of the originals.

Of the fifty poems to Cecchino, only five appeared in this edition. A study of his copies in Archivio Buonarroti Codice XV made while preparing for his edition shows Michelangelo the Younger writing in the margin of folio 28a: "I don't know whether it's wise to carve these epitaphs on the copper plates I'm putting into the chambers, carved there with the other compositions. I don't believe it wise, or at least not all, and emended." He is here speaking of inscribing them in the Casa Buonarroti. On folio 31b he noted: "End of the epitaphs. I'd certainly not carve them all, because there are too many, and then, too, I wouldn't print them." The very name of Cecchino Bracci was expunged from these poems allegedly transcribed from a Vatican manuscript, and the masculine pronouns were changed to feminine. Typical alterations recorded by Girardi were:

Qui reso ha morte: a chi morto ancor m'ama *to*
N'ha reso morte: a chi morta ancor m'ama

Io fui Cecchin mortale, et or son diuo *to*
Io fui mortale, ed or son fatta diua

Di Cecchin di ch' io parlo, in pietra viva *to*
Dell'angelico uolto in pietra uiua

Similarly, when Michelangelo the Younger came to the sonnet "A che piu debb' io mai l'intensa uogla" (G 98), which Varchi had already printed accurately during the artist's lifetime, he was troubled by the reference to Michelangelo's subjection to Tommaso Cavalieri ("Resto prigion d'un Caualier armato"). He wished to change the wording to "Resto prigion d'un cor di virtù armato." For this and a similar sonnet the great-nephew apologised, "Keep in mind that this sonnet, with the preceding and others, concerns, as is clearly shown, virile Platonic love." The editor felt that the bowdlerising was justified, for otherwise "the ignorance of men is given leeway for whispering."[32]

Typical of a Victorian attitude which placed more blame on the editor than on the poet is that expressed by F.-L. Polidori. After mentioning the expurgations of the great-nephew, this Italian editor stated: "Every sagacious reader will understand the reasons for it; we do not spell out these reasons here, not merely for fear of casting a blemish on the fame of Buonarroti, or even that of the aforementioned loving guardian [Del Riccio]; but to avoid stirring up again the disgraceful and wretched talk of that time when the *Rime* in question first came to light."[33]

The excellent Guasti, first editor of a dependable edition of the *Rime* (1863), shows, as does Polidori, how difficult it is for an editor to face up to the homosexual implications of the quatrains to Cecchino. Guasti chides Michelangelo the Younger for tampering with the original autograph versions and even comments ironically that the great-nephew must have expected that no one would ever again inspect the manuscripts. Then he adds, "Nor should I even be blaming him here, had his scruples not been unnecessary. Morality means something more than a variant reading, and as for me, I'd give all of the tales which people talk about for one single heart that they have allegedly corrupted. For those sonnets do not refer to virile love: neither those or others."[34] Then, after these courageous and reassuring remarks, when Guasti comes face to face with the two compromising verses in which Michelangelo mentions the delights of Cecchino embracing in bed, what does Guasti do? He suppresses them!

Now, in the long run it does not matter too much what Michelangelo's sexual or domestic practices were. Of these we might repeat his rejoinder when people complained that the Dukes in the Medici Chapel had not looked as he depicted them: "Who will care a thousand years from now?" Yet it does seem that if we view with equanimity the obvious behavior patterns of other Renaissance figures, like Leonardo, it serves little purpose to alter or misrepresent the evidence which scholarship has brought to light. We know from Michelangelo's tremendous and sustained production, as well as from Condivi's assurance that he was "moderate in eating and in coitus," that the demands of art left little time and few energies for any one man or woman. Michelangelo evidently confirmed and emphasized such moderation, according to Ugo Procacci's paper "Postille contemporanee in un esemplare della vita di Michelangiolo del Condivi," delivered at the fourth centenary of the artist's death ("I have always observed it [moderation], and do thou likewise if thou wishest to lengthen your life"). Yet moderation is not the same as abstinence. Further, we know that late in life Michelangelo repented with agonising sincerity for the little sexual episodes to which we have referred. They were on his conscience when he begged for grace and feared for his salvation, appealing to Christ in words already translated above (p. 125):

> Non mirin con iustitia i tuo sant' ochi
> Il mie passato, e 'l gastigato orechio
> Non tenda a quello il tuo braccio seuero.

His confiteor rings in our ears:

> Uiuo al peccato, a me morendo uiuo! (G 32)

No, it is not Michelangelo we would score in these pages, even for a regrettable affair with a child so young. It is rather those historians, editors, translators, and biographers who even recently have closed their eyes to the obvious character of Michelangelo's sexual practices and would make of him either an ascetic or a woman's man, even to the point of bowdlerising his very words.[35] Papini's heroic effort in this direction leans on the alleged syphilis of Michelangelo; Papini sees it as a proof of Michelangelo's heterosexuality, in patent contradiction to recent studies of homosexuality which show that even in an age of antibiotics the incidence of this disease is greater among deviates than among normal men. Papini also naïvely assumes that two males must outgrow a homosexual attachment if both have reached the age of forty.

The denials, unnecessary and untenable, of Michelangelo's "virile Platonic love," merely accord it an importance which it does not deserve. As for those biographers and editors who would like to screen the facts of his life to suit their preconceptions and principles, I would refer them to a piece of advice phrased by Michelangelo himself late in his life, after he had heard many slurs on his conduct:

> He who does not wish leaves
> Let him not come around in May. (G 278)

NOTES

1 Donato Giannotti, *Dialogi* (Florence, 1939), p. 68.

2 In his edition of the *Opere di Donato Giannotti* (Florence, 1850) II, 385, F.-L. Polidori attributes to Michelangelo another quatrain of the Codice Magliabechiano:

> Il ciel, natura, e fortuna cortesi
> Mi fur d'ogni lor grazia; e farne parte
> Piu non potendo agli altri, il monde e l'arte
> Pativa: onde anzi tempe a lor le resi.

3 Vincenzo Pascale, *Michelangelo Buonarroti poeta* (Naples, 1902), p. 74.

4 Giovanni Papini, *La vita, ed. cit.*, p. 433.

5 Quoted in *Opere di Donato Giannotti, ed. cit.*, II, 382–83.

6 In Petrarch's sonnet, "Lasciato hai, Morte, senza sole il mondo."

7 For the many variants of this theme, see Leo Spitzer, "The Poetic Treatment of a Platonic-Christian Theme," *Comparative Literature*, VI, 3 (1954), 193–217.

8 See *Opere di Donato Giannotti, ed. cit.*, II, 385, and Carl Frey, *Dichtungen des Michelagniolo Buonarroti* (Berlin, 1897), p. 270.

9 Papini, *La vita, ed. cit.*, p. 435.

10 See R. J. Clements, *Michelangelo's Theory of Art, ed. cit.*, Chap. III.

11 Giorgio Vasari, *Le vite* (Florence, 1878–85), VII, 274.

12 Ascanio Condivi, *Vita di Michelangelo* (Pisa, 1823), p. 73.

13 *Le lettere di Michelangelo* (Florence, 1875), p. 534.

14 Arturo Insinga, *Michelangelo poeta* (Palermo, 1919), p. 61.

15 Papini, *La vita, ed. cit.*, p. 434.

16 Carl Frey, *Dichtungen, ed. cit.*, p. 359.

17 Ceriello edition of the *Rime*, p. 201.

18 Valerio Mariani, *La poesia di Michelangelo* (Rome, 1941), pp. 102–03.

19 See Papini, *La vita, ed. cit.*, Chap. CXVII, "L'Aretino suggeritore."

20 In *Biblioteca rara* (Milan, 1863), XII, 183 ff. See also Erika Tietze-Conrat, *Art Bulletin*, XXV (June, 1943), 156–57.

21 P. Langeard, *L'Intersexualité dans l'art et chez Michel-Ange en particulier* (Montpellier, 1936).

22 Pierre de Bouchaud, *Les poésies de Michel-Ange et de Vittoria Colonna* (Paris, 1912), p. 45.

23 Ludwig von Scheffler, *Eine Renaissance Studie* (Altenburg, 1892).

[24] Papini, *Vita*, *ed. cit.*, p. 243.
[25] G. Vasari, *Le vite*, *ed. cit.*, VII, 226.
[26] Benedetto Varchi, *Due lezzioni, nella prima delle quali si dichiara un sonetto di M. Michelagnolo Buonarroti* (Florence, 1549).
[27] Enzo Noé Girardi, "Due ignote sestine di Michelangelo," *Lettere italiane*, LI, X, 333–38.
[28] Frey, *Dichtungen*, pp. 359 ff.
[29] *Ibid.*, p. 361.
[30] D. Giannotti, *Dialogi*, *ed. cit.*, pp. 71–72.
[31] Antonio Mini sold in France many copies of the *Leda* and simple Menighella sold to the peasants of the Valdarno many *santons* (figurines) of Saints Francis, Anthony, and Rocco designed for him by Michelangelo.
[32] In Guasti's edition of the *Rime* (Florence, 1863), p. xlv.
[33] F.-L. Polidori, in *Opere di Donato Giannotti*, *ed. cit.*, II, 384.
[34] Guasti edition, p. xlv.
[35] In reviewing Irving Stone's edition of the letters (*I Michelangelo, Sculptor*) in the New York *Times* on 26 August, 1962, I wrote:

"Thus in an outburst to Febo 'Although you bear me most great hatred, I know not why; I do not believe that it is for the love I bear you, but because of others' gossip, *which you should not believe, having put me to the test; I just can't help writing you this*,' the words in italics are excised. In a most revealing document to Cecchino's uncle Del Riccio, Stone emulates Michelangelo the Younger and suggests that Michelangelo's 'idol' may be a woman. Another letter to Del Riccio is bowdlerised by dropping the last significant reference to Cecchino. The letter to Gherardo Perini is cut almost in half, without deletions indicated. Etc."

In reviewing Creighton Gilbert's *Complete Poems and Selected Letters of Michelangelo* in the *Saturday Review* on 6 July, 1963, I wrote:

"[His attitude on Michelangelo's sexuality] prompts Gilbert to omit two significant letters to Del Riccio (1542) . . . It leads to a mistranslation of a verse in which Cecchino reminisces on his 'lovers.' Gilbert launders this into 'loves.' After the reader has read two revealing poems to young Febo di Poggio (not annotated), he has a right to a less cryptic explanation of a love letter addressed to this *mignon* than 'Who Febo di Poggio was is not known.' "

In reviewing Miss Ramsden's *The Letters of Michelangelo* for the New York *Times* on 19 January, 1964, I wrote:

"In the incriminating letter to Febo di Poggio [September, 1534] the word *amore* is skittishly changed to 'affection.' [Where] Michelangelo characterises himself and Luigi del Riccio as 'men without discretion,' Ramsden bowdlerises this to 'without distinction.' Etc."

Note: In the Archivio di State, Rome, I find an entry of 6, 7, or 8 January, 1544, in a volume of the Visite dei Chirurghi: "Magister Antonino barbierus in Campo Florum declaravit medicavisse Francescum [Pastiriensem?] vulneratum in naso subitantem per murallum Campi Florum in grandis aii." A cross (deceased) was added in the left margin. Whether this clarifies Cecchino's sudden death depends on further study of the indistinct patronym or toponym in question.

7

THE "LOST" POEM ON THE BRONZE DAVID AND THE SCHOLIUM ON THE DAVIDS

IN THE YEAR 1650 Henri Chesneau, poet, advocate, and retainer of Messire Charles, Marquis et Comte de Rostaing, brought out a volume entitled *Bury Rostaing,* whose principal objective was to exalt the dynasty of Florimond de Robertet ("le Grand"), Baron d'Alluye, de Bury, et de Brou, and great-grandfather of Messire Charles on his maternal side. An important section of *Bury Rostaing* consisted of an inventory of the furnishings and art objects present in the Château de Bury shortly after the death of Florimond (1527).[1] As only one known copy of *Bury Rostaing* has survived in recent times, the possessor of that copy, Eugène Grésy, felt that this defective impression of 266 pages and thirteen *planches,* with its faulty pagination and penned corrigenda, was never given a full press run. Since both the original inventory and Chesneau's reprint of it in *Bury Rostaing* had vanished, with the exception of the unique copy mentioned, Grésy proceeded to publish the census in the *Mémoires de la Société Impériale des Antiquaires de France* of 1868, prefacing the text with a statement on Chesneau's relations with the Robertets but leaving many questions still to be posed concerning the inventory.[2] As Chesneau claimed, the cataloguer probably was Florimond's widow, Mme. Michelle Gaillard de Longjumeau, since the compiler not only lists the objects but usually supplies detailed explanations about their provenience as well. The year to which Chesneau attributes the inventory is 1532, a dating which is at the core of the "Ronsard-Michelangelo problem" posed in this chapter.

After Veuve Robertet has made a careful perquisition of the jewels, furnishings, tapestries, paintings, and other treasures of Bury, she arrives at length at the marble and bronze statues. Three of these are of particular significance, since she alleged that Pierre de Ronsard composed a poem on the figure of Porcia, daughter of Cato Uticensis and wife of Brutus, and on the figure of Ptolemy, King of Egypt, while translating a Michelangelo stanza which accompanied the bronze *David*. The background of this claim, and its reliability, must be examined.

As is known, Michelangelo's bronze *David* was executed on commission for Pierre de Rohan, Maréchal de Gié and powerful favorite of Louis XII. After Rohan's headlong fall from royal favor in 1504, when the statue was still unfinished in Florence, his fellow councillor of state, Florimond Robertet—who could have given Machiavelli lessons on how to stay at the helm of government during one reign after another—maneuvered to procure the statue for himself. In 1509 he set it up in his Hôtel d'Alluye at Blois and shortly thereafter had it placed on a pedestal in the center of the courtyard of his recently completed familial castle, the Château de Bury. That it remained there for many years is known, for it is visible in the elevation of the château and gardens drawn by Jacques Androuet du Cerceau in 1576.[3] Veuve Robertet's inventory tells us that there were several lines in Italian at the base of the statue, inscribed by Michelangelo himself. The census reads, "Et faisons aussi beaucoup d'estat des vers Italiens que Michel-Ange, statuaire de ce chef-d'œuvre, fit graver au pied d'estal et que le sçavant Ronsard a traduicts en ce sens:

> Moy David en moins de trois pas,
> Que je fis devant tout le monde,
> Je mis Goliat au trespas
> D'un seul juste coup de ma fronde,
> Et de ma harpe je fis voir
> Qu'avec la charmante Muzique
> L'on repousse tout le pouvoir
> De la ruse diabolique.[4]

There is no echo of Michelangelo's many poems in Ronsard's published works, nor of his art. Other references to David in Ronsard's poetry concern the later years of the Hebrew hero, as king, the mature figure who appears so inconspicuously among the *antenati* of Christ on the Sistine Vault. No mention is made of the young liberator and singer of songs.

An inconsistency is to be explained away if this translation is to be attributed to Ronsard, who was born 11 September, 1524. The inventory containing these poems was said by Chesneau to have been compiled by the widow Robertet on 4 August, 1532. One's immediate conclusion, as was that of my old master Paul Laumonier,[5] is that these stanzas could not have come from the pen of Ronsard. This conclusion occurred also to Grésy, who wrote in a footnote that Ronsard "n'aurait eu que huit ans lorsqu'il composa ce sixain inédit." Indeed, he had not yet reached his eighth birthday. Although accepting the date of 1532 as accurate and noting the chronological dilemma, Grésy expressed no surprise that Madame Robertet could have known of Ronsard's existence in that year or that she could have felt gratification over a poem translated "a few days ago" by Ronsard. Obviously the poems and consequently the inventory in its published version are of a later date, when the "young gentleman Pierre de Ronsard" had established some degree of reputation (and had learned some Italian). That moment could not have preceded 1550, the year of the first *Odes et Bocage.* Since the date of 1532 falls under suspicion, only two explanations are possible. First, Madame Robertet's census was definitively composed or terminated about 1550. Second, Chesneau or some knowledgeable third party between 1532 and 1550 embroidered upon the text of the inventory before it was edited. Since the original manuscript has been lost, there is no way of verifying which of these explanations is the more likely. If either one of them is valid, then we are possibly in the presence of a translation by Ronsard. If neither explanation is valid, the purported translation from Michelangelo is not by Ronsard, but the original inscription preceding the translation loses none of its interest for the light it sheds upon Michelangelo's attitude toward one of his finest creations.

For the moment, let us assume with the record that it was Ronsard who did this translation. The imagination and boldness of Michelangelo's inventions and *concetti* could have well appealed to Ronsard, for it was by this criterion that Du Bellay, who knew something of both men (he frequented the Palazzo Farnese when Michelangelo was putting a new cornice on it) found Ronsard and Michelangelo kindred spirits.[6] From the chronology of his friendships with the descendants of the great Florimond Robertet, Ronsard could have frequented the Château de Bury, the Hôtel d'Alluye, and other properties of the family from about 1550 to 1569, year of the death of Robertet d'Alluye. In the *Nouvelles poésies* of 1563 the grandson and great-nephew respectively of Florimond le Grand, the Baron Florimond Robertet d'Alluye and Robertet Seigneur de Fresne, appear in a pastoral as Aluyot and Fresnet. In this same year Ronsard dedicated *Hymnes* ("Hymne du printemps" and "Hymne de l'esté") to these same friends.[7] The durability of Ronsard's affection for the Robertet family is shown as late as 1584 in an ode where he replaces the name of Revergat with the name of Robertet de Fresne.[8]

Whereas the *David* was still standing in the courtyard in 1576, as Du Cerceau attests, the château itself was permitted by the family to fall into disrepair and ruin within a hundred years, thus serving as an unhappy demonstration of Ronsard's prediction about those who lavish money on castles:

> Qu'à la fin leurs châteaux trebucheront à bas,
> Et qu'en moins de cent ans leurs races incognues
> Se traineront sans nom par les tourbes menues.[9]

The fact that we no longer have the bronze *David* or the original autograph of the census against which to check Ronsard's poetry illustrates another text of Ronsard:

> Mais Dieu ne le veut pas, qui couvre soubz la terre
> Tant de livres perdus, naufrages de la guerre,
> Tant d'ars laborieux.[10]

The Renaissance was the period which saw the *ut pictura poesis* expand from an obscure and restricted five lines in Horace to a quasi-philosophical dictum of the unified aims and processes of painting and poetry. Many a poet was imitating or modeling verse upon contemporary painting and sculpture. Italy furnished such poets in Jacopus Sadoletus, Giovanni Strozzi, Giovambattista Zappi, and eventually Marino. Spain offered the examples of Venegas de Saavedra, Soto de Rojas, and others. It would be pleasant to think that the Frenchman Ronsard lent the prestige of his name to this endeavor, even as translator.

Let us now assume, however, that it was not Ronsard, but a later poet (or poetess) attached to the Robertet family who did the translation under question. As suggested above, the translation from Michelangelo remains of utmost importance to the student of the fine arts, whether it was done by some prince of poets or some lesser rhymer lost in oblivion, perhaps even by Chesneau, who dabbled in verse (see below) and was coincidentally fond of the octosyllabic line.

First of all, were the Italian verses at the base of the bronze *David* written by Michelangelo, as the inventory attests, or by someone else? This question occurred to the student of Michelangelo, Anatole de Montaiglon. "Il pouvait y avoir des vers italiens sur la base de la colonne sans qu'ils fussent pour cela de Michel-Ange."[11] The inscription would not have been found on the column, by the way, but rather on the base of the dado at the foot of the statue and crowning the column; the underpinning marble column seen in the Du Cerceau drawing did not in fact come from Italy with the bronze, since it was agreed that no *fornimento* would be sent.[12] If an Italian poem by someone other than Michelangelo was inscribed on the dado, it would be unique among Buonarroti's productions and certainly done without his knowledge or consent.

It is difficult to confirm or deny the presence of a poem by Michelangelo on the dado or base of this lost *David*. There is no mention of such a poem or inscription in the vast literature on Michelangelo or in the various published collections of his *Rime*. Yet such a poem probably existed. To begin with, there is the general reliability of the inventory set up in the Robertet family, descendants of Florimond Robertet, a man so powerful in France that, in the words of Commynes, he governed the country in the name of his monarchs. Then, too, it was in keeping with Michelangelo's practice to set down a poem lending the gift of speech to one of his statues. As this volume has shown, the stone effigies of Night, of Day, of Cecchino de' Bracci, and an unidentified stone brought down unwillingly from its mountain (G 275) possess such a gift. The whole concept of living, breathing, and talking stone was dear to Buonarroti.[13]

That Michelangelo planned at the very outset to have such a poem—akin to the 48 or 49 quatrains he penned for Cecchino's tomb—accompany this bronze statue may be adduced from the curious distich accompanying the Louvre pen sketch of the bronze *David* and the right arm of the marble *David:*

Dauicte cholla fromba
E io choll'archo (G App. 3)

The word *archo* has been variously interpreted as force, intelligence, effort, or the longtime labor which bent Michelangelo's back "like a Syrian bow" (G 5). The piece "Socto duo belle ciglia" (G 131) suggests the meaning of virile or youthful force, for here he defines old age as "la stagion, che sprezzo l'arco e l'ale."

The inventory which finally appeared in *Bury Rostaing* may help to clarify this mysterious scholium. Around 1502, the date assigned to the distich and signature, Michelangelo must have toyed with the idea of placing on the base of the bronze *David* not only his signature or name but also an inscription or strophe establishing the personal relationship between himself and this figure. The intimate rapport existing between the artist and the work of art was a real thing which he heralded in his poems. Heretofore Michelangelo had placed his name, but nothing more, on his creations (e.g., the *Madonna della Febbre*). We assume that he intended his inscription growing out of the scholium to accompany the bronze *David* rather than the marble "giant" (represented by only an arm), since we learn from Vasari and others that the marble *David* was conceived by the municipal authorities as having an exclusively civic symbolism, a meaning upon which an intrusive inscription of a personal nature would have trespassed. The bronze *David*, done for a private (and distant) patron, could tolerate such a personal stanza. It is possible to suppose then that the distich on the Louvre sketches is actually a perfect hendecasyllabic line and was to be part of a poem heralding his statue and identifying himself as an artist and servant of God. The length of the inscription in her courtyard is not revealed by Madame Robertet or her compilers, and the translation into French need not be conclusive or even informative on this point, since the Renaissance definition of imitation or translation ran the gamut from transverbalisation to the most free and loose *innutrition*. Michelangelo, for example, never adopted the octosyllabic line suggested by the translation, even though it was common enough to Ronsard and his school. One may conclude from the French version that the first product of Michelangelo's afflatus (the Louvre jotting) metamorphosed into a poem differing from his original intention, as happened so often with his sculpture—a poem from which he withdrew mention of himself as an alter ego of David and let the young and triumphant son of Jesse speak only of himself. The *arco* of the scholium then can become *arco* in the sense of harp-frame (as Michelangelo the Younger claimed), and the parallels *fromba/fronde* and *arco/harpe* result. The original theme of David's spiritual and physical strength is retained; mention of his prowess as a musician is introduced. The addition of the element of music, although it had no part in the ideation of the statue, was not foreign to Michelangelo, many of whose madrigals were set to music and who numbered musicians among his acquaintances.

This emergence of the expanding personality of David in the metamorphosed Italian poem, with the attendant crowding out of Michelangelo, coincides with David's increasingly dominant ego as the conception of the statue itself evolved. In its final stage of evolution (if one accepts Du Cerceau's drawing) the figure is informed with the triumphant and dominant note of the lines translated into French, for unlike the conceptions of the Louvre sketch or the callow "giant" in the corner spandrel of the Sistine Ceiling, this David holds aloft "devant tout le monde" the head of Goliath. Michelangelo has progressed far beyond Donatello, Verrocchio, and Ghirlandaio, whose Davids poised a foot on Goliath's head. As for the details of the transformation of the distich (or hendecasyllable) into the longer translated poems, or the motivations behind these detailed changes, it is useless to contrive hypotheses from the available data.

Our chance to verify the precise nature of this transformation leading to the Italian verses at the base of the bronze *David* disappeared by 1650, when Henri Chesneau penned his poetic description of the Château de Bury:

> Autrefois dans cet endroict même
> Il y avait un beau David,
> Mais tout-à-coup l'on le ravit
> A cause de son prix extresme . . .
> Tant il est d'une heureuse fonte.[14]

In 1650 Chesneau thus refers to the quality of the bronze in the present tense. We know that the masterpiece was removed to the Château de Villeroy at Mennecy and had disappeared from that location by mid-century. With it went our last hopes of verifying that Michelangelo Buonarroti brought to full articulation his hermetic thought about David and his sling.

A footnote concerning the David-Michelangelo identity may be permitted. Leone Leoni did a medal of Michelangelo at eighty-eight years, picturing the aged artist, a rosary in his hand, following a dog with the aid of a staff. The motto expressing Michelangelo's sense of artistic mission reads: "Docebo iniquos ut te impii ad te convertantur." The words are from David's psalm, chosen, as Mariani supposes, by Michelangelo himself.[15]

NOTES

1 Two French and one Spanish encyclopaedia set this date at 1522, a date disproved by Robertet's role after Pavia and by available correspondence: *Lettres de Marguerite d'Angoulême* (Paris, 1841), where Robertet is wished a long and happy life in 1525.

2 Eugène Grésy, "Inventaire des objets d'art comprenant la succession de Florimond Robertet, ministre de François Ier dressé par sa veuve," *Mémoires de la Société Impériale des Antiquaires de France*, 3e série, X (Paris, 1868), 1–66.

3 J. A. Du Cerceau, *Les Plus Excellents Bâtiments de France* (1576), p. 125.

4 Laumonier-Lemerre edition of Ronsard, *Oeuvres complètes* (Paris, 1914–19), VI, 511.

5 *Ibid.*, p. 508.

6 Joachim du Bellay, *Oeuvres* (Paris, 1931), VI, 508.

7 Pierre de Ronsard, *Oeuvres complètes* (Paris, S. T. F. M., 1946), XII, 27, 35.

8 Paul Laumonier, *Ronsard poète lyrique* (Paris, 1923), p. 131.

9 Ronsard, *Oeuvres complètes* (Paris, S. T. F. M., 1935), VIII, 292, variant of 1587.

10 *Ibid.*, VIII, 357.

11 Anatole de Montaiglon, *Gazette des beaux-arts*, 2e série, XIII (1876), 245.

12 Charles de Tolnay, *Youth of Michelangelo* (Princeton, 1943), p. 207.

13 Michelangelo, as we have seen, alludes often to such conceits as the "Pietra viva," "figure vive," "immagini vive," etc. See the Frey edition of the poetry, pp. 157, 194, 480, etc.

14 Grésy, *op. cit.*, p. 64.

15 Valerio Mariani, *La poesia di Michelangelo* (Rome, 1941), p. 147.

8

ICONOGRAPHY AND ALLEGORY IN THE RIME

IN HIS ESSAY "Michelangelo poeta" Arturo Farinelli made one of his debatable if challenging generalisations: "Allegory was for him, as for Dante, a poetic coefficient, most valid in its ideas and never cold fiction. In the abstract world he sees luminously all that we see in the real world."[1] It is true that Michelangelo saw art as abstraction and subjects as *typoi* and thus was hardly concerned when his Medici Dukes and his Virgin in St. Peter's were criticised as not realistic or when Aretino cried out against his beardless Christ. Indeed, various of his works were spoken of as allegories. In his lifetime he was admired for informing his *concetti* or symbols with broad philosophical messages. Thus, one reads the pseudo-Aretino's claim in Dolce's *Dialogo della Pittura:*[2]

FABRIZIO: As for the composition of the story, I don't know whether Michelangelo has to cede to Raphael; rather I hold the contrary, that is, that Michelangelo vanquishes him easily, for I have heard that in the order of his stupendous *Judgement* there are contained certain most profound allegorical meanings, which are understood by few.

ARETINO: In this he would deserve praise, since it would appear that he had imitated those great philosophers who hid under the veil of poesy the major mysteries of philosophy.

Certainly the aim of Michelangelo's *concetto* was to contain a density of meaning, an aim carried over to his concentrated poetry. As for iconographical trappings, which were usual to guide the spectator or reader toward the inner meaning, Michelangelo was no more addicted to these than were his fellow artists. In his *Fall of Phaeton,* the river Eridanus becomes a reclining old man, and only a few wavy lines around him identify him as a river-god. Indeed, Michelangelo's fascination with basic form and minimal representation tended to make him disinterested in loading his figures with external symbols conveying additional meaning or identification. Such gratuitous emblems (the horns of the *Mosè*, the owl of the *Notte*) as he added have provoked lively discussion. Scholars have delved into Horapollo, Cartarus, Ripa, and other iconological source manuals available in his time to explain these incremental meanings of his works, from the tiniest fragment to the entire expanse of the Sistine Vault, viewed by De Tolnay as a Platonic *ascensio*.

Michelangelo used allegorical detail as sparingly in his poetry as he did in his painting and sculpture. One of his allegorical poems, vaguely Dantean, was composed *circa* 27 April, 1522. Allegorical forces which make an ordeal for the poet are sea, mountain, fire, and sword. Michelangelo starts to explain them, but does not get beyond the "mountain" comparable to the "dilettoso monte" of the *Commedia*.

A thousand remedies the soul tries out in vain:
Since I was taken from my pristine road,
It has argued in vain how to get me back on the path.
The sea and the mountain and the fire with the sword—
Amid all these I go on living.
He who has deprived me of my intellect and taken my reason
Will not let me ascend the mountain. (G 18)

The sword reappears in his angry sonnet to Julius II ("Signor, se uero è") (G 6) in which the poet regrets that the pontiff has not put his trust in the honest scales and the powerful sword of Justice rather than in the voice of rumor, here allegorised as Echo.

Any discussion of Michelangelo's allegorical bent must consider the dialogue between a Florentine exile and the allegorised City of Florence, "Per molti, Donna, anzi per mille amanti" (G 249). Florence, already emblematised elsewhere as a "precious jewel" (G 71), is here personified as a damsel "d'angelica forma" in the grip of a tyrant. The only human physical attributes specifically given to this allegorical figure are sun-filled eyes and the gift of speech. However, as the patient but firm figure gives reassurance to the exile that she will never be possessed completely by the Medici Dukes, one understands that Michelangelo views her as a sister of the heroic Esther and Judith of the Sistine Ceiling. One also comprehends that these heroines of Hebrew history are allegories of civic virtue, compared by Ollivier to Charlotte Corday. Indeed, the assurance of Florence that while times look bleak the future holds promise suggests the violent retribution executed by Judith and Brutus, two figures of particular interest to Michelangelo.

Another female figure is apparently utilised as an allegory of art itself, just as Michelangelo in the *Diálogos em Roma* views the essential art of design as Dame Painting.

Thus, she decides,
Untamed and savage woman,
That I should burn, die, and fall,
Seeking a favor weighing not even an ounce,
While she drains my blood
Pound by pound from my veins and fibers,
And disarranges my soul and body,
There she enjoys herself and primps
At her looking glass,
In which she sees herself equal to paradise.
Then, turning to me, she settles me properly,
For beyond being old, my aged face
Makes her mirrored face more comely,
Whence I am all the more derided
For my ugliness: and yet it is a boon to me,
If in making her beautiful, I am defeating nature. (G 172)

In this madrigal (1541–44), a contribution by Michelangelo to the contemporary discussions of the relative formative importance of art and nature, the artist is depicted looking into a mirror alongside a harsh woman who torments him. Michelangelo's ugliness merely enhances her heavenly beauty. And yet, as artist, he considers it his good fortune to defeat nature in making her thus more beautiful. The harsh and exacting demands of the lady correspond to the demands laid upon the artist by his profession, demands of which he complained constantly. There are several elements in the poem which justify our accepting it not merely at the foot of the letter, but rather as allegory. The passion and torments to which the lady Art subjects him, the blood which leaves his veins and fibers, and the ruthlessness with which she throws body and soul out of joint—these complaints remind us of Michelangelo's pained outcries elsewhere; "Nelle opere mie caco sangue" (reported in Chantelou's *Journal du voyage du Cavalier Bernin*) and "Non vi si pensa quanto sangue costa" (G App. 40), copied from Dante. The three verses dwelling upon the lady's speculation seem a tribute to the inherent mimetic nature of art which imitates the finest archetypes of nature. Michelangelo's insistence upon his own ugliness and old age, both of which are betrayals nature has visited on him personally (compare also "betrayed by the mirror" in G 51), makes him exult all the more that as artist he can defeat nature.

The most striking use of iconographical figures is, of course, in Michelangelo's *Stanze in lode della vita rusticale* ("Nuouo piacere e di magiore stima") (G 67). This curious poem of 1534–36 hails the simple pleasures of country life and the unambitious, unspoiled character of the husbandman. It adumbrates the praises of bucolic living contained in Michelangelo's letter of 1556 from Spoleto, where he had gone to take the waters and to share the retreat of the monks. The stanzas divide into two major sections. The first describes the pastoral life of country folk, untroubled by the artificialities and insatieties of city life. The second presents a series of allegorical figures parallel to those found in the emblem books and repertories of iconology. These figures are emblematic of the virtues attendant upon country life and the vices which infest the cities. Some, but not all, of the figures are presented in detail: clothing, trappings, general attitude, and even coloration, precisions one finds in Cesare Ripa's *Iconologia* and other sources. The allegories introduced and depicted are respectively: Wealth, Poverty, Doubt, *Perchè* (Why), *Come* (How), *Forse* (Perchance), Truth, Falsity, Hypocrisy, and Adulation. Three other figures (Fraud, Discord, and Lying) are mentioned but not described.

It has been alleged that Michelangelo was influenced in this curious list by Politian's *Stanze per la giostra,* the same sequences which furnished Botticelli with the scene of his *Birth of Venus.* This claim is weakened by the fact that the allegorical figures in Politian never once duplicate those in Michelangelo's stanzas and moreover are never described or amplified.[3] Politian's figures seem closer to those in the Italian poem by Vellutello which lay behind the French *Carte du tendre.* It could be added that the roster of allegorical figures described or mentioned by Michelangelo corresponded more fully to the pages of iconographical manuals than did the more unusual allegorising of Politian.

In this particular instance one may agree with Insinga that Michelangelo's allegories are of the mind rather than the heart, without accepting Insinga's conclusion that this weakens and obscures his poetry. Insinga attributes to Michelangelo's allegories, whose number he exaggerates, the difficulties which we elsewhere attribute to the artist's poetic style. "It was said also that many of his rimes are obscure, as if distilled in the bitter joy of remaining enigmatic, but this derives merely from the symbol or allegory or the awkward use of metaphorical language which spoil their clarity . . . If the expression becomes conceptual, then the thought belongs to the intellect, whereas poetry, that is image, belongs to the heart."[4]

One must not confound allegory and conceptual language. The first is rare in Michelangelo and the second plentiful. Nor should we confuse allegories with mythological figures, which also are rare; the poetry has a bare handful of references to Medusa, Daedalus, Pygmalion, phoenixes, and salamanders, but these are not cultivated as allegorical symbols.

In the interest of establishing Michelangelo's inventiveness, let us examine the figures depicted in the *Stanze in lode della vita rusticale* and see to what extent Michelangelo exhibited or disregarded the iconographical texts at his command.

The first of the figures to appear is Wealth, clad in gems, but "of fearful air," for money does not bring happiness.[5]

> Every wind, every rain saddens her,
> And auguries and prodigies.

Poverty, on the other hand, is happy and carefree, satisfying easily her simple wants, dressed in rustic simplicity, and "free from obligations, cares, and lawsuits."

The next figure in the procession is Doubt (*el Dubbio*):

> Doubt armed and lame is pictured,
> Hopping here and there like the locust,
> Trembling constantly as by his nature,
> Just as a swamp reed shakes under the wind.

The poet has already stated that doubt and uncertainty never trouble the simple and honest husbandman, whose faith is simple and sure, who adores God and who, through prayer, bends heaven's and God's will to his purpose. These graphic lines form an interesting parallel to Michelangelo's powerful sonnet "Vorrei uoler, Signior, quel ch'io non uoglio" (see page 295) in which he compares doubt to a sheet of ice which intervenes between God and the aspiring heart, compromising the soul's chances of receiving grace.

The next allegory the poet describes is Why (*il Perchè*), already an original title for an iconographical figure, which figures are nearly always identified by a generic noun. Even more original, however, is the figure itself, viewed as a lean night watchman or *sereno* with a large assortment of keys:

> The figure Why is lean and round his waist
> Bears many keys, but not the right ones
> Able to fit the keyholes of the door,
> Escorted by darkness, he wanders about the night.

Here the value of night is not that found in the sonnets on night—time of repose and release/time of anguish and restlessness/all-enveloping time withal fragile/(see Chapter V)—nor yet the value expressed in the letter criticising the design of St. Peter's by Sangallo (time of skullduggery and impregnating of nuns). Night here is more clearly a symbol of ignorance (the *épaisse nuit* of Rabelais), as is darkness itself. The difficulty of obtaining the right answers in life, of a moral or a scientific order, and the attendant false keys which resemble the right one, this is the meaning of this curious figure. Michelangelo, who late in life told a cardinal who met him en route to the Coliseum that he was "going to school," who cried on his deathbed that he had only begun to learn the alphabet of his profession, and especially the Michelangelo who groped for the truth and conviction which would earn him salvation, as the poems attest, this is the man who knew how difficult it was to find the key to knowledge.

Michelangelo's *Perchè* is closer than is his congener Doubt to the figure of doubt imagined in Ripa's *Iconologia:* "Un giovanetto senza barba, in mezzo alle tenebre, vestite di cangiante. In una mano tenga un bastone, nell' altra una lanterna, e stia col piede sinistro in fuori, per segno di camminare."[6] This armed man, wandering the dark streets, has a kinship to Michelangelo's figure.

Come and *Forse* (How and Perchance) are equally curious names for allegorical figures, already allowing us to conclude that Michelangelo's iconography was original.

> He has two close of kin, How and Perhaps,
> Who giants are of such a height
> That each to attain the sun seems to delight,
> Even when blinded on gazing at its splendor,
> Whatever parts of cities their proud frames cast in shadow
> Are robbed altogether of what beauty they possess.
> They pick their way over steep and twisted roads, through rocks,
> Testing with their hands which is the most solid.

The poem soars from the deep obscurity of night and ignorance to the blinding brilliance of the sun. How and Perhaps are related not only to each other, but also to Why. Their stature places them near the sun of truth, but they cannot look directly at it. Principally associated with cities, they cast the cities into the same shadow in which they prefer to live. They seek out difficulties, twisted roads paved with rocky obstacles, and advance by groping. Is it significant that these figures are giants whereas lean Why is an allegory of insignificant stature? Apparently, How and Perhaps assume larger proportions in the life of the city.

This is the moment to examine Michelangelo's curious preoccupation with giants. Giants had always assumed an importance in his thinking. He had hoped in 1505 to carve a colossus out of a mountain top overlooking the Tyrrhenian Sea. The first figure to win him prominence was called the Giant by the Florentines. In another of Michelangelo's fragmentary poems, whose verse pattern and date of composition is the same as in these *Stanze*, two giants are described who are evidently allegorical figures. Indeed, some have felt, as did Guasti, that this fragment should be printed in juxtaposition to the *Stanze*.[7] The description of the first (male) giant does not include any moral attributes:

> Still there is a giant, of such great height,
> That his eyes cannot make us out here below.
> Many times has he kicked over and crushed
> An entire city as he set his foot down.
> He aspires to the sun, and towers crumble underfoot

> As he tries to reach the sky, which he cannot see,
> For this tremendous and robust body of his
> Has but one eye, and that set on a heel.

Here again is a towering allegorical figure who does harm to the cities, who thrusts to the sun and heavens without being able to see them, his one eye set along the ground:

> This earthbound eye sees things past,
> Even as he holds his head up firm and close to the stars,
> It would take us two days down here to see
> The strides of his great legs, and hairy is his skin.
> Around his upper regions there is no winter or summer,
> For to him all the seasons are equal and fine.
> And as heaven itself is level with his forehead
> Down on earth his feet tread every mountain flat.

An eye on his heel, he has only hindsight. He towers above even the seasons, since his head attains the heavens.

> As to us are grains of sand,
> So are mountains underfoot to him.
> Within the thick hair of his limbs he carries
> Diverse forms, monstrous and huge.
> Therein a whale but a mere fly would seem,
> And yet he is troubled or saddened, or weeps
> Only when the wind against his single eye doth blast
> Smoke or straw or spinning dust.

Michelangelo becomes fascinated with the same relativity which amused Swift and Voltaire in composing *Micromégas*. To the allegorical giant a whale is a mere fly. Yet size alone is not an advantage, a lesson he derived so fully from the parable of David and Goliath that he executed young David three times (see Chapter VII). There is no agreement over the identity of this giant, further described below as arrogant, bold, and blind. Michelangelo the Younger viewed him as a symbol of Furor. Augusto Conti saw him as "Pride which soars to the stars but sees not God, its heart being earthbound and only earthly things delight or sadden it." The giant could easily represent over-weening pride, indeed, exhibited all over Rome and thus a city vice.

Michelangelo, like the God of the Sistine Vault, decided that his creation should be accompanied by a mate. However, there are two alternate descriptions of her. A first stanza remained incomplete:

> A lady he has with him as his chosen helpmate
> To whom he has recourse in every state of fright;
> When the mighty Jove thunders and hurls his bolts,

> Within her arms alone is he reassured.
> This woman swears to him to take vengeance
> If hail and storms overrun the earth.

The comforting and dominating woman who serves as refuge for her consort during the storms of life is an amusing concept in Michelangelo, who never viewed woman as man's better half. So unlikely is this creation, even as an allegorical figure (Augusto Conti thought her a symbol of Cruelty, despite her generosity and loyalty), that Michelangelo replaced this giantess by another, much less attractive one who understandably reminds Girardi of giantesses in Lorenzo's *Selva Seconda,* strophes 39 and 67.

> With him he has a lazy and slovenly wife,
> Whose breast feeds this horrible figure
> And to her arrogant, bold, and blind husband
> Feeds pride and gives him confidence.
> She stays apart from him in a narrow grotto,
> Within great rocks and behind tall walls,
> Even when he is idle, she dwells in shadow
> And alone casts her spells, impoverishing the people.

This counterpart of the *Madonna che allatta il Figlio* (Vienna, Albertina) or of the gigantic grotto-dwelling Sibyls affords a nightmare-like portrait. In addition to serving as a refuge for her giant spouse (as did the first giantess above), she exercises powers over mankind akin to those of a pagan goddess. Her prescription of poverty has led to her being identified as Avarica, a figure already alluded to in the *Stanze.* However, it is clear that both of these variant female allegories represent a sinister power alien to and effective against the wrath of Jove-Jehovah and a succor to the blind and headstrong arrogance of those who oppose the Gods. (These, in Michelangelo's mind, could include Daedalus, Tityus, Phaeton, Adam, among others.) Thus, she represents a Force for Evil.

As further described, she is more fearsome than the seeresses on the Sistine Vault:

> Pallid and yellow she: and in her grave womb
> She bears the sign of her lord alone.
> She thrives on others' ills, weakens at their well-being.
> Nor is she ever sated, though feeding at all hours.
> Her evil course will ne'er be slackened or stayed.
> Incapable of inciting love, she hates all others.
> Her heart is of stone, her arms of iron.
> Into her belly she gulps mountains and sea alike.

This Eva-Pandora who has given birth to the seven sins is already hatching further evils for the world, sired by the same evil father. Her insatiable appetite is that of a woman who will give birth to huge progeny. Indeed, her entire future will consist of creating more Sins, for her course is unalterable and relentless. Her womb is vast and will teem endlessly.

A final stanza in this sequence relates the past curse inflicted upon mankind by these dread giants: the creation of the Seven Deadly Sins.

> Seven of their first-born wander over the earth,
> Seeking to the reaches of the two poles,
> And war and plot only against the righteous:
> And a thousand members has each one of these.
> The eternal abyss opens and closes for them,
> Such prey do they take from the universal throng.
> And their members slowly clasp around us
> As ivy from rock to rock overruns a wall. (G 68)

Godless pride then is at the origin of the seven sins, just as the ancient Greeks saw *hybris* as the major hamartia. The seven deadly sins, if we are to believe Vasari, were represented by Michelangelo in the *Giudizio universale*[8] as devils pulling souls down to the pit of hell. Two salient points about these are deplorable: their quick dissemination from pole to pole and the thought, expressed so often elsewhere (see Chapter XVIII), that people who try hardest to succeed or to be most worthy encounter the greatest resistance.

The architect who dislikes external nature and foliage, particularly when they attack stone and marble, seizes upon spreading ivy as an image of annoying velocity. At last the *moi haïssable* crops out, the referent (*ci* = us) becomes personal rather than impersonal ("il popolo," "altrui," "universal stuolo"). Michelangelo implicates himself finally, just as he finally imposed his self-portrait on his paintings and statues. The facility with which the seven sins attack him is regretted in those confessional verses where he cries, "Viuo al pechato! . . ." (G 32). The eternal abyss is waiting for the pelt of Michelangelo just as it awaits the "universal throng" in the Book of the Damned.

The curious series of strophes with its vast sweep from lofty heaven to the lowest abyss invites comparison with the contrasting planes of the *Giudizio universale*. The tableau is not Christian, however, in spirit or iconography. It is, most of all, a visionary product of Michelangelo's fascination with gigantism, not to forget his personal concern about salvation.

Let us turn from giants, however, back to the *Stanze in lode della vita rusticale*. After the depiction of *Come* and *Forse*, Michelangelo proceeds to the depiction of one of the most common allegorical figures in the Renaissance, *Veritas:*[9]

> Poor and nude Truth goes about alone,
> Who is so prized among the humble folk,
> Only one eye he has, shining and clear.

His body is of gold and of diamond his heart.
In troubles he grows in stature and becomes lofty,
If he is stamped out in one place, he is reborn in a thousand.
And is with his faithful followers constant and solid.

First of all, one is struck by the initial verse, which seems a recollection of Petrarch's depiction of Philosophy, poor, nude, and alone:

—Povera e nuda vai, Filosofia? . . .
Pochi compagni avrai per l'altra via.

The nudity of Truth was conventional enough. As Panofsky writes, "It is evident that Alberti already imagined Truth as a naked figure of the 'Venus Pudica' type, as she appears in Botticelli's Uffizi panel and many other paraphrases and representations of the Calumny theme. Thus the figure of *nuda Veritas* became one of the most popular personifications in Renaissance and Baroque art."[10] The single eye, which puzzled us on the heel of the giant above, here is understandably the earnest that there is only one true way to look at a thing. The other attributes of Truth in this stanza are clear enough; truth like silence is golden (and rare), truth is stonily objective, truth cannot be stifled, but will keep breaking out faster than dragon's teeth, truth is flourishing like ivy or laurel and shows its external color.

Michelangelo breaks with the Renaissance iconographical tradition (of Alciati) in making *Veritas* or *Aletheia,* obviously feminine figures, into masculine (*vero*). This is consonant with his preference for male figures and his recourse to male models for the execution of female subjects. Throughout this parade of figures, as the reader will have noticed, Michelangelo's preference is for masculine symbols.

If Truth has but one eye, Falseness has two, two "honest eyes cast modestly down." Overdressed in "gold and varicolored raiment" (see p. 75), Falsehood goes about making war only on just men. Here Michelangelo expresses two of his deepest convictions: his disdain for the rich clothing and trappings of the Venetian school and his scorn for the raiments of "clothing mannequins." Clothing itself is a falsifying of the nude body, the "velame di Dio." Ripa's *Falsità,* a female figure, is also "superbamente vestita." Michelangelo's second characteristic thought here is that only the righteous encounter the strong hostility of falsity, the same worthy people who are harassed by the seven deadly sins above.

Actually the remaining lines of the strophe may not necessarily describe a separate allegorical figure, Hypocrisy. They may be a fuller *sfumatura* of the figure of Falseness:

Hypocrite—outwardly he seems to love everyone;
Because he is of ice, in the sun he covers himself and cowers,
He always stays at court but feigns to desire the shadows,

> Having as his fellows and supporters
> Fraud, Discord, and Mendacity.

Michelangelo is thinking of the court flatterers who were a source of irritation to him all his life from those very first days when he saw the gracious Raphael, "the troop captain," turning the head of pope and courtiers. It is very probable that Michelangelo was acquainted with the popular emblems of Andrea Alciati, the learned jurisconsult, which had made their first appearance in 1532. Alciati had devoted emblems to both flatterers ("In adulatores") and insincere courtiers ("In aulicos"). In any case, there was in Latin and in the vernacular a rich literature of anticourtier and antisycophant verse with which Michelangelo was familiar. He disliked adulators and flatterers at court, whether they debased themselves through fawning poetry or through pleasing portraits.

In this context, it is not surprising that his next allegorical figure is Adulation, one already found in Horapollo and Piero Valeriano. Adulation was anathema to the artist, at least adulation of living persons, and he could never be accused of it, from the first moments when he voiced sarcasms to Pope Julius II to the late years when he kept his hat on while speaking with princes of church or state.

> Then next there is Adulation, laden with worries,
> Young, dextrous, and handsome of person.
> She is covered with more color and more clothes
> Than heaven grants to flowers in the spring.
> She gets what she wants with sweet deceits
> And reasons only of those things which please others,
> She turns on tears or laughter at her whim,
> With her eyes she adores even as her hands steal.

Ripa, too, was to emphasise the outer garments of Adulation: "donna vestita di abito artificioso" and "vestita di cangiante," the latter idea deriving from Cicero's *Tusculanae*, ii.[11] One is reminded by the last verse of Paulus Maccius's engraving, "In assentatores," showing a classical figure coaxing a playful dog with one hand while the other holds a concealed stone behind his back: "Altera dat panem manus, occulit altera saxum." We have textual evidences of Michelangelo's distaste for praises heaped on him. We remember such lines in the dialogues with Donato Giannotti as "There is nothing which makes a modest person blush more than praising him in his presence,"[12] or his vehement rebuttal to those who would praise him, "Leave me alone wrapped in my shroud."[13] Michelangelo completes the expression of his scorn for Adulation by dressing this figure in despicable high colors rivaling springtime flower beds. His dislike of fancy clothing is paralleled by his dislike of full color and gold, a conviction of his to which both Vasari and Armenini testified.[14] (See pp. 76–77.) Small wonder then that Fraud and Adulation here are found swaddled in the rich and colorful clothing of a Rigault.

The poet has not entirely finished with Adulation, however. He picks up his pen for a final brief blast. Three lines satisfy him and he writes no further:

> She is not only the mother of all courtly crimes,
> But breast-feeds them along and with her milk
> Increases them, augments them, and defends them . . .

Here again is the curious image of the breast-feeding of wickedness, akin to the evil giantess who suckles the full-grown giant Pride. Michelangelo the misogynist turns again in disgust at the most natural and instinctive function of young motherhood. One remembers the horrid sagging breasts of his drawing supposedly of the aged Vittoria Colonna, a momentary outburst against essential womanhood. One even recalls here *La Notte*. Michelangelo, who so often complained of time and fate, perhaps remembered that death had deprived him of his mother's breast and that he had been turned over to a wet nurse.

In sum, we find that Michelangelo on five occasions between the years 1522 and 1545 indulged as poet in allegory. Even in verse he embellishes his allegorical figures with attributive trappings, with adjectival raiments and symbols. The basic characteristics or attitudes of the figures suffice to depict the quality embodied. Where he wished a pejorative depiction he had recourse to external clothing or adornment.

In general, his descriptions of these allegories departed from that of his contemporaries and showed an original inventiveness. For example, to Da Vinci, connoisseur of the conventional bestiary, *Falsità* was a wolf and Hypocrisy a crocodile. Just as his *Notte*, the sculptured allegory most laden with overt and identifiable symbols, differs from the prescriptions for depiction of Night set down by Cesare Ripa and other iconologists, so are these *figurae* different both in conception (such names as *Perchè*, *Come*, and *Forse* were absolutely autonomous) and in descriptive detail. Michelangelo the poet is consistent once again with Michelangelo the artist.

NOTES

1 Arturo Farinelli, "Michelangelo poeta," in *Raccolta di studi critici dedicata ad A. D'Ancona* (Florence, 1901), p. 331.

2 Lodovico Dolce, *Dialogo della Pittura* (Florence, 1734), pp. 242, 246.

3 The figures in Politian's first list include: Amore, Superbia, Beltà, Leggiadria, Onestate, and Gentilezza; in the second list: Piacer, Insidia, Sperare, Disio, Paura, Diletto, Ire, Paci, Lacrime, Affetto, Magrezza, Affanno, Sospetto, Letizia, Voluttà, Bellezza, Contegno, Angoscia, Errore, Furore, etc.

4 A. Insinga, *Michelangelo poeta, ed. cit.*, p. 14.

5 *Rime*, ed. Girardi, p. 36.

[6] Cesare Ripa, *Iconologia* (Perugia, 1764), II, 271. First edition, 1593.
[7] *Rime*, ed. Guasti, p. 325.
[8] Giorgio Vasari, *La vita di Michelangelo*, ed. Paola Barocchi (Milan-Naples, 1962), V, 244.
[9] E. Panofsky, *Studies in Iconology* (New York, 1939) and F. Saxl, "Veritas filia temporis," in *Philosophy and History* (Oxford, 1936).
[10] Panofsky, *ibid.*, p. 159.
[11] Ripa, *Iconologia, ed. cit.*, I, 38.
[12] D. Giannotti, *Dialogi, ed. cit.*, pp. 45–46.
[13] *Ibid.*, p. 46.
[14] R. J. Clements, *Michelangelo's Theory, ed. cit.*, pp. 248–52.

PART II

The Self-Portrait

9

PHYSICAL AND MORAL SELF-PORTRAIT

It is said that Michelangelo never needed to sign his paintings or sculptures because there could be no doubt of their authorship. *Ex ungue leonem*. To use the words of Sebastiano del Piombo, there was a certain something personal, a cachet, about them. Cellini felt that Michelangelo's sculpture had a special touch which served in lieu of signature. As we have hoped to show in these pages, there are thematic and stylistic traces which enable us to recognise a poem of Michelangelo's. His poetry is by common consent so personal and autonomous (the debated adjective "sincere" comes to mind) that of all the values it may bring to the history of Italian literature not the least is in the area of autobiography. Almost all of Michelangelo's editors and critics have emphasised this "sincerity." Pierre de Bouchaud wrote of the poet, "Son principal mérite est la franchise,"[1] and indeed Michelangelo was franker than the "Victorian" Bouchaud realised. In his edition Amendola rightly asserted: "The *Rime* along with the drawings truly lead us into the intimate spirit of the artist—more internal than the drawings, because they express the soul directly, bypassing the symbol."[2] As if to authenticate this personal quality, Michelangelo on rare occasions signed his poems, just as he signed a few of his works of art. Again, as we have suggested, it was an unnecessary precaution. The *Rime* constitute a self-portrait of the man, physical, spiritual, temperamental, and moral.

Let us take stock of what the *Rime* reveal of the man—as contrasted with the other sources of information: his artistic productions, his letters, and the testimony of his contemporaries. That Homer may never have existed does not diminish our pleasure in reading the *Odyssey*, but the fact that we have so much external data and so little internal means of penetrating Michelangelo's life and works makes even more precious the insight provided in the poems.

Fortunately Michelangelo felt the irresistible urge to project himself into his art, a habit which carried over into his poetry. It has been alleged that "Whenever he set himself to carve a portrait, the only features that would come were his own."[3] It is true that whereas Michelangelo was reticent about doing an *autoritratto* in painting or sculpture, having executed only one or two, he probably did project and identify himself in almost a dozen works of art. He is supposed to have portrayed himself in the *San Proculo* at Bologna, the *Monk* and the *San Bartolommeo* pelt of the *Giudizio universale*, the old man vanquished by the *Genio della Vittoria*, *the Holophernes* on the Judith spandrel, the *Nicodemus* of the Florentine *Deposizione*, the bearded man sketched wearing the coif of a boar's head (see Plate I), and a soldier behind the centurion in the *Crocifissione di San Pietro*. The two mascarons of bearded men under the sepulcher of Cecchino de' Bracci in Santa Maria Aracoeli could be identified as stylised portraits of the master and of Luigi del Riccio, resembling their real-life models as little as the effigies of the Medici Dukes resembled the actual Lorenzo and Giuliano. De Tolnay holds the *Bruto* to be an "unconscious" self-portrayal. Kriegbaum viewed the *San Paolo* in the Piccolomini Altar at Siena as a self-portrait, even though this patriarch was executed by a much younger Michelangelo (guides in the Siena basilica laugh over this attribution). In the present volume we have considered both the marble *David* and the herm of the *Saettatori* as abstract self-projections.

The poetry serves as evidence of Michelangelo's admission that even while painting another, one inevitably paints oneself. In two madrigals he stated that an artist will paint himself and his own moods into the portraits of others:

> If it is true that one working hard stone will liken
> The image of every other model to himself (G 242)
> For if one paints himself when painting another (G 173)

Thus Rodin claimed to find in Michelangelo's figures the artist's own sad withdrawal into himself. Many others have read Michelangelo's moods into his figures, especially the *Mosè*, the *Geremia*, and the *Cristo giudice*.

Nowhere in the *Rime* does Michelangelo state the principle of automatic self-portraiture so flatly as he did when commenting on a painter the best part of whose picture was an ox: "Every painter draws himself well." In the total of 343 poems and fragments Michelangelo "draws himself well," indeed. Even the crude self-portrait mockingly painted in the pelt of *San Bartolommeo* or the unflattering sketch of himself in the coif of a boar does not approach in detail the rough self-portrait found in "I' sto rinchiuso come la midolla," in which a realistic or naturalistic pen turns to his physical appearance and his spiritual depression:

> My loins are strained, I'm out of breath,
> Fractured and broken by my labor, and death
> Is the hostel where I live and eat on credit . . .
> I have a voice like a hornet in an oil jar,
> Coming from a leathern cask and a halter of bones;
> I have three pebbles of pitch [gallstones] in a tube.
> My eyes are rimmed, spotted, and dark.
> My teeth are like keys of an instrument,
> For by their moving the voice sounds or falls still.
> My face has a shape which strikes terror.
> My clothes are such as chase crows to the wind,
> Away from the dry seeds, without aid of other weapon. (G 267)
> (For succeeding lines see p. 266.)

Dissatisfaction with his own appearance was of course intensified after the altercation in the Medici Garden during which Pietro Torrigiani smashed the bridge of his nose. In a deeper way his unhappiness over his appearance emerges again and again in the sonnets where he contrasts his own plainness with the beauty of Tommaso Cavalieri, Febo di Poggio, or even Vittoria Colonna. In his allegorical madrigal "Costei pur si delibra" (G 172) he notes with pleasure that as he and a lady look together in a mirror, his own ugliness heightens her beauty (see above, p. 163). Even in his comic Valentine poem derived indirectly from the *Nencia* of Lorenzo, "Tu a' 'l uiso piu dolcie che la sapa" (G 20), he manages to joke about his own mouth as "una scharsella/Di faguo' piena" (see p. 269). Yet he derived consolation from his Platonism, for, as his verses show over and over, he believed that individuals possessed an inner beauty visible only to the *accorti*. Thus he hoped that he might possess some attractiveness to those to whom he gave of himself.

His physical shortcomings went far beyond his face and figure, if we are to believe the descriptions in the *Rime*. For the poetry provides almost a medical chart of the illnesses and malaises with which he was afflicted (see above, p. 48). The *capitolo* mentioned above lists diarrhea, coughs, catarrh, colds, shortness of breath, snoring, lumbago, hernia, exhaustion, gallstones, dizziness, spotted eyes, weak hearing in one ear and a buzzing in the other; in sum, he would be as well off dead. The fragment (G App. 16) adds: "fever, pains in my sides, weak eyes and teeth," just as though Michelangelo had checked over the previous list and repaired several lacunae.

Yet the *Rime* are more important as a spiritual self-portrait. Even such a *capitolo* as "I' sto rinchiuso," albeit with echoes of the *Rime* of Camelli, reveals behind the irony the low state of morale to which the artist had descended. As we have already begun to see, Michelangelo's religious immersion and his troubled mysticism are detailed and traced chronologically more fully in the *Rime* than in the *Lettere* or anywhere else. We have also dealt sufficiently with Michelangelo's curious eventual renunciation of the fine arts, a purely verbal rejection which did not however impel him to lay down his mallet or his brush.

One aspect of his spiritual self-portrait which we have not yet pointed out was a curious insistence that he was different from other men. This quirk is documented only in the *Rime*. It comes out in such claims as:

> And on what others die of, it is my lot to live (G 73)
> What makes others wise makes me blind and foolish (G 300)
> And what kills others I merely enjoy and thrive on (G 136)

or, more lengthily:

> If fire doth harm all else,
> It burns but sears me not,
> Though not through my great or its lesser power.
> For I alone find health,
> Like the salamander, there where others die. (G 122)

This withdrawal from the norms and patterns of his fellow men was accentuated when questions of judgement were involved. The blindness of the vast majority, incapable of good taste, makes him withdraw from them, even from their praise. He takes pleasure in the concomitant isolation:

> Good taste is so rare that sometimes perforce
> It gives in to the erring crowd,
> Whereas, within itself it derives satisfaction . . .
> The world is blind, and with its titles and honors
> Rewards most who usually need them the least;
> Like a whip, this teaches us as it stings. (G 109)

Michelangelo's feeling that he was a man apart in a world without taste tended to drive him into an ivory tower. As Horace had noted in his *Poetics*, when one hates the vulgar throng, one keeps it at a distance. In the *Diálogos em Roma* Michelangelo gives a lecture on this subject, claiming that certain arts and sciences demand a man's exclusive time and attention. He adds that it is wrong to criticise an artist for his necessary removal from the circle of friends or contemporaries. In the *Dialogi* of Giannotti, Michelangelo explains why he refuses invitations: it is not that he cannot enjoy dinners and good company. Rather, the contrary; he would give too much of himself in the company of men of virtue and genius. Therefore, it is best for the artist to withdraw within himself, to "rediscover and take pleasure in oneself."[4] Perhaps one of the reasons for Michelangelo's dislike of Raphael was that the younger artist seemed the living disproof of his deeply felt conviction about the necessity for artistic solitude. Indeed, Raphael rubbed salt in the wounds by commenting, as Lomazzo recorded it, that Michelangelo was "as lonely as a hangman."

If there is no lecturing on this topic in the *Rime*, there are the inevitable obiter dicta which help fill in the picture. There is the line, superficially Petrarchan, but sincerely felt and experienced: "I walk along untrodden ways, alone." Michelangelo entertained a suspicion that social or courtly life engendered qualities far different from those called for in the *Libro del Cortegiano* or the *Galateo*. Perhaps as he saw the fawning crowds around Raphael at the papal curia, he formulated lines about hypocrites at court he was later to write (see pp. 170–171). Indeed, no document of Michelangelo's expressed better than his *Stanze in lode della vita rusticale* his desire to "get away from it all," to flee from the artificial life of the town and court. So keen is his desire to get off to a campestral ivory tower that he even renounces the fine arts themselves,

> L'auere e 'l dare e l'usanze streme e strane
> E 'l meglio e 'l peggio e le cime dell'arte, (G 67)
> (For translation see below p. 248.)

showing that his ivory towerism was an obsession not merely of the man but also of the artist. One understands that he used his art as a pretext to avoid court and salon like some Misanthrope, only incidentally paint-spattered. The pastoral vein continues, to the discredit of the city:

> Milk, herbs, and water, always at command,
> The peasant recks not of superfluous stores:
> He counts his gains upon his callous hand,
> No other book is needed for his scores:
> Troubled with no accounts of ships or land,
> No usurer's guiles he suffers and deplores;
> He knows not in the world that such things be,
> Nor vainly strives with fortune, no, not he:
> (William Wordsworth)

His workshop-home contrasts meaningfully with the splendid salons about him:

> and even more, were he to see
> My house here among such rich palaces. (G 267)

Michelangelo's withdrawal into his own atelier and into his own ego eventually becomes a withdrawal into his Christian soul, as we have seen. During the years of his several love affairs, he tried to exclude even love from his ivory tower:

in the shadow I remain,
When the sun despoils the world with its rays. (G 2)

The effort, as we know from the *Rime* themselves, was unsuccessful.

The seclusion he sought was trespassed upon by a few good friends. We have always known the identity of these. Papini, in his *Vita di Michelangiolo*, added further names to this privileged group. The *Rime* serve as testimony to the degree of affection and respect he felt for a select group: Luigi del Riccio, Donato Giannotti, Giorgio Vasari, Lodovico Beccadelli, Francesco Urbino, Cecchino Bracci, Tommaso Cavalieri, Febo di Poggio, and Vittoria Colonna. If Michelangelo could write to his brother Buonarroto in 1509, "I have no friends of any sort, nor do I wish any," and if in 1548 he could still write to his nephew Lionardo, "I always go around alone, I get about little, and I speak to no one," we have ample testimony, of which the *Rime* are partial evidence (see Chapter XIV) that his ivory tower walls were successfully breached by a few insistent and understanding friends.

The *Rime* provide minor evidence, as well, of Michelangelo's surliness and quick temper. As he himself put it in the note to one of his madrigals (G 253): "Non ò mele in corpo." Those who write *biographies romancées* of Michelangelo (Stone and Rolland come to mind before others) endow him with the patience of Job, the resignation of Socrates, and the forgiving nature of Christ. His best friends made no secret of his irascibility. Donato Giannotti records the old artist's angry boutades ("Voi mi fate quasi adirare!" etc.) in his *Dialogi.*[5] His saintly friend the Marchioness of Pescara alludes in De Hollanda's *Diálogos* to his "falling into one of those tempers during which he habitually turns upon others."[6] Jacopo Sansovino cried out that to expect kindness from Michelangelo would be the same as wanting water not to be wet, that the day would be cursed when Michelangelo ever said anything good of anyone. There are further evidences of surliness, which we have discussed elsewhere.[7] He often rationalised his irritation or anger toward friends into self-congratulation that eventually everyone would know he, Michelangelo, was in the right. When the founder of his *Giulio II* botched the job, Michelangelo noted with satisfaction that all of Bologna was turning its scorn on poor Messer Bernardino. When Michelangelo had been booted out of Pope Julius's quarters by a lackey, he observed with satisfaction that the act redounded about Rome to the shame of the pope. Thus he felt a sense of superiority which could convert itself, as the *Rime* show, into a comfortable or smug sermonising. When Julius II offended him, Michelangelo penned him an angry but contained sermon—probably never delivered—starting with reproachful moralising:

Signor, se uero è alcun prouerbio antico
Questo è ben quel, che chi puo mai non uuole. (G 6)

(For translation see p. 90.)

His angry sonnet to Luigi del Riccio also is based on a moralising proverb:

> Chi gli omer' altru' 'mpenna e po' tra uia
> A lungo andar la rete ochulta ha tesa,
> L'ardente carita d'amore accesa
> Là piu l'ammorza, ou' arder piu desia (G 251)
>
> (For translation, see p. 149.)

The self-righteous irritation or anger is transparent. It might be added that if the *Lettere* sometimes exploded with bursts of anger against Michelangelo's brothers or even against old Lodovico himself, the filial piety which filled his *capitolo* on the death of his father (also including an expression of the artist's grief over the loss of Buonarroto) is moving and convincing. The father with whom he had exchanged outbursts of anger has transcended such human foibles and haggles and is now seen as no less than divine: "Tu se' del morir morto e facto diuo" (G 86). So, momentarily, has the son.

The next nine chapters review several major components of Michelangelo's *autoritratto* culled from the abundant data in the *Rime*. The principal facets of the master to be dealt with are: his attitudes toward love, his religiosity, his optimism and pessimism, his propensities as a *moraliste*, his moments of coarseness, his disinterest in external nature, his original scientific ideas, his entrenched economic notions, his politics, patriotism, and campanilism.

NOTES

1 Pierre de Bouchaud, *op. cit.*, p. 106.
2 *Le poesie di Michelangelo*, ed. Amendola (Lanciano, 1911; 1931), p. 11.
3 G. F. Hill, "The Portraits of Michelangelo," *Burlington Magazine*, XXV (1914), 345.
4 D. Giannotti, *Dialogi, ed. cit.*, p. 69.
5 *Ibid.*, p. 96.
6 Francisco de Hollanda, *Diálogos, ed. cit.*, p. 188.
7 R. J. Clements, *Michelangelo's Theory of Art, ed. cit.*, pp. 383–85.

10

MICHELANGELO INNAMORATO

The complex relationship of Michelangelo with love is not readily understandable. He fits into no easy pattern. Raphael loved his Fornarina and celebrated her in paint and in sonnets. Rembrandt could fall in love with models and marry them. Titian could fall in love with models and not marry them. Leonardo could render the charms of gracious women while remaining unmoved by those charms. Michelangelo, who sometimes used male models for his female figures, never matured emotionally to the point of having a sustained love affair with a woman. This may or may not have been his hope as a young boy, when an indulgent legend had him enamored of the young daughter of Lorenzo il Magnifico, in whose home he then resided. There are many conjectures about Michelangelo's love for various women, complete with attributive adjectives but without identity, like the faceless princess in Goya's royal group portrait. Some of these are quite shameless as well as inventive. In a wishful article entitled "Michelangelo amante," Guerzoni attributes to the artist a disturbed love for a "diva dagli aurei cappelli," complete with scenes of jealousy.[1] Nicolo Isouard's opera *Michel-Ange* of 1802 centers on our artist's love for Fiorina, daughter of Perugino. We shall return below to these conjectural ladies.

The many-sidedness of this poet-lover, mirrored in the *Rime*, is well noted by Insinga in his *Michelangelo poeta:* "Surely, loving and tumultuous as he was, Michelangelo was to mirror in his rimes the rough sweetness of his great, soft, indocile, and meditative heart, in a brusque and disdainful form, eager and iracund, which mirroring sets him apart from the poetasters of his time."[2] As this statement suggests, the moods and attitudes of Michelangelo's love poetry are many. The styles and vocabularies of earlier writers on love infiltrate these *Rime:* Dante in his stilnovistic period, Petrarch, Politian, Plato as rephrased in Ficino, and even Lorenzo of the joyous "Nencia."

If the ladies who haunted the love lyrics (with the exception of Vittoria

Colonna) cannot be identified or even authenticated, the same is not true of the men. They were, in succession: Gherardo Perini (never mentioned by name), Febo di Poggio (probably more "Apollinic" pieces were addressed to him than hitherto supposed), Tommaso Cavalieri, and Cecchino Bracci (the infatuation discussed in Chapter VI). We shall discuss these poems to men below, and review briefly the probable nature of Michelangelo's sexuality.

The *Rime* are abundant testimony to the fact that, as Condivi asserted, the artist reasoned often about love. Certain themes intrigued him. Our perquisition of these themes follows the order below:

I. The categories of love in the *Rime*
II. The union or identity of true lovers
III. True love versus sensual love
IV. Love and reason
V. The suspense of love
VI. The power of love
VII. Dialogues with love
VIII. Generalities about love: anxieties / suffering / jealousy / unfairness of love / martyrdom / peril / bondage / love's blindness / redemption through love
IX. Poems to Vittoria Colonna
X. The alleged Bolognese
XI. Other women
XII. Love of men
XIII. Tommaso Cavalieri
XIV. Gherardo Perini and Febo di Poggio
XV. Love and death
XVI. September loves
XVII. Renunciation of love

I. Let us distinguish early between categories of loves which will come under our scrutiny. There was first the *amor umano* (*amour passion*, as Stendhal put it), Petrarchan and human. There was *amor onesto*, a transcendental emotion elevated by Platonism and by the alembication of the *dolce stil nuovo*. Finally, there was the *amor bueno* of Christians and mystics alike, the love of God and Christ which becomes intense and even anguished. Michelangelo, we have seen (p. 81), keeps the first category strictly apart from the others: "Unbridled desire is sense, not love, and kills the soul" (G 105). The extent of *amor bueno* in the poetry is demonstrated in Chapters III and XI. Sometimes the three categories are kept apart with difficulty, with more difficulty than in Michelangelo's art. The profane loves are abundant in the art: armed Venus and Cupid, Samson and Delilah, the running Satyr, Leda and the Swan. There are Tityus, who represented, as we have seen, "the pangs of a shameful amorous desire," and Phaeton, who carried a physical desire to excessive heights. Judith and Holophernes represented passion spent through self-immolation, as did Esther and Haman of the "Miraculous Salvations of Israel." The Ganymede symbolised honest love, the sublime rise of two lovers to heaven as illustrated in the artist's verse "If one spirit, one will, dominates two hearts," quoted more fully below. Other examples of the *amor onesto* are the many-progenied ancestors of Christ on the lunettes of the Sistine Ceiling, many of these with children in or at hand. The drawing of the *Archers Shooting at a Herm* is certainly an example of the *amor onesto* which stands firm against mere passions (see Chapter V).

Of these three categories of love, it is obvious that divine love is most frequent in the *Rime*, the *amor onesto* next (addressed to Vittoria Colonna and Tommaso Cavalieri), with mere passion or "falls" the least portrayed. The constant occupation with love in the *Rime* results inevitably from the relentless return and ceaseless attacks of one love after the other during the course of a man's lifetime:

> Love, which uses its every snare and lime
> That I may not break its bonds . . . (G 44)

II. As though mindful of the androgynous ideal, Michelangelo believed that love depended on a perfect union and fusion of equals. The necessity of compatibility and similarity of age is succinctly stated: "C'amor uuol pari stato e giouanezza" (G 255). Here, as so often, one suspects that Michelangelo is thinking of the love of two men, for in counseling his nephew Lionardo on the choice of a bride, the artist had stipulated that the groom should be a decade older than the bride. As for compatibility, love further insists:

> For love limits friends, and for this they are rare,
> To those similar or equal in fortune and virtue. (G 252)

The selfless love which unites lover and beloved (who must be "equal") is the theme of a revealing sonnet, "S'un casto amor," (1532), admirable in its idealism:

> If one pure love, if one supreme devotion,
> One fate unite two hearts in harmony,
> If grief of one the other's sorrow be,
> If by two minds is felt one spirit's motion:
> If one eternal soul is made for twain,
> Uplifting both, and in one flight to heaven;
> If by one burning shaft two breasts are riven,
> Which deep implanted doth for aye remain:

If, self forgotten, each the other love,
With joy, that such sweet intermingling hath,
Each for his own the other's will doth take;
If all twice-told the hundredth part would prove
Of such great love, and bond of mighty faith:
Shall wrath avail to loose it, or to break? (G 59)
(Elizabeth Hall)

Romain Rolland hailed this as "one of the most beautiful songs to perfect friendship." This sonnet, with its insistence on fused lives, wills, and bodies shows how difficult it would have been for Michelangelo ever to find the sort of love he longed for, a love like that which had united Giovanni Cavalcanti and Ficino, who shared only one soul, as De Tolnay reminds us.[3] Michelangelo's intense feelings for the recipient Tommaso Cavalieri gave the younger man, who preferred to accept the more normal life of a husband and father, understandable concern.

The completed fusion of lover and loved one is equally described in another magnificent sonnet, "Veggio co be uostr' ochi" (1530–34), dedicated to Tommaso, which Sheffler claims to be "the most beautiful lyric poem of sixteenth-century Italy."

Through thee I catch a gleam of tender glow,
Which with my blind eyes I had failed to see;
And walking onward, step by step with thee,
The once-oppressing burdens lighter grow.
With thee, my groveling thoughts I heavenward raise.
Borne upward by thy bold, aspiring wing:
I follow where thou wilt—a helpless thing.
Cold in the sun and warm in winter days.
My will, my friend, rests only upon thine;
Thy heart must every thought of mine supply:
My mind expression finds in thee alone.
Thus like the moonlight's silver ray I shine.
We only see her beams on the far sky.
When the sun's fiery rays are o'er her thrown. (G 89)
(Fanny Elizabeth Bunnett)

These two poems, which answer most affirmatively the question of whether Michelangelo merited the title of poet, show how thoroughly the artist abandoned himself to an affair. We reject Bevilacqua's retrospective criticism of the latter poem: "But how filled with seventeenth-century conceptualism!"[4] Hamlet, before long, will mock this idea of the fusion of lovers while saluting his stepfather as "mother." The poems restate in lyrical fashion the artist's admission to Donato Giannotti and his friends that once he found someone of exceptional quality and virtue: "I am constrained to fall in love with him and give myself to him as prey, so that

I am no longer mine, but his."[5] This is restated in the line "Se l'un nell'altro amato si trasforma," which occurs twice in the poetry (G 193 and 194), and echoes Petrarch, 94: "ch'io vidi duo amanti trasformare." Perhaps analogous to Michelangelo's general deficiency in ease and grace, his lack of *sprezzatura*, was his inability to take a love affair lightly. When things did not work out, the seriousness with which he regarded the affair led him to feel both guilt and a greater awareness of the distinction between love and sin, a dichotomy mentioned several times in his *Rime*. The words *peccato* and *colpa* recur from his youthful poetry to that of old age.

An early sensation of an affair not going well, of its being less than idealistic, was hastily recorded on the back of a letter from Stefano di Tomaso in Florence, 20 April, 1521:

> Cruel, bitter, and pitiless heart,
> Clad in sweetness and full of love,
> Thy faith is slowly born, to last less time
> Than do the flowers in a mild winter, etc. (G 17)

This cynical and incomplete draft bespeaks a passion experienced, whether for a man or a woman. Perhaps the sensitive Michelangelo, prone to injury, feared afterwards to give himself completely to a love capable of inflicting such great hurt.

III. There are times when the poet cannot help himself, even though he knows that his love is carnal and that the senses are not sufficient for love. He plummets to a new abasement:

> Fallen am I there where truth lies silent;
> Sense survives that from which it is separated. (G 78)

He is not sure whether he himself or the loved one is at fault.

Michelangelo will often be moved to deny the senses in wishful poetising:

> Not always to all is so prized and precious
> That which satisfies the senses,
> For at least one person there will be who feels
> That behind its sweetness it is evil and bitter. (G 109)

The same disclaimer of sensual desire toward Cavalieri is repeated in a poem apparently designed for Vittoria Colonna:

> Love forbids my iniquitous and depraved desires
> And elevates me, heretofore weary and base,
> Up among rare spirits and demigods. (G 254)

To guarantee that sin will not contaminate a relationship, one must find a love which will accomplish a fusion and union of heart, soul, and body. Even after death, one of the partners will perpetuate such a love:

> Thus I remain alive in him who loved me so. (G 203)

The legend of the androgyne, so entertainingly recounted by Aristophanes in the *Symposium*, assumed that every lover had one ideal mate with whom he had enjoyed a perfect union to be sought anew. Michelangelo enlarges the choice to candidates who resemble the perfect mate:

> And wishes me to live and burn
> Not only for you, but for whoever resembles you. (G 81)

IV. The opposition of love and reason, which provided conflict in so much classical and neoclassical tragedy, occasionally occupied Michelangelo's thought. Love deprives him of reason, thwarting his anabasis up an allegorical mountain (G 18). Love makes rash promises of which reason soberly disabuses him (G 294). In a sonnet from *circa* 1529 Michelangelo remonstrates with reason for disapproving of his indulgence in a shameful earthly love; reason shames the artist by the "true words" that from Michelangelo's "living sun" he will win only death (G 43). Reason conspiring with love and habit can leave the poet unable to erase a loved one from his mind (G 28). Understandably the artist felt that the more he saw a loved one the more he risked losing his rationality and objectivity. If in his heart he pictures him or her as beautiful, inner vision takes over and the image emerges more beautiful than ever (G 155), beyond the appraising eye of common sense or reason. Michelangelo here conciliates Platonism with Stendhal's "crystallisation."

V. Michelangelo's inability to find peace in love surprises no one who stops to consider how difficult it would have been for him to give himself to a man or woman and to make the tributes which love requires. Thus, it is no surprise that one of the *Rime*'s recurrent themes is precisely the suspense, the ups and downs of love. The poet records, for example, that love gives him not an hour's respite from awareness of the double perils which menace him awake or asleep: imminent death and exhaustion from the searing attrition of love (G 232). Love favors him only rarely, "con breue riso" (G 40). The on-again, off-again progress of love is a torment, for to be kept on tenterhooks is unbearable:

> Whence with equal anguish
> I recognise that both help and injury are mortal;
> And the half-way state, for him who loves, is always the worst. (G 157)

This murderous *mezzo* makes the poet suffer in the same way as will Molière's Alceste. The madrigal above, dating from about 1546, was addressed to Riccio.

The suspense of love can drive one to the point of renouncing guarantees of love:

He who gives himself to someone, let him make no promises;
Behind an excessive pleasure death awaits us. (G 148)

Michelangelo led too busy a creative life to tolerate such anxiety. The poet used an awkward and conceivably scatological image to explain that favor and disfavor are the lover's harvest:

> He who rides by night, him it befits during the day
> To spend some time in rest and sleep. (G 53)

This thought in an amorous context is reminiscent of the passage in Ovid's *Heroïdes* iii:

> Arcus et arma tuae tibi sunt mutanda Diane
> Si quanquam cesses tendere mollis eris, etc.

Michelangelo could have read this passage and seen the image in many a Renaissance emblem book.[6] A curious rationalisation of the suspense of love is found among the poems destined for publication by Riccio:

> Let doubt be sweet to him who is hurt by truth (G 141)

This possibly cynical reminder is similar in spirit to the poet's blunt: "Chi non uuol delle foglie/Non ci uenga di maggio" (see p. 152). The curious figure of Doubt, allegorised in the rustic *Stanze*, is even more meaningful when considered in the context of love.

VI. Another dominant theme is love's miraculous power. We have already alluded to a curious—sacrilegious, if you like—tribute to this power, phrased in the language of Christ as recorded in the Evangels. This is the power of one who is loved to bring light to the blind and heal wounds with his sputum (G 90). Another parareligious notion found in the *Rime* is that love sends *messi* on visitations, announcements parallel to those divine annunciations which all the artists were painting and which Michelangelo sketched on only one occasion (the *Annunciation* in the British Museum).

A better known poem on the power of love is the sonnet "La forza d'un bel uiso a che mi sprona?" translated by Wordsworth, Emerson, and so many others. There is no resisting the power of love; Michelangelo darts to love like a fish to the lure:

> to thee I arrive
> Like a fish drawn on by the bait on the line. (G 15)

Love is capable of several miracles which transcend logic and reason. One of these which finds constant expression in the *Rime* (and on one occasion is explained by Love itself) is the admission of the outer image of the beloved through the eye to the soul, where it expands, is purified, and transcends to an ideal. That this is not a mere metaphysical process but an actual physical reality with a shattering impact is clear from the following tercet:

Lord, if thy power is in heaven as it is among us,
Make thou of my whole body one single eye;
Let there then be no part of me that doth enjoy thee not. (G 166)

We have noted elsewhere that Ficino, before Michelangelo, wrote of heavenly beauties too overwhelming to be taken in by "the small pupil of the eye."[7] To Tommaso the artist wrote: "Think, if the eye were to have its share as well, in what a state I should be!"[8]

Other powers are miraculous, too. The ardent ray of beauty pierces through the closed eyes of the lover (G 30). Love's psychagogy is such that it can pierce the poet's heart without touching his flesh (G 8). Love transmits a power to the arms, which lift weight without moving (Frey CVIII and G 88). One of Michelangelo's tributes to love's miracle-working is not solemn and awed, but gay and gladsome. It is in the strophe (1529–32) we like to describe as his Pygmalion poem, evocative of a familiar piece by Cecco Angiolieri:

Methinks, though thou wert stone, the charm I'd know
(So strong and faithful is my love for thee)
To lead thee with me wheresoe'er I go:
If thou wert dead, I'd make thee speak to me:
Wert thou in heaven, I'd draw thee down below
With sighs, and prayers, and tears of agony:
But since as living flesh thou here dost dwell,
What hopes may not be his who loves thee well? (G 54)
(Channing)

To this magnificent tribute, sometimes characterised as Bernesque, we shall return below.

A few other reminders of love's power are worth pointing out. A splendid little fragment on the *omnia vincit amor* consists of two lines of proverbial brevity:

He who is armed with love wins over every anger,
Every misery, every power, every fortune. (G 29)

Just as a tree uprooted dries in the summer heat, so the poet's soul withers when removed from his love (G 26). Love is the lodestone of the lover; to find peace he must follow its pull to the center of attraction (G 254). Finally, the power of love is sufficient to defeat the wisest counsel (G 135).

VII. Michelangelo's poems are sometimes cast in the form of dialogues with Love, a form perhaps influenced by the Neo-Platonic dialogues on love available to him. These usually constitute a question or provocative observation by the artist and a reply from Love. He who was so proud of his imagined descent from the counts of Canossa will wonder, for example, how his mistress can give herself to plebeian rivals (G 146). He warns Love that its harshness will succeed only in spurring him back to virtue (G 114). He will resort to flattery and address Love as a perceptive power which elevates spirits to more worthy concerns (G 38). Michelangelo finally acknowledges to Love that his late tears are useful now to lave away his sins (G 231). Weary of the ordeal of his passion, he asks Love in desperation if not exasperation, "What can and must I still undergo at thy insistence?" (G App. 39). Chagrined over a liaison which is getting nowhere, Michelangelo addresses an I-told-you-so to Love, "non tel diss'io?" (G 169).

It is amusing to find the mature artist expressing in these poems an ingenuousness about Love. He wonders typically:

So dissimilar and so unlike
My every daily wont,
How can this infinite beauty and sovereign glow
Fail to burn even as I am burning? (G 113)

Sometimes Love pities his state and counsels him wisely, as when casting such pearls as: it is better to have loved and suffered than never to have loved at all; life without love is death (G 38). This Love whom the poet addresses is, by the way, conventionally winged (G 49). The painter who removed wings from angels (except for the *Annunciation* drawing) leaves them on his Cupid.

When Michelangelo is not involved in dialectic with Love or with his beloved he suddenly recalls Dante (perhaps also Boccaccio); we find him addressing "ladies" ("Donne, amor, chome uedete") (G 3). Now he avows that Love, the relentless archer who is to pursue him all his life, is catching up with him.

VIII. There are a number of observations on love, stressing its peculiar psychology or the anguish it inflicts. This anguish lasts a lifetime, "Dal primo pianto all'ultimo sospiro" (G 119). Love is a bondage which holds him like a slave (G 7). Love is a martyrdom (G 12 and 119). Love is a peril (G 130). Love is a habit (G 130). Love is blind, which explains why it does not kill the poet straightway:

So in killing me, Love
Perhaps because it is blind,
Delays, trembles, and fears. (G 91)

Honneste amour, so lauded in the Renaissance, shows openly its real nature and intent. Unfortunately, a beautiful woman is more likely to deceive, says the worldly poet, and one might as well make the best of it and enjoy her (G 174).

The anxieties of love are expressed in four baroque lines which seem to cry out "Come on in, the fire is fine." "E chi uiuer non sa d'angoscia e morte/Nel foco uenga ou'io mi struggo . . . (e *ardo*)" (G 56). Destructive flame is the theme of another piece laden with the same baroque paradoxes:

> If I thrive best on what burns and sears me,
> The more fire doth burn from wood or wind,
> The more the one who slays me doth succor me
> And help me most where he harms me most. (G 57)

The *canzoniere* is thus a catalogue of sufferings inflicted by love. There are of course Petrarchan sighs, plaints, tears, frozen hearts, and burning hearts as well. Tears flow out, not inward where they are needed to quench the inner fires of the lover (G 136). Some of the sufferings are Dantean, especially when they are continuous and without respite, like those of a damned soul:

> My soul, which trembles and roars,
> As does a man who dies unjustly,
> Complains to me of the wrongs it eternally endures. (G 135)

The punishments of hell do not always bother lovers who are already suffering. Perhaps thinking of Paolo and Francesca, Michelangelo conjectures that being even in hell with his loved one would be sweet (G 139). If they go to hell, the poet will be consoled by the other's presence; if instead they go to heaven, he will enjoy God less; "Fie men fruire Dio" (G 140). He fears that his mistress is actually incapable of love (G 11). His cruel mistress keeps her dagger in his wound, so that he feels life and death at the same moment (G 124). Obviously, love makes one live more fully even while one suffers more: "Life increases where the hurt increases" (G 39).

A line describing the defeated, unsuccessful lover is worthy of the unhappy gasp of a Werther: "Prostrate on the ground I lament and weep" (G 2). Since this is from Michelangelo's second extant poetic effort (1503–04), it may be charged to juvenile hyperbole.

Curiously, both the *pietà* and *mercè* of the beloved can be just as murderous as his or her *durezza* and leave equally mortal a wound (G App. 37). Love's *mercè* can even be "troppo molesta" (G 252).

One common experience of love poets is jealousy. Though not often expressed in the *Rime*, it does make token appearances. We have already mentioned the poem voicing the poet's surprise that his lover could grant favors to a plebeian rival. In this piece to a flirtatious woman, "Gli sguardj, che tu strazij" (G 146), he excoriates coquetry as theft and murder. In dismissing his rivals ("brutj," "'l uulgo," "gente stolta"), he accuses his lady of a breach not only of faith but of taste as well. The sad truth, sometimes engendering jealousy, is that love comes easily to one of a pair and drags its feet (*zoppa*) toward the other (G 113). Thus, love is often one-sided and unfair, a charge to which we return in a moment.

Death of a loved one occasions grief and pathos of the highest order. This loftiness of sentiment was communicated to the poems written after Vittoria's death. Through such suffering love achieves a katharsis, like the purgation accomplished by fire itself. There are two expressions of this idea in the *Rime*:

> If grief o'er death makes beautiful, as they say,
> Weeping and deprived of a beautiful human face,
> The unwell being is made well,
> My misfortune yields life and grace. (G 244)

and again:

> Kindled love, by which the soul is released,
> Drawn as to a magnet by its kindred fire,
> Or like gold purged in fire returning to God (G 243)

The unhappy situation of the lover enmeshed in an unshared affection is common enough in poetry from Sappho down. Michelangelo's personal conviction, expressed several times, that he who tries hardest fails most often has no less meaning in the context of love. This is the unhappy situation pictured in an incomplete sonnet which dates from *circa* 1524–34 since it accompanies drawings possibly intended for the Laurentian Library.

> About here it was that my love, with his usual mercy,
> Took my heart and what is more, my life;
> Here with his beautiful eyes he promised me solace
> And with those very eyes he chose to deny me.
> There beyond he bound me, here he loosed me,
> I wept for myself, and with infinite grief,
> From this rock I saw him take leave
> Who took me from myself and then wished me not. (G 36)

A variant form of "My Love" reads "My Lord." We may have here, as my former student Donald Remstein has pointed out, one of the few pieces inspired by Poliziano. It could derive from the Montepulciano poet's *canzone a ballo:*

> Deh, udite un poco, amanti,
> Se io son bene suenturato.
> Una donna m'ha legato,
> Or non uuol udir mie" pianti
> Una donna el cor m'ha tolto,

Or no' 'l vuol e non me 'l rende;
Hammi un laccio al col auuolto;
Ella m'arde, ella m'intende;
Quand' io grido, non m'incende;
Quand' io piango, ella si ride,
Ecco il core, ecco la vita . . .

The binding quality of love, the placing of the heart and life itself in jeopardy, the irrevocable rejection, the ensuing weeping—these are elements appropriated by the later poet, who changes the loved one's sex.

As we leave the topic of the unfairness of love, we must add one final, brief complaint of the poet about the demands of love:

Thou givest me only what is convenient for thee
And demandest from me only what I do not have. (G 270)

In these isolated two lines is another admission of Michelangelo's that he cannot, given his demanding profession and his personal psychology, make the sacrifices and tributes requisite to sustenance of a love affair.

Love, we have seen, can be a purifying experience, a katharsis. Carrying this thought to its logical and Christian conclusion, love can become a means of redemption, of salvation. Sometimes Michelangelo worried as much about his insufficiency to win love's salvation as about the salvation of his soul (G 148). Another popular sonnet on the redeeming powers of love is "La uita del mie amor' non è 'l cor mio." The paradise promised by love is the Christian-Platonic empyrean recalled in anamnesis, there where the two had first known each other before their souls descended to earth. It is in this sonnet that we find the verses,

As heat cannot be separated from fire,
My esteem is indivisible from the eternal beauty
Which exalts, there whence it came, who most resembles him. (G 34)

In likening the inseparability of true lovers to that of heat and fire perhaps Michelangelo had remembered the following lines of Guido Guinizelli:

e prende amore in gentilezza loco
così propiamente
come calore in clarità di foco.

In any case, here is still another demonstration of the inseparable union or fusion which Michelangelo held to be inherent in a true love.

IX. The love of Michelangelo for Vittoria Colonna could not fail to gather legendary accretions. Once, on the island of Ischia, I was solicited by guides to come and see the residence of the Marchioness where the great artist "came to pay court to her." The facts themselves need no such elaboration. This great lady accomplished two miracles of equal importance in the life of Michelangelo. First, she inspired a great affection which did indeed perform a katharsis of his soul. For this it did not matter that she was another's loyal widow, a woman combining the qualities of Penelope, Griselda, and Isabel la Católica all in one. Second, she was the first woman whom Michelangelo ever considered anything near an intellectual equal.

When this Platonic love first started is not known. Amico-Mantia, in his *L'amore e le Rime di Michelangelo* (1899) sustains the thesis that "it is impossible to admit that Michelangelo loved for the first time only at the age of sixty."[9] He reasons that Michelangelo must have known Vittoria as early as 1508–09 when the public was first admitted to witness the wonders of the Sistine Ceiling. According to Amico-Mantia, Vittoria, like any well-bred young lady of eighteen or nineteen, came to admire this chapel, met the painter, and the two knew and loved each other from then on. More probably the two met around 1536 and had become mutual admirers by 1538 when Michelangelo was sixty-three and the lady over forty-six. She was a devout if hard-thinking, mature woman, endowed with few feminine beauties, as both her contemporaries and her portraitists agree. Michelangelo himself suggested this lack of femininity, when he wrote of her: "A man in a woman, or rather a god, speaks through her mouth." The point is made by Condivi that after Michelangelo went for the last time to see the deceased Marchioness "he regretted that he had not kissed her forehead and face as he kissed her hand." We may assume that this was the only time the artist kissed the widow other than in a formal *baciabasso*.

Nevertheless, many love poems were composed to her by the artist, both during her lifetime and after. Ugo Foscolo, impressed by the number and the intellectual quality of these poems, wrote in his English essays (see Bibliography): "Michelangelo was excellent and even most rare in poetry and in the true science of love, which is like a vast and perplexing forest, so that whoever enters therein without the safe-conduct of great learning and wisdom, must after many windings lose his way." Walter Pater, echoing the soaring language with which he discovered for Anglo-Saxons the mysterious smile of the Gioconda, was also struck by the even tone of the verses for Vittoria Colonna: "It was just because Vittoria raised no great passion that the space in his life where she reigns has such particular suavity; and the spirit of the sonnets is lost if we once take them out of that dreamy atmosphere in which men will have things as they will, because the hold of all outward things upon them is faint and uncertain. Their prevailing tone is a calm and meditative sweetness. The cry of distress is indeed there, but as a mere residue, a trace of bracing chalybeate salt, just discernible in the song which rises like a clear, sweet spring from a charmed space in his life."[10]

The outpouring of sonnets to an individual woman required that Michelangelo improvise new themes or variants on the exhaustible topic of the affective relationships between man and woman. One of the most spontaneous themes, one encouraged by the current Platonism, was the loftiness and nobility for which Vittoria was celebrated. Paolo Giovio dedicated an emblem to her steadfast virtues. Indeed, she is generally believed to be the Virgin in Veronese's *Nozze di Cana*. Vittoria's inaccessibility to him led Michelangelo to place her on a pedestal or altar, to crown her like a demigoddess or like one of those tiared iconographical figures of virtue toward which Renaissance poets aspired during a grueling anabasis. This, for example, is the burden of his unperfected madrigal "Al' alta tuo lucente diadema" (G 156) which voices the poet's hope that she will descend slightly to his level, even though it is a "sin" to hold such a hope. Henri II voiced the same thought to Diane de Poitiers. This inability to ascend to Vittoria's level is a fitting theme in poetry occupied with the ascensions of both Platonism and Christianity. Even with the wings lent the poet by his Donna he cannot raise himself to her (G 154). The inability to soar upward—

> Never did any wise man try,
> Without elevating and spurring himself,
> To enjoy that which is beyond his power, (G 148)

—will remind him elsewhere of that tragic phoenix which cannot soar. Neither his *ingegno* nor his art can raise him to her level (G 149). For she is as unattainable as a star (G 119). Indeed, she shines as brightly as a faraway star (G 129). Sometimes he rationalises that since he cannot attain her heights,

> But since I have no value of my own
> To open the path to ascend to that goal, (G 159)

he will remain wiser, more chastened, after his defeat. Certain it is that Michelangelo looked up to the Marchioness of Pescara and to Tommaso Cavalieri as he never looked up to princes of church and state.

Thus it is natural that Michelangelo, bewildered like Dante on a *via smarrita,* should have turned to the Marchioness for guidance and purpose. In his quest for moral and psychological salvation he sees his own poetic confessions as valueless. Her poems will be able to show him truth:

> Between vice and virtue
> My confused heart in travail doth weary me;
> Like one who sees not the sky
> And loses himself and misses every trail.
> I offer a blank sheet
> For your sacred writings,
> That I be disabused of love and pity inscribe truth thereon. (G 162)

He asks of Vittoria, as he usually interrogates Love, whether a repentant sinner has much less chance of salvation than a sovereignly good man.

The madrigal which accompanies the piece above shows how spiritually dependent at times Michelangelo became on Vittoria Colonna. He deplores his unworthiness to the point of self-hatred, but his soul does not fear for its redemption provided he can be near her (G 163).

We have mentioned that Michelangelo referred to Vittoria as "un uomo in una donna." (Knowing only defective editions, Foscolo quoted this verse as "un nume [divinity] in una donna.") The sonnet in question tells how thoroughly Vittoria's words to the poet draw him out of the introversion and introspection which was characteristic of his later years and which he defended to Donato Giannotti.

A man within a woman, nay, a god,
Speaks through her spoken word:
I therefore, who have heard,
Must suffer change, and shall be mine no more.
She lured me from the paths I whilom trod.
Borne from my former state by her away,
I stand aloof, and mine own self deplore.
About all vain desire
The beauty of her face doth lift my clay;
All lesser loveliness seems carnal mire.
O lady, who through fire
And water leadest souls to joys eterne,
Let me no more unto myself return. (G 235)
(J. A. Symonds)

This last verse is a parallel to the imprecation closing a sonnet to Christ: "Tom' a me stesso, e famm' un che ti piaccia" (G 161). It has been observed by others that Michelangelo viewed Vittoria as a link to divinity. The pious widow was frequently called "divina," an adjective habitually applied to Michelangelo as well. Of this sonnet Mariani writes: "This miraculous sentiment which he harbors in the years of his late maturity casts a penetrating ray of light on the vexed world of the artist: there emerge from it other nostalgic characteristics, hope for faith, feverish anxiety over work; but especially is light shed on that nucleus of religious thoughts which, stirred up when the artist was still young by the inflammatory words of Savonarola, were allayed but not stamped out by his passionate love for Beauty."[11]

Michelangelo's own inner vision or *sensus visivus*, as the Platonists put it, enabled him to view reality in his peculiar way, empowered him to convert the image entering through the eye into something finer as it reached the soul. He wrote of this incoming and expanding image, "crescie, poi ch'a miglior loco sale,/Se per gli ochi mortali all'alma corre" (G 42). It was easy for him to visualize Vittoria Colonna as beautiful. Indeed, many are the poems which pay tribute to this physical beauty as well as beauty of soul.

As in one of the quatrains Cecchino Bracci boasts that beauty was withheld from other men to be granted him (which will be apparent at the Resurrection), so Michelangelo feels that beauty was reconstituted to form Vittoria Colonna. This beauty was not modeled part by part from several women, as Zeuxis formed the Crotonian Venus, however:

> Pure and unsullied beauty Heaven lent
> Unto one noble, lofty, fair alone,
> Beneath a spotless veil, that when through death
> Reclaim'd, it should not have to leave so many.
> If Heaven indeed had shared it among all
> That mortal are, it scarce could have withdrawn
> It back, and re-enrich'd its treasury. (G 265)
> (John E. Taylor)

In another stanza, reminiscent of Shakespeare's query about Silvia, Michelangelo asks Love if Vittoria is as *pietosa* as she is beautiful:

> Pray, tell me, Love, if milady's soul
> Be as kind as she is fair of face,
> And if anyone would be so foolish
> Not to take and give himself to her? (G 147)

Whatever contemporary comment exists concerning Vittoria's unloveliness (Papini reminds us of Filonio Alicarnasso's remark that even when young Vittoria was not "di gran beltà posseditrice"), her face displayed for Michelangelo that unique combination of beauty, piety, and goodness which the Greeks had grouped under the term *kalakagathon.* Thus, her face and blond beauty (G 129) elevated and inspired him and, as stated above, cleared away his excess (*soverchio*) making him a finer man.

> The more I flee and hate myself still,
> The more, milady, I have recourse to thee
> With great hopes, and less doth my soul fear,
> So long as I stay near thee.
> In thy face and fair eyes
> I aspire to heaven's promised bounty,
> Assured of every salvation. (G 163)

When Vittoria died at the age of fifty-six, harassed and persecuted as a critic of the Church, Michelangelo was saddened for a longer period than deaths usually affected him. He even foresaw when she was to die, for his "Ochi mie, siate certi" (G 229) adumbrates her early death. Like

Petrarch, he was inspired by her death to compose a corpus of new poetry. Three years later he sent a few of these commemorative pieces to Giovan Francesco Fattucci with the apologetic but revealing note: "So that this letter will not be so brief, having nothing further to write, I enclose one of my little novellas [poems] which I used to write to the Marchioness of Pescara, who was most fond of me and I no less of her. Death took from me a great friend" (CDLXVII). The simplicity of these words, evocative of Montaigne's stark explanation of his friendship with Étienne de la Boétie ("parce que c'était moi, parce que c'était lui"), has the density of his poetry itself. "Amico" in Michelangelo's tribute has much more force than "amica" would have had.

Even in death the face of the Marchioness elevates him:

Rapt above earth by power of one fair face,
Hers in whose sway alone my heart delights.
I mingle with the blest on those pure heights
Where man, yet mortal, rarely finds a place.
With Him who made the Work that Work accords
So well, that by its help and through His grace
I raise my thoughts, inform my deeds and words,
Clasping her beauty in my soul's embrace.
Thus, if from two fair eyes mine cannot turn,
I feel how in their presence doth abide
Light which to God is both the way and guide:
And kindling at their luster, if I burn,
My noble fire emits the joyful ray
That through the realms of glory shines for aye. (G 279)
(William Wordsworth)

Another powerful tribute to the beatitude bestowed by Vittoria concludes a madrigal claiming that no beauty but hers is mirrored in his eyes and soul:

Even at this late hour, you succeed in making me blest,
Me, to wretchedness born.
If grace and good fortune prevail over my cruel destiny,
By you both heaven and nature will be vanquished. (G 234)

Perhaps one other of the sonnets occasioned by Vittoria's death might be added here, "Quand' el ministro" (1547), one of the most powerful:

When the prime mover of my many sighs
Heaven took through death from out her earthly place,
Nature, that never made so fair a face,
Remained ashamed, and tears were in all eyes.
O fate, unheeding my impassioned cries!
O hopes fallacious! O thou spirit of grace,
Where art thou now? Earth holds in its embrace

Thy lovely limbs, thy holy thoughts the skies.
Vainly did cruel death attempt to stay
The rumor of thy virtuous renown,
That Lethe's waters could not wash away!
A thousand leaves since he hath stricken thee down.
Speak of thee, nor to thee could Heaven convey,
Except through death, a refuge and a crown. (G 47)
(H. W. Longfellow)

(Longfellow's image of "Lethe" does not occur in the original.)

I should venture to propose that at this point Michelangelo's realism and irony—directed more at himself than at Vittoria—come to the fore. The sonnet is written on the verso of a folio containing, among other drawings, a curious sketch of Michelangelo, in a boar's coif, staring at a sad elderly woman with sagging breasts. Between the two heads is a hand making the vulgar gesture of the *fica*, a surprising touch found also in Da Vinci's drawing of Envy astride a crawling skeleton. Most commentators identify the heads as those of Michelangelo and Vittoria, but ignore completely the deprecating gesture which separates the two. It seems to me that the enforced chastity which governed their relationship, like that troublesome negativity of Tommaso Cavalieri, occasionally disturbed the artist. Association with a saint must inevitably have its trying moments. Perhaps even, he reflected on her dead husband, the prototype of Renaissance gentleman, who had paid so little attention to the Marchioness and with whom she was now rejoined in death. One thinks of Aretino, also surfeited with Vittoria's reputed saintliness, who, for his own reasons, insinuated that she was promiscuous with monks:

Cristo, la tua discepola Pescara
Che favella con teco faccia a faccia,
A te distende le chetine braccia,
Ove non so che frate si ripara.

The mutual admiration which Michelangelo and the Marchioness shared had many bases. I should merely like to add that their esteem for each other's poetry was very real. If it is true that such important writers as Castiglione submitted their works to Vittoria Colonna, soliciting her criticisms, she read none of these with more interest than she read Michelangelo's. We know that Michelangelo actually helped to collect her substantial *canzoniere* and preserve it for posterity. The artist wrote to his nephew on 7 March, 1551, of her sonnets—"which I had bound in the same libretto and lent to many persons at that time" (CCXLIII).

There is of course a general similarity in the spiritual outlook of Michelangelo's religious poems and those of the Marchioness. As we note below, Façon emphasized early that both were influenced by Valdés, whom Vittoria knew at Naples. Papini, in his excellent study of Michelangelo and his circle, claims that at the very most there may be just two allusions to Michelangelo in her poetry, but he is not sure. These would be in her sonnets, "Perchè la mente vostra ornata e degna" and "Quando intender qui puote umano ingegno," which refer to a painted or sculptured Christ. Papini overlooks, however, a few direct points of contact, such as Michelangelo's sonnet on the Redeemer, "Non fur men lieti che turbati e tristi" (G 298) and Vittoria's "Gli angeli eletti e quel bene infinito." There are further *rapprochements*, which we point out in our discussion of Michelangelo's sources and originality (Chapter XIX).

x. One poem of Michelangelo appears, indeed, to be addressed to an actual woman, purportedly a young Bolognese whom he met around 1507 and who could have consoled him in those days when he was feuding with the local artists and trying to win back the favor of Julius II. Many have romanticised this conjectured infatuation. In 1502 Vincenzo Italo Pascale had no scruples about identifying her as the daughter of a goldsmith and clarifying: "Seeing up there a beautiful and blond girl, he burst into a flame of love for her."[12] Papini is tempted by this same fiction: "We have reason to believe that right around the year 1507 Buonarroti fell in love again, almost certainly with a beautiful and young Bolognese."[13] It is fruitless to mention the many further conjectures about the girl, such as her re-creation in a recent American novel as a hot-blooded relative of Michelangelo's protector Giovan Francesco Aldovrandi.

The poem, composed in 1507–08, is interesting in that it eschews Petrarchan and Platonic conceits to describe the actual figure and physical charms of the damsel. The theme, which reappears in Waller's "On a Girdle" and Tennyson's "The Miller's Daughter," concerns the lover's jealousy of the tight embrace of his mistress's girdle. Even when treating a theme which interests other poets, Michelangelo views in his special sculptor's way the emergence of the body from under its veil of clothing.

> How great must be that happy garland's bliss,
> That wreathes with flowers the hair of one I know:
> Each flower would swifter than its neighbor go,
> That he may first those golden tresses kiss.

Hermann Grimm conjectured that Michelangelo was here describing a *ghirlanda aurea* designed by Domenico Ghirlandaio's father, a goldsmith. Passing from the description of the head to the body, the poet continues:

> All day contented with its happy lot
> That bodice clasps her breast, or with it heaves:
> And what the name of golden thread receives
> Her cheek and neck from touching ceaseth not.

After dwelling on her close-clinging clothing, Michelangelo insists,

> But joy more exquisite then aught beside
> That ribbon hath, with golden fringes gay,
> Which on the breast it laceth, resteth so;

In the final tercet the embrace is mentioned a further time and the lover's longing is intensified:

> And the neat girdle round her waist that's tied,
> Saith to itself, "This let me clasp away":
> What then remaineth for my arms to do? (G 4)
> (Elizabeth Hall)

Three verbs, *serrare, stringere, premere* are employed to stress the slight pressure which clothing exerts upon the human body. We remember Michelangelo's rhetorical question (see p. 76) in the *Diálogos em Roma,* which dismissed clothes as an inferior accompaniment to the human body.[14] We know of Michelangelo's rejection of the sumptuous clothing with which the Venetian painters garbed their subjects. We have noted also that his dislike of elaborate clothing led him to portray such allegorical figures as Wealth and Fraud in rich raiments. We know that such a knot as holds the young lady's clothing together here was quickly cut off the unfinished marble figure which Michelangelo was to transpose into the gigantic and quite nude David.

This strange little sonnet, constituting in Calero's words "the first phase of Michelangelo's poetic activity,"[15] thus presents several problems to the student of Michelangelo's mind and taste. First of all, it is his only poem which sings the specific charms of a young woman's physical beauty, with the possible exception of the two facetious love poems, "Io crederrei, se tu fussi di sasso" (G 54) and the comic "Tu a' 'l uiso" (G 20). Second, it seems to show a sensual longing absent from all his other *Rime.* Finally, it shows an interest in clothing which would be most unusual in his aesthetics were it not for the particular treatment he gives the drapery. Michelangelo's great-nephew, solicitous as he was about the homosexual suggestions of the *Rime,* refused to accept even the heterosexuality of the last verse and revised it to "Or che farebber dunque l'altrui braccia?" ("What then remaineth for a man's arms to do?")

What impelled Michelangelo to undertake this sonnet? I do not subscribe to the unlikely existence of a young lady friend who (as an American novelist's purple passage describes it) was responsible for the artist's loss of innocence. For one thing, Michelangelo decided to express in verse a thought which obsesses him as an artist: clothing has no more meaning than has the *soverchio* of a statue, the excess material which encases true form. Clothing has form only as it outlines the contours of the figure it embraces—indeed, has form only when cloth gives way to the flesh and muscle of the body. The importance of this belief to Michelangelo is most apparent in the figures of Giuliano and Lorenzo in the Medici crypt, for the military tunics of these two dukes disappear from their torsos, muscular bodies emerging to supplant them.

Valerio Mariani feels that the *Studio di Donna* in the British Museum illustrates the sonnet "Quanto si gode" (G 4).

The experiment of transferring this basic tenet of sculpture to poetry so fascinated Michelangelo that he tried it again in a poem dating from after 1535 and doubtless addressed to Tommaso Cavalieri. First he wishes he were the silkworm which sacrifices its cocoon for the making of an elegant silk glove, thus living again on Tommaso's hand. He wishes he he could shed his skin like a snake and dying clothe Tommaso with it. Finally he wishes that his skin were the garment and the shoes which embrace the young nobleman:

> Oh, if only it were mine, the hairy pelt
> Which, with its plaited fur, makes such a coat
> That fortunately embraces such a fine breast.
> I'd clasp it all the day. Or the slippers
> Which make for him a base and a column,
> I'd carry him on them for at least two winters. (G 94)

Again the verbs *contessere* and *stringere* appear.

Since the poem to the "Bolognese girl" is intended as an exercise in making an aesthetic point in rhyme, its value as an autobiographical document is certainly diminished. Such value is further denigrated if the poem turns out to be merely a plagiarism of another writer.

It has been proposed that this sonnet is an evocation of one of Luigi Alamanni's *Rime:*

> Per farti una ghirlanda, la mia Clori,
> Vado cogliendo in questo prato i fiori,
> Deh t'abbracciasse io come
> Questi ti cingeran le belle chiome.[16]

Luigi, however, was only thirteen in 1508.

It is rather my belief that Michelangelo had in mind a pleasant word picture by the humanist Politian of Simonetta Cattaneo, found in the same stanzas which apparently inspired the artist's allegorical figures in his *Stanze in Praise of Rustic Life:*

> Candida è ella, e candida la vesta,
> Ma pur di rose e fior dipinta e d'erba:
> Lo inanellato crin dell'aurea testa I, 43
> Scende . . .

Ell' era assisa sopra la verdura
Allegra, e ghirlandetta avea contesta
Di quanti fior creasse mai natura,
De' quali era dipinta la sua vesta . . . I, 46

Ch'e' suoi crin biondi e crespi all'aura spiega
E mille fiori in ghirlandetta lega . . .
Questa con ambe man le tien sospesa
Sopra l'umide trecce una ghirlanda
D'oro e di gemme orientali accesa . . . I, 102

There is no doubt about Michelangelo's knowing these lines, and especially the last three verses. These describe the woodcarving on the temple of Venus, and particularly the wafting of Aphrodite onto the strand. One nymph covers Venus's hair with a garland as other nymphs clothe the goddess. The same could easily inspire lines of Michelangelo's poetry, just as they incited Botticelli to paint the scene as *The Birth of Venus*. Michelangelo even borrows the very rhyme words (*vesta/contesta/testa: ghirlanda/spanda*). Michelangelo supplied, however, the feature which was lacking in Politian: the emergence of the human figure and the recession of the clothing itself. Furthermore, he added the concupiscence mentioned by Luigi Alamanni and the later poets. In sum, Michelangelo's "poem to the Bolognese girl" reminds us of Horace's *Epodes* 8 and 12, which were not personal or confessional documents after all, but imitations of Archilochus's invective against his former betrothed.

XI. Were there other women in Michelangelo's life? Even those who propose the compromise theory that Michelangelo was ambisexual are at a loss to find any woman whom he loved or with whom he had an affair. Various editors have invented ladies out of adjectives occurring in Michelangelo's *Rime*. They talk of the "donna aspra e fiera," "donna altera, bella e crudele," or the "donna bella e dispietata," the latter evocative of Guittone's "Spietata donna e fera." They seem unconcerned that these similar attributes could refer to the same individual, most possibly theoretical. Others talk assuredly of an "unknown, elegantly-attired, much-bejeweled lady," reminiscent of Michelangelo's allegory of Wealth and who would have been equally incompatible to him. There was conjecture about the vain and exacting lady of "Costei pur si delibra," before it became apparent that she was most probably an allegorical figure representing the fine arts. Girardi groups together a series of poems for a "donna altera, bella e crudele" with the early (1536–38) pieces to Vittoria Colonna. Yet it is easy to conclude that Michelangelo, in his fleeting moments of withdrawal from this saintly woman (see above) might easily have considered her *altera* (cf. G 156).

Evidences of Michelangelo's misogyny are numerous, even down to his use of male models for female figures. There are little traces of misogyny in his correspondence, such as his boutades that all servant girls of Rome are whores, that girls without families easily become whores at court. Witness also the haste of Sebastiano del Piombo to inform the artist that he, Il Piombino, has given up his *comare*. The haughtiness of the women in his exercises of love poetry is no endearing trait. Even the little country lass in the *Stanze* on rustic life stands apart in a hostile mood ("in contegno"). Michelangelo's playful poem "Tu a' 'l uiso piu dolcie che la sapa" pokes fun at woman's most sacred and praised physical charms: skin shiny, hair the color of leeks, teeth like beans, teats like cucumbers in a sack (paralleling the weakened breasts ridiculed in Michelangelo's sketch of Vittoria Colonna). Ironically, the poet adds that this parodied woman excites him. The poem is in a sense a *contr'amour* (see Chapter XII).

Michelangelo's friendships with living women were as inconclusive as were those vaguely mentioned in his poetry. As for the legend circulating that he was as a child smitten by Contessina de' Medici, every sort of circumstance would have prevented such a romance from developing. The widow of his assistant Urbino, Cornelia Colonnelli, felt that she knew him well enough to be insistent and even contentious, but no affection was involved. He knew and respected Ammannati's wife, Laura Battiferro, and he admired her poetry as he admired that of Vittoria Colonna. Papini demonstrates very convincingly that Michelangelo had a real affection for the young painter Sofonisba Anguissola when she was not yet thirty and he had reached his eighties. Again their mutual admiration could not develop into an affair, and at best such a young woman could only have inspired some of the September songs in which he complains that the fire of passion makes quick work of seasoned wood.

If it is true that Michelangelo never had a known affair with a woman, why then did he write so many poems giving evidence of heterosexual love? In the first place, his study of models in poetry centered on Dante, Petrarch, Lorenzo, and Poliziano. If as a young man he is already addressing a Donna in his poetry, it is a purely traditional exercise. It is a turnabout from the Renaissance love poems to men—including Shakespeare's—by poets who were not homosexuals. The poems, moreover, do not celebrate a completed union with a woman—only sing of unfulfillment, unattainability, and rejection. Platonism and Petrarchism dominate, and both of these may deal with love in the most abstract way. Never does this painter who was obliged every time he painted a woman to fill in all the physical details, such as hair style, color of eyes, and the rest—never does he give us such details about the women to whom he allegedly sings his songs. They are abstract *typoi* and their very existence may thus be doubted.

XII. The recital in Chapter VI of Michelangelo's infatuation with Cecchino Bracci casts light on Michelangelo's sexual mores. As we turn now to the poems to Tommaso Cavalieri, Gherardo Perini, and Febo di Poggio, it is not our purpose to stir up spent coals. It might be useful, however, to assess the various self-justifications which are found in Michelangelo's poetry, explanations rather than exculpations from the pen of a man disturbed by the Malebouches among his fellows. As we have written elsewhere, Michelangelo in general felt that he lived in a world of wagging tongues, yet found it difficult to heed the advice of Sebastiano del Piombo to shrug off such talk. Yet when the talk descended to Michelangelo's relations with younger men, he found it hard to remain silent. Let us review his disclaimers in chronological order and relate them to events in his life.

XIII. As early as 1532 Michelangelo stipulates in a sonnet to Tommaso Cavalieri that he is inspired by the young man's face to sentiments which outsiders could never appreciate—which, indeed most human beings would have to die first before understanding. One variant, however, does not limit the inspiration to Tommaso's face, but reads:

What from thee I long for and learn to know deep within me
Cannot be well understood by outward acts and signs. (G 60 var.)

Already there is the defensive thought that outsiders will only misunderstand his feelings for the younger man. Another variant reads:

It is scarcely understood by the minds of men.

Over ten years before, Michelangelo had met Gherardo Perini, and gossips may then have included him in their indoor sport. By 1534 talk had begun about Michelangelo's affection for Tommaso, and we know from Michelangelo's letters that such talk discomfited the younger man even more than it did the artist, who entered into such relationships more completely and blindly, as he stated in the dialogues of Giannotti. Partly to explain his feelings and partly to reassure Tommaso, the artist wrote:

Read by my thoughts, thy features seem to shine
With that which human words can ill explain,
A soul still compassed with its earthly chain,
But beauteous bright and fired with Love divine;
And if the base and envious world malign
And point with scorn at those who think like thee,
Unchanging still with firm fidelity,
My heart, my faith, my preference, are thine. (G 83)

Michelangelo, as his poetry and art point out, was less concerned by the pointing fingers of his contemporaries than by the upraised arm of Christ. He urges Tommaso to share his Horatian scorn for the vulgar, chirruping crowd. Remember also that by this time his relationship with Febo di Poggio was several months old, which made the artist more defensive about the gossip.

In 1536–42 Michelangelo wrote his successful sonnet to Cavalieri "Per ritornar la, donde uenne fora." There are at least seven variants to this piece, showing its importance to him. The final tercet, generally preferred, reads:

Ne Dio, suo gratia, mi si mostra altroue
Piu che 'n alcun leggiadro e mortal uelo;
E quel sol amo, perch'in lui si spechia. (G 106)

(For translation see p. 146.)

It is clear that Michelangelo views Tommaso's physical beauty as nothing less than an incorporation of God's beauty itself. One of the variants of the last line stresses the chastity of this love:

Nel casto amarti, da chi piu se' bello.

A madrigal, "Per fido esemplo," composed during the period 1541–44, again reveals that Michelangelo is sensitive to opinions about his personal life:

For faithful guide unto my laboring heart
Beauty was given me at birth,
To be my glass and lamp in either art.
Who thinketh otherwise misknows her worth,
For highest beauty only gives me light
To carve and paint aright.
Rash is the thought and vain
That maketh beauty from the senses grow.
She lifts to heaven hearts that truly know,
But eyes grown dim with pain
From mortal to immortal cannot go
Nor without grace of God look up again. (G 164)

(George Santayana)

In 1545 Aretino wrote his damaging slur (see below) about Michelangelo's consorting with Gherardo Perini and Tommaso Cavalieri. By this time, one assumes, the talk was not only widespread but commonly accepted. Accordingly, Michelangelo writes one more brief *apologia pro vita sua*, in a sonnet which begins:

In one instant there passes through the eyes to the heart
Every sort of beautiful object which exists,
On such a vast and capacious field of vision
That a hundred, nay, a thousand, are caught up,
Of every age, of each sex, whereat I am bewildered. . . (G 276)

This last line in the first version had read, by the way, "d'ogni sorte e fortuna" (of every fate and fortune). By this time the friendships with men had all begun—with Gherardo, Febo, Tommaso, Cecchino. There would be less "voice of Echo" (G 6) in the future, but there will be more poetry in which Michelangelo will look forward anxiously to his judgement by Christ and worry ingravescently about his salvation. This last sonnet dates probably from 1547–50. Explanations of Michelangelo's affection for these younger men will be undertaken in 1550 by Vasari and in 1553 by Condivi.

In a letter (28 July, 1533) to Tommaso, a man almost forty years his junior, Michelangelo made this amazing declaration of love: "I could as easily forget the food which only nourishes my body miserably, as your name, which nourishes both body and soul, filling the one and the other with such sweetness that neither weariness nor fear of death is felt by me while memory preserves you in my mind. Think, if the eyes could also enjoy their portion, in what condition I should find myself." (CDXVI, Symonds' translation.)

Posterity should be grateful for Michelangelo's friendship with the Roman nobleman Tommaso Cavalieri. Without it we should be the poorer by many fine poems and several important sketches. If Flamini, in the *Cinquecento,* finds "abnormality" in Michelangelo's tenderness for Tommaso, it was apparently not in the nature of consummated pederasty. At the outset Tommaso was troubled at this dedicated love and uncertain how to deal with it. When Michelangelo realised that he was frightening the younger man away, he hastened in letters and in poems to present a chastened view of his feelings, sought to allay suspicion and concern. Gossip has made Cavalieri pitiless (*spietato*) toward the anguished poet and Tomai has apparently turned down an appointment (*giornata*) with him:

> Then, alas! how shall ever be heard
> The chaste wish that flames within my heart,
> By him who always sees himself in another's words?
> My precious day will not then be spent
> With my lord, who gives heed to falsehoods.
> For when one tells the truth, the liar is he who believes not. (G 58)

Nothing less than holy is the artist's love for Tommaso, if we accept the sincerity of a sonnet from 1546:

> For if every one of our affections displeases heaven,
> To what purpose would God have made the world? (G 259)

Let us by all means accept the Platonic and chaste nature of this love, whose character was surely determined by Tommaso rather than by the artist. Indeed, Tommaso married around 1548 and became a loyal father and even grandfather. (His firstborn son, Emilio, as Papini discovered, was a musician and pioneer of the Camerata dei Bardi.) In any case, the holiness of this affection for Tommaso, which evidently germinated in 1532 (the date of the first letters) did not prevent Michelangelo from entering into his relationship with Febo di Poggio by the following year. One is almost tempted to wonder whether in 1533 Tommaso might not have been converted into a *chandelier,* to cover up more unworthy loves like that of Febo. Thus, one is amused to read Michelangelo's song on his attainment of such a firm and solid love for Tommaso that he hopes for perdition should he look longingly upon another:

> May I burn if I do not love thee with my heart,
> And lose my soul, if I feel for any other. (G 96)

Certainly Michelangelo attained new heights in his poems for Cavalieri. We have quoted from some of the finest of these which illustrate his belief that true love denotes a complete union and fusion of mind, soul, and body. Throughout the poems to Tommaso recur the adjectives *casto* and *onesto,* which are the *imprimatur* of the innocence of his tremendous affection. Such a poem is the following sonnet, "Se nel uolto per gli ochi," in which Michelangelo addresses Tommaso in language he would use to the Christus Iudex when longing for the tender embrace of the once upraised arm:

> If through the eyes the heart speaks clear and true,
> I have no stronger sureties than these eyes
> For my pure love. Prithee let them suffice,
> Lord of my soul, pity to gain from you.
> More tenderly perchance than is my due,
> Your spirit sees into my heart, where rise
> The flames of holy worship, nor denies
> The grace reserved for those who humbly sue.
> Oh blessed day when you at last are mine!
> Let time stand still, and let noon's chariot stay;
> Fixed be that moment on the dial of heaven!
> That I may clasp and keep by grace divine,
> Clasp in these yearning arms and keep for aye
> My heart's loved lord to me desertless given! (G 72)
> (J. A. Symonds)

This sonnet, which we have already associated with the Christ of the Universal Judgement, increases in interest in light of the possibility that Tommaso's face was painted as that of the Christus Iudex.

Of the many pieces addressed to Cavalieri evocative of Benivieni's love sonnets to Pico, two additional ones might be reproduced here. The first, "Non so, se s'e" (1533) shows that even an ideal love has moments of suspense and uncertainty as well as a bittersweet quality:

> I know not if from uncreated spheres
> Some longed for ray it be that warm my breast,
> Or lesser light, in memory expressed,

Of some once lovely face, that reappears,
Or passing rumor ringing in my ears,
Or dreamy vision, once my bosom's guest,
That left behind I know not what unrest,
Haply the reason of these wayward tears.
But what I feel and seek, what leads me on,
Comes not of me; nor can I tell aright
Where shines the hidden star that sheds this light.
Since I behold thee, sweet and bitter fight
Within me. Resolution have I none.
Can this be, Master, what thine eyes have done? (G 76)
(George Santayana)

The sonnet "A che piu debb' io mai l'intensa uogla" develops the theme of the lover's helplessness, ordained by heaven, and the uselessness of protest. The sonnet's theme is interesting enough, but more striking is the fact that Michelangelo puns in Petrarchan fashion on the nobleman's name. The last tercet reads:

If vanquished and imprisoned, I am to be blest,
It is no marvel if, nude and alone,
I remain the prisoner of an armed Cavalier. (G 98)

Varchi early identified the object of the poem as this noble Roman youth, whom the artist had found endowed with great charm and beauty. This final line has been adduced to explain the cryptic meaning of Michelangelo's *Genio della Vittoria* (see Chapter V).

Many other poems to Tommaso Cavalieri appear in this volume, illustrating further moods, themes, or styles in the *Rime*.

XIV. In November, 1545 the trouble-making Aretino (whom recent scholars try in vain to whitewash) wrote a letter to Michelangelo on the nudities of the *Giudizio universale*. He makes a gratuitous allusion to two of the young men loved by Michelangelo. "[L'invidia] vuole che non si possin disporre se non Gherardi e Tomai." Having already dealt with the poems to Tommaso Cavalieri, we now must weigh those to Gherardo Perini and Febo di Poggio.

Gherardo Perini became a close friend of Michelangelo around 1520. Giovan Francesco Fattucci and the goldsmith Piloto (Giovanni di Baldassarre) were mutual friends of theirs, as was Vincenzo Perini, brother or relative of Gherardo. We possess three letters from Gherardo to the artist, written on 11 January and on 6 and 18 July, 1522. In February, 1522, Michelangelo sent the following reply to Gherardo's first courteous letter:

All of your friends as well as I, my most dear Gherardo, were overjoyed, and especially those whom you recognise as loving you most, hearing of your good health and welfare through your last letter delivered by the faithful

Zampino; although your kindness in this letter obligates me to reply, I do not feel sufficient to the task; I shall say merely this: that we your friends are likewise, that is in good health, and we all send you our respects and especially Ser Giovan Francesco and Piloto. Knowing that you will shortly be here, I hope to do this more fully by mouth and to satisfy myself about every particular, because it is a matter of importance to me.

On some date or other in February, according to my biddy,
Your most faithful and poor friend.

There is in this letter the same indefinable personal insistence which is found in letters to or concerning Cavalieri, Febo di Poggio, and Cecchino Bracci. A similar vague but revealing admission of the sway of Gherardo over the artist is the jotting (translated on p. 145) on a folio showing a *putto* urinating into a vase, a preliminary sketch dated at some time between 1522 and 1530. Under the Petrarchan line "Valle locus clausus toto mihi nullus in orbe" a listless and lonely Michelangelo penned: "Io vi prego che non mi facciate disegnare stasera perchè e' non c'è el Perino."

Giovanni Papini, indignant at the slur by Aretino, attempts to explain away any overtones of homosexuality in this relationship. In the registry of the Baptistery of the Opera of the Florentine Duomo he finds a Gherardo di Domenico Perini, baptised on 12 March, 1480. Perini was thus forty-two at the time Michelangelo replied to his first letter. As Papini concludes derisively: "The forties are not the ideal age for an *efebo* and a *cinedo*." We cannot share Papini's conclusion, but since we are here interested in the poetry, we must admit that any references to Gherardo in the *Rime* are never specific or by name. The poems expressing penitence or regret at past sins may well refer to the relationship with Perini, however.

Puns on the name of Febo di Poggio are much in evidence, nevertheless. So also is a revealing letter to this young man from December, 1533 (Ramsden proposes the alternate date of September, 1534):

Febo,—Although you bear me great hatred, I know not why, I can hardly believe it is because of the great love I bear you, but because of the words of others, words which you should not believe, having put me to the test. I cannot help, however, writing you this. I am leaving tomorrow and go to Pescia to meet the Cardinal de Cesis and Messer Baldassare. I shall go with them to Pisa and then to Rome. I'll not return here again. I want you to understand that so long as I live, wherever I shall be, I shall always be at your service with loyalty and love, more than any other friend you may have in this world.

I pray to God to open your eyes for a while longer, so that you may recognise that he who desires your welfare more than his own salvation knows how to love and not hate as an enemy.

The artist who once signed a letter discreetly as "Piero"[17] appends no signature whatsoever. Again the constant fears about others' calumnies which have led us to conclude elsewhere that Michelangelo believed himself surrounded by Malebouches.[18] A reply arrives from Febo the following month. After some details on his comings and goings, the young man assures Michelangelo that he could never become angry with the artist, whom he considers a father to him. Furthermore, Michelangelo's behavior toward him was not of a sort to breed hatred. The young man, perhaps a model, then adds that Michelangelo had promised him money which he still is expecting. "Here I find myself in need of money for clothes and to go to the Monte and see the fights, for Messer Vincenzo is there . . . So I beg you to provide and help me with however much you think you can." Certainly this cajoling letter is an unsettling document, even if Aretino forgot to mention Febo in his reference to the *mignons* of the great artist.

Whereas Gherardo Perini is never specifically named in the *Rime*, Febo di Poggio, like Tommaso and Cecchino, is directly involved in at least two sonnets (one incomplete) which pun on his name. When the exaltation of his affair with Febo had passed, when Michelangelo probably realised that the young man was exploiting both his fame and his finances, the artist ruefully wrote:

> Well might I in those days so fortunate,
> What time Phoebus lightened my path above,
> Have soared from earth to heaven, raised by [his] love
> Who winged my laboring soul and sweetened fate.
> The sun hath set, and I with hope elate
> Who deemed that those bright days would never move,
> Find that my thankless soul, deprived thereof,
> Declines to death, while heaven still bars the gate.

Although some editors incredibly believe the recipient of these lines to be Vittoria Colonna, among them being Guasti, Frey, and Ceriello, Michelangelo repeats the young man's full name (Febo/Poggio) in the first of the tercets:

> Love lent me wings, my path was like a stair [Poggio];
> A lamp unto my feet that sun [Phoebus] was given;
> And death was safety and great joy to find.
> But dying now, I shall not climb to heaven;
> Nor can mere memory cheer my heart's despair—
> What help remains when hope is left behind? (G 99)
> (J. A. Symonds)

Grimm, with heavy pedantry, sees the poem as political allegory, Febo representing Florence. However, Symonds, Girardi, and others acknowledge the patent meaning of past excitement and present disillusionment. The sonnet concludes that all is over, that his soul no longer ascends to Heaven; today love and he are as dead. All is so far past that even the memory of it now fails to stir the heart. Consolation is no more after the damage is done. Even his fidelity to Febo had served no purpose. This memory of a probably deviated relationship is glossed in Neo-Platonic imagery and vocabulary: winged soul, ladder of love, and identification of love with light.

At the same time, or possibly earlier, Michelangelo penned his incomplete sonnet, "Ben fu, temprando il ciel":

Heaven was surely devoid of pity toward me,
Fusing thy keen ray on two eyes alone,
While with its swift and eternal motion,
I gave to us the light and to you the journey.
Happy bird, with such advantage over us,
To thee is known Phoebus and his fair face,
And even more than this grand sight, it is further granted thee
To fly to those heights [poggio] whence I fall
to my ruin. (G 100)

After the second quatrain the flow of thought breaks off. There is nothing substantive to add after the recollection of disaster. There is only the remembrance of Febo's "beautiful face" (the phrase is used also with both Cecchino and Tommaso). Michelangelo falls like Phaeton before the searing rays of Phoebus, and envies the phoenix to which he now contrasts himself. The young man's name provides two puns, the idealised Phoebus and the heights from which the poet falls.

Certainly there may be other echoes of young Febo in Michelangelo's writings and art, such as the reproach to Febo ("perchè a mme sol ti scuri") in a rejected variant of G 246. The *Fetonte* was apparently given to Tommaso Cavalieri, but its message coincided with the sentiments of the poetry (*rovino* e *caggio*) to Febo. One recalls Febo on reading such a fragment as:

In such a wretched state, your face
Doth lend us, like the sun, gloom or light. (G App. 36)

Febo is mentioned by name in a variant of "Te sola del mio mal contenta ueggio." In this variant the adjective becomes masculine (*contento*). Herein he calls Febo *sole*, reinforcing our surmise that in other poems "sun" may actually refer to this young friend.

Oh sun which warms the world on every side,
Oh, Febo, oh light eternal of mortal men,
Why dost thou obscure thyself to me alone and not to others?

Despite the masculine gender of the variant, some editors would have this poem directed to Vittoria Colonna. If it were true that Michelangelo used feminine forms even when patently addressing Febo, this opens up the possibility that many of the poems apparently written for ladies were actually intended for men. The sentiments here are the same ones evidenced in his other poetry to men: pride, humility, sense of sin, etc. Indeed, the version with the masculine *contento* was originally written under a letter to Febo di Poggio of September, 1534, leading Girardi to conclude that the *capitolo* was in fact directed to Febo.

In the British Museum there is a page of black chalk and pen studies: a nude seen from behind, two *putti*, leg study (1859–6–25–564 *recto*). The central figure of a nude young man is not so boldly drawn as the *putti*, nor does it have their hatchings. Various scholars date the drawings from as early as 1504 (date of the Pitti tondo and the *Battaglia di Cascina*) while others fix the date at 1520–25 or later. The folio contains four lines written in the same dark-grey ink of the leg study:

> Only I remain burning in the dusk
> After the sun has stripped the world of its rays:
> Whereas other men take pleasure, I do but mourn,
> Prostrate on the ground, lamenting and weeping. (G 2)

In his edition of the drawings Goldscheider supposes that the poem dates from "the time of Michelangelo's friendship with Perini, after 1522; the handwriting is not that of the early period."[19] Whether one accepts the earlier dating (1503–04) of Wilde and Girardi or that of Goldscheider, it is probable that the piece was composed before the friendship with Febo. Thus, one finds the poet in advance of Febo addicted to the theme of the flaming sun to whose dazzling heights the lover dare not rise.

Another fragment recorded by Girardi recalls incoherently a "charming and beautiful soggiorno" under the influence of Febo. Even in this garbled profusion of scattered words one finds that the brilliance of Febo led only to pain: "mi addolora" (G App. 10).

Whatever one may think of the little "blackmailer" who condoned Michelangelo's behavior, who claimed to hold Michelangelo "in a father's place," and who dunned the old artist for money, he did inspire poetry, melancholy and confessional, in Michelangelo. Thus he won an immortality more identifiable in the *Rime* than somewhere in the works of the artist for which he served as a model.

XV. A persistent theme of the *Rime*, as indeed of all poetry, is the relationship between those stern realities love and death. Sometimes their hostility works to the advantage of the poet, sometimes to his disadvantage. Love and death are often viewed as similar menaces, death being an immediate dissolution and love a lingering one (G 11). The attacks of love are frequently mortal:

In the blows of love, a mortal wound (G App. 37)
The fire stings and the wound is mortal. (G 27)

If death and love are normally at odds, "Che doue è morte, non s'appressa amore" (G 127), if death comes "inuidiosa e fella" between the poet and love (G 125), death is sometimes a boon to the lover. Death delivers the poet from the snares and pains of love. Michelangelo keeps the image of death firm in his heart as a shield against love, that image which sufficed also to dispel even thoughts of his art (G 127). Divine grace may also accompany death (G 128), which intensifies his preference for death to love. Indeed, the rain of grace can extinguish forever the flames of love.

In death the poet will no longer have to face the mockery of the one who makes him weep (G 127). Just as Michelangelo envied the heavenly host for being above the stresses and strains of earthly life (in the *capitolo* on his father's death), so does he suppose that these blessed souls love without turmoil. He addresses them directly and receives confirmation:

> Our eternal quiet,
> Outside all time, is deprived
> Of envy, loving, and of anguished weeping. (G 134)

The poet replies that the thought of living so long on earth in the travails of earthly love frightens him:

> For a little is too much to him who serves well and strives.

Since death assumes the role of counselor or even saviour, the older Michelangelo grows, the more easily does death ward off love's attacks (G 231). The certainty that love is a slow death and that his only salvation will be a rapid one permits the poet to indulge in baroque contradictions and playful logic: "I should be deadly except for my death. Nor against death doth any other force prevail than death, etc." (G 118). In the series of late sonnets and madrigals on love's tyranny over the aged during those last short hours when "the fruit is fallen and the rind is dried," the poet grants that if love dispels thoughts of death, disturbing though love is, it mitigates and makes love sweeter thereby (G 158). Thus he is grateful for such loves as that for Tommaso Cavalieri which rid him of thanatophobia ("nè timor di morte posso sentire").

XVI. Some of the finest poetic monuments Michelangelo left behind are his September songs, whether intended for some younger men or for a young woman like Sofonisba Anguissola. He was even capable of rationalising that late loves are the finest, for what has been waited for longest is most rare and cherished:

> For everything rare has greater force and value,
> The less near it is and the most desired. (G 257)

In a *sonetto caudato* on servitude to love (G 25) he denies that an old man cannot love. Love returns him to his "less green" age, warms and nurtures him, restores and rekindles him, and in sum rejuvenates:

> And if some make idle talk and feign,
> Saying that it is a shame in one's old age
> To love something divine, it is a great lie.

Old age was to him merely the "eta men uerde" (G 142), for the flame of love is never spent. An old man has as much right to love as any if he observes "weight, limit, and measure." "Perche l'eta ne 'nuola" (G 268) admits that while the artist is already tired, near his last word, and reconciled with death itself, love still incites and fills him with fire and hope. In the piece "Or d'un fier giaccio or d'un ardente foco" (G 269), however, this hope dims and he is a mere mirror of old age, woes, and shame. "Amor, se tu se' dio" (G 262) finds Michelangelo "close to dying," wondering whether death, which is so harsh to the unfortunate, will be any less pitiless to "him who dies on the threshold of his greatest happiness." A truly pathetic note is struck in the sonnet "Tornami al tempo, allor che lenta e sciolta" (1547), a vivid and painful evocation which has proved predictably popular with translators. Here the aged poet, "almost arrived on the other shore," begs for a recollection of his past love. Even though it will be a melancholy review *du temps perdu*, his old age will protect him:

> Oh give me back the days when loose and free
> To my blind passion were the curb and rein,
> Oh give me back the angelic face again,
> With which all virtue buried seems to be:
> Oh give my panting footsteps back to me,
> That are in age so slow and fraught with pain,
> And fire and moisture in the heart and brain,
> If thou wouldst have me burn and weep for thee!
> If it be true thou livest alone, Amor,
> On the sweet-bitter tears of human hearts,
> In an old man thou canst not wake desire;
> Souls that have almost reached the other shore
> If a diviner love should feel the darts,
> And be as tinder to a holier fire. (G 272)
>
> (H. W. Longfellow)

His advanced years and his full experience as well will dim the stings of memory. Not that the lessons of experience will always protect one from new exposure to beauty; he is less confident in the following "September song," notable for its unusual metaphorical variations upon the theme of imminent death:

The young beauty of a woman
Spurs, incites, and whips me on,
Even though not only is tierce hour passed,
But nones and vespers and the eve is nigh.
My birth and my fortune—
The one already plays with death,
Nor can the other here give me entire peace.
I, who was well adjusted
To both my white head and my many years,
Already held in hand the plow of the other life,
As is promised to one with a contrite heart.
He loses most who fears the least
In the last round of the game,
Having trust in himself and his own power
Against the accustomed ardor:
If only the ear is left of memory,
It is of no avail, without grace, to be old. (G 263)

In the madrigal "No' salda, Amor, de tuo dorati strali" the weakened defenses of the aged lover are again described ("no longer helmet or shield"). It is a hopeless struggle against love, one which would attack the dead themselves. Michelangelo, exposed as the bare herm of the *Saettatori* drawing, decides that his defeat is inevitable:

Weak, old, and late. And the flight
Is slow in which I've placed my trust.
He who wins by fleeing, let him not stay on the field. (G 175)

There are some further observations of interest on the hardships of an old man in love. Old men suffer the hardest in love and are the quickest to be destroyed: "Piu presto ancidi quante uien piu tardi" (G 232). Love's arrow plants itself more fatally in the old man's heart (G 142). This despite the point of his madrigal, "S'i' fussi stato ne prim'anni accorto" (G 253), that he who has been burned in youth by love can handle the better such attacks in old age. The thought that habits which are entrenched in older men make it harder to adjust to love affairs finds several modes of expression:

For heaven lends no aid
Against old habits in such a brief span of time. (G 143)

For entrenched error
Grows ever stronger as I advance in years. (G 92)

If a long span of unworthy and foolish habits
Needs even more time to be purged for the better,
Death already nigh doth grant it not,
Nor doth evil desire find a curb on what it wished. (G 297)

There is an increasing consciousness that the amour passion is a weakness and more frequent are mentions of *onore* and *vergogna*.

XVII. Thus, it is no surprise that we arrive at the absolute renunciation of love, as something unworthy in the eyes of God:

> Once fire used to burn in the cold ice,
> Now the ardent fire for me is naught but cold ice;
> Loosened, Love, is that indissoluble knot.
> Death to me now is what was once merriment and sport. (G 281)

In 1544 he again echoed this thought that the time was past for "flaming hearts" (G 231). Even more than physical exhaustion and disappointments, the realisation that old age is the time to press for one's salvation drove him toward a renunciation of love. As he put it in a late, somber sonnet:

> Thoughts on love, once carefree and happy,
> What may they be now, as I approach two deaths? (G 285)

We have already noted that one of his poems turning away from pursuit of the fine arts includes almost automatically a rejection of earthly love:

> Love, the Muses, and the flowery grottoes . . .
> My scribblings and drawings now are used
> For inns, for privies, and for brothels. (G 267)

Finally, in his very last poetic effort of which we have record (1560), he admits his loss of will and acknowledges that He who cleanses and heals the soul can alone save the old artist from:

> Love, perilous and vain emotions. (G 302)

NOTES

[1] In *Lettere ed armi* (Milan, 1883), II.
[2] Arturo Insinga, *Michelangelo poeta, ed. cit.*, pp. 9–10.
[3] Charles de Tolnay, *The Medici Chapel* (Princeton, 1948), p. 114.
[4] Enrico Bevilacqua, *op. cit.*, p. 648.
[5] D. Giannotti, *Dialogi, ed. cit.*, p. 68.
[6] See R. J. Clements, *Picta poesis: Humanistic and Literary Theory in Renaissance Emblem Books* (Rome, 1960), p. 202.
[7] See R. J. Clements, *Michelangelo's Theory, ed. cit.*, pp. 7–14. We find an unusual parallel of Michelangelo's lines in Gabriela Mistral, *Lagar* (Santiago de Chile, 1954), p. 13:

> Todo el cuerpo hecho pupila.

[8] *Lettere*, ed. Milanesi, p. 467.
[9] Antonio Amico-Mantia, *L'amore e le Rime di Michelangelo* (Trapani, 1899), p. 6.

[10] Walter Pater, *The Renaissance* (New York; Modern Library, n.d.), p. 70. See also, for a Victorian view, Pierre de Bouchaud, *Les poésies de Michel-Ange et de Vittoria Colonna* (Paris, 1912).
[11] Valerio Mariani, *La poesia di Michelangelo, ed. cit.*, p. 165.
[12] Vincenzo Pascale, *op. cit.*, p. 44.
[13] G. Papini, *La vita, ed. cit.*, p. 163.
[14] R. J. Clements, *Michelangelo's Theory, ed. cit.*, p. 77.
[15] Giuseppe Calero, *Michelangelo poeta* (Turin; S. E. I., n.d.), pp. 26–48.
[16] In *Rime inedite del '500* (Bologna, 1918), p. 36.
[17] In 1942 Poggi unconvincingly attributed this letter to an assistant.
[18] See R. J. Clements, *Michelangelo's Theory, ed. cit.*, pp. 375–83.
[19] L. Goldscheider, *Drawings of Michelangelo* (London, 1951), p. 29.

11

POETRY AS PRAYER AND CONFESSION

MICHELANGELO COMPOSED TWO, and possibly three, prayers which have come down to us. He was a firm believer in prayer, as we know. He admitted in a letter complaining of his painful gallstones that he had more confidence in prayer than in medicine. When embarked on a new commission he prayed for its successful outcome and urged that his father pray likewise. Describing the simple, enviable husbandman in his idyll on the Golden Age, he alleges:

He honors, loves, fears, and prays to God. (G 67)

The artist's creative urge could thus naturally find an outlet in prayer. A minimal orison in his handwriting is a surprising addition to a pen sketch of torsos:

Deus in nomine tuo salvum me fac!

The youthful hand would indicate the early age at which Michelangelo feared for his salvation. A jubilant poem prayer or paean of utter simplicity from 1505–06 reads:

Praise, little ones (*parvoli*),
Our Lord.
Praise Him ever. (G App. 15)

Quaint and curious—an opportunity missed by those romanticising painters who filled the Casa Buonarroti with their evocations of the master—is the picture of the thirty-year-old artist exhorting youngsters to prayer.

Finally, there is the longer prayer found among his autographs, not in his handwriting but accompanied by some of his jottings. Guasti, who reproduced it, could not claim it to be Michelangelo's composition, but the spirit of this *Orazione* corresponds closely to the religious effusions among his late poetry (see Chapter XVII):

O most lofty father, through whose kindness I was made a Christian only to bring me into Thy kingdom; Thou didst create my soul out of nothingness, and didst imprison it in my wretched body; give me grace, so that as long as I stay in this prison inimical to my soul, in which Thou alone dost hold me, I may exalt Thee; for if I praise Thee, Thou wilt give me grace to benefit my fellow men, and in particular to do good to mine enemies and to commend them to Thee. Grant me grace once more, O holy God, since having to endure corporeal sufferings, I may recognise that these will not offend my soul; remembering Thy most holy Son, who for the salvation of humanity died so shamefully; from this I shall take consolation, and I shall always praise Thy holy name. Amen.[1]

This effusion is typical not only of Michelangelo's vocabulary and syntax and spelling but of his innermost thoughts: his fixation with the Crucifixion, his fear for his own carnal sins, and even his attempts to pardon his enemies, real and imagined ("Vn generoso, alter' e nobil core/Perdon', et porta a chi l'offend' amore") (G 147).

One of Michelangelo's incomplete sonnets of 1555, expanded in English by Wordsworth from a fuller if inaccurate earlier reading, is a hymn of praise which he tentatively wishes to express as a prayer:

The prayers I make will then be sweet indeed
If Thou the spirit give by which I pray;
My unassisted heart is barren clay;
That of its native self can nothing feed;
Of good and pious works Thou art the seed,
That quickens only where Thou say'st it may:
Unless Thou shew to us Thine own true way
No man can find it: Father! Thou must lead.
Do Thou, then, breathe those thoughts into my mind
By which such virtue may in me be bred
That in Thy holy footsteps I may tread;
The fetters of my tongue do Thou unbind,
That I may have the power to sing of Thee,
And sound Thy praises everlastingly. (G 292)
(William Wordsworth)

It is difficult to separate the elements of prayer and those of confession in Michelangelo's *Rime*, for avowals of moral inadequacy are accompanied by requests for salvation. The importance of confession as a sacramental rite is demonstrated by two letters on the deaths respectively of his brothers Giovan Simone and Gismondo; he inquired immediately in each case whether the brother had died "confesso." None could dispense with the need of prayer and few with the need for confession. Man is born in sin. So was Michelangelo, as was his father before him (G 66). He retained free will, however. We can assume that as a young man Michelangelo went occasionally to confession, that as an older man he found poetry the medium for his *confiteor*. Even as architect and artist he was constantly providing the means for this sacramental act to be carried out. Whether meditating on floor plans for St. Peter's or the Gesù (which he did not finally execute) or contemplating the decoration of a little Franciscan church at La Magliana, creating atmosphere for prayer and space for confession were on his mind.

In his later years, in fact, he developed a mystical or personal relationship with Christ and God which we have earlier characterised as baroque. This sense of immediate proximity, symbolised by the solicitous nearness of Nicodemus to Christ in the Florentine *Deposizione*, eventually did away with the necessity of intermediaries. Even if priests themselves shrived one another in the confessional, Michelangelo elected to purge himself in his poetry and art. Just as artists begin to feel a familiarity with their models, Michelangelo came to know Christ. Poems, mere *goffagini* when treating of profane topics, became a serious thing when they conveyed his religious passion; sufficiently serious to become the language of the *culpa*.

We have already seen evidence of his fear of the Dies Irae in the brief poem from 1505–06. As early as 1532–33 he composes the first real confessional outpouring to Christ, written in pale ink on the back of a letter from Figiovanni. The thoughts are anything but pale. The judgement of Christ on the Cross (*legno*) and his own unworthiness occupy his thoughts, a reminder swelling to a crescendo which will become deafening during his long span of life. If the following piece was from late 1533 it could allude to his passion for Febo, but if it coincided with his first contacts with Tommaso Cavalieri, one must assume that Michelangelo's sin was rather one of intention than commission. Although he partakes of the consequences of Original Sin, his own fall from grace causes him great anxiety:

> Perchance that I might learn what pity is,
> That I might laugh at erring men no more,
> Secure in my own strength as heretofore,
> My soul hath fallen from her state of bliss:
> Nor know I under any flag but this
> How fighting I may scape those perils sore,
> Or how survive the rout and horrid roar
> Of adverse hosts, if I thy succor miss. (G 66)

Michelangelo's interest in secondary causes (so obvious in Giannotti's *Dialogi*) leads him to look for indirect justifications—even for sin; his sins were necessary to teach him greater humanity and humility.

O flesh, O blood, O cross! O pain extreme!
By you may those foul sins be purified,
Wherein my father's were, and I was born!
Lo! Thou alone art good; let Thy supreme
Pity my state of evil cleanse and hide—
So near to death, so far from God, forlorn. (G 66)
(J. A. Symonds)

Still and always the sense of imminent death, coupled with a feeling of unworthiness.

Late in life he shows gratitude for heavenly uplifting; he hopes that it may be intensified as his need is doubled:

From day to day, back to my very first years,
Thou hast been, Lord, my succor and guide,
Whence my soul still trusts
In double assistance in my double concerns. (G 287)

Sometimes Michelangelo's guilt feelings are based on some imprecise offense which he is unable or unwilling to recall. An example is his confessional poem (ca. 1555) petitioning the Redeemer to forgive a vaguely remembered sin which must be known to Christ.

Worried and confused, my soul finds within itself
No motive other than some grave sin,
Scarcely recognised, and yet not concealed
From [God's] immense compassion which looks after the fallen.
I speak to thee, Lord, since every trial I endure
Cannot make man blessed without intervention of thy blood;
Take pity on me, since I am born
Unto thy law; it will not be the first time. (G 280)

The last four words, which have been variously interpreted and translated, mean "it's the same old story," and are an acknowledgement that the artist has worriedly been petitioning forgiveness for over half a century. Artistically, they constitute an admission that the old poet has long abused this same motif. The same *Schuldcomplex* disturbs him in a somewhat later poem:

I think and even know that some pressing guilt,
Hidden from me, holds my spirit in martyrdom.
By its sense and its own burning is my heart
Deprived of peace, of all desire for salvation. (G 291)

Here the poet turns to Divine Love to save him through its intercession.

The most guilt-ridden verses Michelangelo ever wrote (1525) are of necessity repeated here, for their centrifugal power and meaning force their presence into other chapters:

I live in sin, I live dying within myself;
Now is my life not my own, but of sin.
My grace was given of heaven, my evil of myself,
My will dissolved, free will have I no more. (G 32)

At times the confessional poem is so insistent as to become demanding, an imprecation. One of the most pitiful of Michelangelo's sonnets is the late "Vorrei uoler, Signior, quel ch'io non uoglio," in which he complains bitterly of the veil of ice which God has permitted to intervene between them. The artist, who as iconographer saw Doubt as an allegorical figure "armato e zoppo," wants no more of it. The first tercet reaches a paroxysm of emotion:

Rend thou the veil, O Lord, break down this wall,
Which by its hardness keeps retarding so
Thy holy sunshine, in the world blacked out. (G 87)
(J. S. Dwight)

This piece, which we have met and shall encounter again as one of the "trembling-hand" sonnets in Chapter XVII, echoes similar demands for reassurance in the poetry of Vittoria Colonna. The unfortunate Marchioness, persecuted for her religious beliefs, had even greater reason for wishing assurance from God that she was in the right. Both poets are longing for the inner peace and surety of salvation sought also by Juan de Valdés, who first influenced the Marchioness during her Neapolitan-Ischian days.

Prayer need not always be confession or petition. It may be thanksgiving. The following two tercets, addressed perhaps to Christ rather than to some earthly *beatrice*, attain one of the highest points of the *canzoniere:*

In me my death, in thee my life,
Thou dost distinguish and divide and assign the time;
My life is brief or long, however much it please thee.
Happy am I within thy courtesy,
Blessed my soul, where time courses not,
Through thee it has come to contemplating God. (G 37)

Throughout the confessional poetry there is, as we have seen, a constant awareness of the error of the poet's way; "I' conosco e mie danni e 'l uero intendo" (G 43). Sometimes, however, his prayers will shift some of the responsibilities onto God himself. Such hints of a shrugging despair —one sampling follows—come during his later years.

My infinite thoughts, with error filled,
In the last years of my life
Ought to settle down to one alone,
To guide me to the serene days of eternity.
But what can I do, O Lord, If Thou comest not
To me with Thy wonted ineffable graciousness? (G 286)

As God the Father was less a subject of Michelangelo's art than was Christ, similarly, Christ is the recipient of more of these confessional and prayerful poems than was God. As the *Rime* show, the image of the *Christus Iudex* loomed large in Michelangelo's vision ever since the turn of the century. There are many hints in the poetry assuring us that the tremendous task of painting the *Last Judgement* was one he knew he must inevitably undertake. The claim that the mature artist painted every inch of the *Judgement* with the aid of only a paint-mixer must be accepted as indication, perhaps akin to Loyola's flagellation, of a penance and a petition for grace and *cortesia*. The largest fresco in Rome centers upon the Christ to whom his poems flow. He was too scrupulous to paint that Christ as other than austere. Indeed, the anger of his *Christus Iudex* is the proof that in 1534 Michelangelo was by no means sure that his poetic petitions would be granted. It was while pausing from the labors of painting his pessimistic fresco of humanity that he pondered (1534–36) man's fate and wrote, "then I recognise well/the error and wrong of humankind" (G 132). It was at that time he recognised "the old, sweet error/through which he who lives too long/kills his soul and helps not his body" (G 133); then that he meditated on the "eternal damnation of the soul" (G 135), on man's "harsh lot" (G 136). There was the reclothing of man's soul on Judgement Day naturally on his mind:

> If the soul returns at last
> Into its sweet and desired body,
> Heaven, as is believed, either damns or saves . . . (G 140)

Indeed, the love poetry of the years 1534–39 is balanced by fleeting recollections of the solemn and august theme which was occupying his work days. The Last Judgement and the reclothing of souls are also a principal theme when Michelangelo is obliged a few years later to write fifty epitaphs on the death of Cecchino.

The long-suffering and righteous Christ invades the late "trembling-hand" sonnets, of which the most imposing is the "Non fur men lieti che turbati e tristi" (see p. 132). Of lofty inspiration is also "Scarco d'un'importuna e greue salma" (1555), a hymn to the wounded and grieving Saviour. Except for one tercet, it is less reminiscent of the *Christus Iudex* than of the artist's sketches of the stations of Christ's Passion and the *pietàs:*

> Eternal Lord! eased of a cumbrous load
> And loosened from the world, I turn to Thee,
> Shun, like a shattered bark, the storm, and flee
> To Thy protection for a safe abode.
> The crown of thorns, hands pierced upon the tree,
> Thy meek, benign, and lacerated face,
> To a sincere repentance promise grace,
> To the sad soul give hope of pardon free. (G 290)

This poet, who once objected symptomatically that he was "lapidated every day as though he had crucified Christ," achieved in these lines a closeness to his divine confessor which he could never have achieved through a priest. Here again the Crucifixion is recalled, including the nails which are absent from Haman's crucifixion but present on the British Museum drawing of the Crucifixion presented to Vittoria Colonna. In the verses translated by Wordsworth above, Michelangelo seems to be thinking of all the Christs he had drawn, painted, or sculpted, except that of the Day of Wrath. However, the first tercet, quoted earlier (see p. 125), is an intrusive outcry against the upraised arm of the *Christus Iudex:*

> With justice mark not Thou, O Light Divine,
> My fault, nor hear it with Thy sacred ear;
> Neither put forth that way Thy arm severe;
> Wash with Thy blood my sins; thereto incline
> More readily the more my years require
> Help, and forgiveness speedy and entire.
> (William Wordsworth)

In his spiritual drouth Michelangelo prays for the "rain" of grace. How impossible it was for his contemporaries—the Aretinos, the Gilio da Fabrianos, the Pope Pauls, and all the others who criticised it at one stage or another—to fathom the deep, almost convulsive, personal meaning of the *Giudizio!* The *Rime* which held the secret were at that point scattered on random sheets, on folios of sketches and designs. Michelangelo's exclusive interest in religious themes of art was not merely the product of his working as artist-laureate of the Church of Peter, as a Tolstoy would claim, but grew out of his anguished conviction that during his unfortunately prolonged life greater pains and efforts were necessary to offset the increasing obstacles and deterrents to his own salvation. When Pope Paul complained about the nudities in the *Giudizio,* Michelangelo replied that the Pope's *Last Judgement* could be easily arranged ("che le pitture si acconciano presto").[2] His own personal final judgement, he knew, would not be that easily arranged.

NOTES

1 Michelangelo, *Le Rime*, ed. Guasti, p. xl.
2 Vasari, ed. *cit.*, VII, 240.

12

PLATONISM

WHEN LORENZO DE' MEDICI took the boy Michelangelo into his garden, it was not merely to furnish him with the necessities of his craft mentioned in Alberti's *De Statua* or to give him casual instruction on mimesis (e.g., "old fauns, like old men, have not retained all their teeth"). It was equally to give the unschooled boy some of the learning necessary that his art might have substance. This explains why the Magnifico admitted the boy also to his home, just as Cosimo before him had taken in the eighteen-year-old Marsilio Ficino. Michelangelo would not otherwise have come into direct commerce with the greatest of the early Platonists. Ficino had recently terminated the *Theologia Platonica* and Pico completed his commentary on the *Enneads* in 1491, precisely when Michelangelo was living in the home of Lorenzo. The boy was thus a witness to the excitement caused by the arrival of Plotinus's work in Italy. If there are constant evocations of Plato in Michelangelo's work, there are also some passages which would indicate that he knew Plotinus. Unschooled in Latin, he could nevertheless avail himself of the Platonic discussions in the Medici household. These discussions made of him (for the efforts to make Michelangelo an Etruscan seem endless) a "platonico etrusco."[1] As time went on he could read the Italian versions of Ficino's commentary, and such Platonic works as his patron Lorenzo's poetry, Benivieni's *Canzona di amor celeste e divino,* Diacceto's *Libri d'amore*, Bembo's conversations, and the poetry of his friend and counselor Poliziano, whose octave "Costei ha privo il ciel d'ogni bellezza" is, in Nesca Robb's words, "prophetic of Michelangelo." If many pages have been devoted to the Platonic interpretation of Michelangelo's works of art—especially the Medici Chapel, which has inspired at least three books dwelling on its Platonism—the poetry remains no less Platonic. Miss Robb wrote, "It was left for Michelangelo to inform the Petrarchan-Neoplatonic lyric with something of the fire and vigour that distinguishes his art."[2] The success of Lorenzo's immersion of the young sculptor into the atmosphere of the Platonic Academy is nowhere better measured than by Berni's perceptive comment on Michelangelo's artistic and poetic Platonism:

> Ho visto qualche sua compositione:
> Sono ignorante e pur direi d'havelle
> Lette tutte nel mezzo di Platone.
> (For translation see p. 262.)

Berni, with his usual sagacity, localised in this *capitolo* the one element of Platonism most exploited by Michelangelo as a poet: the *kalakagathon*—the idealistic system expounded by Platonists and Neo-Platonists. This area of Platonism—involving the ideal world above zones and spheres/perception and reminiscence of that world/the meteorisis of the soul—informs a major segment of his *Rime*. It is applied to his outpourings of love, his pieces on art, his theorising on beauty, and even his sonnets anticipating death. For this reason, Michelangelo's literary Platonism can hardly be limited to a single chapter of this volume. It is very evident as well in Chapters IV, V, VI, X, and XVII. In view of the general infusion of Platonism in so many of the poems treated in our pages, the present chapter will limit itself to considerations of Platonic vision, of the winged soul, and, more briefly, of reincarnation and the Anteros. To complete the inventory of imagery which Neo-Platonism placed at the disposal of the Renaissance poets, we might mention those which Michelangelo as poet rejected. There is no mention in the *Rime* of such familiar Platonic elements as the ladder of love (though the ascents to Febo's *poggio* are suggestive of it), the androgyne, the unchecked steed, the four furies, demons, the Great Year, or the torches that light the path to heaven.[3]

As we have mentioned in Chapter IV, the concept of prototypical form which exists and remains in heaven but whose reflection or imitation may be perceived on earth by those endowed with a special vision is at the basis of most Renaissance Platonism. It was particularly appealing to Michelangelo, engaged in the mimetic arts. The archetypal art-form, which Michelangelo called *idea, concetto, immago,* or *immagine,* existed by God's grace on earth within the very materials of art. This is best expressed in the famous quatrain "Non ha l'ottimo artista alcun concetto" (see Chapters IV and XX), which Varchi first discovered and which launched Michelangelo's fame as a philosophic poet. (It is an amusing irony that Varchi's labored commentary on this quatrain views it continually as essentially Aristotelian, no doubt a surprise to Michelangelo, who [see Chapter 1] hailed the commentary nevertheless as "coming from God.")

The four words describing the prototypical art-form crop up throughout the *Rime*, always in a Platonic sense: "il buon concetto," "un concetto di bellezza," "l'immagine vera," "l'immagine uiua in pietra alpestre e dura," "d'un'immagine uiua," "l'immagine del cor," "ho concetto alcun immago," etc. The *concetto* then becomes the artistic objective, the perfect coupling of form and content, which the talented artist knows is possible for him to achieve. It is as true for the goldsmith as it is for the painter and sculptor:

> Only with fire does the smith bend iron
> Into his cherished *concetto* and fine work. (G 62)

And it is true even for the writer, as we suggested earlier. The sonnet "Si come nella penna e nell'inchiostro" (G 84) assumes that artistic creations exist within the ink of his inkwell. Tityus, Orlando, Panurge, all preexisted in the ink of their creators.

The perception of the *concetto* is restricted to those with a special endowment of vision. The eye in Plato and Plotinus may have an inner, intellectual power as well as the outer vision given to all. The elite which possess this inner vision are called *accorti:*

> Every beauty which is to be seen here below
> Resembles that merciful source whence we are all come
> More than anything else, if one is a person of perception. (G 83)

The object perceived by the outer eye passes through the retina and becomes lodged in the heart; here it grows into a larger image corresponding to the *typos* in heaven of which heretofore it has been the mere reflection. The image swelling within the heart may grow to such size that it occupies the entire body, an idea which could explain Michelangelo's curious thought:

> Make of my entire body one single eye, nor let there be
> Then any part of me not taking pleasure in thee. (G 166)

In the very Platonic sonnet, "La uita del mie amor'," God transforms the poet into a whole eye: "Me fe' san ochio e te luc'et splendore" (G 34). This mechanism is best explained in the dialogue between the poet and Love, "Dimmi di gratia, Amor, se gli ochi mei" (G 42). Like Phaedrus interrogating Socrates, the poet asks if true beauty is contained in the object or person before his eyes or whether it is something within him. Love replies with the lesson in Platonism translated above on page 79, explaining how beauty is converted into something finer as it passes from the outer to the inner eye. This conversion of the outer into an inner vision is again described:

> As I draw my soul, which sees through the eyes,
> Closer to the beauty which I saw at first,
> The image therein grows, and the other recedes
> As though unworthy and without any value. (G 44)

The implication seems to be that whereas the earthly image makes the poet tender, the heavenly archetype makes him feel greatness and possibly more power. This expanded inner image has a tremendous effect, even against death, when the image is of a loved one:

> But the true image
> Which keeps me alive, then rises to the heart
> So that love might not be vanquished by death. (G 112)

When Michelangelo looked upon the beauty of Tommaso Cavalieri, the image of this patrician was converted into that of his lofty *typos*, already known through anamnesis.

> That, friend, which in thy gracious face I see
> Scarce in this present life may man express;
> The spirit, wearing yet its fleshly dress
> By this upborne has looked on deity.
> And though the throng, malign and brutish, free
> Its gibes and scoffs at what the few possess,
> There fails no joy from this warm eagerness,
> This chaste desire, this love, this fealty.
> For every beauty that we look on here
> Brings, to wise souls, in recollection clear
> The merciable fount whence all things flow;
> Nor other pledge nor other fruit have we
> Of heaven on earth. Who loves thee faithfully
> To God ascends, and makes death precious so. (G 83)
> (Nesca Robb)

Within this idealistic context, as we noted on page 145, the poet manages to revile those slanderers who gave Tommaso concern. Of this particular sonnet, "Veggio nel tuo bel uiso" Whitfield claims: "It is of Shakespeare rather than of Bembo that he reminds us."[4] Once the eyes have transformed the earthly image to the heavenly one, the soul itself ascends to its source of origin:

> The soul, the whole and sound intellect,
> Through the eyes ascends more free and loose
> To thy lofty beauty . . . (G 166)

The eyes themselves begin to long for the heavenly beauties, for the *accorti* weary easily of mere earthly beauties, which arrive accompanied by thoughts of death rather than everlasting life:

> Ravished by all that to the eyes is fair,
> Yet hungry for the joys that truly bless,
> My soul can find no stair
> To mount to heaven; save earth's loveliness.
> For from the stars above

Descends a glorious light
That lifts our longing to their highest height
And bears the name of love.
Nor is there aught can move
A gentle heart, or purge or make it wise,
But beauty and the starlight of his eyes. (G 107)
(George Santayana)

We have examined the splendid sonnets to Cavalieri extolling the union of two perfect lovers, with their fusion of wills. "Veggio co be uostr'ochi" (G 89) implies that a fused vision is best able to give the weaker lover the acuity needed to witness the sweet splendors ("dolce lume") of heaven.

The special Neo-Platonic conception of vision espoused by Michelangelo gives deeper meaning to two seemingly banal lines of the *Rime*. "Nessun uolto fra noi è che pareggi/L'immagine del cor" (G 49) would seem at first glance to mean that a person's face seems handsomer to those who love him; Platonically, it portends that the expanded image in the heart is metamorphosed from that captured by the outer eye. Similarly, the curious single line: "Che mal si puo amar ben chi non si uede" (G App. 26) carries not only its apparent, superficial meaning, "out of sight, out of heart," but implies also that love comes not with the outer vision but after the conversion of the inner vision. This same tribute to the power of the *visus interior* is contained in a madrigal probably addressed to Vittoria Colonna:

Since man's thought falls late in love
Through that eye which cannot see
[Divine things] through its own power. (Frey CVII)

Let us turn now to the theme of the winged soul longing to return to the paradise from which it descended. Imprisoned in the body, its wings weakened, it remembers the joys of the empyrean, and this makes it impatient. As Francesca sighed to Dante and Vergil, "Nessun maggior dolore."

Because the half of me which comes from heaven
Thereto with great longing wings its way back. (G 168)

The wings which Plato assigned to the soul are viewed by Ficino not as plumes but actually as lights, one innate and one divine, which carry the soul about as though they were wings. "Lumen igitur habet geminum; naturale alterum, sive ingenitum; divinum alterum et infusum, quibus una conjunctis ceu duabus alis per sublimen pervolare valeat regionem."[5] Michelangelo, like most of the Cinquecento poets, knows Ficino's special view of these wings, but favors the traditional view of Plato himself.

One of the poems best illustrating this theme was probably inspired by Cavalieri. "Non uider gli occhi miei" does not exist in manuscript form, but appeared in the *Due lezzioni* of Varchi, who explicated it before the Florentine Academy. The sonnet expresses a conviction that an ideal love will spur the soul's return to heaven. Having shown the heights to which true love can carry us, the poet dispatches with three lines the tawdry imitation of sensual love:

> Mine eyes beheld no thing of mortal shape,
> When the first gleam of thy serene regards
> Shone on me, and the soul, that aye ascends
> To its end, had hoped to find in them its peace.
> Stretching its wing toward Heaven, from whence
> it came,
> It aims not only at the beauty which
> Pleases the eyes; since that is frail and weak,
> It passes on to universal form. (G 105)
> (John E. Taylor)

The rise of the earthly image to its archetypal phase is the transition from a particular to a universal. In this sonnet the wings which operate the ascension, as is often the case, are not specifically mentioned. An excellent example (1536–42) of the wingless soul is found in the following quatrain referring to the descent and imprisonment of a soul (wingless as the angels of the Sistine Vault):

> The immortal soul, aspiring to that height
> It stooped from, to your earthly prison came,
> An angel of compassions infinite
> To heal all hearts and bring our earth good fame. (G 106)
> (Nesca Robb)

When the fusion of two lovers is achieved, their souls, like their wills, are joined and may wing their way back to heaven as one:

> One soul in two bodies is made eternal,
> Raising both to heaven with equal wings. (G 59)
> I fly with your wings and without plumes, (G 89)

Lofty thoughts are precursors of the *ascensio*. As in Bernardino Daniello's "Se 'l viver nostro è breve giorno oscuro" and Du Bellay's "Si nostre vie est moins qu'une journée" the poet eyes heaven longingly; such thoughts spur the soul's wings to spread:

> Now, weary, I raise my thought on wings, and spur
> Myself on to a more secure and noble place. (G 271)

The winged soul may return not only to the empyrean but also to its own star of origin:

> But since the liberated spirit
> Returns to its star . . . (G 121)

When the lofty thoughts are missing, the soul no longer has the will to ascend on its wings:

> My soul is plucked and shaved of its plumes. (G 267)

The general idea of the ascent of the soul was known to Michelangelo from a host of sources both Christian and Platonic. At times it is uncertain whether his use of the image is Christian or Platonic, or a fusion of the two, as in its occurrence in poetry of his idol Petrarch (in "Quel antico mio dolce mio Signore"):

> Anchor, e questo è quel che tutto avanza,
> Da volar sopra 'l ciel le avea dat' ali,
> Per le cose mortali,
> Che son scala al Fattor, chi ben l'estima.

The staircase mentioned in Petrarch was also a Dantean image, for his St. Thomas Aquinas speaks of the ray of grace as leading only upward: "quella scala/U' senza risalir nessun discende" (Para. x, 83 ff.). Other writers known to Michelangelo used the image of the stair: Pico, Lorenzo de' Medici, Ficino, Giambattista Lapini, and Leo the Jew.[6] Michelangelo, despite his preoccupation with the stairs of the Laurentian Library, of the Capitoline, and so on, does not associate his image of ascent with *scale* or *gradi*. The idea of soaring ascent, a preoccupation of his art, is most evident in his drawings: the several resurrections of Christ, the more limited rearising of Lazarus. He did not portray Daedalus, but mentions him in the two-line fragment translated earlier (G App. 24). (We omit Michelangelo's interest in the soarings of angels, visible in the drawings of the *Sogno* and the *Sacrifice of Isaac* or in the *Conversion of Paul* and the Sistine *Creations*.) If the lofty elevations of the soul describe an ideal love or one going well, the inability to soar (the phoenix, the apathetic soul) or the plunging fall describe an unhappy or disastrous love. Thus, the three drawings of the *Fall of Phaeton* (who wished to fly with Phoebus) symbolise the fall of Michelangelo after the break with Febo di Poggio ("Onde io rouino e caggio"). The casting of Tityus into hell has a similar personal meaning, as we have noted in Chapter V.

The idea of soaring and plunging, Christian and Platonic and mythical in origin, comes thus to have a principally psychological meaning in Michelangelo's love poetry. This is an easy transition, in any case, for most of the Ficinian reasoning on Plato was centered in the context of love, and Neo-Platonism's re-emergence in Renaissance literature was principally in amorous poetry.

Two minor themes will conclude our passing discussion of Platonism. The concept of Eros and Anteros which was picked up by Renaissance literature and art was so closely affiliated with Platonism that Antoine Héroët held it to be "aultre invention extraicte de Platon." If Plato never told the tale of the sibling loves popularized by Héroët, he did use the word *anteros* in the sense of reciprocated affection. By the Cinquecento the notion had evolved to one of two conflicting loves, one divine and one carnal. It is in this sense only that the Eros-Anteros concept found its way into Michelangelo's *Rime:*

> The love of which I speak aspires to the heights—
> Too unlike that for a woman; it ill befits
> A heart wise and virile to burn for a woman.
> The one draws you to heaven, the other down to earth;
> The one inhabits the soul, the other the senses,
> Aiming its bow at base and vile things. (G 260)

Eros or Cupid has by now become the god of passion, while Anteros symbolises the pure love which elevates one as do the wings of the soul.

The other development of the Anteros, entirely different, is the *Contr'-amour*, the poem emphasising the ugly or ridiculous features and characteristics of a mistress or ex-mistress. Poliziano's "Una vecchia mi vagheggia" is a perfect example. Such poems, a product of the antifeminine viewpoint expressed in Boccaccio's *Corbaccio* and become common coin in the misogynistic literature of the Renaissance, frequently bore the title of "Anteros." It is inevitable that Michelangelo should have been interested in this vogue of misogynistic verse. Michelangelo's two parodies of love poetry ("Io crederrei, se tu fussi di sasso" [G 54] and "Tu ha' 'l uiso" [G 20]) may contain one or two misogynistic touches ("Perchè non basta a una donna bella/Goder le lodi d'un amante solo,/Che sua belta potre' morir con ella") (G 20), but in general they mock love poetry rather than mocking the woman addressed.

The Platonic (and Pythagorean) doctrine of metempsychosis makes a brief appearance in the *Rime*. Like so many of the Renaissance poets, Michelangelo availed himself of this theme variously described in the *Republic* and the *Phaedrus:*

> If it is true that the soul, from its body freed,
> In some other person may return,
> For a short and brief sojourn,
> To live and die another time . . . (G 126)

And, as with the Pléiade poets in France[7] and the Platonists in Italy, his adaptation is fitted into a love poem. Michelangelo seemed to feel that beauty and form are kept in the storehouse of nature; they are given prodigally to men and women at youth, but slowly taken back with the passage of time.

I believe that nature takes back unto itself
All that which day by day disappears from thee,
That it may serve for the birth from a greater womb
With a better fate and with more extreme care
To form anew another person
Who will have thy angelic and serene face. (G 230 var.)

There is no hint of the time which will elapse before the beauties are utilised again in a reincarnation, although Ficino had associated the doctrine of transmigration with the Platonic Great Year. Platonic and Ficinian thought on palingenesis varies from Michelangelo's treatment, for in Plato and his exegete the emphasis is on the transmigration of the soul, not of the body. Michelangelo evokes the reincarnation of souls on the Day of Judgement, a repeated theme of the epitaphs to Cecchino Bracci.

There is in addition to G 83 (see above) another, clearer suggestion of the Platonic doctrine of reminiscence. Just as the individual's soul may recall prenatal experience, so may one experience racial memory, the "déjà vu." Michelangelo senses that it may be some primeval beauty out of racial memory which so affects him:

I know not if it is the desired light
Of its primordial maker which the soul feels,
Or whether out of the memory of the race
Some other beauty shines within the heart . . . (G 76)

In concluding this brief chapter we do not take leave of Platonism, a subject reappearing throughout this volume. We have seen that Michelangelo's origins in Medicean Florence continued all his life to be apparent in his poetry. As Miss Robb concludes, "One is tempted to say that if the Academy had done no more than supply him with a language it would have justified its existence."[8] And even if Panofsky never quotes from the *Rime* in his interesting essay on "The Neoplatonic Movement and Michelangelo,"[9] the poetry illuminates the Platonic character of much of Michelangelo's art.

NOTES

[1] Giovanni Amendola, *Le poesie di Michelangelo, ed. cit.*, p. 18.
[2] Nesca Robb, *Neoplatonism of the Italian Renaissance* (London, 1935), p. 240.
[3] For a demonstration of the literary employment of these themes, see R. V. Merrill and R. J. Clements, *Platonism in French Renaissance Poetry* (New York, 1957).
[4] J. H. Whitfield, *A Short History of Italian Literature* (Hammondsworth, 1960), p.163.

[5] Marsilio Ficino, *Commentarium*, iv, 4.
[6] R. V. Merrill and R. J. Clements, *op. cit.*, pp. 79–81.
[7] *Ibid.*, Chap. VII.
[8] Nesca Robb, *op. cit.*, p. 261.
[9] Erwin Panofsky, *Studies in Iconology* (New York, 1939), pp. 171–230.

13

POLITICAL, SOCIAL, AND SCIENTIFIC IDEAS

MICHELANGELO HAD LITTLE interest in and less stomach for the politics of church or state. Had he pronounced himself on politics in some tract, he would doubtless have revealed the same cynicism about politicians and their motives as is apparent in his townsman Machiavelli. The vicissitudes of fortune, the shiftings of power, the vindictiveness of new regimes, these were indeed menaces to men of good will and deterrents to creative endeavor. Michelangelo was by no means so certain as would be the school of Burckhardt that his generation was elevating statecraft to an art comparable to the arts of design or the art of *cortegiania*. Unfortunately, Michelangelo was destined to live in a century when political factionalism was rife and a country which, as Michelangelo ironically mentioned in the *Diálogos em Roma*, was singularly blessed as a battlefield. Michelangelo tried to stay close to his atelier and eye the political and social turmoil without involving himself. Disregarding Alfieri's unfounded comment that Michelangelo was forced in his evil times to paint heroes whose battlefield was the bed, it is nevertheless true that the artist assiduously had to avoid the company of the bellicose leaders of his time. It was rather they, Charles V, Bayazid the Turk, Francis I, and the rest, who sought him out, either through correspondence or personal pilgrimage. As he tried to keep his distance, an occasional aphoristic comment escaped him. He watched as great political figures rose high in the firmament, only to plummet and crash like the Daedalus or Phaeton who figured in his drawings or verses—Savonarola, Lorenzo de' Medici, Alessandro de' Medici, the Maréchal de Gié for whom the bronze *David* was intended. He shrugged and remembered setting down to Luca Martini the following observation: " 'Tis better to keep still than fall from high!" (Letter CDLXIII.) He watched warfare raze parts of his beloved if ill-defined country, shook his head, and wrote to his father in October, 1512, that wars "are very contrary to our art." Even when he was engaged on the fortifying of Florence, he took what the English call "French leave" and their Gallic cousins call "filer à l'anglaise." (He did, however, return voluntarily to Florence in November, 1529, six weeks after the siege by the Spaniards had begun.) Indeed, civil disturbances twice caused him to flee Florence. He advised his family in writing to flee these outbreaks "as from the plague," cautious counsel to give a family which was to produce the political activist Filippo Buonarroti (1761–1837). Michelangelo's political prudence even leads him to observe in the presence of several *fuorusciti* from Tuscany that to kill evil princes is "great presumption."[1]

There are echoes of this tergiversation in the *Rime*, of course, although never vehement or sustained. Witness such familiar lines as:

> He who wins by flight, let him stay not on the field (G 175)
>
> He who seeks disaster, God will give it to him (G 267)

There is at least one fragment condemning insatiable tyranny:

> Lend an ear for a moment to my words:
> He who rules the world and is so great
> Doth ever desire more and hath not peace (G 67)

There is a passing jibe at the *Fuehrerprinzip:*

> For in equality there's no room for lordliness. (G 160)

To such expressions of disapproval one must add his pessimistic stanza

> When the master with harsh bonds chains the slave . . . (G 25)

with its unhappy conclusion that people constrained under tyranny become inured to their condition and even unaware of their bondage.

Michelangelo's attempts to remain aloof from politics were not always successful. His entire career was affected by fluctuations in the fortunes of such dynasties as the Medici and the Della Rovere. Well might he copy Petrarch's line about the death of Giovanni Colonna ("roct'è l'alta colonna e 'l verd . . .") after he lost the protection of Lorenzo il Magnifico. As a youth he was caught in the struggle for power between Savonarola and this patron. His second major patron, Julius II, longed to be a *condottiere* under the *vexillum* of the Church. Guasti held that Michelangelo's outcry against those who make helmets and swords out of chalices ("Qua si fa elmi di calici e spade") dates from the period of Julius's expansionist ambitions. Politics, like war, sought out this artist. He held political office in the Gran Consiglio of Florence. When the siege of Florence followed the sack of Rome, he was drawn into the conflict not only as a fortifier of San Miniato and Florence but also as a political figure. At one point he had the unhappy experience of waiting out this tumult in the belltower of San Niccolò, his life perhaps at stake. Subsequent to his flights from Florence in fear for his life, he stayed away from this town for a period out of a conviction (shared by some modern historians) that Duke Alessandro wished to kill him.

If the 1540s marked the one period when Michelangelo was admittedly an *engagé* sculptor and carved the *Bruto* (whose political significance is clearly presented in the *Dialogi* of Donato Giannotti, for whom the bust was intended), it was then too that Michelangelo penned his most politically imbued poetry. He could hardly shrug off politics at this stage of his life, for his constant commerce in Rome with Giannotti, Del Riccio, Antonio Petreo, the Strozzi, and other *fuorusciti* may have led him to feel that he too was a voluntary exile from his Tuscany, as did his refusals to return to Florence under the Medici Restoration. His chiding of Cellini for Benvenuto's lack of freedom under Cosimo, his allusions to Baccio Bandinelli as a court favorite and lackey, and of course his dialogue "Per molti, Donna, anzi per mille amanti" (1545–46) contribute to this view of his own status as exile. The sordid murder of Duke Alessandro in 1537, evocative of the murder of Giuliano de' Medici by the Pazzi, turned everyone's attention to politics. Michelangelo's disappointment with the policies and abuses of Duke Cosimo made him aware that even an artist must think sometimes about public welfare. Though he did not pick up the challenge in his other arts—excepting the aforementioned *Bruto*—he did become momentarily committed as poet.

The most vehement of these poems of protest was the dialogue mentioned above in which the artist commiserates with the allegorised figure of Florence over her having been made the unwilling mistress of a tyrant and denied her true lovers. These are the worthy men of Florence.

The Exile: For many, Milady, for even a thousand lovers
Wast thou created, angelic of form.
But now it would seem that heaven sleeps
While one lone man takes for himself what was given to so many.
On hearing our plaints, give back to us
The beauty of thine eyes, that gift seemingly denied
To him born in the wretched state of exile.

The adjective in the second verse recalls the tyrannised city described in Leo Ferrero's antifascist tragedy *Angelica*. Michelangelo's piece concludes with the wishful thought that the republic of Florence cannot remain under a tyrant, that the lady is freeing herself from her bondage and that a usurper cannot enjoy his despoliation:

Florence: Pray, trouble not your righteous desires,
Since he who seems to despoil me and deprive you of me,
Fearful as he is, enjoys not his great sin.
For the state of lovers whose great desire
Is checked by the very abundance of their ill-got gains
Is less happy than a wretched state yet full of hope. (G 249

On the autograph of this madrigal Luigi del Riccio made the gratuitous comment, "Di messer Michelangnolo Buonarroti, intendendo Fiorenza per Donna." The reassurances of the allegorical lady recall the political heroines Esther and Judith of the Sistine Ceiling, intent upon the salvation of Israel. The dialogue reminds us also of two passages in his beloved Dante: "Ah, serva Italia, di dolor ostello" and "Che le città d'Italia, tutte piene son di tiranni" (*Purg.* VI, 76 and 124).

Another stanza which may have political meaning is the madrigal "Io dico, che fra noj, potenti dej":

I tell you that among us, powerful gods,
It is meet that every reversal be endured.
After thou wilt be dead
Of a thousand injuries and wrongs,
She will love thee, as now thou burnest for her,
Thou shalt take a righteous vengeance.
Alas! weary is he who waits too long,
As I must to his solace arrive so late! (G 147)

Guasti held these obscure lines to be a political allegory, although this has been doubted by Frey, Girardi, Ceriello, and others. If Guasti was correct, then the burden of the piece would be a plea for the pardon of political offenses, the message contained in the final couplet:

A generous, lofty and noble heart
Pardons and bears love to its offender.

The political content of the famed quatrain on the *Notte*, believed to describe the "danno e vergogna" of the Medici Restoration, has been fully discussed in Chapter V.

It has been alleged that one of the epitaphs for Cecchino Bracci bears an indirect political condemnation of the Medici Restoration. This is the piece:

I was of the Bracci, and if portrayed and deprived
Of my soul, now death is sweet to me,
Since that work of art has the happy fortune
To enter depicted where I could not when living. (G 202)

This quatrain, with its typically elliptical expression in the last two lines, could of course refer merely to the fact that the lad was about to receive sculptured immortality in the Church of Aracoeli, a holy setting for which his mores had ill prepared him. Pascale read a "political reminiscence" into the four lines: "This youngster, son of an exile, could not enter alive into Florence, but after his death the image executed by Michelangelo's hand will enter there."[2] This claim is weakened by the fact that Cecchino apparently lived in Florence between 1529 and 1534, the year he came to Rome. However, the greatest objection to Pascale's theory is that Francesco's sculptured image was designed to repose in Rome, on the Capitoline Hill, where it may be seen today, and not in his native Tuscany. Michelangelo may have seen in Cecchino a child victimised by those *fuggiguerra* tendencies which he himself shared, for the boy's father Zanobi had been arrested in 1530 for fleeing the besieged city of Florence.

Both Levi, in his *Mente di Michelangelo,* and Vincenzo Pascale believe that the sonnet "La ragion meco si lamenta e dole" dates from the siege of 1529 and contains a political meaning. Their hypothesis is strengthened by the fact that this poem was found on a sheet referring to the date of 6 January, 1529. The ambiguity of certain verses allow for considerable conjecture.

> My shame reproaches me and says:
> —What shalt thou bring us back from the living sun
> Other than death? And not that of the phoenix.
> But it avails naught, for him who insists on falling
> The quick, liberating hand of another sufficeth not.
> I know my wrongs and I understand the truth;
> On the other side I lodge another heart
> Which kills me more the more I surrender. (G 43)

The self-recrimination of these verses could, of course, apply to Michelangelo's regret that he had fled from the homeland in need of his services. To Calero, however, there is no political allegory. "He speaks of two hearts, the one which heeds reason and the one heeding love. He speaks of two deaths: he doesn't want one [physical death] and he doesn't understand the other [death of the soul]."[3] The Petrarchan custom of viewing love as warfare beguiles one into interpreting victories and surrenders in a political context.

There have been suppositions that other works of Michelangelo were conceived with a political motivation. Vasari notes that the marble *David* was intended as a symbol of Florentine strength and civic virtue. De Tolnay supports this claim by noting that the statue was commissioned on 16 August, 1501, twelve days after the adoption of the new constitution. The anger of the *Christus Iudex* has been interpreted as churning against the French and Spanish invaders of Italy rather than against sinning mankind. The same patriotic lesson has been attributed to the cartoon of the

Noli me tangere. The *Leda* has been held to be a political bribe to influence Francis I, as was Michelangelo's offer of July, 1544, to execute an equestrian statue of that monarch in the Piazza della Signoria if Francis would liberate Florence. If most of these conjectures and reports are not supported by any extant statement of the artist, written or quoted, the same is not true of the *Bruto*. Michelangelo's interest in Brutus and in tyrannicide was amply clarified in the *Dialogi* set down by Donato Giannotti after a heated discussion of politics occurring in the latter's Roman home, perhaps while Michelangelo was carving the *Bruto*. Several of the artist's observations on tyranny and political murder herein are of interest to us, since they were made without his usual caution on this subject. His general exculpation of assassination of cruel tyrants is modified by the reminder that fortune often conceals future good under apparent evil, as illustrated by the case of the Emperor Silla. It is further modified by his belief that tyrants like Caesar are nevertheless symbols of majesty, sometimes elected by God: "Whoever betrays the majesty of the Roman Empire must be punished in the same way and with the punishments as he who betrays divine majesty . . ." Since this dialogue was provoked by a discussion of the *Divine Comedy*, Michelangelo was perhaps recalling here Dante's canto entirely devoted to Justinian's explanation of the divine nature of the Roman Empire. He continues: "Brutus and Cassius killed Caesar and in his person betrayed the aforementioned Roman Empire."

Michelangelo's seemingly ambivalent attitude in Giannotti's record of their conversation is commemorated by the Latin distich which the Grand Duke Alessandro de' Medici is said to have placed on the bust: "Dum Bruti effigiem sculptor de marmore ducit,/In mentem sceleris venit et abstinuit." The implication is that the rough surface revealed a change of heart on the part of the artist, who then abandoned the bust. The magnificent head, with its *disprezzo eroico*, stands as a monument to the political murderer Lorenzino, currently hailed by Michelangelo's friends Filippo Strozzi, Varchi, and Molza as the "new Brutus" and the "second Brutus." De Tolnay reminds us that the phrase was applied to every Florentine who had killed or tried to kill a Medici: Cola Montano, Pietro Boscoli, Rinuccini, and others. Despite the inconsistencies and rationalisations about Brutus in the *Dialogi* of Giannotti, Michelangelo's statement therein that he who kills a tyrant kills a beast is his final say on the matter. The evidences of the poetry confirm this conclusion.

The *Rime*, then, betray an occasional evidence of political prudence and even timidity, as do the *Lettere*. More than the *Lettere* and even more than painting and sculpture, the poetry shows us that Michelangelo, a loyal Medici supporter since his apprentice days in the Giardino Mediceo, was moved by his association with the Florentine exiles in Rome, by the coddling of such rivals as Bandinelli under the later Medici, and by his own deliberate but sure sense of right to administer at least three or four rebukes to the evil scions of the Medici Restoration.

Living in a country which during the artist's lifetime fitted Metternich's unfortunate description of a "geographical expression," Michelangelo left us no stirring paean to Italy, as did his beloved Petrarch. He did use the word "nazione," however, to describe central and northern Italy (Letter CDLXXXVIII), and he took pride in an Italy which served as school to all the artists of Europe. In this sense he could, as De Hollanda chronicled, speak of "Italia, onde ha a perfeição das cousas." In the *Diálogos em Roma* he considers Italy the universal heir of ancient Greece, and swears that no one can copy the Italian manner successfully; "And if through some great miracle such a one should succeed in painting well, then, even though he did not do it to imitate Italy, one could say that he painted like an Italian." This pride in Italy as homeland of the arts may explain why Michelangelo could never bring himself to leave its confines, either to accept commissions from Francis I and Sultan Bayazid or even to make a pilgrimage he momentarily planned to St. James of Compostela. Some historians have tried to extend the meaning of Michelangelo's quatrain (G 247) spoken by the statue of the *Notte* ("Mentre che 'l danno e la vergogna dura") to apply to the wretched situation of the entire Italian peninsula overrun by French, Spanish, Swiss mercenaries, and even Turkish raiders. Indeed, the first English translator of this quatrain insisted on this interpretation by rendering the line as "while shame and misfortune overwhelm my country" and by holding the poem to be as worthy an example of patriotic fervor as Vincenzo da Filicaia's "Italia, Italia, e tu . . ."[4] However, we must rather agree with Insinga, who regretted the lack of a national consciousness in Michelangelo's *Rime:* "No allusions, then, to the fatherland in Michelangelo's *Rime,* neither in those of bright coloration nor even less in those others clouded by the lazy mist of symbol or allegory."[5] Only Galeozzo di Tarsia, adds Insinga, could salute Italy in a sonnet worthy of Petrarch.

Instead of one vast homeland, Michelangelo wrote in the *Rime* of two *patrias chicas,* both of which had great sentimental claims upon him.

Even his feelings of loyalty to Florence and Rome were based on artistic thinking. Florence was to him a "pretiosa gioia" (G 71) as the stronghold and showpiece of the Tuscan artistic tradition. Rome was another museum where he felt thoroughly at home, so much so that he wrote his nephew that if he left Rome and its conveniences he would be dead in three days. He accepted honorary citizenship in Rome and yet declared to Donato Giannotti and his friends that he was a "cittadino fiorentino." He owned property in Rome and even more property in Florence.

There are many diverse evidences of Michelangelo's twin loyalties which drew the two cities into a *gemellaggio* in his own mind.[6] The *Rime* contribute only one important evidence, the depth of the passion which these two cities could stir in him. Michelangelo made a habit of turning upon those he loved when he assumed that they were failing him or were ungrateful. We have evidence of this in the letters to his family and, indeed, in his poems to Luigi del Riccio and Julius II. This curious anger he turned against the two cities he loved best. Perhaps, as with the case of his friends, only the depth of his campanilism could explain the extent of his anger.

Rome was subjected to one outburst, the sonnet we have discussed in connection with the *Cristo giudice:*

> Qua si fa elmj di chalicj e spade,
> E 'l sangue di Christo si uend' a giumelle,
> E croce e spine son lance e rotelle,
> E pur da Christo patientia cade.
> Ma non c'arriui piu 'n queste contrade,
> Che n'andre' 'l sangue suo 'nfin alle stelle,
> Poscia ch'a Roma gli uendon la pelle,
> E cosi d'ogni ben chiuso le strade. (G 10)
>
> (For translation see p. 127.)

Even this condemnation of Rome, similar to other excoriations we mentioned in Chapter V, turns to the symbolism of art objects (*chalicj*) to emphasize its point.

We have shown that this sonnet echoes a Dantean rancor against Rome. Nor were Dante's outbursts against Florence forgotten. In both of Michelangelo's sonnets on Dante he stresses the ingratitude and insensitivity of the Florentines, traits which he still found among them in 1512, as one reads in a letter (XXXVII) to his father:

> Di Dante dico, che mal conosciute
> Fur l'opre suo' da quel popolo ingrato,
> Che solo a giusti manca di salute. (G 248)
>
> Biasmar si puo piu 'l popol che l'offese,
> C' al suo men pregio ogni maggior salire . . .
> E le porte, che 'l ciel non gli contese,
> La patria chiuse al suo giusto desire.
> Ingrata, dico, e della sua fortuna
> A suo danno nutrice, ond' è ben segnio
> C' a' piu prefecti abbonda di piu guai. (G 250)
>
> (For translations see pp. 316–17.)

The thanklessness and diffidence had considerable personal meaning to Michelangelo. He could recall the aftermath of the siege of Florence when he had to hide in a belltower, reassessing his "campanilism." He also remembered how Florence had a way of confiscating the properties of her favorite sons—Dante and Petrarch came to mind—and he had come to possess several properties in Florence during the latter part of his life. Yet Florence was the *patria*, "Fiorenza mia," as he put it in a rejected variant verse, even while scolding the Florentines (G 248 var.).

As we have pointed out above, the tyrannies of the Medici Restoration mollified his anger and even led him to write expressions of pity for Florence, in "Per molti, Donna, anzi per mille amanti" and probably "Io dico, che fra noj, potentj dej." Remembering Dante, he was even moved to pen a diatribe (1532–34) against the Pistoiesi, sent to his friend Giovanni da Pistoia:

> Since parting from you, I have learnt, 'tis true,
> That Cain hath in your pedigree a place,
> Nor do you your greatest ancestor disgrace.
> Your neighbor gaineth ought? 'tis loss to you.
> The foes of heaven, with hatred filled and scorn,
> Mercy's sweet face is loathsome in your sight,
> Who to your hurt alone have fealty sworn.
> Enough if that which Dante once did write
> Of your Pistoia in your mind be borne—
> And you would flatter Florence! Hypocrite!
> A jewel of delight
> She is; but not to you her worth she shows,
> He knows her not, who little virtue knows. (G 71)
> (Elizabeth Hall)

The Dantean fulminations against Pistoia are, of course, from *Inferno* VI, XV, XXIV, and XXV. It is probably true, as suggested, that this piece is addressed to Giovanni da Pistoia (see pp. 128–30), although the recipient is addressed as *voi* rather than the *tu* used in the extended sonnet addressed to "Giouanni, a quel propio da Pistoia" (G 5, note).

There is no tribute in the *Rime* to little Caprese nel Casentino, near Arezzo, in 1964 renamed Caprese Michelangelo, where Michelangelo was born. Yet we cannot refrain from noting the artist's letter to Vasari that any good qualities he possessed were due to his inheritance of the *sottilità* of Giorgio's homeland of Arezzo. One thinks of Du Bellay's "douceur angevine," also contrasted with the hectic life in Michelangelo's Rome.

The poetry informs us even of Michelangelo's understanding or misunderstanding of science. He who attended the creation of the sun and the moon in 1508 had strange ideas about those planets. One of his notions was that the sun which heats the world is not hot itself:

Fa forse come 'l sol, se nol permetti,
Che scalda 'l mondo e non è caldo lui. (G 88)

He considered the sun and moon as contrary forces, each negating the power of the other and thus preventing the earth from igniting or freezing:

Cosi taluolta i nostri eterni lumi,
L'un caldo e l'altro freddo ne ristora,
Accio che 'l mondo piu non si chonsumi. (G 45)

He knew that in the upper regions of the atmosphere "there is no winter or summer" (G 68). He suspected in traditional fashion that the sun and moon would halt their course on Judgement Day:

O felice quel di, se questo è certo!
Fermisi in un momento il tempo e l'ore,
Il giorno e 'l sol nella su' antica traccia, (G 72)

There are only vague suggestions that he believed in the Ficinian-Platonic cycle of the Great Year, that cycle—as explained in the *Timaeus*—required for the planets to depart from and return to their original conjunction.

The Pythagorean-Platonic notion of metempsychosis was of course known to Michelangelo (see Chapter XII). All in all, Michelangelo's disinterest in science was yet another example of his polaric differences of opinion and interest from those of Leonardo da Vinci.

Michelangelo was troubled not so much by the fact that artists do not make a good living as by the necessity of their ever having to haggle over or ask for money. Like Alberti before him, he was more interested in acquiring distinction and fulfilling his potentialities in his art rather than in winning abundant financial rewards. He wanted earnestly to be as unconcerned about *quattrini* as Paolo Pino theorised that an ideal artist should be. Yet his *Lettere* return again and again to the subject of money (and banks, which he mistrusted), as did of necessity the *Richordi*. Indeed, this artist who wrote to Riccio of his "great debt and little money" scarcely abandoned the subject of money in his letters. From the letters we learn: the artist is penniless (1510 and 1512); money is at the root of all evil (1560); honor is worth more than wealth (1549); banks are fraudulent (1545, 1547, 1549); money brokers are fools (1515); taxes are a punishment worse than hell (1524); moneylending is hazardous (1518); etc.

The *Rime*, therefore, in contrast to the insistence in the *Lettere*, are important in showing Michelangelo's theoretical disdain for riches. The stanzas on rustic life (1534) condemn the quest for wealth as a typical big-city evil:

O Avarice blind, O mean and base desires
O those who pass the gifts of Nature by!
For gold alone your wretched pride aspires,
Restless for gold from land to land ye fly;
And what shall quench your never-sated fires,
Ye slaves of Envy, Sloth, and Luxury,
Who think not, while ye plot another's wrong,
Man wants but little nor that little long? (G 67)
(William Wordsworth)

These lines confirm his letter LXXXV, of *circa* 1511: "Avarice is a very great sin." His portrait of wealth in the rustic stanzas is scarcely an enviable one;

Wealth, sad at heart the while, and full of dread,
Goes all adorn'd with gems and gay with gold;
And every cloud which passeth overhead
As ominous of change doth she behold;
But Poverty her happy days hath led,
Vex'd with no hope to have, nor fear to hold;
Amid the woods in homely weeds bedight
She knows no cares, no quarrels, no affright.

the modest possessions of the husbandman provide a happy contrast. He cares not for the commerce of the city and the "summits of art."

You can count their riches one by one,
They have no locks and fear no harm . . .
Their loftiest treasure is a plow,
And the plowshare the gem which they prize;
A pair of baskets is their buffet
And shovels and hoes their golden vases.

These stanzas are not important for their superficial praise of the farmer's life. In actual fact Michelangelo wrote that his brother should stop working his farm, since he did not wish to be known as having a relative who followed after oxen. The verses are important simply in their expression of an unconcern for money, preached in the *artes pictoriae* of the time, a disinterestedness which Michelangelo hoped to achieve.

Michelangelo, we know, was extremely sensitive to being called a *ciurmatore, giuntatore,* or *usuraio,* epithets from which he defended himself in his correspondence.[7] There is an almost excessive protestation that he is no "thieving usurer." To these protests there is an additional condemnation of moneylending, percentages, and usury in the *Rime:*

And the ten and the hundred and the accounts and the records
Of usury, which spread over the land. (G 67)

The Christian attitude toward usury and toward money itself shows up in the *Rime* where Michelangelo makes a distinction (1545–46) between spiritual and material wealth:

> The soul is not unworthy, as it awaits
> Eternal life, in which there is peace and quiet,
> Where one is enriched by the only coin
> Which heaven mints for us, and nature here spends. (G 238)

It is revealed in the three drawings of Christ expelling the money-changers which implicitly condemn this trade. It also shows up in the fresco of the *Last Judgement*, where the presence of moneybags indicates that some of the damned sinners are usurers.

Thus, the *Rime* express the Christian and humanistic unconcern for wealth to which Michelangelo wishfully subscribed. They show him noting almost with pride his simplicity of dress and his simplicity of living: "la mia casa qua fra sì ricchi palagi" (G 267). His Poverty in the rustic stanzas is the happiest of the allegorical figures described therein. The continuous outcries of poverty and hardship in the *Lettere* have a curious echo in the *Rime*. When Michelangelo, late in life, receives a gift of sugar, candles, wine, and a mule from a friend (presumably Vasari) he claims, out of long habit, that he is not in a position to reciprocate:

> Al zuchero, a la mula, a le candele,
> Agiuntoui un fiascon di maluagio,
> Resta sì uinta ogni fortuna mia,
> Ch'i' rendo le bilance a San Michele. (G 299)

(For translation see p. 255.)

This inability is contrasted with his moral inability to reciprocate: "Che 'l debito pagar non è presente."

Michelangelo tried hard to be diffident about money, and on several occasions was even capable of great generosity. But as he reminded his nephew (Letter CLXV), "money isn't found in the streets."

In his essay "Michelangelo poeta" Farinelli states that Michelangelo is constantly filling in the profile of himself: "Michelangelo speaks with singular constancy to and of himself."[8] One who studies for long Michelangelo and his work becomes convinced that he projected himself and penetrated deeply into every work he created, in whichever medium. If this chapter has shown how many detailed views of the artist on society may be gleaned from his poetry, it is equally true that each of the master's works of art mirrors him similarly. To arrive at the complete *autoritratto*, one must sometimes supplement the art with the poetry and at other times supplement the poetry with the painting, sculpture, or even architecture. For this specific purpose of self-portraiture, poetry is certainly no less important than the other. Perhaps this is why Michelangelo continued turning out his own *turpissimi inchiostri* almost until his death.

NOTES

[1] Donato Giannotti, *Dialogi, ed. cit.*, p. 96.
[2] Vincenzo Pascale, *op. cit.*, p. 75.
[3] Giuseppe Calero, *Michelangelo poeta, ed. cit.*, p. 45.
[4] G. Melchiori, *Michelangelo nel Settecento inglese, ed. cit.*, p. 74.
[5] Insinga, *op. cit.*, p. 54.
[6] R. J. Clements, *Michelangelo's Theory, ed. cit.*, 259–62.
[7] *Ibid.*, pp. 380–81.
[8] Arturo Farinelli, "Michelangelo poeta," *loc. cit.*, p. 317.

14

EPISTOLARIO POETICO

IN THE RENAISSANCE the personal letter was not merely a medium for the exchange of ideas but was often a conscious work of art as well. An anthologist of Italian Renaissance letters, who significantly entitled his collection *The Gentlest Art*, reminds us that after the late Quattrocento cultured people accepted the prose or metric epistle as the lofty literary form it had been in Augustan Rome. They supposed, indeed hoped that their letters would be published as well as circulated. Many letters were written to our artist with this expectation. (Frey's *Briefe an Michelangiolo* are being supplanted by Paola Barocchi's fuller edition.) Perhaps Aretino's were the most conspicuous examples. If one reads the artist's letters first collected by Milanesi, a few with variants and false starts, one might think that Michelangelo entertained such lofty hopes for his letters. A closer examination of the letters belies this, however. Most of the letters are prompted by an immediate situation or by another missive requiring a burdensome reply, and were not intended to be read *sub specie aeternitatis.*

Letters for which Michelangelo anticipated a wide circulation were the brief, impatient epistle to Varchi on the Paragon of painting and sculpture, the textbook lesson on architecture (authorship currently disputed) cribbed from Vitruvius, sent to Pope Paul III, his ribald blast at Clement VII's plan to erect a colossus in Florence near the Stufa Palace, and certain defensive letters justifying himself to his patrons. There were a few letters to people so famous—the note to Francis I is an example—that the artist knew they would be passed around and read by an entire court or coterie.

If Michelangelo did not usually choose to make his prose epistles into models of the genre, he fell back on an old tradition and chose poetry for his loftier epistles of a more public sort. There are a few poems to friends which stand apart from the remaining corpus of religious, amatory, patriotic, and satirical pieces. It is to these that we now address ourselves.

There are several correspondents to whom Michelangelo often sent letters during the early stage of his career: Giuliano da Sangallo, Domenico Buoninsegni, Piero Urbano, Lionardo di Buoncompagno, Donato Benti, Bernardo Dovizi, Sebastiano del Piombo, Giovanni Francesco Fattucci, and Battista della Palla. Single letters went to such important figures as Lorenzo il Magnifico and Clement VII. These are the principal correspondents up to the 1530s. It is noteworthy that to none of these early friends does Michelangelo address poetry, whereas the friends who receive letters after January, 1533 are often the recipients of verse-letters as well. Before that date there is only the missive to the "prudente giovane Gherardo Perini" (February, 1522), involving someone who may have received anonymously one or more of the early love poems. It may be concluded that Michelangelo was in his mid-fifties before the notion really took root of communicating in verse to his friends. We shall examine the epistles to Giovanni da Pistoia, Pope Julius II, Gandolfo Porrino, Luigi del Riccio, Giorgio Vasari, and Lodovico Beccadelli.

There are two or three earlier examples of a special character, the earliest being the *sonetto caudato* on the painting of the Sistine Ceiling, addressed to Giovanni da Pistoia. This sonnet (see page 91) is impersonal despite its gaiety and its concluding appeal for Giovanni to come to the defense of his painting. Such a "defense" would be a written one, for Giovanni di Benedetto da Pistoia was a writer of verse and comedy. A second sonnet to Ser Giovanni picks up the Dantean invective against Pistoia and its inhabitants. In it Michelangelo writes that he has read Giovanni's latest message "twenty times":

> I' o pur, poi ch'i' ui lasciai, saputo
> Che Cain fu de uostri anticedenti,
> Ne uoi da quel tralignate altrimenti;
> Che s'altri a ben, uel pare auer perduto. (G 71)
>
> (For translation see p. 246.)

Giovanni Papini was the first to identify fully this correspondent.[1] He theorised that the reference to Cain implies some betrayal of Michelangelo, real or imagined. Michelangelo then echoes Dante with a general condemnation of the Pistoiesi:

> Envious, haughty, enemies of heaven,
> The charity of your fellow man vexes you,
> And only of wrong are you friends.

It would appear from this that the camaraderie with Giovanni broke up over the same sort of misunderstanding which strained almost to breaking point the friendships with Sebastiano del Piombo and Luigi del Riccio. This despite the five letters in verse sent by Giovanni to Michelangelo, with their fulsome protestations of affection:

> Michelangelo mine, if being with thee
> Has been a sweet consolation for me in this life,
> Thou hast escorted me through a thousand emotions,
> So that without thee I scarce can stand by myself.

Michelangelo's final vilification of Giovanni is that this Pistoiese is unable to appreciate the "precious jewel" of Florence; a curious attempt to rib or to alienate this friend, for, as Papini discovered, Ser Giovanni was for forty years chancellor of the lieutenant of the Supreme Magistrate of the City of Florence and three times Chancellor of the Accademia degli Umidi.

The same envy of which Michelangelo accused Giovanni was bothering him when he wrote his second-earliest verse epistle to Pope Julius II, "Signor, se uero è alcun prouerbio antico." This piece, to which Frey assigned the date of 1511, was written at such a pitch of bitterness that it was certainly never sent to the irascible pontiff. The young artist charges that the pope has been listening to slanderous remarks ("fauole e parole", "uoce d'eco") about him and has rewarded the slanderers.

We have reproduced and discussed this sonnet (see p. 90) accusing the artist's enemies. Who the enemies were is not certain, but they could have been the Bramante-Raphael clique, of course. Michelangelo was so aware of his enemies at this early point of his career that he refused to work on the Sistine Vault on a suspended platform. In any case, as we have written elsewhere,[2] Michelangelo's writing leaves us with the impression that he lived in a world of hostile, wagging tongues. The verse epistles to Giovanni da Pistoia and Julius II would both so testify.

The onerous task of turning down commissions frequently required tact. Even a letter of rejection couched in such gracious language as Michelangelo's refusal to execute a commission for Francis I could not soften the decision so graciously as could a reply in verse. Thus, on two occasions Michelangelo turned to poetry to write messages of rejection. The first was the letter to Gandolfo Porrino of Modena and the second the letter to Luigi del Riccio declining to execute a bust of Cecchino Bracci.

Gandolfo Porrino had won Michelangelo's friendship by praising the *Giudizio universale* in a sonnet. In 1543 his friend Faustina Lucia Mancini Attavanti, wife of Pier Paolo Attavanti, died at an early age. Despite tributes to her by Porrino, Molza, the respected Annibal Caro, and Atanagi (who called her "nobilissima e pudicissima"), historians for centuries dismissed her as a courtesan with whom Michelangelo may have had intimate relations. When Porrino asked the artist to execute her bust, Michelangelo responded with a weak epitaph of four verses based on a pun (Mancini/mancina = "left-handed") and with another piece containing a direct refusal:

For you alone was she born; I could not do her
With chisels in stone, on paper with brush . . .   (G 178)

This sonnet, upon which we have commented (see p. 74), concludes that only God could do justice to such beauty. The formula of refusal is not unlike that adopted for Luigi del Riccio, except that in the latter case Michelangelo did at least design the bust.

In the 1530s began the friendships with Febo di Poggio, Tommaso Cavalieri, and Vittoria Colonna. The poems to them, epistolary and other, have been discussed in Chapter X.

Michelangelo had every reason to be grateful to Luigi del Riccio, host during the artist's illness (1545), intermediary with the musician Archadelt, guardian of Michelangelo's beloved Cecchino, and so on. Yet the temperamental artist could turn on even Del Riccio.[3]

Among the letters for 1545 we find him quarreling with Del Riccio over the latter's refusal to destroy a certain print (*stampa*), possibly of one of Michelangelo's works, but just as possibly a printing of poems to Cecchino. A quarrelsome sonnet of this period, which we have already reproduced (p. 149), is one of the most vehement of Michelangelo's verse epistles.

A curious fragment found over a drawing of a Christ's head may have been, as Girardi conjectures, the conclusion of a playful verse-letter to Riccio: "another evening, for this evening it is raining/and he can speak only badly who is awaited elsewhere." He notes the resemblance between these lines and a letter of 1545 to Luigi: "As for being together with you tomorrow I must beg off, because the weather is bad and I have chores to perform at home." Michelangelo's notes to Riccio, as we have seen, tend sometimes toward the cryptic and conspiratorial.

Unlike other friends, Giorgio Vasari managed to remain continually on the good side of the master. In general, Michelangelo commented favorably on his painting.[4] It was to Vasari that he occasionally offered the first inspection of one of his sonnets, along with offhand disclaimers about their being "clumsy things" which attested to his having arrived at second childhood. Michelangelo was never more appreciative of Giorgio than when the latter came out with his flattering biography of him in the *Vite*. Indeed, he was even more grateful when the second edition was issued (after Condivi's) with more ample information. When Michelangelo read his gift copy in April–May, 1550, he wrote with satisfaction to his friends that Giorgio who equaled nature in his art now surpassed her as a writer. For if nature takes the lives of even the greatest artists, Vasari grants them immortality:

Now the memory of others, already extinguished,
You have revived and joined with that of yourself,
To be despite everything eternally alive.   (G 277)

To Vasari, Michelangelo apparently addressed another sonnet of thanks (1555). This sonnet is to be compared with the bitter sonnet to Del Riccio explaining that gratitude is a magnificent virtue, but one which can be destroyed by a discourteous act:

> Sugar thou givest, lamps, a mule to ride,
> And add'st thereto a flask of ruddy wine:
> Gifts which do so outrun all needs of mine,
> That with St. Michael I the wealth divide.
> Lapped in a calm too deep, my little boat,
> With idle sails, upon a windless sea,
> Is like to lose its way, and seems to be
> A straw upon the rolling waves afloat.
> With kindness such as thine, and bounty rare,
> The food, the drink, the riding to and fro.
> The thought wherewith my every want is met:
> Dear friend, the present would as nought compare.
> Could I myself and all I have bestow:
> No gift he gives, who only pays a debt. (G 299)
> (Elizabeth Hall)

The sonnet concludes with a maxim: "Che 'l debito pagar non è presente," usually interpreted as meaning "For to pay what is owed is not giving," but which could also mean "For I do not have it in me to repay you as I ought." Line 4 also is translated literally as "That to St. Michael I'll restore the scales." As evidence that Vasari was the intended recipient (the sheet has a letter to Ammannati and a sketch of the stair of the Laurentian Library with the two dates 1 January, 1554 and 26 December, 1555) is the revelation by Vasari. "He, Vasari, noted that he did not use wax, but candles of pure she-goat suet, which are excellent; so he sent Michelangelo four bunches of them."[5]

Poetry could be used as a missive to acknowledge the receipt of gifts or favors, as demonstrated by the effusive thanks to Vasari for the candles, sugar, and mule. Verses could accompany gifts as well, and a playful posey went along with a gift of perfume (or flowers) to some young man or woman in the period 1520–34.

> I've bought for thee, though it cost me dear,
> A little something fragrant as can be,
> By its odor I'll learn to find my way,
> Wherever thou may be, wherever I shall be.
> Without any doubt I'm certain and clear of this.
> If thou hidest away from me, I'll pardon thee.
> Bearing it wherever thou go'st always with thee,
> I could find thee even were I quite blind. (G 55)

Such a fragrant gift might well have been addressed to Febo di Poggio, who liked agreeable clothes and entertainments. Even if the recipient is not known, the stanza is an epistle and forms an amusing contrast in spirit to most of Michelangelo's surviving poetic letters.

The name of Lodovico Beccadelli, Archbishop of Ragusa, figures in the late poetry as a fellow-Christian humanist who exchanged sonnets with the artist. Having begun as a law student at Bologna, he left this "thorny" field to cultivate the Muses. A friend of the famous Giovanni della Casa in Florence, he studied the classics there, continuing at Padua. He became secretary of Cardinal Contarini, and then of Cardinal Reginald Pole, so admired by Vittoria Colonna and her group and revered by Michelangelo for his virtues and goodness (Vasari). After a career as Church diplomat Beccadelli came to Rome in 1554 as "Vicar-elect and one of the four prefects of the Saint Peter's Workshop," an authoriative post which indirectly set him over Michelangelo. A poetic exchange between the prefect and artist includes seven extant sonnets of Beccadelli and two of Michelangelo, addressed to the former in his post as Archbishop of Ragusa. Having made a pilgrimage to Vaucluse while serving in Southern France and having written a life of Petrarch, *Epiteti di Dante e Petrarca*, as well as sonnets and epistles in the Petrarchan manner, he thus shared two of Michelangelo's idols. It was to Beccadelli that Michelangelo sent his splendid sonnet of renunciation of the world's vanities: "Le fauole del mondo m'anno tolto" (see p. 86). The fact that Beccadelli was an active reformer who later (in 1562) associated with the Council of Trent helps to explain the Tridentine mood of Michelangelo's sonnet.

In response to the sonnet of renunciation Beccadelli sent from Austria the following riposte (late March, 1555). Only the example of Christ's sacrifice sustains him, on the threshold of death, as he hears the Christian message far from Rome:

Con passo infermo e bianca falda al uolto
et per lungo camino et tempo rio
lascio uoi, Buonarroti, et la m'inuio
oue 'l nome romano è mal accolto.
    Dura è la strada e piu la causa molto,
ch'al andar mi faria dubbio et restio:
se non che miro a chi per noi morio
sul duro legnio, e fu per noi sepolto,
    e reuisse per noi, fatta immortale
la nostra carne. In lui spero et consolo
la uirtu del mio cor, quassi smarrita;
    e se per uia questa mia spoglia frale
manca, pregate che felice uolo
l'anima porti al suo Fattor unita.[6]

Michelangelo and Beccadelli are visited by the same Christian Muse, and the verses of his friend remind one of the artist's (and Vittoria Colonna's) hymn to the Redeemer.

In February, 1556 Beccadelli sent another sonnet to Michelangelo, from Ragusa. Here again is the ring of renunciation, further demonstrating an affinity between the two men, the artist fifteen years the senior of the cleric. A divine voice keeps urging the prelate to "take this new cross as a ladder to heaven," where he will abide with the artist.

> Solo mi regge una superna uoce,
> che parla dentro al cor ad hora ad hora,
> dicendo: Piglia questa nuova croce
> per scala al cielo, oue farai tu anchora,
> se uiuo passi la terrena foce,
> co 'l Buonarroti tuo lieto dimora.[7]

Again Michelangelo took pen in hand. He alleged that he had intended to visit Beccadelli in the company of Urbino, his assistant. That Michelangelo at eighty-one should make such an arduous trip, over terrain as described by Beccadelli, is unlikely—even as a gesture of pious or ascetic self-imposition. In any case, the painful death of Urbino (3 December, 1555) had made such a project impossible. Michelangelo consoled his friend Beccadelli with the assurance that the two of them would meet in heaven. The news of Urbino's death, the secondary theme of the sonnet, is introduced in the sestet; it has been widely and justifiably quoted as evidence of Michelangelo's love and compassion for his assistant, confirmed also in his letter (CDLXXX) to Urbino's widow Cornelia.

Michelangelo echoes Beccadelli's reference to the Crucifixion as the passport to heaven:

> Through grace divine, after the Cross and woe,
> We surely shall in Heaven each other greet,
> But ere we yield our latest breath, 'twere meet
> We should awhile be happy here below.
> Though rugged mountains frown and oceans roll
> Between us twain: yet never fervent hearts
> Winter with all its frosty rigours parts,
> Nor fetters may the wings of thought control.
> Wherein I evermore with thee do stay
> And of my dead Urbino speak and weep,
> Who living would be with me by thy side,
> As once I thought: his death another way
> Doth draw me now, where he his watch doth keep,
> Till coming thither I with him abide. (G 300)
> (Elizabeth Hall)

The intent of the letter is clear. Beccadelli waits for him in Ragusa; Urbino waits for him in heaven. It is not the rigors of the trip which make Michelangelo give up his trip to Ragusa (as he once renounced his plan of visiting Santiago de Compostela) but rather his impatience to rejoin Urbino in death. Indeed, man's redemption through Christ will enable them both to rejoin Urbino. To the archbishop Michelangelo writes with more certainty of his own salvation than when he writes to Christ or God. The quickening of his desire to die after the loss of Urbino is confirmed in two compassionate letters on the latter's death. To his nephew Lionardo the old artist wrote in part: "It has left me with much affliction and tribulation, so much so that it would have been easier for me to die with him, because of the love I bore him; and he deserved no less, for he had made himself a worthy man, full of devotion and loyalty. Thus it seems to me now that I have been left lifeless through his death, and I cannot console myself" (CCLXXXIV). In a letter to Vasari he added to the expression of his intense grief a curious admission which relates to much of his late poetry, including this sonnet: "The consolation [*grazia*] has been that whereas in life he kept me alive, in dying he taught me to die, not with displeasure, but with a desire for death" (CDLXXVII).

To the 495 letters in prose which are a memorial to Michelangelo's evolving feelings for family, friends, and associates one may then add many more in verse, included in the present and other chapters of this volume. All but two date from after the early 1530s when Michelangelo began to feel mastery of the poetic craft.

NOTES

[1] G. Papini, *La vita di Michelangiolo, ed. cit.*, pp. 192–94.
[2] R. J. Clements, *Michelangelo's Theory of Art, ed. cit.*, pp. 379 ff.
[3] See E. Steinmann, *Michelangelo e Luigi del Riccio* (Florence, 1932), 66 pp.
[4] R. J. Clements, *Michelangelo's Theory, ed. cit.*, p. 281.
[5] G. Vasari, *Le vite, ed. cit.*, VII, 249.
[6] In Girardi edition, p. 455.
[7] *Ibid.*, p. 471.

15

BERNI AND MICHELANGELO'S BERNESQUE VERSE

FOR THE READER who has worked his way through the exalted love poetry or the Christian-Platonic meditations of Michelangelo, the occasional coarse strains may be disturbing, those strains which indicate that a rivulet of salt water has somehow infiltrated the Pierian spring. Although the family of poets who popularised the current vogue of crude and burlesque verse included Bini, Mauro, Molza (author of the *Ficheide*), and Bronzino, the genre was given the name of *bernesco* after Francesco Berni. We grant that the adjective might be considered arbitrary and even slightly retroactive when applied to the artist, as Girardi claims (*Studi*, p. 111). That the great comic poet was a friend of Michelangelo should not by now surprise us. That Michelangelo admired Berni we know from a direct encomium (see below) and from the indirect compliment of imitation. Whereas much of the Bernesque poetry which flourished even around the court of Lorenzino de' Medici leaned for its humor on the *double entendre* and innuendo of sexual conduct and misconduct, Michelangelo rather inclined toward clinical or latrine humor. The most conspicuous example is the long *capitolo*, "I' sto rinchiuso," with its malodorous description of his maladies (see p. 266). Bernesque also is the *sonette caudato* depicting the bodily strains involved in painting the Sistine Ceiling ("I' o gia facto un gozo") (G 71), the isolated fragment "Febbre, fianchi dolor', morbi ochi e denti" (G16), as well as such unexpected lines encountered *passim* as:

> Like one dying to void his belly,
> Who has greater comfort for first having had the pain. (G 54)

These efforts correspond in spirit to such little gems as Aretino's *capitolo* on the quartan fever, Mauro's on beans and Priapus, Dolce's on spittle, and Bini's on venereal disease. The poems of Michelangelo mentioned form a counterpart to the continuous complaints about ill health which one reads in the later letters.

We know, and have been reminded by Tolstoy and others, that the princes of the Renaissance liked a good belly laugh. We know that the bawdy *Heptameron* was composed to titillate the aging Francis I, who had worked through the ten days of Boccaccio. We also know that the racy *Mandragola* was supplied a special theater by a cardinal. Michelangelo's love of Bernesque humor was not restrained by his position as papal employee. Whether or not he intended his poems to be seen by the succession of popes for whom he worked, one of his letters stands as proof that he could express outrageously funny outhouse humor for the pope's special attention. Writing in December, 1525, to his friend Fattucci for the attention of Pope Clement VII, Michelangelo ridicules the papal project of erecting a colossus in the Piazza San Lorenzo of Florence.[1] The poet suggests that the colossus be set over a barber shop on this square, and that the "living statue" be made to sit down over the barbershop. The Bernesque thought follows: "And since there might be objections to carrying off said barbershop out of love for the income [*entrate*] it affords, I have thought that said statue might be made to sit down. The behind would be placed so high that, making the work empty on the inside, as befits something constructed of pieces, the barbershop could stay underneath and not lose income." Fortunately, Michelangelo's objections prevailed, although the pontiff did not appreciate Michelangelo's wit, and Florence was cheated of a statue to rival the Manneken Pis of Brussels, a child's figure, incidentally, which the artist drew.

Among the parodies on contemporary people and events which constitute, along with a *rifacimento* of Boiardo's *Orlando Innamorato*, Berni's chief claim to fame, there is a panegyric to Michelangelo. There is no doubt that Berni knew his man, as did Aretino, and he might have aimed the same shafts at the artist that he did at others. Berni, by the way, wrote a *rima faceta* against the slanderous Aretino, predicting Pietro's death by the "knife, sewer, or the knot" (*pugnale, cesso, nodo*). Yet Francesco admired and obviously loved his fellow Tuscan, Michelangelo. Then, too, Berni's chief aim in life was to entertain, and he brooked the comedian's admiration for the resolute artist whose aim was almost never to entertain.

Perhaps aware of stepping out of character and wishing to avoid the banalities of Renaissance encomium, Francesco expressed his praise of Michelangelo in a curious and indirect way. He sent from Venice a long *capitolo* to Michelangelo's erstwhile painter-friend Sebastiano del Piombo, Keeper of the Papal Seal. The poem antedates 1537, for in that year appeared the first edition of his works. Girardi shows that it must be assigned to between 1531 and 26 September, 1534, the date of the death of Clement

VII. A few words on the relations of Sebastiano and Michelangelo may be in order here. The published exchange of letters between Michelangelo and Sebastiano del Piombo gives eloquent testimony to this well-weathered friendship. Indeed, Michelangelo assisted his friend by supplying the design of such a painting as the *Resurrezione di Lazaro*. There were reciprocal services. Sebastiano interceded with the pope in the effort to release Michelangelo from pressures by the Duke of Urbino to complete the Tomb of Julius II. Il Piombino's letters show him giving continuous encouragement and solace to the older artist. His was that splendid piece of advice to Michelangelo, who suffered under criticism: "Le acquile non degnano delle mosche" ("eagles deign not to notice flies"). If Michelangelo shortly after 1534 decided that Sebastiano was indolent and pampered by over-indulgent patrons (cf. De Hollanda's *Diálogos em Roma*, October, 1538), Sebastiano remained loyal to the artist, even when "boiled in oil" by him (an allusion to Il Piombino's working in oils, for which Michelangelo mocked him to De Hollanda, and to Michelangelo's resentment that Sebastiano urged the pope that he adopt oil for the *Giudizio universale*).

In his lengthy tribute, Francesco Berni hails Michelangelo, in the phrase used also by Bembo and Varchi, as a new "Apollo-Apelles."

> Father, "reverend" to me more than the others
> Who are called reverendissimi—
> About their reverence I am in the dark.
>
> Father, more famous than all the friars
> The world has today, or ever had,
> Including the stupid Inghiesuati.

Berni apparently assumes that Michelangelo shared the current scorn for the new flood of friars and orders, like the Inghiesuati, founded by Giovanni Colombini. The jibe brushes Fra Sebastiano, a new friar more interested in women than in religion. Michelangelo's recorded remarks about friars are limited to two; first, that the habit does not make the monk[2] (cf. Berni's third verse, above), and second, that certain friars have "spoiled the world,"[3] a reference to such schismatics as Luther. The artist, who almost became a friar in Savonarola's order, as did his brother, was less critical of friars than of other intellectuals and academics with whom he associated. Least of all was he critical of Loyola and the Jesuits; despite his advanced years he indicated his willingness to design the mother Church, the Gesù, a fact proudly communicated to members of the Order by a circular letter of Loyola himself. Berni continues:

> What have you been doing since I last left you
> With that fellow to whom we are so devoted?
> He's not a woman and yet I fell in love with him.
> I mean Michel' Agnol Buonarroti:

> Whenever I see him, I'm seized with desire
> To burn incense to him, put up *ex votos* to him.
>
> I believe that this would be a more devout act
> Than donning beige or white for a day or so
> When one recovers from a malady.

Berni compares Sebastiano's vocation as friar to the temporary wearing of token Dominican or Franciscan garb as an *ex voto*. There was inevitably a slightly mordant touch in the first tercet, recalling Michelangelo's love of males. Berni then hails Michelangelo as the living symbol ("idea") of architecture and sculpture. He turns to the Platonic imagery familiar since the days of Ficino, but now associated with Michelangelo's poetry and even art. It is interesting that Berni does not make the artist also the "Idea della Pittura," the phrase reminiscent of Lomazzo's treatise, even though Michelangelo despite frequent disclaimers eventually considered himself consummate in all three arts. Michelangelo seldom used the word *idea*, preferring the word *concetto* in the Platonic sense of prototypical art-form. Berni proceeds to expound on Michelangelo's Platonism:

> You know yourself what a gentleman he is,
> How he has judgement, genius, and discretion,
> How acquainted with the true, beautiful, and good.
>
> I have seen some of his compositions;
> I am ignorant, and yet could claim
> To have read them all in the middle of Plato.

Similarly, the Platonic *nous* becomes in Michelangelo *intelletto*, rather than the "ingegno" used here. After this tribute to Michelangelo's knowledge of the *kalakagathon* follow three tercets which betray further discernment of Michelangelo's artistic style and prejudices. The Apollo-Apelles does not trifle with themes of pale violets, limpid pools, and slim sylvan beasts. He deals not in verbiage, but in concrete things more real than words: "He says things, you say words." Taylor and Bevilacqua[4] agree that this is a reproach of the empty language of the Petrarchists especially. Bevilacqua adds: "A verse worthy of close inspection. For, if we interpret literally the idea which it contains, it could even rightly and profoundly hit upon the essential difference between the Petrarchism of the eminent follower and the Petrarchism of the sheep-like herd."[5] Both Contini (see Bibliography) and Girardi (*Studies*, pp. 92–93) speak of the artist's obsession with "things" and materials (*legno, fuoco, ghiaccio, cenere, zolfo, ossa, medolla*, etc.), although Girardi correctly adds that such seemingly concrete things are often transmuted into symbols. Michelangelo's poetry, Berni suggests, has the solidity of the stonecarver's art. Artists should turn to him and sell their colors to the ladies. Berni's understanding of Michelangelo's disinterest in color (see p. 76) and his definition of painting as design or contours approximating sculpture confirm the opinions in Michelangelo's letter to Varchi and his testimony in the *Diálogos em Roma.*

Berni then pays tribute to the devotion of Sebastiano to Michelangelo. He wishes that both could be rejuvenated, disbelieving, "that you two, who bring alive logs and rocks/Should then like asses have to die." Although the phrase "living rocks" may seem a commonplace, it was so inherent to Michelangelo's aesthetics that it again reveals remarkable perception on Berni's part, as does his awareness of Michelangelo's preoccupation with senescence (see Chapter XVII). Oaks, olive trees, crows, ravens, and dogs live on, but geniuses die. Berni then reproaches himself for descending to trivia and for rambling like Mamelukes and Lutherans. He urges Sebastiano to convey his greetings to the old artist, as well as to the Vicar of Christ (Clement VII, to whom Berni addressed several poems), to three cardinals in the consistory, to Francesco Molza, and to his fellow gourmet Monsignor de' Carnesecchi (Michelangelo's answer clarifies which cardinals are meant). These references to hearty eaters (Cardinal Hippolytus and Carnesecchi) form a contrast to Michelangelo's frugality of diet (he was, says Condivi, moderate in eating). Berni's poems clarify this point, for he alludes to Cardinal Hippolytus's gourmandise in his *capitolo* to Bartolomeo Cavalcanti, while his parody on Archbishop Buondelmonte hails Michelangelo symptomatically as a painter who "dipinge la quaresima e la fame" ("paints Lent and hunger"). Berni closes his amiable missive with an admonition to Fra Sebastiano not to work too hard, rightly certain that this would elicit a wry smile from Michelangelo.

In his reply Michelangelo projects himself into another person and personality, just as he could in his art. He assumes the identity of Fra Bastiano and is thus able to speak of himself in the third person. There is only one slip-up, as we shall see, when he speaks directly for himself in a modest aside. Dealing with a professional wit, he will be sprightly and indulge (twice) in his Petrarchan habit of punning on names in his nineteen bantering tercets. (Berni had composed exactly nineteen also before turning his attention to the other personalities whom Sebastiano was to greet! Michelangelo calculatingly disregards those other tercets.) Michelangelo manages to include several fleeting thoughts of importance to an understanding of his own mind.

In his exordium he explains that he, as Sebastiano, has conveyed Berni's greetings to the pope and several dignitaries as requested.

> When I got your letter, my Lord,
> I went off seeking among all the cardinals
> And said to three on your behalf: "A Dio."
>
> To the greatest Medic of our ills
> I showed your note, whereat he laughed so
> That his nose split his glasses in twain.

The holy and worthy man served by you there
And here took such pleasure at how you write
That he laughed over it just as much.

To him who holds the deepest secrets
Of the lesser Medic I've not as yet shown it;
It would have the same effect on him, were he a priest.

Here there are many others denying Christ
Since you are absent, and without a twinge;
For he who believes not is less unfortunate.

With this letter of yours
I'll relieve their tedium; he who isn't satisfied with it
Can founder under the hangman's hand.

The Meat [Carnesecca] that is cured and dried with salt,
(He would also be good on a grate)
Remembers you, it seems, more than himself. (G 85)

Michelangelo is at his gayest. The two Medici, major and minor, are Clement VII, whose laughter shakes his glasses, and Cardinal Ippolito. Michelangelo has displayed Berni's letter widely except to the scandalous Molza, who would have enjoyed it were he a priest. The poet then picks up the anticlerical tone of Berni's letter and of his own imprecation against Rome, "Qua si fa elmi" (see pp. 127–30). Sebastiano (Michelangelo) has exhibited Berni's *capitolo* around, and if anyone is not happy about the anticlerical lines, let the "executioner" take care of him. Michelangelo, known by Raphael's epithet as the "hangman," will stand against any who are opposed to Berni. A Petrarchan pun divides Monsignor Carnesecchi into *Carne* (meat) and *Secca* (dried).

Michelangelo proceeds to his personal message with considerable grace for a man supposedly lacking social finesse. He is conscious here that he has assumed the name and person of a gracious courtier, Sebastiano.

Our Buonarroto, who adores you,
Since he read your letter, if I may believe my eyes,
Seems wafted heavenward a thousand times each hour.

And he says that the life in his marbles
Would not suffice to make your name as eternal
As your divine songs make him.

Neither summer nor winter can harm your songs,
Exempt from time and cruel death,
Which cannot govern virtuous fame.

Our artist merely regrets that Berni's writing about his works will not make Berni immortal. He does not add that if he did a portrait of Berni he could immortalise that poet. Whereas the rush of time is more frequently measured in Michelangelo's mind by nights and days, here the index is the eternal cycle of the seasons. Unlike his Petrarch, he concludes (but here only) that death has no triumph over fame.

Michelangelo now returns to Berni's desire to light votive candles to him, and affirms that such tributes are better paid to the works themselves than to the painters and poets. "Ai dipinti, uisti i uersi belli,/S'appiccon uoti e s'accendon candele." Thus he himself is honored as a painting, yet a poor painting daubed by an ignorant painter:

> Thus I am but one in the number of those
> By a clumsy and worthless painter,
> Extracted from his paintpots and brushes.

He then asks to have his gratitude transmitted to Berni, "who alone among so many knows the real truth about me," unlike those who mistakenly praise him. This admission about Berni's knowledge of his personal life and innermost thoughts must reflect a genuine surprise. In any case, Michelangelo could be happy that the shafts of Berni, potentially as sharp as those of Aretino, were withheld by the former if not by the latter. He then flatters Berni as he flattered Aretino. Continuing with the thought that he is a poor painting, Michelangelo seems to promise a moral regeneration in order to live up to Berni's opinion of him:

> But his teaching can become to me
> As a bright light; it will be a great miracle
> To make a painted man into a real one.

"Sebastiano" then states that Michelangelo will be the bearer to Berni of these verses. "Sebastiano," however, proceeds to sound precisely like Michelangelo himself when slipping into another of the many and familiar Buonarroti disclaimers:

> While I write this, verse by verse
> I blush the more, thinking to whom I send it,
> Coarse and crude and out of my profession.

This very denial of competence, as we have pointed out here and elsewhere,[6] is repeated throughout Michelangelo's poems, letters, conversations and is applied to the fine arts as well as to the trades and crafts. If Michelangelo was seriously pretending to assume the person of Sebastiano, he gave himself away in the next tercet, which begins the close (*raccomandazione*) of the *capitolo*. For here he states "altro non accade," the very phrase which concludes a number of his personal letters. Michelangelo recovers Sebastiano's identity for the final salutation in which he asks Berni, author of the virulent sonnet "Contra li preti," not to look down on him for his becoming a friar. It is amusing to have Michelangelo insert this apology to Berni, who spent his lifetime among cardinals, bishops, and apostolic protonotaries. There is in this insertion a slight complacency, also, for Michelangelo in his early years decided that an artist worth his salt should best devote himself to God through his art, without the financial security and attendant loss of freedom brought about by wearing the surplice. The final line, like the *pointe* of an epigram, is worthy of Berni himself:

Command me and then act on your own!

The most Bernesque of Michelangelo's poems is typically a *capitolo,* "I' sto rinchiuso come la midolla," addressed to Luigi del Riccio and bearing corrections by Donato Giannotti. Dobelli wrote that this lengthy piece fuses Bernesque influence with that of Angiolieri,[7] and Pascale euphemistically calls it the work of a "studioso d'anatomia."[8] Michelangelo enumerates the physical ills which are the bitter harvest the fine arts have brought him (see also pp. 84–87):

Here I am poor and alone
Enclosed like the pith in its rind,
Or like a spirit holed up in a decanter;
And my dark tomb affords little flight,
Where Arachne and a thousand spiders labor
And in spinning make of themselves spindle-racks.
About the exit are dung-heaps of giants,
As though all those who have taken of grapes or physic
Do not go elsewhere to stool. (G 267)

This outrageous verb (*cacare*) is not unknown in Michelangelo's poems and letters (*caco sangue, cacastecchi,* etc.). Having descended to the level of the vespasian, the poetry tarries there.

I have become well acquainted with urine
And the tube whence it issues through the crack
Which summons me before the morning sun.

(One supposes that Michelangelo has read Berni's *capitolo* "Dell' orinale.")

Cats, carrion, beetles, or cess—
He who comes to change me never fails to find them
Heaped up by the housekeeper.
My soul has this advantage over the body,
That if the obstruction gave way to let out stench,
It could not hold it in with bread or cheese.
Coughs and cold do not let the soul die,
For if it cannot issue forth from the exit below,
It can scarce come forth with the breath of the mouth.
My loins are strained, I'm out of breath,
Fractured and broken by my labor, and death
Is the hostel where I live and eat on credit.

After announcing that discomforts and melancholy have become so commonplace to him that they are now comforts and happiness—the same truth about "conditioned reflexes" noted in his poem "Quand' il seruo il signior d'aspra catena" (see p. 108)—Michelangelo seems to evoke two lines of Berni's "Sopra la mula dell'Alcionio"; both locate a pessimistic truth at Twelfth Night:

Michelangelo:

> Che chi cerca il malanno, Dio gliel dia.
> Chi mi uedess' à la festa de Magi
> Sarebbe buono;
> (To him who asks for disaster, let God give it;
> Whoever saw me at the feast of the Magi,
> Good for him!)

Berni:

> il dì di Befania
> Anunzio il malan, che Dio gli dia;
> (The day of Epiphany
> Announced disaster, and let God give it to him.)

This curious unnoticed *rapprochement*, best observed in the original Italian, was neither accidental nor probably even intentional. It merely demonstrates that Michelangelo enjoyed and absorbed some of the most comic passages in Berni. The pessimistic belief that heaven turns especially against those (i.e. himself) who try to rise above their fellow men to accomplish something worth while is repeated in other poems (G 6, 68, 248, 250) and was a staple of Michelangelo's aphorisms (see Chapter XVIII).

It is very possible that Michelangelo composed this long poem while recuperating at the home of Luigi del Riccio, the original possessor of the manuscript. Therefore Michelangelo could draw a sordid contrast between his benefactor's home (actually the *palazzo* of the Strozzi) and his own now-vanished lodgings in Macel dei Corvi. As Papini observes of this *capitolo,* "When one thinks of the fine large palace which Raphael had built in Rome and of the houses of Titian at Venice, or of the even more luxurious one of the sculptor Leone Leoni in Milan, one will understand better the humor and tenor of Michelangelo's life."[9] Or perhaps Michelangelo here was merely evoking Horace's *Ode* III, 16, 18, 24.

The *capitolo* returns directly to its original clinical intent, as the poet couples his disenchantments with his physical disabilities. He is too sore to think of the pains of love:

> No flame of love has remained within my heart,
> For the greater pain always expels the lesser,
> And the wings of my soul have been clipped and shorn.

Even though Berni had read Plato in everything Michelangelo wrote or painted or sculptured, the statement that the poet has shorn his soul's wings is a blunt rejection of a favorite Platonic image, common in other Platonic poems including his own.

We have quoted earlier (p. 179) the next three terzine with their complaints, especially about Michelangelo's painful *mal della pietra*, which he tried to cure through prayers, mineral waters, and the good offices of Realdo Colombo. Then he continues:

> A spider web lies hidden in my one ear,
> While all night long a cricket chirrups in the other.
> At my catarrhous breathing, I neither sleep nor snore.

In the letters this continuous cricket chirruping is redefined as an unflagging "sonaglio" which prevented him from thinking straight (CCCL).

The *capitolo* ends with a rejection of love, of poetry, and even of art, which merely keeps him subjected to the power of his patrons. The final line longs for death, not death which reunites the mystic with his God, but death the refuge from despair and exasperation. The renunciation of the fine arts will appear again in his poetry, among the "trembling-hand" sonnets of 1550–60, but the renunciation will be the result of religious scruples.

Of this *capitolo* Saviotti has written: "Certainly there is exaggeration and perhaps the intention of treating one of the themes dear to all burlesque poets, from the earliest ones (depiction of one's own miseries, unfortunate life, heavy harness, etc.). But this exaggeration has in Michelangelo something grandiose and impressive."[10]

As we have seen, Michelangelo practiced the *sonetto caudato* form dear to Berni, as well as the *capitolo*. Both of the extended sonnets to Giovanni da Pistoia are Bernesque. The sonnet on the pains and discomforts of painting the Sistine Ceiling ("I' o gia facto un gozo in questo stento") (G 5) dwelled on the unpleasant anatomical features of Bernesque verse—goiter, belly, backsides, leathery skin, rump, and so on—with the same complementary admission of mental anguish and twisted thinking. The Bernesque image of the "archo soriano" is found here. Bernesque also is the mocking extended sonnet to Giovanni da Pistoia: "I' l'ho uostra mercie, per ricieuuto," (G 71) voicing a Dantean disapproval of the Pistoiesi.

Bernesque is the 1531–32 sequence of octaves beginning "Io crederrei, se tu fossi di sasso," which contain the lines on the relief of defecation which we quoted at the beginning of this chapter. Amid the many bantering stanzas on love, there is one moment when Michelangelo seems to be recalling Berni:

Michelangelo:

C'una uagina, ch'è dricta a uedella,
Non puo dentro tener torte coltella.

Berni:

Un gran coltel uuol una gran guaina

Michelangelo's gay octaves beginning "Tu ha' 'l uiso piu dolce che la sapa" (G 20) must be qualified as Bernesque in their comic and incongruous adjectives. There are certainly evocations of Berni's sonnet to his mistress, "Chiome d'argento fino, irte e attorte," which has been accepted as a parody of Bembo's sonnet on the beauties of his lady (eyes of pearls, lashes of snow, lips of milk, teeth of rare ebony).[11] This striking piece couples adjectives and images absurdly and humorously and is a parody of the conventional descriptive love sonnet. However, Michelangelo was inspired by the "Nencia di Barberino" of an older friend, Lorenzo de' Medici, with its line "Tu sei piu bella che non è una papa." The resemblances are striking, although Gino Saviotti qualifies: "Whereas Vallera is content to bear to heaven the appetizing graces of his Nencia, the rustic innamorato of Michelangelo succeeds in setting up a casuistry of love, Petrarchan style. A family vice!"[12] The comment seems less than just. The spontaneous awkwardness of the two simple lovers and their utter joy and excitement, as well as a common vocabulary, bring the two together. Both find their mistress literally "piu bella ch'una papa": to Vallera, Nencia's teeth are as white as a horse's, to Michelangelo's lover, white as parsnips. Each mistress' cheeks are red: (in Michelangelo, like poppies on fresh cheese, in Lorenzo, like roses on white crystal). The delight afforded by Michelangelo's gay (incomplete) stanzas is not much diminished by confrontation with his model, or models. Girardi (*Studi*, p. 147) lists two further variants of the first line, in Pistoia's sonnet "Tu lustri piu che non fa l'or filato" and a sonnet (Codice Miscellaneo Riccardiano 2868), "Tu sei più dolce assai della senapa . . . Tu sei più dolce che non è la sapa." As Auguste Barbier wrote, in retrospect Michelangelo seems one who never laughed. It is good to see his lighter moods, however brief. Let us not be deluded into believing that Michelangelo was writing to a real woman; this poem is merely an exercise in facetious verse. Despite Berni's admiration of Michelangelo's Platonistic sonnets and madrigals, wherever the artist followed Berni and wrote *capitoli, sonetti caudati,* or octave stanzas, chances were excellent that they would be humorous and lively; despite Berni's famous tribute that Michelangelo said things rather than words in his *Rime*, the "words" could sometimes be sufficiently entertaining so that the "things" were not missed.

NOTES

[1] *Lettere*, ed. Milanesi, p. 448.
[2] Vasari, *Le vite*, *ed. cit.*, VII, 279.
[3] *Ibid.*, VII, 279.
[4] J. E. Taylor, *Michelangelo Considered as a Philosophic Poet*, *ed. cit.*, p. 26.
[5] Bevilacqua, *op. cit.*, p. 643.
[6] R. J. Clements, *Michelangelo's Theory*, *ed. cit.*, pp. 411–12.
[7] *Rime*, ed. Ceriello, p. 212.
[8] Vincenzo Pascale, *op. cit.*, p. 62.
[9] G. Papini, *La vita*, *ed. cit.*, pp. 503–04.
[10] Gino Saviotti, *op. cit.*, p. 49.
[11] E. H. Wilkins, *A History of Italian Literature* (Cambridge, 1954), p. 202.
[12] Gino Saviotti, *op. cit.*, p. 41.

16

MINOR THEMES AND MOTIFS

OUR CHAPTERS have now completed a perquisition of the major motifs of Michelangelo's poetry. There are a few minor themes which emerge more slowly, like minor concetti contained full-formed at the bottom of the poet's inkwell. Although they occur but a few times, they are sufficiently central to his thinking that we must consider them respectively: fire, the phoenix, the mirror, fame, and external nature.

There is no reason to anticipate that fire would be an important element in the poetry of Michelangelo. Although he refers often albeit vaguely to the Platonic notion of the ascension of the winged soul through the four zones toward the empyrean, there is no particular mention of the zone of fire. Fire and flames, which are to play such an important role in baroque painting, are not featured in his art. Indeed, we know (see Chapter IV) that he disapproved of and rejected vivid reds, golds, and yellows. True, certain subjects demanded fire, just as this antibucolic artist could not paint the Fall of Man without including a tree. Thus, there can be no *Giudizio universale* without the scorching flames of Hell, although the vast fresco, often repaired or retouched, has just the suggestion of distant glow beyond the *terra vacua* of the lower foreground. Only the most dubious incandescence of fire is present on the spandrel of the Brazen Serpent.

Fire was nevertheless a lively theme of his verse, and part of the baroque baggage (see p. 52). He devoted three poems in succession to it. Fire fulfilled at least four functions.

The most prominent exploitation is the figurative fire of passion. Here of course Michelangelo, "predestined to fire" (G 97), had old traditions behind him, including the Petrarchan, with its plaints of the searing (*cocenti*) stings of love. A curious example of this conceit is a sonnet, "Se da prim' anni aperto," dating from about 1544, when the artist was nearing seventy. Fire, he explains, is more destructive to an aged lover:

If some mild heat of love in youth confessed
Burns a fresh heart with swift consuming fire,
What will the force be of a flame more dire
Shut up within an old man's cindery breast?
If the mere lapse of lengthening years has pressed
So sorely that life, strength, and vigour tire,
How shall he fare who must ere long expire,
When to old age is added love's unrest?
Weak as myself, he will be whirled away
Like dust by winds kind in their cruelty,
Robbing the loathly worm of its last prey. (G 233)

Michelangelo's consciousness of the nothingness of his body, one of the baroque characteristics of his poetry, is nicely adapted here to the image of highly inflammable seasoned wood.

A little flame consumed and fed on me
In my green age: now that the wood is dry,
What hope against this fire more fierce have I?
(J. A. Symonds)

As we have pointed out in discussing the facetious footnotes to the epitaphs for Cecchino Bracci, the afterthoughts penned under these poems have nothing to do with the content or the moment of the poem. Thus, the playful note "Per una delle buctagre" ("for the mullet eggs") does not diminish the tragic burden of the sonnet.

The time comes when even a complacent will and a tenacious body must eventually renounce the fiery passions of love. The coldness of death chills these very ardors:

Arder sole' nel freddo iaccio il foco.
Or m'è l'ardente foco un freddo iaccio . . . (G 281)
(For translation see p. 219.)

Another madrigal (G 171) picks up the theme: the icy touch of death turns fire into ice and laughter into tears, while the memory of a dead love can nevertheless be as dried wood fed to a burning fire.

The flames of a pure passion can have a purifying function. A lover, just as the phoenix, is restored through flames. As a goldsmith refines with flames, so does love:

Not without fire can any workman mold
The iron to his preconceived design,
Nor can the artist without fire refine
And purify from all its dross the gold:
Nor can the phoenix revive, we are told,
Except by fire. Hence if such death be mine
I hope to rise again with the divine,
Whom death augments, and time cannot make old. (G 62)

The exaltation of love, which lifts the soul "to its element," may elevate Michelangelo, transmuted into fire, along with it (1532):

> O sweet, sweet death! O fortunate fire that burns
> Within me still to renovate my days,
> Though I am almost numbered with the dead!
> If by its nature unto heaven returns
> This element, me, kindled by its blaze,
> Will it bear upward when my life is fled.
> (H. W. Longfellow)

Needless to say, this katharsis effected by pure love of a man or woman is accomplished even more easily by divine love.

Fire is of crucial value not only to the art of gold- and silversmith; it is essential as well to sculpture and architecture in making the lime so necessary to knit stones together:

> So friendly is the fire to flinty stone,
> That, struck therefrom and kindled to a blaze,
> It burns the stone and from the ash doth raise
> What lives thenceforward binding stones in one:
> Kiln-hardened, this resists both frost and sun,
> Acquiring higher worth for endless days—
> As the purged soul from hell returns with praise,
> Amid the heavenly host to take her throne. (G 63)
> (J. A. Symonds)

Michelangelo, like the stone itself, is consumed by this inner fire. Out of a burnt and spent condition he will evolve to a new life (no mention of the phoenix here). "Therefore if I live, made smoke and dust, I shall yet be eternal; if I endure beyond the fire, it is as gold and not iron that I am converted."

The function of fire in the making of lime is adapted to further love poems. Just as water dissolves lime instantly, so will the poet's tears dissolve his stout heart:

> But enclosed in a narrow space
> Hard rock turns to lime,
> Which water then dissolves in but a moment . . . (G 170)

It is better that his heart be dissolved than for him to go on burning without dying. Once again (G 143), love concentrates its fire within him, fire which not even a stone could withstand, much less his poor heart ("circumscribed by a fire/In which stone itself could not preserve its nature").

A second poem begins with the premise "Se 'l foco fusse alla bellezza equale" (G 77). Here the treatment of the fire motif is more banal. If the fire of Tommaso's glance were equal to his beauty, no frozen region of the earth would fail to burn under the kindling ray. Yet heaven in its infinite mercy has reduced Michelangelo's visual powers so that he is less affected. If the younger man feels that Michelangelo is not burning or dying for him, it is because advanced age has impaired the artist's capacity for suffering. It is reassuring to find the artist writing to Tommaso of a more disciplined passion, a tonal modification which the younger nobleman certainly welcomed. (It is of course equally possible that this piece was addressed to a man other than Cavalieri, one whom Michelangelo considered unworthy of a deep passion.)

The hellfires which glow dimly in the background of the *Giudizio universale* blaze openly in one quatrain which may have been the beginning of an unfinished sonnet. This is the third poem beginning "Se 'l foco."

If fire reduces stone and liquefies iron,
The child of their selfsame hard core,
What will the most fiery flames of hell then do
To a dried and hostile sheaf of straw? (G 64)

Fire as the ally of the goldsmith appears in two further poems of differing tone and intention. In a comic sequence of octaves, Bernesque in inspiration, Michelangelo's amorous sighs would fan the flames of even the hottest oven:

No oven or furnace ever raged so fiery
That it would not grow ever hotter from my sighs.
And when it happens that I have my loved one nearby,
I sparkle like iron in a burning blaze . . .
I cannot think how thou dost burn my heart,
Passing on the way through eyes always wet
That should quench the fire even more than thy glances. (G 54)

This unlikely image of Michelangelo shooting off sparks in amorous excitement typifies the comic vigor of the entire piece. A more serious adaptation is made of the smithy's fire in the following madrigal:

Not only does the mold, empty of completed work,
Of silver or gold melted by the fire,
That only breaking the form could remove,
Wait then to be refilled;
I, too, with the fire of love still within,
Refill the empty desire for infinite beauty,
For the woman whom I adore,
The heart and soul of my fragile life. (G 153)

In his madrigal "Si come per leuar, Donna, si pone" (G 152) Michelangelo credits love with accomplishing the sculptor-like task of clearing away the dross (*soverchio* or *superchio*) which surrounds and beclouds his soul. Here the *concetto* theory is exploited by means of the goldsmith's art. Michelangelo himself becomes the *soverchio* which, like the mold of the smith, contains and brings forth a perfect work, the mistress herself who has descended into him as into a mold. To bring her to fulfillment he must be shattered and cleared away.

Before passing on to the complementary motif of the phoenix, we turn to Michelangelo's most meaningful poem on fire. Michelangelo, who gazed and meditated on clouds, patches of water, fishes' fins, must have stared with fascination at flames. The flickering of a flame was intimately connected with his conception of dynamic form. Michelangelo once advised Marco da Siena to execute figures serpentine in form. Lomazzo elucidated this remark by stating that Michelangelo's notion of serpentine derived from a flame flickering and endeavoring to ascend to its sphere.[1] This is the flame described in the isolated three verses:

> As a flame grows brighter the more assailed
> By the wind, every virtue which heaven exalts
> Shines all the more, the more it is offended. (G 48)

These lines served as an inspiration to the artist; with them he assured himself that from all the obstacles which beset his life he would emerge more resplendent and successful than ever. The life of Dante illustrated this lesson, and indeed three verses of Dante (see p. 318) inspired these three lines of Michelangelo. Suffice it to note that calm, vertical flames in a setting of still air do not interest the poet, but rather flames whipped into an extended serpentine.

Fire reappears in various guises throughout the *Rime:* the fire of the sun or of Phoebus (Di Poggio), the burning heart so dear to Santa Teresa and the baroque mystics, and the appearances just mentioned. Two related themes dear to Michelangelo the poet concern creatures that dwell in fire, the phoenix and the salamander. Before proceeding to the important theme of the phoenix, let us tarry for a moment over the one salamander which slithered into the *Rime*. Not so famous as the salamander exhibited to Cellini by his father as a moral lesson, this salamander is important as an image of Michelangelo, a being toughened and conditioned by the earthly ordeals of fire and emerging stronger than ever:

> If fire harms all else,
> It burns me without searing,
> Not because of my great or its lesser power,
> But because I alone find safety
> Like the salamander, there where others die: (G 122)

Though in this particular case, the testing fires are those of love, the lines have broader application to all the ordeals of his life, as well.

The phoenix was obviously more conspicuous in his iconography than was the salamander.

The idea of ascension preyed upon Michelangelo, who hoped to soar to paradise as did Christ himself. The Platonic *ascensio* was equally present in his consciousness; De Tolnay claims that the entire nine histories of the Sistine Ceiling were conceived (and should be read) as an ascension from the *Drunkenness of Noah* to the *Separation of Darkness and Light*. Michelangelo even thought of himself as a soaring Daedalus ("Non altrimenti Dedal si riscosse") (G App. 24) and of Febo as a Phoebus plunging through the skies. Thus it was easy for him to identify himself with that most miraculous of creatures, the soaring phoenix. Before making the association, he toyed several times with this iconological oddity which appeared in the contemporary emblem books with such appropriate posies as "Perit ne pereat" or "Uritur, ut vivat."

First there is his denial that man shall ever rise like the phoenix after death, enunciated almost as a maxim. Indeed, it is this dissimilarity between man and the phoenix which gives him pause when he reflects on suicide:

> But because man is not like the phoenix
> Which in the sun's light rearises and returns (G 52)

He is also deterred when his reason tells him that some loves, like his for the living sun Phoebus, will bring only death:

> —What will you bring back to us from the bright sun
> Other than death, and not that of the phoenix! (G 43)

In a sense man's reclothing at the Day of Judgement is like the phoenix reassuming its form. Among the several pieces on Cecchino Bracci's reassumption of his beauty on the Day of Wrath, one compares the lad to this fabled purple-red bird from the Arabian desert:

> If it happens that like the phoenix, even more admired
> The beautiful face of Bracci is restored,
> It will be for the best that he who did not know it
> Should lose it for a while and then recover it. (G 217)

The heat which gave new life to the aged phoenix is generated within the aged artist by the new love for Tommaso Cavalieri. Could he have believed that this love would renew him, he would have sought it wholeheartedly:

> If I had believed at the first sight
> Of this beloved phoenix in the warm sun
> That I'd be renewed by fire, as is happening,
> In my extreme old age, whence I'm all afire . . .
> I'd have rushed to it, whereas now I'm quick too late. (G 61)

In this instance Cavalieri is the phoenix. In the other occurrences of this motif, Michelangelo himself becomes either the phoenix or like the phoenix.

The blinding heat generated by Phoebus was sparked by the God's namesake, Febo. For a while the poet hoped that he would rise like the phoenix:

> Ben mi doue' con si felice sorte,
> Mentre che Febo il poggio tucto ardea,
> Leuar da terra . . . (G 99)
> (For translation see p. 120.)

However, sometimes the phoenix lies inert among its splendid ashes, unable to rise:

> What a marvel it is, if next to the fire
> I was destroyed and burned, if now outwardly spent
> It inwardly afflicts and consumes me,
> And gradually reduces me to ashes? . . .
> A burning coal I remain, but covered over. (G 266)

Even from his earthbound and immobile plight he envies the lofty meteorisis of the phoenix:

> Felice uccello, che con tal uantaggio
> Da noi, t'è Febo e 'l suo bel uolto noto,
> E piu c'al gran ueder t'è ancora arroto
> Volare al poggio, ond'io rouino e caggio. (G 100)
> (For translation see p. 120.)

Some commentators have interpreted this bird as the eagle. However, this incomplete sonnet still toys with the tragic motif of the phoenix which cannot rise.

Along with the theme of the injured phoenix which cannot soar, Michelangelo improvises on the theme of the phoenix too old to rise—that is, the lover no longer exalted by love:

> Nor do I hope, like a new phoenix in the sun,
> Ever to return; for time doth grant it to us not. (G 108)

Finally, we have already (p. 272) mentioned the sonnet on the purifying properties of fire (G 62), akin to the purgative action of love ("Ne l'unica fenice se riprende"), which recalls the necessity of fire to the flight of the phoenix.

The theme of the *arco* (bow) which recurs frequently both in an amatory sense (G 20 var., 23, 24, 175, 272, 285) and as a symbol of force (G App. 3, 5, 131) is discussed in Chapter VII, as it affects the meanings of both the marble and bronze *Davids* and the *Saettatori*.

The motif of the mirror intrigued Michelangelo as poet; however, it performed no auxiliary function for him as artist, as it did for Alberti, Leonardo, and other technicians who employed it, like a sextant, to capture or verify a semblance of reality. Indeed, Michelangelo must have been surprised at the curious compliment which Vittoria Colonna wrote to him after she had received his finished drawing of the Crucifixion. She explained that she had examined the drawing with a magnifying glass and with a mirror, and had found in it no mistakes.

Among the ancestors of Christ on the smaller spandrels of the Sistine Ceiling we discover the pony-tailed wife of Naasson, mother of Salmon, contemplating herself in a hand glass. This seems to be the one appearance of a mirror in Michelangelo's art. It was long thought that Michelangelo's carved figure of Leah held a mirror in her left hand. This, as Foscolo and others believed, was a reference to Dante's line: "Here in my glass I take joy in my array" (*Purg.* XXVII, 103). However, Goldscheider (*Selected Drawings*) assumed that Leah is holding a diadem "through which she has already drawn the tresses of her hair."

In the *Rime* the mirror is a measuring device designed by nature for moral purposes. Its main function is to remind man of the passing of time. Youth is described in "S'i' fussi stato ne prim' anni achorto" (G 253) as "the green age when there is light and mirror." The mirror is "loyal" to youth, but a traitor to old age:

> Alas! Alas, for I am betrayed
> By my fleeting days and by the mirror. (G 51)

A madrigal declares that no beauty but that of Vittoria Colonna is mirrored in his eyes, that any attraction unlike hers is lost to him as though unreflected by unleaded glass (G 234). Finally, true to his habitual self-projection, Michelangelo transforms himself into a mirror (G 269); as in a glass his past woes are reflected as present vicissitudes and future hopes.

One place in which the mirror motif could have been exploited but was not is the playful poem (G 75) accusing Tommaso Cavalieri like a "Medusa in Mauro" (G 10) of destroying people who look directly upon him.

Finally, a full account of the allegorical madrigal in which the figure of art mirrors herself,

> In her faithful mirror
> Where she sees herself equal to paradise, (G 172)

has been given in Chapter IV.

As Berni might have put it, fire, the phoenix, the salamander, the bow, and the mirror are "things," whereas fame is a "word." Seldom was an artist more certain of his fame by the term of his life than was Michelangelo. One way for a talented artist to assess his posthumous fame is to live almost into his ninetieth year. So many and so extravagant were the contemporary testimonies to that fame that the "divine" Michelangelo became surfeited with them. He could only wince under the effusive encomiums typified by Doni's accolade: "O divine man, everyone considers you an oracle . . . You ought to be adored by men and, dying in no other way, raised by the angels to one of the most beautiful seats of Paradise . . . Most surely I hold you for a God . . . Etc., etc." The extent to which the Renaissance was nurtured on such hyperbole has been treated by many historians, most recently in O. B. Hardison's *The Enduring Monument.*

Living in an age when the words "Painter" and "Poet" were spelled with a capital letter, when painters and poets were beginning to enjoy new social prestige, when artists began to sign their works and insert into them their own self-portraits, Michelangelo was as eager as any other for recognition; the *Rime* inevitably give us clues to the artist's cult of fame.

First of all there is an evidence in his poetry paralleled in his art. Michelangelo broke with the past in signing several of his works (the bold inscription on the *Madonna della Febbre,* the autograph on the *David* sketch, etc.). The poetry introduces the same novelty. The angry sonnet "Qua si fa elmj di chalicj e spade" (G 10) bears his signature: "Vostro Michelangniolo in Turchia" (see p. 129) and two of the quatrains to Cecchino (8th and 45th) bear accompanying notes with signatures.

As an introduction to the subject of fame in the *Rime,* the most obvious is the tercet accompanying a drawing of the two Medici sepulchers. It is dated without wide discrepancy by Frey (1523), De Tolnay (1520–21), and Wilde (1519–21), with Girardi in general agreement. As Michelangelo was commending to eternity the two Medici scions, his thoughts (1520–23) turned to fame and immortality. He wrote:

> Fame holds the epitaphs lying still;
> Fame goes neither forward nor backward,
> For they are dead, and their activities stayed. (G 13)

These verses, set out as prose, have been variously interpreted. One explanation (Girardi) is that fame renders epitaphs useless; they afford no advantage or harm, being dead and thus unable to operate in any way. This view of the epitaphs being dead is in contradistinction to Michelangelo's view of living epitaphs (Cecchino) and living stones (the *Notte,* etc.). Another obvious message of the lines is that with death, the die is cast; the reputation of the dead figures is set for all time. It is equally true that Michelangelo may have been thinking of the *Trionfo della Fama* (I, 7–13) of his beloved Petrarch, that is, of fame which takes men at death and keeps their image intact: "Che trae l'uom del sepoloro, e 'n vita il serba." In his *Studies in Iconology* Panofsky states that Michelangelo's first line above must be translated "Fame holds the epitaphs in position." Noting that the original study for the double wall-tomb which carried the lines above did not include recumbent statues of the Dukes, Panofsky supposes that the word *epitafi* refers merely to the memorial tablets appearing on that study.[2]

Christian modesty notwithstanding, it would be difficult to receive such a torrent of praise for so many years without believing it well grounded. After all, Michelangelo's Platonic theory of art holds the true artist to be one of an elect granted the gift of *intelletto*. "Po' c'a destinguer molto/ Dalla mie chiara stella/Da bello a bel fur facti gli ochi mei" (G 173). His resentment at the servitude imposed by the Maecenate system increased his consciousness of his own talent, "sculpturing divine things here" (G 282).

Fame as a theme in the *Rime* most often relates to the Pindaric notion that art and poetry confer double immortality, on the artist and on his subject. The ability of the artist to confer life and win immortality himself was noted in Berni's *capitolo* to Michelangelo; "A ogni modo è disonesto a dire/Che voi, che fate i legni e i sassi vivi,/Abbiate poi com' asini a morire."[3] (See page 263.) Similarly, Michelangelo hailed Berni's poetry as deathless (G 85). Another friend recalled this obvious truth to him; the Marchioness of Pescara said in the course of the *Diálogos em Roma* that the painter gives life for many years to him who dies. He later wrote in return to the Marchioness:

> Dunche posso ambo noi dar lunga uita
> In qual sie modo o di colore o sasso,
> Di noi sembrando l'uno e l'altro uolto;
>   Si che mill'anni dopo la partita
> Quante uoi bella fusti, e quant'io lasso
> Si ueggia, e com' amarui i' non fu' stolto. (G 239)
> (For translation see p. 72.)

Even that *enfant gâté* Cecchino Bracci, in Michelangelo's words, knew that he was to be immortalised in painting:

> I' fu' de Bracci, e se ritracto e priuo
> Restai dell'alma, or m'e cara la morte,
> Po' che tal opra ha si benigna sorte
> D'entrar dipinto, ou' io non pote' uiuo. (G 202)
> (For translation see p. 241.)

Perhaps similar satisfaction at attaining such heights through art invested those young models who saw themselves as *ignudi* on the Sistine Ceiling. A friend or model of whom the artist apparently made a sketch, possibly Febo di Poggio, finds himself not only immortalised but ennobled through art as well: "Contrary effects illumine the paper with life,/More than was their custom when he lived,/Dead, he now possesses heaven, whereas before he had no part of it" (G 47).

Although Michelangelo was thus gratified by the diuturnity of art, including the cold stone monuments of architecture ("in some way it [fire] lives on, binding stones together into an eternal monument") (G 63), he knew his Horace well; the theme of the *scripta manent* or *monumentum aere perennius* appears several times in the *Rime*. He was convinced that Vittoria Colonna would have lasting fame as a poetess through her solemn and religious verses:

> Although her body is dead,
> One cannot assign to oblivion
> Her sweet, charming, and holy inks. (G 265)

Michelangelo's predictions for the literary success of Berni and Vasari proved to be better grounded. His tribute to Vasari's literary endeavors has already been quoted. He conceded that Berni's *carmi* would outlast his own marbles:

> Ai quali non nuoce nè state nè uerno
> Del tempo esenti e da morte crudele,
> Che fama di uirtù non ha in gouerno. (G 85)

(For translation see p. 264.)

In sum, Michelangelo willingly accepted the kudos of his century (especially if the praises were not spoken in his presence) and shared them with a select few writers and artists of his country. Only in later life (see Chapter XVII) did moments of doubt and depression cause him to wonder whether all works of art were merely *bambocci* and art itself a waste of the time which might be better spent in contemplating God. This renunciation of art was merely a part of a tergiversation on life itself. More usually, Michelangelo took consolation that like his *David* he had won glory for himself and his people through his self-disciplined strength (*arco*) or that like a Daedalus he had shaken off the shackles of weakness and poverty and risen high in the firmament (G App. 24). This pull toward the sun by the figure of Fame was depicted by Francesco Curradi in a portrait housed in the Casa Buonarroti.

Michelangelo's biographers have asked in genuine wonderment why the artist was so disinterested in external nature. Was he not born in the hills near Arezzo, raised at Settignano with that panorama of Tuscan slopes still to be beheld today? Was he not always beckoned by the paths and flowery lanes around Florence? Even the annoyances which beset him at Carrara and Pietra Santa must not have diverted his attention entirely from the magnificent spectacle of mountains skirting the blue Tyrrhenian Sea.

Furthermore, those poets who influenced him extolled external nature with enthusiasm. Dante and Petrarch should have drawn him closer to a deep appreciation of nature and landscapes. Indeed, one of his jottings seemingly inspired by nature, "Chiare, fresche, e dolci acque," is merely the *incipit* of a famous Petrarchan *canzone*. Again, he copied the bucolic line of Petrarch to Vaucluse ("Valle lochus chlausa toto michi nullus in orbe") on a sheet containing sketches of *putti* (G App. 22). The modern poets whom he knew well, Lorenzo de' Medici and Poliziano, on occasion were joyous nature poets. One might even expect more nature poetry of Michelangelo, since he was willy-nilly an habitué of the courts and lived in an age when the pastoral and idyll entertained the princelings and their guests as lyric poems, as playlets, and even as ballets. We have already theorised (p. 89) that the artist who acknowledged this new mode by a *Bacco* may very well have written a Bacchic ode replete with the fauns, satyrs, nymphs, and other sylvan dwellers described by Tasso, Guarini, and Marino.

We know all too well the little importance external nature held for Michelangelo as artist. We remember his statement to Vasari that the human body made a better decorative motif than did foliage or fronds. Better also than landscapes themselves, a conviction so well revealed by the Doni *Madonna* and the *Ignudi*. We know of his complaint to Francisco de Hollanda that the Flemings indulged in cluttered panoramas of external nature, *lontani* as they were called ("patches, masonries, plants in the fields, shadows of trees, rivers, and bridges").[4] It was Vasari who pointed out that in the Cappella Paolina Michelangelo neglected landscaping and trees as one who perhaps disdained to lower that great genius of his to such things.[5] Michelangelo's lifelong production of art affords the best testimony of all. Only three trees grace his work, two in the *Diluvio* and the Tree of the Knowledge of Good and Evil triptych, an indispensable prop of the Original Sin diptych. A stump appears for good measure in the *Creazione di Eva*, and a branch behind *Giona*.

Trees are correspondingly absent from the *Rime*, appearing only as withered symbols of the decline of love or affection. In other subjects which required fewer trees and less vegetation than the Garden of Eden Michelangelo managed to avoid this vein of nature entirely, notably in the *Battaglia di Cascina* and the *Centauromachia*. The painters who first influenced and guided Michelangelo—Giotto, Masaccio, Schongauer, Ghirlandaio, and later Signorelli—were not great *paysagistes*, but none disdained nature as Michelangelo was to do. The most cogent illustration of the artist's disinterest in nature are his confessional drawings of the *Fall of Phaeton*, who, according to myth, cascaded into the river Eridanus. The river is here depicted as a husky river god, about to experience, like Aeschylus, death from above.

The perceptive Berni, whose assessment of Michelangelo as poet, artist, and man was so acute, alluded in his *capitolo* to Sebastiano del Piombo to this side of the artist's character. Mindful of the "liquido cristallo" of such bucolic poems as Petrarch's "Amor, che meco al buon tempo," he claims:

> He is then a new Apelles and new Apollo—
> Fall silent, pale violets, for aye,
> And you, crystal liquids, and fleet woodland beasts,

External nature is not so entirely absent from the *Rime*, however, as it is from his art. To begin with, there was his fragment written, as Girardi notes, in an elegant juvenile handwriting:

> To the sweet murmur of a streamlet
> Which a limpid shadow casts into green shade . . . (G App. 5)

It is useless to attempt a literary evaluation of such a Petrarchistic fragment, as does Insinga: "In its impossible verbal coincidence, it is merely mnemonic, insincere, and flaccid."[6] The fragment indicates that at least in younger days Michelangelo paused to reflect upon what he was missing; perhaps he was anticipating the Vaucluse he never visited, the ideal *podere* of the several he was to purchase, or perhaps he was just practicing during his poetic apprenticeship. In any case, it is typical that his sylvan muse deserted him in mid-inspiration.

There is evidence of a similar desertion in the lengthy *Stanze in lode della vita rusticale*, one of Michelangelo's rare exercises in the *ottava d'oro*, the octave sequence. Again the first stanza starts out as refreshingly as a deep draught of mountain air:

> And sweet it is to see in summer time
> The daring goats, upon a rocky hill,
> Climb here and there, still browsing as they climb,
> While far below, on rugged pipe and shrill
> The master vents his pain: or homely rhyme
> He chaunts: now changing place, now standing still;
> While his beloved, cold of heart and stern!
> Looks from the shade in sober unconcern. (G 67)
> (William Wordsworth)

True, Pan or the Faun is changed into a rustic goatherd and Oenone converted into a swineherdess. True, the essential note is less like Sannazaro or Guarini than like Luigi Alamanni's *Coltivazione* or Luigi Tansillo's *Podere*. The inspiration is actually Poliziano's first stanza for the joust depicting a Golden Age.

> Quando giova a mirare pender da un'erta
> le capre, a pascer questo e quel virgulto
> e 'l montanaro all 'ombra piu conserta
> . . .

destar la sua zampogna e 'l verso inculto
veder la terra di pomi coperta
ogn' arbor da' suo' frutti quasi occulto,
veder cozzar montone, vacche mugghiare
e le biade ondeggiare come fa il mare . . .[7]

The depiction of small farmers and a rustic *paysage*, not unlike the Flemish genre scenes which Michelangelo disliked, continues for two more octaves. After that the direction of Michelangelo's poem changes. The countryside is no longer the great fertile miracle of nature which poets have ever extolled, but simply the setting of a peaceful way of life reminiscent of a Golden Age, which contrasts with the hectic, artificial, and unethical life in the city. Michelangelo, like the protagonist in his patron Lorenzo's *Altercazione*, is the city man envying the husbandman's way of life. Further stanzas, presented in Wordsworth's free version, sing of the happy simplicity of the rustic life:

Nor less another sight do I admire,
The rural family round their hut of clay,
Some spread the table, and some light the fire
Beneath the household rock, in open day:
The ass's colt with baskets some attire:
Some tend the bristly hogs with fondling play;
This with delighted heart the old man sees,
Sits out of doors, and suns himself at ease.
The outward image speaks the inner mind,
Peace without hatred, which no care can fret;
Entire contentment in their plough they find,
Nor home return until the sun be set:
No bolts they have, their houses are resign'd
To Fortune—let her take what she can get.
A hearty meal then crowns the happy day,
And sound sleep follows on a bed of hay.
In that condition Envy is unknown,
And Haughtiness was never there a guest.
They only crave some meadow overgrown
With herbage that is greener than the rest;
The plough's a sovereign treasure of their own;
The glittering share, the gem they deem the best;
A pair of panniers serves them for buffette;
Trenchers and porringers for golden plate. . . .
They in old time who drank the streamlet clear,
And fed upon the fruits which Nature sent,
They should be your example, should appear
Beacons on which your eyes should still be bent:
O listen to my voice with willing ear!
The peasant with his herds enjoys content . . .

In addition to Poliziano's stanza for the joust, there is another source which should be mentioned here, a source less direct but in pages which Michelangelo knew well: Petrarch's sunset scenes of Vaucluse so beautifully described in the *canzone* "Ne la stagione che 'l ciel rapido inchina." (Indeed, later in his life Michelangelo knew equally well his friend Beccadelli's praises of Vaucluse.) Petrarch's *zappador* sings at his hoeing and then sits down at table to simple fare (acorns, as in Michelangelo). The pastor herds his flock and then sleeps *à la belle étoile* untroubled by the cares of city folk ("there without a care he relaxes and sleeps"). Such insouciant sleep is a motif of Petrarch's verse; whereas the old lady, the peasant, the shepherd all enjoy it, Petrarch cannot because of his "obstinate worrying." In Michelangelo the husbandmen are able to sleep on hay, whereas Petrarch's shepherd slept on fronds or reeds (*giunchi*). Other similarities between Michelangelo's and Petrarch's halcyon tableaux could be pointed out. In view of the echoes of Petrarch and Poliziano here, we must conclude that, unlike most Renaissance poets, Michelangelo was incapable of being stirred to verse by the miraculous aspects of external nature.

Frey and his generation thought that Michelangelo's discovery of the happy, natural life of the monks at Spoleto inspired these verses. Indeed, a letter from Michelangelo to Vasari (28 December, 1556) is the most solid evidence we possess of a love of nature (discovered late) on the part of the artist: ". . . With considerable difficulty and expense I have had during these days a great enjoyment in the mountains of Spoleto, visiting the hermit monks. As a result, less than half of me has returned to Rome. For truly one cannot find peace except in the woods" (CDLXXIX). The circumstances of this escape to Spoleto, to avoid a rumored military invasion of Rome, coincide with the spirit of the stanzas on rustic life. Not only do they laud the peace of the country, but also proceed for eleven stanzas to decry the evils of city living, including wars and political ambitions. Girardi's study of the autographs shows, however, that the verses date from *circa* 1534.

To complete our brief register of Michelangelo's nature poetry, we should recall those poems involving the sun and moon which we discussed in Chapter V and especially a sonnet (1534–38) addressed to Vittoria Colonna, a sonnet ("Rendete a gli ochi mei") which anticipates John Donne's "The Message" ("Send home my long-strayed eyes to me"):

> Restore, ye springs and rivers, to mine eyes
> That stream, not yours, which doth not cease to flow,
> And you so richly nourisheth, that so
> Beyond your wont with swift increase ye rise.
> And thou, dense air, made heavy with my sighs,
> That from my sad eyes shadest heaven's light,
> Restore them to my heart and let my sight

Pierce to the brightness which thy mists disguise.
Let earth its footprints to my feet restore,
The herb spring up again, which they did press,
And dullard Echo send back my lament.
And let thine eyes give back my looks once more,
That I one day some other loveliness
May love, since thee so little I content. (G 95)
(Elizabeth Hall)

Michelangelo has already evoked Echo in his complaining stanza to Julius II (G 6), where Echo is synonymous with slander. Here Echo takes her proper place as a sylvan oread. In the mid-1530s, after having consistently avoided the bucolic baggage introduced by Theocritus and left by Sannazaro as a legacy to the Cinquecento and Secento, Michelangelo "tries it once" just to show that he is capable of writing in this vein.

NOTES

[1] R. J. Clements, *Michelangelo's Theory of Art*, *ed. cit.*, pp. 175–77.
[2] Erwin Panofsky, *Studies in Iconology* (New York, 1939), p. 200.
[3] Francesco Berni, *Rime facete* (Milan, 1959), p. 156.
[4] Francisco de Hollanda, *Diálogos em Roma*, *ed. cit.*, p. 189; also, Rezio Buscaroli, *Il concetto dell'arte nelle parole di Michelangelo* (Bologna, 1945), p. 9.
[5] Vasari, *Le vite*, *ed. cit.*, VII, 216; see Clements, *Michelangelo's Theory*, Plate IX.
[6] Arturo Insinga, *Michelangelo poeta* (Palermo, 1919), p. 23.
[7] A. Poliziano, *Stanze per la giostra*, I, 18.

17

OLD AGE, APPROACHING DEATH, AND RENUNCIATION

DEATH, AS THE ARTIST WROTE to Vasari, was sculptured in Michelangelo's every thought (CDLXXVI). In Chapter III we met the constant evidences of his concern and fascination with death. It is an irony that Michelangelo, who worried about his "propinqua morte" most of his mature life and who feared that one's chances for salvation decreased as his life span increased, should have lived to within a fortnight of his ninetieth year. His belief in the greater security afforded by a short life he voiced in several poems:

Thus the longer one sojourns here below, the less grace he has
For he who lives less, returns lightest to heaven. (G 132)

For the longer the span of time the less good will endures, (G 296)

and elsewhere (see pp. 97 and 306). He thus had not only a more protracted old age but also, as we shall see below, a longer period of renunciation during which to question the values which had sustained him during his youth and maturity.

From the testimony of the poems, Michelangelo rarely viewed senescence and death with the equanimity of some philosophic author of a *De Senectute*. Almost never did he see old age as a "golden period" of his life, although there is a hint of such imagery in the lines:

But perhaps, even though I am at the end of the day,
With the sun already almost set in the West
Amid the thick shadows and the cool gloom . . . (G 261)

Most usually old age was a period to contemplate death. Since Michelangelo considered himself old by the 1530s, such contemplation began early. Around 1534–35 the artist drew an upright skeletal figure of death bearing a crude box on its back on the stair landing of his Roman home, where it might grin at him every time he retired. The box carried the following *memento mori:*

> I say to you, who to mundane things have given over
> Your soul and body and spirit as well;
> In this dark box is your lot. (G 110)

Although we can only imagine how this painting looked, the grinning skulls of the depths of the *Giudizio universale* afford an idea.

Lest one be surprised that Michelangelo should thus force himself to daily speculation upon death, one must remember the words he uttered to his Tuscan friends in the *Dialogi* of Giannotti: "And I remind you that in trying to find oneself again and to enjoy oneself, it is not necessary to seek such delights and pleasures, but one must think on death. That is the only thought which makes us recognise ourselves, which keeps us united within ourselves, without letting us be robbed by relatives, friends, great masters, ambition, avarice, and other vices and sins which rob a man from himself and keep him scattered and dissipated, without ever letting him find himself again or become whole. And a marvelous thing is the effect of this thought of death, which by its very nature destroys all things—preserves and maintains those who think on it, and defends them from all human passions."[1] By Montaigne's definition Michelangelo here became a philosopher, for he had learned how to die. If we give credence to these sentiments, they explain why Michelangelo was content to devote so much time to the planning and execution of sepulchers and mortuary chapels.

In another sense this monologue, worthy of an old Savonarolian Piagnone, is an exegesis of one of the artist's madrigals, "Non pur la morte." For no sooner has he recited it than he remembers he has pointed out its lesson in a "madrigaletto" on the conflict between love and thanatophobia:

> Not death indeed, but the dread thought of death
> Saveth and severeth
> Me from the heartless fair who doth me slay:
> And should perchance some day
> The fire consuming blaze o'er measure bright,
> I find for my sad plight
> No help but from death's form fixed in my heart;
> Since, where death reigneth, love must dwell apart. (G 127)
> (J. A. Symonds)

The original lines confirm that fear of death is as destructive as death itself; that if fear of death saves one from love, then the lady's image lodged in his heart is already a protection against love, for death is in that heart and love will not enter therein. The convoluted logic of this piece makes it more difficult than most. The sestet "S'a tuo nome ò concecto alcuno inmago" (G 284) acknowledges that the specter of death also makes art and genius vanish, an observation rephrased elsewhere as "L'arte e la morte non uan bene insieme."

Among the most prominent themes of Michelangelo's art and poetry are these (senescence, illness, withering of the flesh, concern for salvation, the phoenix) which reveal him no less aware of oncoming death than a man of the Middle Ages darting fearful glances at the M's (*memento mori*) in the folds of his palms or practicing for his chess game with Death. In no poet more than in Michelangelo are the motifs of his poetry the very motifs of his everyday thought.

Mediaeval, too, was his ballad of the dead (1515–30), that distinctive ballad which stands apart from all the other poetry like the two skeletons terrifying their fleshy neighbors on the Acherontic bank in the *Giudizio universale*. Reminiscent of Villon's *Ballade des pendus*, several cadavers speak, insisting on their dried skin and empty eye sockets and echoing their grim ritornello: "Ogni cosa a morte arriua."

Whoever is born arrives at death
With the flight of time; and the sun
Leaves not a single thing alive.
The sweet and painful alike pass away,
And the thoughts we have thought and the words spoken.
Our generations gone by are like shadows
In the sun or smoke on the wind.
Like you, we were men.
Like you, happy and sad.
And now we are, as you see,
Lifeless earth under the sun.
Everything comes at length to death.
Once were our eyes whole
With pupils in their sockets;
Now they are empty, horrid and black,
And that is the portent of time. (G 21)

This ballad, akin to carnival songs and to verses accompanying German woodcuts, illustrates as well as any other work of Michelangelo the horror which the thought of death conveyed to the Renaissance's greatest artist. The artist's great-nephew thought the verses inspired by religious poems of Castellano de' Castellani or of Antonio Alamanni. (Of interest is the scoring of this poem for voice and chamber orchestra by the leading twelve-tone composer Luigi Dallapiccola [*Tre poemi*, 1949]. In this work, dedicated to Arnold Schoenberg, dodecaphony heightens the forlorn mood and desperation of the plaint.) This ballad of the dead was written early, during the 1520s or before.

Even among the Petrarchan poems of this period one finds Michelangelo worrying about old age and death. In "Oilme, Oilme, ch'i' son tradito," the artist laments that he has not heeded the warnings of the mirror and has postponed thinking of repentance and taking counsel with himself. Now, in "un giorno uecchio," he finds himself with death at hand.

> Inimical to myself, I pour forth
> Useless tears and sighs,
> For there is no wrong equal to
> wasted time. (G 51)

His reflection on time lost coincides with his awareness of the three years he had sacrificed on the Façade of San Lorenzo. In reporting on the latter to the Vatican, Michelangelo complained, "I have lost three years, I am ruined." In the "song" Michelangelo returns in the third stanza to the physical and moral changes wrought by old age, to the aimlessness of senescence. Life is an adagio death march to eternal punishments. As frequently in the *Rime*, death is not the only specter. There is the attendant prospect of the Day of Wrath.

Michelangelo wrote and talked of his senescence to friends and correspondents. Francesco Berni—who penned his "Capitolo a Fra Bastiano del Piombo," actually addressed to Michelangelo—proves to have an unusual perception of the artist's habits of thinking and feeling, curries favor by regretting that the master is now in his fifties and wishing that somehow Michelangelo and Sebastiano del Piombo could be rejuvenated:

> We'd have to have that cauldron
> Where Medea cooked her father-in-law,
> To snatch him from the hand of old age.
> Oh, would that the wife of Ulysses were alive
> To rejuvenate the two of you
> And make you live longer than Titan did live.

In extreme old age Michelangelo had the cruelty of death brought home to him every time someone dear to him died. We remember the admission in the *Lettere* that he has no friends left with whom to share his wine. These painful moments found their way into his poems, some Petrarchan and others more independent. Even the early deaths of the Duke Giuliano de' Medici, Savonarola, and Pope Julius II found echoes in his *canzoniere*. The deaths of the members of his family—he outlived his four brothers—his dear friends Vittoria Colonna, his assistant Urbino, Cecchino Bracchi, Faustina Mancini, and all the others are reflected in his poetry. As we saw in Chapter VI, the death of the adolescent Cecchino elicited an entire *canzoniere-fiume* of thoughts and improvisations on death. Michelangelo could have further explained his belief that a short life is best by adding that from an old man "death takes many a great friend," to recall his sentence to

Fattucci about the deceased Marchioness of Pescara. From the testimony of the poetry we learn that Michelangelo derived lessons from the deaths of his friends: that death is not something to fear, but the occasion of rejoining friends (G 300), that a dying friend's eyes reveal God's presence making him wish to meet God himself (Frey XXX), that the Final Resurrection will take place (epitaphs to Cecchino), and so on.

That the death of friends and family did not shake his faith but rather confirmed it causes the one plea for reassurance to stand out. From the spring or summer of 1547 (Vittoria Colonna having died on 25 February) Michelangelo felt at a low ebb. He wrote an appeal to God which anticipates the anguished tones of the great imprecations and jeremiads which were soon to follow:

> Oh, make me see thee, Lord, in every place!
> If burns my heart, to mortal beauty bent,
> Near thine will be that earthly ardor spent,
> And I aflame again with heavenly grace.
> Oh, my dear Lord, thee I evoke and call
> Against my blind and unavailing pain
> Without, within. Thou canst renew again
> My will, my sense, my strength so prone to fall!
> Thou gavest once to time this spirit divine,
> Clothed in this frail and heavy dress;
> Imprisoned here, and subject unto law,
> What can I do to change this state of mine?
> Nought without thee avails my heart to bless:
> A power divine alone for me new lot can draw. (G 274)
> (Ednah Dow Cheney)

Usually, however, the death of a friend makes the artist more eager to join him in death than he was in life.

The poetry occasioned by the deaths of his assistant Urbino, of Vittoria Colonna, and of Cecchino is treated in other appropriate chapters. It was the death of his father, however, which inspired him to his longest outpouring of grief.

Old Lodovico occupied a special place in his son's heart. Without having known his own mother (even the artist's stepmother Lucrezia degli Ubaldini died in 1497), Michelangelo lavished all his filial sentiments upon him. As a child he must have been proud of the humble municipal posts held by Lodovico at Chiusi, Caprese, and Castelfranco—a model of success to emulate until the boy heard the great Lorenzo il Magnifico's ironic (and possibly thoughtless) remark that Lodovico "would always be poor." If old Lodovico deserted Castelfranco and fled to Pisa in troubled 1529, he was merely anticipating the advice of his son to flee politics "like the plague." The number of letters of the artist to his father over the years (Lodovico, like his son, lived almost nine decades) even more than their content attest to this devotion. The words "carissimo" and "reverendissimo" are common enough. Michelangelo could still be angry with his aged father for not quashing rumors concerning him, impatient with him for talking politics indiscreetly, for not disciplining the other sons, especially the adventurous and world-traveling Giovan Simone (in Michelangelo's words a "beast" for "threatening" their father).

Papini, often the antischolar and iconoclast, felt that Michelangelo entertained no great affection for his father: Lodovico had renounced his paternal authority by turning Michelangelo over to the Magnifico in 1490; Michelangelo always referred to his father as Lodovico in letters to his brothers; the letters to his father treated only domestic and financial matters; and so on. To Papini, Michelangelo inherited from his father only the less noble of his traits: tendency to flight, snobbist pretensions, overconcern for money. Yet Michelangelo's poem on his father's death shows that in the final balance he felt admiration as well as deep filial affection.

In 1528, shortly before the death of Lodovico, Michelangelo lost his brother, the merchant and prior Buonarroto. The father's death has until recently been given as occurring between 11 June and 23 September, 1534, although Wilde and Ramsden have persuasively set the year as 1531. A *capitolo* of 1534 (in the usual *terza rima*) laments this double passing: "Non so, qual pena piu m'affligga o noi." Throughout the poem there runs a series of reflections on death: the roots and veins of fortune are fattened and swollen by death; death leaves memories behind engraved like paintings or sculptures; one should grieve less over those who die late (contrasting with his belief that one should rejoice at the death of a young person, more innocent and certain of salvation). The dominant theme of the poem is that one is wrong to fear death, for the souls in heaven are emancipated, free of concern and pressure, and exempt from vicissitudes:

> Fortune and Time which bring us grief so sure
> With joy uncertain, claim no more their right,
> Their fickle changes enter not your door.

Lodovico's death, like that of Urbino, has taught him how to die, how not to fear death and dissolution. In fact, he has confidence that he will see again in paradise his ever-loving father:

> And if 'twixt son and father, Love's best art
> Grows yet in Heaven, as every virtue grows. . . . (G 86)
> (Ednah Dow Cheney)

Here the poem breaks off, leaving the tercet rime in disarray. Perhaps the poet realises that an analogy involving the Heavenly Father and Son is too audacious to develop. Even more than for its filial piety, the *capitolo* is important for its rare display of equanimity in the face of the incubus of death.

No loss of a loved one, nor indeed any other tragedy or duress, could drive Michelangelo to thoughts of self-destruction, as we have seen. Michelangelo decried suicide (1531) not merely because it was a mortal sin, but also because it would require a tremendous effort of will:

> If it were permitted to anyone in this world
> To kill himself, thinking thus to gain heaven,
> It would be only fair that it be he who serves love
> Wretched and unhappy, and yet with such loyalty.
> But since man is not like the phoenix
> Who rearises and returns at the light of the sun,
> I stay my hand and my foot doth tarry. (G 52)

Michelangelo the Younger thought that the poet was here "reasoning about Cato." The lines were actually inspired by Petrarch (see p. 24).

Between the years 1550 and 1560 Michelangelo produced a series of magnificent effusions which have been called the "trembling-hand sonnets." They reach a high peak of religious passion, making one feel that it was just as well that the Donato Giannotti–Luigi del Riccio edition of Michelangelo's *Rime* did not appear as planned in the mid-1540s, for these later poems are in some ways the jewels of the *canzoniere*. Whereas the quality of Michelangelo's sculpture inevitably declined, as the last *Pietàs* attest, the quality of the poetry soars.

It is worth noting that in these last efforts Michelangelo turns usually to the more demanding and disciplined medium of the sonnet. The looser madrigal form, as Michelangelo practiced it, was not adequate to the purpose of these last verses. The predominance of sonnet form here might be explained as the influence of Vittoria Colonna's 334 devotional exercises in sonnet form, so dear to him. However, in so far as effusive emotions, fears, and regrets of these poems struggle against the firm confines of the sonnet, one prefers to conclude that Michelangelo decided, as a special votive offering to God, to once more wed the most elusive content with the most rigid form. Three were *non finiti*. Perhaps, too, he was attempting a final demonstration of his ability to fit *concetti* into *hyle* (materials), an accomplishment so much more difficult for him as an old artist who unceasingly designed projects for others to carry out.

Since these rich sonnets make many other appearances in the pages of this volume, I should like merely to record them, making most concise remarks on their content.

"Le fauole del mondo m'anno tolto" (G 288) strikes the note of renunciation which we shall consider shortly below. "Non è piu bassa o uil cosa terrena" (G 289) contains the suggestion of two baroque images, that of God dropping the chain of faith for the poet to grasp and that of heaven as a citadel to which one may be admitted only with the key of mercy. There is an evocation of Christ's shedding blood, a familiar, baroque insistence (see pp. 44–45). "Scarco d'un' importuna e greue salma" (G 290) views heaven not as a citadel, but as a haven from the tempests of life. Its affinity to the *Christus Iudex* has been discussed in Chapter XI.

"Ben sarien dolce le preghiere mie" (G 292) consists of only two quatrains and is conventional, merely acknowledging that God is the seed of all good actions. "Carico d'anni e di pechato pieno" (G 293) regrets the artist's evil and poisonous habits and urges Christ to indulge him as he nears his "first and second deaths"; the poem is evocative of Petrarch's introspection: "Io son si stanco sotto 'l fascio antico/de le mie colpe e de l'usanza ria." "Mentre m'atrista e duol, parte m'è caro" (G 294) again views Christ's blood as the sinner's only salvation: "And yet Thy blood helps us to understand." The sonnet "Di morte certo, ma non gia dell'ora" (G 295) is a jeremiad containing an almost Calvinistic view of man's inevitable perverseness. God is the only refuge against man's evil nature and the Creator is slow to act. This piece uses the phrase "il mondo è cieco" in a moral sense, the same words Michelangelo has employed in reference to art and to love.

"S'auien che spesso il gran desir promecta" (G 296) is rich in aphoristic thoughts and paradox ("Tanto piu nuoce quante piu dilecta," "Che con piu tempo il buon uoler men dura," etc.). One must not hope for a long life, but for admission to heaven, since Death inexorably approaches. Michelangelo's second-last poem extant is a two-quatrain lamentation found on the back of a letter (CDXC) to Cardinal Ridolfo Pìo da Carpi (1560) defending the artist's architectural plans against his detractors. The poem's tragic note of pessimism ("Di piu cose s'actristan gli ochi mei") (G 301) reminds one of another letter to the Cardinal of the same period (13 September, 1560). The latter document, perhaps the most poignant of the entire correspondence, marks the close of a career. In it Michelangelo admits to his failing talents, although accusing others of falsifying to the Cardinal the situation in the Vatican workshop, and requests to be relieved of his administrative post there. In the poem Michelangelo acknowledges his moral failings, as he admits in the letter his professional ones. The final sonnet, also incomplete, appropriately ends with an invocation to Christ. Once again the poet refers to the saving blood of the Redeemer, so prominent a theme in the "trembling-hand" sonnets.

Dear my Lord, Thou who alone doth clothe and denude,
And with Thy blood purge and heal souls,
From the infinite blows and guilts of mankind . . . (G 302)

It is fitting that the culmination of the poetry by the artist whose last sculptural project, unfinished, was a slumped figure of Christ be a poem, equally unfinished, referring to the Crucifixion.

One sonnet, so close in spirit to the "trembling-hand" sonnets that Frey assigns it to the years 1550–54, dates (in Girardi's words) from the "Cavalieri period." One of the most powerful of the effusions to God, "Vorrei uoler, Signior" (1534–40) reveals the poet's doubts as to his own worthiness and his ability to communicate with God, as well as doubts of God's own willingness to grant him grace.

> Fain would I will, O Lord, what I'm not willing!
> 'Twixt fire and heart a veil of ice is hidden,
> Damping the fire: agreement thus forbidden
> Between my pen and works makes false each leaf.
> I love thee with the tongue, then count it grief
> That love reach not the heart: since so is hid
> The door to grace, whereby the heart were rid
> Of impious pride its inmost temple filling.

Having bared his soul in this manner, the poet, in his anxiety, makes three commands, two of which we have noted earlier (p. 225):

> Rend thou the veil, O Lord, break down this wall,
> Which by its hardness keeps retarding so
> Thy holy sunshine, in the world gone out.
> Oh, send the light, so long foretold for all,
> To thy fair bride, that so my soul may glow,
> And feel thee inwardly, and never doubt! (G 87)
> (John S. Dwight)

Although Dobelli has compared this sonnet with a psalm of David, its demanding tone is rather that of a mystic, especially as the speaker indulges in the practice common to the male mystics of considering themselves "brides" of Christ. The language often parallels that in the love poems to Cavalieri, to whom Michelangelo made the similar demand: "Let the wall between the one and the other be broken!" Before the heart can be inflamed by God's love, a veil of doubt, egotism, and timidity must be snatched away. The heart must be *ready* for grace. Its baroque intensity and *angoisse* make this one of Michelangelo's most unusual outcries. The fourth line reminds us of Michelangelo's admission in a letter to Cavalieri, "The pen cannot even approach one's intent." The imagery of the sonnet contains echoes of Vittoria Colonna's poetry (see Chapter XIX).

In Chapter IV we found that religious scruples, world-weariness, and discouragement led our great artist to renounce the fine arts and to wish that he had devoted his life to the making of sulphur matches. A deeper abdication of life itself is found in poems earlier than the "trembling-hand" sonnets where we observed its presence. In a madrigal of 1534–36 our poet renounces all human concerns and passions:

> When my past is present before me
> As it comes before me now,
> Then, o false world, I recognise clearly
> The error and damnation of mankind. (G 132)

Here Michelangelo is echoing the late regrets and uneasiness of Petrarch, who, in 1356, expressed doubts about this life, love, and works in the same antiworldly fashion:

> Ma ben veggio or sì come al popolo tutto
> favola fui gran tempo, onde sovente
> di me medesimo meco mi vergogno;
> e del mio vaneggiar vergogna è 'l frutto,
> e 'l pentirsi, e 'l conoscer chiaramente
> che quanto piace al mondo è breve sogno. (Sonnet I)

Petrarch's "ben veggio or" is echoed in Michelangelo's "allor conosco bene," and more closely in the "conosco or ben" of his powerful sonnet of Christian renunciation: "Giunto è gia 'l corso della uita mia." This espousal of the *vanitas vanitatum* reveals the old artist, surfeited with honors and prestige, bringing his fragile bark (cf. Petrarch, CXXXII, "frale barca") into the port where his every action on life's voyage will be questioned.

> Whence the affectionate fantasy
> Which made of art my idol and monarch,
> I recognise well now how laden it was with error,
> And what in spite of himself every man desires. (G 285)

It is curious how, at this late date, other reminiscences of Petrarch seep into the poet's memory: "si lieve di saver, d'error si carca" (CXXXII), "poco prezando quel ch'ogni uom desia" (XIII). There are other similarities to Petrarch's "Passa la nave mia" and "Chi è fermato di menar sua vita."

The refuge of art no longer serves to ward off fears of death. The final tercets (see p. 85 for the complete Longfellow translation) show that only the intervent on of Christ has this power. This "puritanical" denigration of the arts made the sonnet most popular with nineteenth-century Englishmen and New Englanders. Including Longfellow's and Wordsworth's versions, ten translations of it exist in English. Of the last terzine Bevilacqua wrote: "It is no longer a matter of poetising; that is cast aside; the soul never attained calmness."[2]

Like Michelangelo's "Mentre che 'l mie passato m'è presente," discussed on p. 226, his madrigal "Chondocto da molt'anni all'ultim'ore" (1536–46) sermonises that earthly life promises pleasures not in its power to bestow:

Borne to the utmost brink of life's dark sea,
Too late thy joys I understand, O earth!
How thou dost promise peace which cannot be,
And that repose which ever dies at birth.
The retrospect of life through many a day,
Now to its close attained by Heaven's decree,
Brings forth from memory, in sad array,
Only old errors, fain forgot by me—
Errors which e'en, in long life's erring day,
To soul destruction would have led my way.
For this I know—the greatest bliss on high
Belongs to him called earliest to die. (G 133)
(Fanny Elizabeth Bunnett)

Michelangelo is especially qualified to know this, for he has sampled honors and material rewards. Indeed, having at last seen the world for what it really is, the poet realises once again that the most fortunate mortals are those whose very cradle is attended by death.

Renunciation, then, is one of the persistent themes of Michelangelo's *Rime*; renunciation of life, art, and love. That it was more than a mere poetic motif one may be especially sure when the chronicle of the letters explains the circumstances behind the mood. Ceriello finds that this deep-grained spirit of renunciation contributes to Michelangelo's stature as a poet: "Enough to guarantee his glory as poet are these moments in which, after having intuited the lofty image of Beauty, the infinity of Art, the sublime intimacy of love, he senses all their proud strength crumbling, in the diffuse despair of a heart which must renounce love and art irrevocably and enclose itself with resigned faith in the most gloomy solitude."[3]

NOTES

[1] Donato Giannotti, *Dialogi*, *ed. cit.*, p. 69.
[2] Enrico Bevilacqua, *op. cit.*, p. 640.
[3] Ceriello edition of the *Rime*, p. 11.

18

APHORISMS

Praised as a gymnosophist by the learned Lomazzo, Michelangelo was nonetheless anything but a philosopher. He had neither the patience nor the faith in words required of philosophers.[1] Yet Michelangelo was a thoughtful man and an attentive if guarded witness to a period more hectic than halcyon. He stayed close to his atelier, without desire to participate in the political and social turmoil outside (see Chapter XIII). Occasionally an aphoristic comment escaped his lips or his pen. He noted the worldly designs of such contemporaries as Charles V and Julius II, reflecting, "It seems to me that things which have a bad beginning cannot come to a good end."[2] He watched the maneuvering and self-abasement of the courtiers, including artists, and scoffed that "those who start out early as the asses of princes have their burden set out for them until after their death."[3] He saw Christianity split in twain during his very lifetime, muttered a remark about "heretical monks spoiling the world,"[4] and possibly even painted Luther among the *Dannati.*

Thus, we find certain sententious conclusions, sometimes hopeful but more often unhappy or cynical, forming in his mind concerning man's ceaseless struggle against fate—often inherent in the word *parto,* "birth," as Girardi notes—fellow men, or even providence itself. He did not record these conclusions in philosophical essays, but condensed them into maxims. Many of these are couched in his *Rime,* and the reader will recognise them as verses he has encountered in the preceding pages in broadened contexts. They are usually to be found at the end of a poem, like the quip of an epigram, and introduced by *chi, chè,* or *che.* Since Michelangelo disliked making outright generalisations, he employed the conjunction *che* to shift the aphorism into indirect discourse and to render his responsibility for restatement indirect. He could sometimes obliterate or pluralise himself by a prefatory formula:

Milord, if an ancient proverb is true
This then is a case in point, for . . . (G 6)

If it is true, as it is, that . . . (G 192)

If it be that . . . (G 111, 117, 242)

If grief, then, as some say, makes
beauty . . . (G 244)

(Note that a rejected variant of this last verse reads: "For there is a proverb that grief makes one beautiful.") Usually he avoids the temptation of reminding us so obviously that he leans on folk wisdom. Indeed, if his aphoristic mentality betrayed his humble beginnings in Caprese and Settignano, most of the maxims which he presented were of his own composition. That they were something more personal than a studied literary device is apparent from their spontaneous appearances in his hasty love letters. In one single letter (CDLV), for instance, we find three of them: "Love does not accept a master," "He who loves sleepeth not," and the Dantean "He errs who forgets soon so much loyalty." Other typical aphorisms culled from the *Lettere* are "One must not laugh when the whole world is weeping" (CDLXXII), on the birth of his first grandnephew; "the pen cannot even approach the right intent" (CDXI), written to Tommaso Cavalieri and set in quotation marks; and a third with the impersonal prefatory phrase, "It is said, he who does kindness to the good man makes him better, and to the bad man makes him worse" (CXXVII), written in anger to his brother Giovan Simone.

If in the *Rime* Michelangelo minimised his assertiveness by frequently shifting the maxims into *che* clauses, the thought they condensed remained most important and usually summarised the burden of the madrigal or sonnet which it concluded. In fact, the maxims express an even fuller philosophical content, reminiscent of the view of those Renaissance emblem writers who claimed (after Cicero and Petrarch) that the *Iliad* could be condensed into a nutshell.[5] The reader will have come across many of the foregoing passages and will thus understand them in their full context.

Most of Michelangelo's maxims contain truths applicable to man in general. They are usually the product of experience recalled in an autobiographical poem. In a few cases the projection is so intense that Michelangelo cannot subtract himself in time and comes himself to figure in the maxim. Such instances not being the rule, however, they will generally be omitted in these pages. Leaving aside the political maxims mentioned, the aphorisms divide themselves into five identifiable groups: general truths displaying an objective or even optimistic outlook, pessimistic truths, speculations on causality, conclusions about love, and finally, reflections on old age and death.

1. Perhaps the most optimistic of these many affirmations is Michelangelo's claim (from 1521 to 1524) that man's soul turns naturally toward the good:

> The soul caught between two turns to the worthier. (G 15)

Another hopeful last-line thought is that great happiness can sustain equally great misfortune:

> A great pleasure can support a great trouble. (G 23)

A final optimistic aphorism concludes a letter of 1512 to his father Lodovico: "He who would do wrong harms himself." Here the maxim occupies the summary position of so many maxims in the *Rime*.

It proved hard for Michelangelo to maintain this sanguine tone, however. A more "realistic" note begins to interject itself in:

> The more one believes in himself, the more he is deceived. (G 165)

or the *pointe:*

> For he cures all ills who takes life. (G 137)

There is a variant of the proverb "out of sight, out of mind" which, set in a context of love, prepares the way for Casanova's cynical: "The absent always fare ill":

> Seeing rarely is close to forgetting. (G 163)

Another sententious nugget which would seem to contradict this, however, was set down in a more optimistic or idealistic moment:

> As a thing was never so beautiful,
> So also was it never so painful,
> As when one no longer hears or sees it. (F XVI)

On the folio containing these lines there is a variant form of the first two verses where "simile amore" replaces "tanto dolore," lessening the possibility that Dante's "nessun maggior dolore" inspired this reflection. To this aphorism on beauty one must juxtapose the aforementioned verse concerning katharsis: "Se 'l duol fa pur, com'alcun dice, bello" (G 244). If Michelangelo weakened the force of this affirmation by preceding it with one of those forty-six "ifs" with which he began stanzas (see p. 50), his choice of subjects as artist (pietàs, martyred saints, and general *terribilità*) attest his belief in it.

A curious and objective maxim, analogous to nothing in English save the remote "love me, love my dog," reads:

> He must love the slave who the master adores. (G 117)

A final "realistic" maxim crops out in a letter urging Luca Martini to find the appropriate way to thank Varchi for the latter's praises: "He who is in good repute must not tempt fortune" (CDLXIII).

II. The maxims which convey outright pessimism or cynicism are more numerous, as was the case in the works of the *moralistes* of the following century. The cynicism is not grounded, however, in the belief of La Rochefoucauld and his generation that man is weak and self-centered, but rather in the conviction that forces operate ceaselessly on and against man:

> Now I clearly see that in this life
> The hours of fortune and grace are brief. (G 269)

Life thus seems at times a "dolce stanza nell'inferno" (G App. 7). There is a series of pessimistic maxims on man's struggle, set as baroque paradoxes:

> But the truth does not help him who wishes his error. (G 43 var.)
>
> Evil harms far more than goodness helps. (G 124)
>
> He never dies who keeps lingering on the road to health. (G 120)

Hostile forces could emanate from one's fellow men. Michelangelo, who broke with some of his friends, such as Sebastiano del Piombo and momentarily even Luigi del Riccio—not to mention his family—concluded, as we have seen, that good will was a passing thing:

> The longer the span the less good will can last. (G 296)

More than once did he allege, after Petrarch, that "Loyalty is brief and beauty lasts not" (G 17), a bitter phrasing from one of his first poems.

One of his maxims about concealed woes would not be denied by a modern psychiatrist—or a modern priest:

> Suppressed misfortunes have a double strength. (G 60)

A frequent concern of these maxims is that nature seems most intent upon holding down men of greatest merit. The most economical expression of this grievance is contained in a letter (LXIII) to his brother Buonarroto explaining how the competent smith Messer Bernardino failed to cast the bronze statue of Julius II:

> He who acts, fails.

Yet it was the fate of his idol Dante, whom he considered a creative mind without peer (see below, p. 317), which impressed this truth upon him most deeply:

> Only the worthy are not blessed with good fortune. (G 248)

Another occurrence of this pessimistic thought, cast in epigrammatic brevity, is found in his allegorical poem on the two giants and their offspring, the seven deadly sins (see p. 169). Michelangelo meditates on the vices' endless struggle against mankind and finds that they intrigue and war against (here he repeats the phrase) "only the worthy":

The seven deadly sins intrigue and war against only the just (G 68). Writing his other sonnet on Dante, Michelangelo is again embittered by the fact that the Trecento poet was singled out for persecutions:

> The most perfect abound in the greatest ills. (G 250)

The only example as conspicuous as Dante was unfortunately himself. This is the unhappy burden of his bitter sonnet (see p. 90) dating from his first troubles with Julius.

III. Michelangelo found it hard to bear his ultimate realisation that his artistic genius was not to safeguard him from headaches and disappointments of many sorts. During much of his life he laid blame on the doorstep of patrons, family, various cardinals, or professional rivals and enemies. Yet he incubated the uncomfortable belief that heaven or providence itself had turned against him. As his life progressed, the doubt lurked no longer but came out in the open: heaven turns against the individual who tries hardest to demonstrate his worth. After recording his loyalty to Pope Julius and his legitimate expectations of that patron, he sets down a "proverb," "chi puo mai non uuole," and a pessimistic reproach:

> Ma 'l cielo è quel ch'ogni uirtu dispreza
> Locarla al mondo, se uuol c'altri uada
> A prender fructo d'un arbor, ch' seco. (G 6)
> (For translation see p. 90.)

In a religious context this pessimistic thought remains valid. If a man has faith and sees his hopes to be in vain, Michelangelo wrote to Berni (see above, p. 264), he would be better off with no faith at all:

> For he who believes not is less unfortunate. (G 85)

Granted that the man of worth is so often discriminated against, nature or heaven, too, often contrives for him to endure his harsher fate longer than other men. This conclusion reached him, curiously enough, as he pondered the premature death of Cecchino Bracci:

> Less favor and less bounty last longer,
> For to the ill-starred death is lazy and late. (G 208)

Pondering his years spent in the attempt to serve Christianity through painting and architecture, years which brought only poverty and misery, he concludes ironically:

He who seeks disaster, God will give it to him. (G 267)

Nor should one forget the hostility originating in stars and planets, the "personifications" of heaven; two lines, never developed, stand as a stark accusation of the celestial powers which rob man of his power and even sometimes of free will. Man is left with that abulia so visible in Michelangelo's figure of the *Sogno della vita umana* or in the face of the Adam of his *Creazioni,* without will until visitation by God:

Cruel star, and even cruel will,
Which restrict and bind my power and desire. (G 70)

The futility of the worthy man's effort to do well is reflected in letters of varying date from 1518 to 1549, again showing the consistent thinking of this artist who claimed "I do not contradict myself": "Today it is a sin to do well" (CXVI) and "He who is better suffers more" (CCXIII).

If many of these pessimistic maxims center on hostile outside forces which rob man of his power and even of free will ("sciolto uoler"), two of them do refer to flaws in human character. Juxtaposed, they tell us that if one is fortunate, one may learn from experience, whereas one seldom learns from wise counsel:

He gains much who learns by losing. (G 116)
Wise counsel is vanquished by bad habits. (G 135)

After the maxims on stinginess and ingratitude comes a curious affirmation in the note to Del Riccio: "To him who wishes only a half loaf of bread, it ill befits to give a palace" (G 148).

IV. At best destiny is unpredictable. Michelangelo was well aware that during our lifetime we must choose the best perspective from which to face life, as in painting we must accept a *veduta unica*. Even if we are to make of our lives a work of art, as Michelangelo himself endeavored to do, we occasionally wonder how things might have worked out had we made different decisions at the critical moments. How might we have improved our fortunes, fulfilled our potentialities, or justified more fully our existence? Michelangelo wondered late in life how it might have been had he become a Dominican friar like his brother Lionardo. He even wondered, in a moment of wrath, if he might not have had a more tranquil life had he apprenticed himself in boyhood to a sulphur-match maker.[6]

So Michelangelo, devotee of sibyls and prophets, was given to speculation on causality. As we are now aware, the first and foremost conjectures he entertained concerned his own life. What if he had been Dante, for example, damned with such an uphill struggle against destiny?

Fuss'io pur lui! c'a tal fortuna nato,
Per l'aspro esilio suo con la uirtute
Dare' del mondo il piu felice stato. (G 248)

(For translation see p. 316.)

Causality intrigued him into his old age. In the dialogues recorded by Donato Giannotti, which center loosely on the chronology and itinerary of Dante's trip through hell and purgatory, the discussion turns to the freezing punishment of Brutus and Cassius. Whereas Michelangelo must concede to his fellow Florentines (still mindful of Lorenzino's murder of Duke Alessandro) that tyrannicide is not a crime, he wonders aloud about the need or value of this murder of Caesar. For one does not always know, he reasons, just how things will turn out—whether Caesar might not have performed such good deeds if spared that his murder would have been unfortunate.[7] As Michelangelo put it in an incomplete sonnet:

Evil doth not endure where goodness endureth not,
But often the latter is transformed into the former. (G 53)

He stated this hypothesis in another context:

Best could be worst. (G 145)

The same idea seizes him as he thinks of the early death of his Giuliano. Michelangelo makes the statues of Night and Day share his speculations. In their choral recital, they wonder aloud:

What would he have done with us, then, had he lived? (G 14)

Is it any wonder then that Michelangelo began forty-six of his poems with *se!* The vacillation which is such a baroque characteristic of many of his religious poems is reflected in his considerations of causality.

v. Some of the maxims, while set in the context of a love poem, are applicable to life in general. One of these is the fatalistic:

He who grows up wanting, 'tis good that he die. (G 204)

or

Let doubt be sweet to him whom the truth can hurt. (G 141)

A curious thought contained in a sonnet to Vittoria Colonna has universal value. Its sense in this passage is not that every individual has his price, but that a great favor, like a great disfavor, can be mortal to a lover:

Weak virtue dies at a great gift. (G 150)

Another variant of this truth reads in two rejected variant lines:

A sovereign pleasure can kill him who loves strongly
More easily than can a thousand deaths. (G 148 var.)

Three verses refer in differing ways to the process described in Stendhal's *De l'Amour*, the inevitable enhancing of a loved one's beauty by time and habit:

The heart loves late what the eye sees not. (G 258)
Habit heals every defect for the eyes. (G 256)
In love habit heals every defect. (G 256 var.)

The second example is further explained by the artist's Platonic belief that images captured by the outer eye are converted within the inner eye, "l'inmagin dentro crescie" (G 44), into something greater and finer.

Three aphorisms note in differing ways that unrequited service to love makes life drag along even more slowly, that the habit of servitude is hard to break:

A little is too much to him who serves well and strives. (G 134)
One hour does not vanquish the habit of many years. (G 131)
The habit of many years is not overcome by a day. (G 130)

Destiny closes in on man like a narrow sheath and man cannot do other than adjust himself to its forms. This depressing observation is coupled with a remark (Italian version on p. 269) about man's subjugation to love:

For a sheath which is straight to the eye
Cannot hold within a twisted knife. (G 54)

That Michelangelo held love to be one of the hostile forces mentioned in our previous paragraphs is apparent not only from his poems urging young and old to flee love's attacks but also from his curious drawing of the *Saettatori* and from armament worn by Venus in his drawing of *Venere, Marte e Cupido*.

The natural excesses of passion's victims are stated:

Halfway measures, for him who loves too much, are
always the worst. (G 157)

Cynicism about the durability of love strengthens his pessimism. Faithfulness in love is short-lived, indeed, briefer "than any flower in a mild spring" (G 17). This image of the spring flower provides him elsewhere with a maxim about flowers in winter (also *verno*):

A gentle wind suffices to destroy a winter flower. (G 218)

The higher sense of this example is that a crushing fate is imposed even more easily on the young or weak or innocent.

As Michelangelo aged, he discovered that old men are all too susceptible to the incendiary attack of love:

Fire makes a poor test on burnt wood, (G 272)

that it is folly for an old man to fall in love with a younger man or woman:

Love requires equal status and youth. (G 255)

VI. Since old age and death were endemic themes of Michelangelo's *Rime*, they naturally lent themselves to sententious treatment. One of the *pointes* which links the motifs of love and death stresses the mutual antagonism of the two:

For, wherever death is, love approacheth not (G 127)

Another closes a poem affirming the hostility of youth and old age:

For verdant youth abhors the ways of extreme old age (G 167)

Death makes even life seem a mere dream, the theme Michelangelo placed into a drawing (*Il Sogno della vita umana*) and the maxim:

For what has been seems never to have taken place (G 200)
(For comment and original Italian see p. 53.)

Another truth he twice condensed into a maxim, apparently after an interval of over a decade. As suggested above, this consistency should not surprise us in the neoclassical, intense character of Michelangelo who, like an ideal Aristotelian hero, changed and evolved ethically almost not at all. In any case, it was after the death of his beloved father Lodovico that he wrote:

For one should not mourn him who dies old (G 86)

On the occasion of the unexplained death of the boy Cecchino Bracci, two days after Epiphany, 1544, he sat down to write his fifty epitaphs to the lad. Certainly without realising it, this artist who (as his biographers boasted) never repeated a line in his art, repeated this line of poetry with negligible variation:

For one will not mourn more him who dies old (G 205)

Indeed, one should welcome death, even an early one, for the sooner one dies, the greater are his chances of salvation, a thought he expressed several times:

For he who lives least returns lightest to heaven (G 132)

. . . he who lives too long
Kills his soul and helps not his body (G 133)

He who lives least may hope for more pardon (G 226)

One of Michelangelo's maxims about death gave hope to those like himself who would slip into paradise despite their many peccadilloes. Christ the Judge would lower his wrathful arm and beckon to them:

> For in heaven there is no harm in being least blessed (G 140)

Again, as throughout, this truism is placed at the end of a poem.

A final, paradoxically phrased aphorism on death alludes to the endless sufferings one risks by playing such dangerous games as love:

> For he who feeds on death never dies (G 74)

In the balance sheet of his maxims Michelangelo shows himself more cynical and pessimistic than optimistic. In an essay "Il pessimismo di Leonardo e Michelangelo,"[8] De Lorenzo found Michelangelo a pessimist, although not consistently so. It could not be otherwise. Whether or not he was, as D'Annunzio alleged, "l'uomo più triste di nostra gente," he was not hopeful about man. On the fresco of the *Giudizio universale*, as we have noted, the Book of the Damned is infinitely thicker than the Book of the Elect. He was too convinced of those hostile forces, mentioned above, aligned against man. This world, he wrote to Vasari (Letter CDLXXVII) is a "mondo traditore." Given the inexorable opposition of God, fate, and fellow men, one too often capitulates. He becomes too often a slave not only to destiny but also to other men. This theme informs several other passages, just too long to be aphorisms and yet sufficiently brief to be the product of an aphoristic mentality. The following lines surely grew out of the artist's panoramic view of the artistic servitude in his homeland, even at the courts of benevolent Maecenases. Perhaps they were an echo of conversations with the Florentine exiles in Rome, wondering why Tuscany had not cast off the Medici yoke:

> Quand'il seruo il signior d'aspra catena,
> Senz'altra speme in carcer tien legato, etc. (G 25)
> (For translation see p. 108.)

It was in this spirit that Michelangelo carved six slaves, only one of which, the so-called *Atlante*, shows any sign of revolt. Michelangelo may also be thinking of the way artists like Cellini, Vasari, and Baccio Bandinelli end up by working without complaint for the tyrant Cosimo. (He even goaded Cellini on this subject in a letter.)

It was for these Florentine *fuorusciti*, by the way, that he penned his foremost political aphorism:

> In equality there's no room for lordliness (G 160)

At times Michelangelo deluded himself that one may propitiate such hostile forces by passive acceptance:

Good treatment takes away the bite of serpents
As the sour grape sets teeth on edge. (G 54)

But it is better to face up to facts, even when unpleasant—so says one of his most delightful and versatile maxims:

He who doesn't like leaves
Let him not come around in May. (G 278)

This blunt message is found on the design for a window. (Michelangelo the Younger thought it was to enhance a portal.) Girardi is reminded of the Shakespearean "Ripeness is all." To us it is a spirited reminder to face up to the facts of life, and to avoid consciously its most unpleasant realities.

Sometimes Michelangelo Buonarroti sought to console himself with the thought that a flame burns brighter when assailed by a contrary wind. Once again the tercet in which the thought appears is isolated, out of any orientating context. It would not seem to be a poetic *non finito*, then, for he apparently intended to say nothing more.

Come fiamma piu crescie piu contesa
Dal uento, ogni uirtu che 'l cielo esalta,
Tanto piu splende quant' è piu offesa. (G 48)

(For translation and comments see p. 275.)

Its likely source is a tercet of Dante. Twice Michelangelo prided himself that he could triumph over these hostile forces when other men buckled under:

And on that which kills others I merely live and thrive. (G 136)

And on that which kills others, it is right that I live. (G 73)

He admittedly had more to contend with than most:

My worst is my good fortune. (G 143)

When the hostility comes from man himself, one must rise to Christian forgiveness:

A generous, lofty, and noble heart
Pardons and bears love to its offender. (G 147)

This lofty thought inspired Archadelt to set to music the madrigal which contains it.

When Michelangelo was painting the pensive *Geremia* on the Sistine Vault, he turned again to the Old Testament to refresh himself on the plaintive thoughts of this prophet (see pp. 104–106). Some of these jeremiads seem to ring out anew in the *Rime*. There are the outcries that the world is blind ("Il mondo è cieco") found more than once in the writings. There is a deploring of the vulgar throng: "Al uulgo maluagio, isciocho e rio" (G 83). There is the very real jeremiad of "viuo al pechato, a me morendo uiuo":

> Servile my freedom, mortal my God
> Has become to me. Oh unhappy state!
> To what wretchedness, to what a life was I born? (G 32)

or the world-weariness, previously quoted on page 105, of a seer for whom the world of the Old Testament was already ancient:

> Di piu cose s'actristan gli ochi mei, etc. (G 301)

God's cruelty to his own decried in these maxims had already been deplored by Jeremiah (*Lamentationes ii*, 4): "Tetendit arcum suum quasi inimicus, firmavit dexteram suam quasi hostis, et occidit omne quod pulchrum erat visu in tabernaculo filiae Sion . . ." The upraised right arm of God turns in wrath against man, as does that of the *Christus Iudex*.[9]

Michelangelo, who always sought minimal expression in art—the bare *concetto* without unnecessary elaboration—was drawn to the aphorism. He who sought an exact correspondence between form and material preferred succinctness and density in poetry as well as art. For this reason, the maxim, which he did not inherit from his literary models, was his own literary innovation. Often his poems culminate in a maxim. But a few times the drive toward brevity was so urgent that when a sententious thought began a poem, its impact left little or nothing to add; the minimal thought was the important thing and the project was abandoned, just as in art itself Michelangelo's main interest was density of thought. The finishing process, with its decorative effects, was of less interest to him.

Among the maxims in the *Rime*, there are more formulations about the difficulties of the human condition than about their solution. Yet if the number of aphorisms about man's destiny is a considerable one, and if there are not many outright counsels for taking up arms against troubles, the reader is at least forewarned about what man must face. Nor do contemporary philosophers accomplish more than this. The same messages concerning life, love, religion, and death which are explicit in the maxims are implicit in his paintings, drawings, and sculptures.

NOTES

[1] In Dolce's *Dialogo della Pittura* Michelangelo is compared to "those great philosophers who hid under the veil of poetry the greatest mysteries of philosophy" (Florence, 1734), pp. 242 and 246. Taylor's *Michelangelo Considered as a Philosophic Poet* (London, 1852) was one of the earliest assessments of the artist's Platonism.

[2] Letter CCLVII to the artist's nephew Lionardo, 21 November, 1552.
[3] See above, Chap. V, n. 18.
[4] G. Vasari, *Le vite, ed. cit.*, VII, 279.
[5] See the amusing emblem, after Pliny vii, of Sebastián de Covaruvias Horozco, *Emblemas morales* (Madrid, 1610), p. 214.
[6] Letter CDXXXIV to Luigi del Riccio, October, 1542.
[7] Giannotti, *Dialogi, ed. cit.*, pp. 96–97.
[8] G. de Lorenzo, "Il pessimismo di Leonardo e Michelangelo," *Revista d'Italia*, April, 1919, pp. 389–93.
[9] Cf. Michelangelo's two sonnets, G 285 and 288, and *Prophetia Jeremiae*, X, 14–15, etc.

PART III

Evaluations

19

SOURCES AND ORIGINALITY

"I walk along untrodden paths alone."

MICHELANGELO'S LINE has a deeper meaning than the verse on Petrarch's protoromantic wanderings, "solo e pensoso." Even the most grudging literary historians who entertain reservations of one sort or another concerning Michelangelo's poetry are agreed on the autonomy of Michelangelo's muse. Calero is typical: "He is alone among the almost always imitative rhymers of his century."[1] Considering the widespread acceptance of plagiarism in the Renaissance, one would expect Michelangelo's pastime of poetry to be imitative, even though his sculpture might not be. Bishop Marco Girolamo Vida, often hailed as the third great literary theorist after Aristotle and Horace, wrote in 1527, just before Michelangelo's greatest poetic activity, three books of poetics which not only permitted but incited poets to plagiarise from established or classical authors. For that matter, Michelangelo, who knew his Horace well enough to quote the verses on the licenses of poets and painters, remembered the Horatian advice about absorbing day and night the best writings of the past.

The counsel Vida was giving the poets was being repeated for artists by Vasari and Lodovico Dolce—and indeed by every artist who consented to take pupils into his studio. If the fledgling artist Michelangelo copied from Giotto, Masaccio, Schongauer, the sculptors of the *Laokoön* and others, he was much more cautious about borrowing from others even as a "Sunday poet."

In principle Michelangelo was against plagiarising. Vasari quotes him as declaring:

> He who trails behind another cannot pass ahead of him, and he who cannot do well by himself cannot make good use of others' works.[2]

He thought that imitations of other poets or painters could not fail to exhibit one's own weaknesses. Thus, to adapt three of his verses, a weak poet who copied from Homer would only be wasting his time:

> For he who would without wings
> Follow an angel, in vain he casts
> Seed on rocks, words on wind, and intellect to God.[3] (G 80)

One could not hope to rival or better Dante since "the artist can be surpassed only by himself."[4]

The poets of his generation were copying from individual models—"classical" poets from Homer, Hesiod, and Pindar down to the neo-Latin Marullus and Navagero. Like Bramante over at the Colosseum pillaging marble blocks for his own new buildings, they ransacked the riches of Petrarchism—in Petrarch, Serafino d'Aquila, Tebaldeo, Pamfilo Sasso, Cariteo, and the rest. They dipped into Platonism—Plato, Plotinus, Ficino, Bembo, Leo the Jew, and others—to find imagery to adopt as their own: the androgyne, the winged soul, anamnesis, and so on. Being affiliated with no literary pleiad or *camerata* of poets, Michelangelo could of course remain freer from influences than most of his generation. He could fix his eyes on the sun, blind to all the rest, like Shakespeare's eagle: "Fermar gli ochi com' acquila nel sole" (G 80).

Indeed, one of the advantages of not having his *Rime* published during his lifetime was that no admirer could copy from them to the degree that contemporaries copied from his frescoes in the Sistine Chapel, until the master cried out, "How many must make something clumsy of this work of mine!"[5] This is indeed one of the few consolations afforded poets whose works are published posthumously.

The most independent spirit, however, cannot resist influences. Literary sources affected his art. Such sources, primary and secondary, as were operative on his painting and sculpture we have listed in Chapter V and in *Michelangelo's Theory of Art:* the *Cratylus*, the *Phaedo*, the Old and New Testaments, the *Dies Irae* of Tommaso di Celano, the hymns of St. Ambrosius, Dante, Petrarch, Villani, Guicciardini, Poliziano, Ficino, Sannazaro, and Savonarola. It has been noted by De Tolnay that Michelangelo's *Phaeton* follows the text of Ovid's *Metamorphoses*, while Goldscheider finds the *Tityus* originating in Vergil, Ovid, and Lucretius.

Some of these same sources are echoed in the *Rime*.

Let us acknowledge at the outset that little of the detectivism to which Michelangelo's art has been subjected has been devoted to the *Rime*. A few scholars have searched for sources, particularly Rizzi, Façon, Giuseppe Ferrero, Amico-Mantia, and Insinga. The most thorough is Girardi, whose *Studie sulle Rime* appeared as this volume was going to press. However, most of the works dedicated to Michelangelo as poet (typical are the essays of Giuseppe Calero and Vincenzo Italo Pascale) seem innocent of any belief that the *Rime* reflect writers other than Dante and Petrarch. One of the first to point out the need for a study of literary sources of Michelangelo's poetry was Arturo Farinelli, but this enthusiastic essayist did no more than suggest without proof that others than Dante and Petrarch might have influenced him. "More than one echo comes back from Boiardo, Tebaldeo, Aquilano, Ariosto, Bembo, and Molza."[6]

This chapter, inevitably duplicating some of Girardi's researches, will attempt a brief recapitulation, as well as propose a few sources hitherto unnoticed—notably in Petrarch, Poliziano, Berni, and Vittoria Colonna. It is interesting to observe that Greek and Roman authors, who influenced Michelangelo's works of art and were so widely plagiarised by his contemporaries, figure almost not at all in his poetry. Of this only a partial explanation at best lies in the fact that Michelangelo knew no Greek and, as he admitted to Giannotti's guests, almost no Latin. For he avoided imitation—even of classic works in translation.

The first and foremost influence on Michelangelo was of course Dante. In his learned discourse to the Florentine Academy on two of Michelangelo's sonnets the eminent and pedantic Benedetto Varchi paused to acknowledge the enduring influence of Dante on Buonarroti. "Our Poet has been most studious of Dante and just as he has followed and imitated him in his verses, so in sculpting and painting he has jousted and combatted with him, and perhaps rivaled him sometimes as they say Apelles did Homer."[7] Again, in the third *disputa* of his *Della maggioranza delle arti*, Varchi wrote: "And as for me, I do not at all doubt that Michelangelo, as he imitated Dante in his poetry, imitated him as well in his works of art, giving them not only that grandiose and majestic quality found in Dante's concepts, but striving also to achieve in either marble or paint what he had succeeded in doing with his words and sentences."[8] After Varchi it became common enough to find analogies between Dante and Michelangelo, a custom which has lasted through Foscolo and Farinelli to the present. In the passage of his *Trattato* coupling artists and poets of kindred spirit, Lomazzo paired Michelangelo with Dante. Carlo Lenzoni dedicated to Michelangelo his dissertation *La difesa della lingua fiorentina e di Dante*. Yet the first contemporary to hail Michelangelo as a Dante specialist was none other than Leonardo, who called upon his younger rival in the street to adjudicate an argument about Dante. According to the *Codice Magliabechiano*, the implied compliment was unfortunately misunderstood by the young artist, who made an insulting remark and turned on his heel. Later in life he was not embarrassed at being considered a Dante specialist. We have the verbal record of his meeting with Donato Giannotti and other friends in Rome to discuss certain fine points about Dante's trip through hell and purgatory. In the presence of these Florentine humanists, the septuagenarian has a fine time contradicting and correcting the other learned scholars, including the great Cristoforo Landino, on even minute points of Dantean chronology and cosmology. This discussion has a particular value, as we have stated, in revealing Michelangelo's persuasions about Brutus, whom Dante eternalised in ice and Michelangelo in marble.

No scholar has ever demonstrated the ascendancy of Dante over Michelangelo any better than did the artist himself in two sonnets composed to his idol, sonnets which must at last be translated fully. The first, "Dal ciel discese," expressed an absolute veneration for the Trecento poet and a wish that the artist might demonstrate a similar virtue, even if this meant accepting a harsh, Dantean fate. In the last tercet the poet tentatively identifies himself with his spiritual ancestor:

> He from the world into the blind abyss
> Descended and beheld the realms of woe;
> Then to the seat of everlasting bliss,
> And God's own throne, led by his thought sublime,
> Alive he soar'd, and to our nether clime
> Bringing a steady life, to us below
> Reveal'd the secrets of eternity.
> Ill did his thankless countrymen repay
> The fine desire: that which the good and great
> So often from the insensate many meet,
> That evil guerdon did our Dante find.
> But gladly would I, to be such as he,
> For his hard exile and calamity
> Forgo the happiest fortunes of mankind. (G 248)
> (Robert Southey)

A second sonnet, "Quante dirne si de'," judged by Bevilacqua "inferior by far to the first,"[9] hails Dante as a genius without peer and again laments his fate:

> What should be said of him cannot be said;
> By too great splendor is his name attended;
> To blame is easier those who him offended,
> Than reach the faintest glory round him shed.
> This man descended to the doomed and dead
> For our instruction; then to God ascended;
> Heaven opened wide to him its portals splendid,
> Who from his country's closed against him, fled.
> Ungrateful land! To its own prejudice
> Nurse of his fortunes; and this showeth well
> That the most perfect most of grief shall see.

Among the thousand proofs let one suffice,
That as his exile hath no parallel,
Ne'er walked on earth a greater man than he. (G 250)
(H. W. Longfellow)

These sonnets on Dante's misfortunes, both from 1545–46, remind John E. Taylor[10] of Dante's "noble exclamation" to Latini: "Ch'a la fortuna, come vuol, son presto" (*Inf.* XV, 79). Pascale believed that the sonnets dated from 1519, when the artist signed a petition to Leo X to bring Dante's ashes from Ravenna to Florence, but Girardi corrects this to late 1545 or early 1546. Girardi (*Studi*, p. 103) speculates that the sonnet's themes may have been suggested by a reading of Boccaccio.

Certainly there was every reason for the artist to sense an affinity with Dante. Intensity of feeling, nostalgia of an "expatriate," deep-felt religiosity, dedication to an art, these were only a few of the many components of their characters which allied them. Probably no poet so affected him in the reading; we know that he ingratiated himself as a young man with the Venetian nobleman Giovan Francesco Aldovrandi by reading to him passages of Dante, and are told that he enthusiastically filled with drawings a copy of the *Divina Commedia*, a copy which a friend lost in a shipwreck between Livorno and Civitavecchia.[11]

Turning to an evaluation of Dante's influence on Michelangelo's creations, a few words must be said about the works of art, for here the inspiration is most apparent. If the *Giudizio universale* owed much technically to Luca Signorelli, it owes most ideologically to Dante. Vasari described not only the Dantean information of this great fresco, but also its Dantean effect. "He gave so much strength to the paintings of this work that he verified the wording of Dante: 'The dead appeared dead, the live alive,' and therein one recognises the misery of the damned and the joy of the blessed."[12] Several people in recent years, including an amiable and persuasive Venezuelan diplomat, Joaquín Díaz González, have advanced the theory that the central mass of the *Giudizio* is contoured to suggest a profile of Dante's head.

It was Condivi who first informed us that the statues of Leah and Rachel, or the Active and Contemplative Lives, were inspired by Dante. "In these works Michelangelo, always a zealous student of Dante, has followed the poet, to whom in his *Purgatory* the Countess Matilda appears as personification of the active life in a flowery meadow."[13] Michelangelo had in mind two Dantean passages: *Purgatorio* XXVII, 100–05 and XXVIII, 118 ff. As suggested earlier, considerations of Dante's Brutus and Cassius in his discussion with Donato Giannotti's group apparently led to Michelangelo's carving the *Bruto*. In his edition of the drawings, Goldscheider traces the origins of the drawing *Il Sogno della vita umana*, with its background of sinners, to Dante's anthology of those who have transgressed through passion.[14]

Reflections of Dante in Michelangelo's poetry, cited by Varchi as numerous, are indirect rather than direct. One more poem mentions Dante by name, a jocose piece addressed to Giovanni da Pistoia (translated on p. 246). Another direct reminiscence of Dante is the verse "Non vi si pensa quanto sangue costa" (*Paradiso* XXIX, 91) that the artist inscribed on the *troncone* of the cross of a Pietà in relief, which is now lost but which was executed for Vittoria Colonna before 1546.[15] On another occasion he copied as a fragment "Rachoglietele al piè del triste ciesto," of *Inferno* XIII, 142, as Girardi has written. We have already called attention to the similarity of the following moral metaphor and its Dantean source:

> As a flame grows brighter the more assailed
> By the wind, every virtue which heaven exalts,
> Shines all the more, the more it is offended. (G 48)

> For if the will willeth not, it cannot be crushed,
> But doth as nature doeth in the flame,
> Though violence wrench it aside a thousand times. (*Para.* IV, 76–78)

Dante's verse "Amor e cor gentil son una cosa" finds a diffuse echo in Michelangelo's tercet:

> Amore è un choncecto di bellezza
> Immaginata, che sta dentro al core,
> Amica di uirtude e gentilezza.

Many further inconclusive borrowings have been alleged. The unfinished sonnet "Se sempre è solo e un quel che sol muoue" has reminded one translator of Dante's opening of *Paradiso*, and Michelangelo's image

> Il ciel porgie le chiaue;
> Amor le uolgie e gira
> E apre a iusti il pecto di costei; . . . (G 254)

has brought to mind

> Io son colui che tenni ambo le chiavi
> del cor di Federigo, a che le volsi,
> serrando e desserrando, si soavi. (*Inf.* XIII, 58–60)

A number of other less conclusive *rapprochements* might be added here. Certainly the poetic skill of Dante, praised by Michelangelo in the dialogues of Giannotti, influenced Michelangelo's vocabulary and metaphor in a general way. There are various stilnovistic passages, such as:

> Passa per gli occhi al core in un momento
> Qualunque obbietto di beltà lor sia, etc. (G 276)

Various authors (Farinelli, John Robert, B. H. Sumner, and others) have written on various facets of the affinity between Dante and Michelangelo as artist. The Dantean influences on the art have obviously been studied more fully than those on the poetry. We have listed the few most likely juxtapositions, including one on the earth's convulsions at the Crucifixion (see above, p. 132). Actually, there are by far fewer borrowings from Dante than from Petrarch in the *Rime*. Michelangelo, spending eternity in Santa Croce, need not feel uncomfortable alongside Dante Alighieri's cenotaph, just a few steps away.

There is no mention of Petrarch by name in the *Rime*, no acclaim of this itinerant poet as "without peer," no tentative identification with him. The influence of Petrarch on Michelangelo was not so dramatic or seminal as was that of Dante. Yet, in its diffused way, it was more sustained—especially up until the mystical poems of Michelangelo's last years. Petrarch was a good master. He taught the artist a vocabulary of poetry. He taught Michelangelo that poetry could be a refuge against the vicissitudes of love and loneliness. He instilled in him an occasional moral truth; in the *Diálogos em Roma* the artist echoes the Petrarchan thought: "Vulgi enim laus apud doctos infamia est." Petrarch taught him especially how to write reflective or triumphant stanzas to commemorate the death of a beloved friend. Unlike most of the Cinquecentisti, Michelangelo was less influenced by the Petrarchists than by Petrarch himself. Michelangelo's habit was not to read widely, but to read a few books well. *Rapprochements* between Michelangelo's *Rime* and Petrarch's verse may be found, but only vague similarities link them with Daniello, Cariteo, and the rest. Unlike Dante, Petrarch had many qualities which distinguished his temperament and character from Michelangelo's: extreme erudition, love of external nature, Latinity, grace, and the rest. Yet Michelangelo must have sensed that he might profitably possess more of these qualities. He studied the *Canzoniere* and the *Trionfi* and tended to copy from them unconsciously rather than in the deliberate manner advocated by Vida. Occasionally, and for reasons not certain, he copied directly, literally, as when he penned on the Louvre sketch of the *David*, "Roct'è l'alta colonna e 'l verd . . . ," Petrarch's line deploring the dual loss of Laura and the Cardinal Giovanni Colonna. On a folio with a sketch of *putti* he penned Petrarch's Latin praise of Vaucluse: "Valle clausa, a place like none other to me in the whole world," an area Michelangelo never saw but which was praised eventually to him by such eyewitnesses as Beccadelli. Perhaps this dream valley symbolised a refuge from the headaches of Florence and Rome, a country retreat he was to discover later among the hills of Spoleto. Probably in May, 1501, he wrote in a youthful script on a sheet of sketches the first line of the fragment from the *Trionfo della morte* (II, 34–36):

La morte è fin d'una prigione oscura
all'anime gentili; all'altre è noia,
ch'anno posto nel fango ogni lor cura.

Michelangelo does not copy the tercet, but as the years passed his poetry would become heavily laden with this renunciation of earthly values as well as with a mystic's desire (see Chapter III) to escape from the prison of this world. On the right side of a sketch of St. Anne, the Virgin, and Child Michelangelo twice started to write the first verse of Petrarch's "Di pensieri in pensier (di monte in monte) mi guida Amor."[16]

On a letter to his assistant Urbino's widow Cornelia Colonnelli (28 April, 1557), a letter charged with affection for his dead friend, Michelangelo set in *incipit* position the appropriate thought: "He does wrong who doth so soon forget such loyalty." How did the master recall and dignify this originally banal verse from the *Canzoniere* (206, verse 45), a plaintive line from an uninspired lover's lament, stronger in mediaeval poetic techniques than sincerity of feeling? Here Michelangelo ennobled the words of Petrarch, as he did when he added the Petrarchan line again as epilogue to a letter to Vittoria Colonna during the spring of 1539. (Milanesi dates this letter—CDLV—as of 1545.)

Similarly, concluding his angry sonnet to Del Riccio (see above, p. 149), Michelangelo copies the moral sermon "Mille piacer non uaglion un tormento" from Petrarch's sonnet "Io mi vivea," a plagiarism hitherto unnoticed.

Like the fledgling artist who practiced by copying from Giotto, the young poet Michelangelo turned to Petrarch's sonnet 271, "L'ardente nodo ov'io fui d'ora in ora," and copied it on the verso of sketches of a slave, *putto*, and cherubim. However, he does not improve it, for he replaces *interi* by *ardendo*, an unwelcome repetition:

L'ardente nodo ou' io fu' d'ora in ora,
contando anni uentuno ardendo preso, (G App. 13)

There is a curious paraphrase of Petrarch, as Frey has noted, in the octave of a sonnet, "Signiore, io fallo e ueggio":

Signiore, io fallo e ueggio el mio [fallire],
ma fo com'uom' che arde e'il foco a 'n seno . . .
chè 'l duol pur cresce, e la ragion uien meno
ed è gia quasi uinta dal martire.
Sole' spronare el mio caldo desire
per non turbare el bel uiso sereno
non posso piu, di man m'a' tolto 'l [freno],
e l'alma disperando a preso ardire. (G App. 31)

Lord, I fail and recognise my failure,
But I act as does a burning man with the fire in his breast

For the pain increases as reason gives way
And is now almost vanquished by martyrdom.
I used to put the curb to my hot desires
Not to disturb that beautiful serene face:
I can do it no longer; from my hand thou hast taken the reins,
And my soul despairing has caught on fire.

Modified in three lines, this is the residual form of the first eight verses of Petrarch's sonnet 236:

(1) *Amor*, io fallo, e veggio il mio fallire,
(2) Ma si com' uom ch'*arde* e 'l foco ha 'n seno,
(5) Solea *frenare* il mio caldo desire

Michelangelo's variant, written on the verso of a penciled architectural sketch, poses a curious problem. Frey held that the few changes make the poem expressive of Michelangelo's own feelings, an assumption Girardi denies. This is the only time that Michelangelo appropriated a block of verses for slight, personal modification. His borrowings from Politian and others conveyed more personal alterations. Yet this slightly altered variant does tell much of Michelangelo's importunate feelings toward Tommaso Cavalieri, and is akin to his apologetic letters to the young nobleman. The change from *frenare* to *spronare* is significant as an admission that Michelangelo charged right into this emotional relationship with the future paterfamilias ("la ragion vien meno" becomes appropriate). This habit of giving of himself utterly he admitted in a confessional statement to Donato Giannotti and his friends.[17] (See above, p. 134.) There remains of course the less likely possibility that Michelangelo, who committed to memory favorite poetic fragments (in the *Diálogos em Roma*, for example, he quotes lines from Horace) may be quoting with slight inaccuracy or with unconscious "correcting."

The octave of a would-be sonnet is addressed to a man (*colui*), possibly Gherardo Perini, as Frey believes. It relates to Michelangelo's broken affair with Gherardo (or possibly with the cajoling Febo, since the autograph page contains some financial accounts):

It was about here that my love laid hold of me,
And, thanks to him, of my heart and even more, my life.
Here with his beautiful eyes he promised me solace,
And with those very eyes he tried to take it away from me . . . (G 36)

It has been suggested that this piece derives from Petrarch's "Nova angeletta sovra l'ale accorta," in which love snares the poet with a silken noose. Here, however, we turn into the labyrinthine path of indirect plagiarism and influence. Once we have begun to accept such "innutritions" (Faguet) of Petrarch in the artist's *Rime*, the process can continue indefinitely.

Indeed, Petrarch's conceits, vocabulary, and protobaroque paradox and oxymoron (see Chapter III) had become so much a part of the poetic lexicon that it would be surprising if Michelangelo did not echo them. They crop out in such resemblances as the lines on Cecchino's death (at a moment when "the fountain was dry" and the artist was casting around for ideas to assist his poetic distillation of grief):

> Only this rock rejoices, for it possesses him,
> While the entire rest of the world then weeps for him, (G 222)

comparable to Petrarch's generous thought on Laura's death in his "Lasciato hai, Morte, senza sole il mondo: . . . Non la conobbe il mondo mentre l'ebbe/Conobbil' io, ch'a pianger qui rimasi." Vague Petrarchistic echoes, then, inform many verses, as Foratti has claimed of "Non salda amor de' tuoi dorati strali." There are repercussions of the Petrarchan chronological progressions—"Benedetto sia 'l giorno, e 'l mese, e l'anno," etc.—in the *Rime*, not to forget a wonderful outburst in the *Lettere:*

> Let time and the hours halt for a moment,
> The day and the sun on its ancient round. (G 72)

> Oh cursed a thousand times the day and the hour
> when I felt Carrara! (CXVI)

Other borrowings which have been alleged by scholars are:

Michelangelo:	*Petrarch:*
Colui, che'l tucto fe, fece ogni parte	Il motor eterno . . . Degnò mostrar del suo lavoro . . . (72, 17–18) (Also *Tr. Morte* I, 15–17)
La ragion meco si lamenta . . .	Sennuccio, I' vo' che sappi in qual manera (112)
Oltre qui fu, doue'l mie amor mi tolse	I' vo pensando, e nel penser m'assale (264)
Oilme, Oilme ch' i' son tradito Da giorni mie fugaci e dallo spechio.	In questa passa 'l tempo, e nello specchio mi veggio andar ver la stagione contraria. (168)
Per più doglia darmi	e con un riso, per più doglia darme (*Tr. Amore* III, 96)
A quel pietoso fonte, onde sian tutti	Tu partoristi il fonte di pietade (366, 43)
S'un casto amor, s'una pieta superna	S'una fede amorosa, un cor non finto (224)

The following *rapprochements* with Petrarch are included in Amico-Mantia's thoughtful little volume, *L'amore e le Rime di Michelangelo*

Buonarroti (Trapani, 1899) pp. 31–32, and the numberings of the Michelangelo poems are those of the Guasti edition: in the case of Petrarch, Amico-Mantia adopts both of the traditional types of numbering, within given genres and within the total *canzoniere*.

Michelangelo:	*Petrarch:*
Ch' io cerco in un momento Del me' di loro, e di poi il peggio piglio (Mad. lxxxvi)	E veggio il meglio e al peggior m'appiglio (Canz. 17)
Che chiusi el dì de l'ultima partita Gli aperse in cielo a contemplare Iddio (Sonetto viii)	Quando mostrai de chiuder, gli occhi apersi (279)
Se 'l foco in ghiaccio e 'l riso volge in pianto (Mad. xvii)	Vedrem ghiacciar il foco, arder la neve (Sestina 2)
Quand' ogni or fugge il giorno che mi resta (Mad. lxxxix)	Quanto più m'avvicino al giorno estremo (Son. 19)
Che 'l tempo passa e l'ora si avvicina (Mad. xliv)	Il tempo passa e l'ore son sì pronte (Canz. 3)
Nel freddo petto dell'età men verde (Mad. xlii)	Dal freddo tempo e dall'età men fresca (Ballata 3)
. . . onde è peggio al sezzo strale La ricaduta che 'l mio primo male (Mad. xlii)	E temo no 'l secondo error sia peggio (Ballata 3)
Se io fussi ne' primi anni accorto (Mad. lxxxviii)	Lasso, che mal accorto fui da prima (Son. 42)
Quanto di fuor coi begli occhi prometti (Mad. xxix)	Promettendomi pace nell'aspetto (Son. 50)
Che cosa è questa, amore, Ch'al cor entra per gli occhi (Mad. xxv)	Quando giunge per gli occhi al cor profondo l'immagin donna (Son. 63)
Spirto ben nato in cui si specchia e vede (Son. xxiv)	In qual parte del cielo, in quale idea (159)

To this conscientious list, Pascale (p. 163) adds:

O felice quel dì, se questo è certo	O felice quel dì, che, del terreno (349)

Such minute textual confrontations are collected also in the second essay of Girardi's *Studi sulle Rime*.

The possibility of self-destruction, recalled from Sappho and other love poets, occurred to Michelangelo. It suggested itself to him both as mystic poet longing to break out of this earthly prison and as lover. The immorality of suicide preached to him by Dante seemed lessened in such cases. As a Petrarchan lover, he contemplates suicide. Petrarch himself had done so:

S' io credessi per morte essere scarco
del pensiero amoroso che m'atterra,
colle mie mani avrei già posto in terra
queste membra noiose e quello incarco. (XXXVI)

Petrarch hesitates because it would be a mortal sin, bringing about a transition from the infernal stings of love to the eternal punishment of hell. Michelangelo poses this thought inevitably in a context of Petrarchan suffering, but while the Trecento poet rejects the idea in eight lines (followed appropriately by a sestet), Michelangelo dismisses it in seven (see p. 24 and 293).

Michelangelo's warning "Fugite, Amanti, amor, fugite 'l foco" (G 27) has an immediate source in Poliziano (see p. 111), and a very real secondary source in Petrarch's "Poi che mia speme è lunga a venir troppo," (see p. 111) with its urgent warning to those falling in love to turn back while there is still time.

Girardi believes that a variant form of "S'egl' è, che 'l buon desio" is copied not from Petrarch, but from a sonnet of Pietro Dietisalvi to Petrarch.[18]

Finally, there are those poems with which no textual confrontation is possible, but whose major preoccupation is Petrarchan, as when Michelangelo pleads to God for grace, when he triumphs over the thought of death, when he rails at Rome (Turkey) as Petrarch decried Avignon (Babylon), when he puns on names of friends, or when he indulges in the burning-freezing, living-dying paradoxes with which Petrarch anticipated European baroque poetry (see Chapter III).

Many are the scholars who have placed Michelangelo among the Petrarchists. Other students have insisted on the artist's independence of the group. Farinelli's early essay on "Michelangelo poeta" separates him from the Petrarchists and claims that the *Rime* lacked the "easy endearments, graces, tendernesses, incenses, and swoons" of the Cinquecento Petrarchists. Pascale rejoices that the artist has abandoned the Petrarchists' "golden hair, alabaster shoulders, and shining eyes."[19] Pierre de Bouchaud assents: "But let us hasten to add that he is far from that profusion, that overflow of stars, suns, gleams, sparkles, flashes, darting arrows, which offered to Laura's lover and his imitators an inexhaustible subject matter."[20]

In any case, Michelangelo did not imitate the *intent* of the Petrarchists in more than a score of poems even while sharing with them Petrarchan techniques and vocabulary in many.

Boccaccio seemed to bequeath little of interest to Michelangelo, but Girardi's *Studi sulle Rime* (p. 103) offer two echoes of the great storyteller's poetry:

Michelangelo:	*Boccaccio:*
S' io avessi creduto al primo sguardo	ardendo spero
Di quest'alma fenice al caldo sole	Nel foco rinnovar come fenice
Rinnovarmi per foco . . .	
or di pari a volo	e che m'impenna l'ali
seco m'impenna a seguir sua virtute	Nell'alto vol con penne di virtute.

It is widely accepted that Agnolo Poliziano both influenced and encouraged Michelangelo when the youthful artist and the older humanist broke bread together with Lorenzo il Magnifico. It is commonly supposed that Poliziano suggested to Michelangelo the theme of the *Centauromachia* or *Ratto di Deianira*. Whether Michelangelo's *Bacco* was inspired by Poliziano's famous Bacchic song we shall never know. Two specific influences have been heretofore alleged: Michelangelo's use of the allegorical figures in his *Stanze in lode della vita rusticale*, figures which only vaguely resemble the two outcroppings of allegorical figures in Poliziano's *Stanze per la giostra*, and (as we have seen in Chapter XVI) Michelangelo's use in the *Stanze* of a landscape with goats and swine which seems inspired by a word picture of Poliziano.

The accomplished humanist from Montepulciano was also gracious and able in poetry, a role in which Michelangelo competed on an equal footing. Poliziano's lyrics are spontaneous, sincere, and free of the cold alembications of the later Petrarchists. As such he was bound to appeal to Michelangelo. If Michelangelo could not read the Greek works of his mentor, he could decipher slowly the Latin *opera* and, as we shall demonstrate briefly, was acquainted with the vernacular works. A total of four works of Poliziano, which the artist may have heard declaimed under the Medici roof, influenced Michelangleo as poet.

One of Michelangelo's *non finiti* was his incomplete, penciled sonnet, "Fugite, Amanti, amore, fugite 'l foco," of 1524 (Frey). While Michelangelo knew only too well the pangs of a frustrated love, this sonnet did not grow autonomously out of his own experience. His warning reads:

Flee love, Lovers, flee its flame;
Its burn is harsh and the wound is mortal;
For after its first assault naught avails,
Neither force nor reason nor moving away.
Flee, now that you have before you many examples
Of love's deadly arm and its sharp arrow.
Read in me what will be your ill fate,
What will be its game, without respect or pity.
Flee, and do not tarry at the first glance.
For I had always thought I could come to terms with love.
Now I suffer, and you see how I burn. (G 27)

(For original Italian, see above, p. 112.)

Michelangelo, blessed with the retentive memory recalled by his biographers, must have had in mind as he composed his truncated sonnet an octave of Poliziano,

> Take heed, you who follow love,
> At my own so bitter and harsh death!

the octave reproduced above in Chapter V. Both of these pieces, as stated above, are evocative of course of Petrarch's "Poi che la mia speme è lunga a venir troppo," with its similar counsels to avoid the shoals of love (see p. 111). Although Michelangelo's wording is closer to Politian's, both the artist and Petrarch caution specifically against unwise delay ("non tardate"/"non v'indugiate").

One borrowing from Poliziano has especially interesting implications. This is the poem of Michelangelo supposedly addressed to a young Bolognese girl, whom he met in that city in 1506 or 1507 (see Chapter X). Even when treating a theme exploited by other poets, Michelangelo views the emergence of the body under its veil of clothing in his own personal manner as sculptor: "Quanto si gode, lieta e ben contesta" (see pp. 202–205).

The sonnet was written in a hasty, youthful scrawl on the back of a letter sent him in Bologna from his brother Buonarroto under the date of Christmas Eve, 1507. Since the piece is in relatively finished form, it may have been composed earlier. A further note lending an appearance of youthful passion was the jotting alongside: "La m'arde e lega e tienmi e parmi un zuchero."

To assess fully the originality of the sonnet, we must look into one or two authors. First of all, there is the inevitable Petrarch, who paints his word picture of Laura in "Chiare, fresche, e dolci acque." A quatrain by Luigi Alamanni contains this expressed wish for an embrace, a piece contained in *Rime inedite del '500* (see above, p. 204).[21]

However, it is my belief that Michelangelo had in mind or before his eyes a poem of Poliziano he found in the abundant library of his Bolognese host Aldovrandi, a pleasant word portrait of Simonetta Cattaneo. This occasional poem was Poliziano's *Stanze per la giostra*. Furthermore, we have every reason to believe that he drew upon the stanzas for his octaves on rustic life, as we have noted. The reader will see the resemblances on even a hasty comparison of the Italian texts (see pp. 204–205).

A final confrontation with Poliziano was made in Chapter X (see p. 194). The humanist's *canzone* (9), "Deh, udite un poco, amanti" has the similar plaint of the rejected lover found in Michelangelo's "Oltre qui fu, doue 'l mie amor mi tolse."

Michelangelo certainly read and heard the poems of his host Lorenzo il Magnifico, and one influence already noted should be repeated at this point:

Michelangelo:	*Lorenzo:*
Tu ha' 'l uiso piu dolcie che la sapa (G 20)	Tu sei più bella che non è una papa, etc. (La Nencia di Barberino)

Girardi (*Studi*, pp. 104–07) finds influences of Lorenzo on the artist's poems of "autobiographical meditation": numbers G 2, 22, 33, 38, 39, 40, 61, 67, 68, 229, and 266. Very similar are Michelangelo's "Qual merauiglia è se prossim' al foco" (G 266) and Lorenzo's "Qual meraviglia, se ognor più s'accende."

The influence of Berni was great, even though specific borrowings were few (see Chapter XV). Both Lorenzo's "*Nencia di Barberino*" and to a lesser extent Berni's "Alla sua Donna" are the models for Michelangelo's parody "Tu a' 'l uiso piu dolcie che la sapa." Other general influences from Berni cannot be doubted, although only one direct confrontation of the poets has been presented in Chapter XV.

Michelangelo:	*Berni:*
Che chi cerca il malanno, Dio glielo dia.	. . . il dì di Befania Anunziò il malan, che Dio gli dia.
Chi mi uedess' a la festa de' Magi Sarebbe buono; . . .	

If Arturo Insinga is correct, Michelangelo did considerable borrowing from Bernardo Accolti, called "l'Unico Aretino" ("the unique one from Arezzo"), whose *Virginia* appeared in twelve editions between 1513 and 1584. Insinga feels that Michelangelo may have been acquainted with him.

Michelangelo:	*Accolti:*
Come puo esser ch'io non sia piu mio?	Vale, madonna mia, oh dura sorte, Da te mi parta no; ma da me stesso . . .
Com'aro dunque ardire Il cor lasso con voi, che non è mio	Come potrò mai fare ch'io mi comparta se io ti lasso Non lasso te ma la trista alma el core
O gran martire D'una doglia mortal senza morir.	L'hora ch'io morirò senza morir
Le fallaci speranze e 'l van desio; Piangendo, amando, ardendo e sospirando.	Amando, ardendo, pregando, piangendo
Nel tuo morire el mio morire imparo	Ond' io non danno te, ma la mia sorte Che m'ha fatto in amarti amar la morte.

Insinga adds two or three more such dubious possibilities, noting that Michelangelo's borrowings from Accolti reveal an imitative tendency "not generic and superficial but voluntary."[22]

Girardi's *Studi,* finally, record minor affinities of Michelangelo's *Rime* with Burchiello, Cei, Tebaldeo, and Serafino d'Aquila.

Certainly many of these parallels which we have included in the interests of completeness are rather evidences of the stereotypy of Renaissance vocabulary and metaphor. It is no more possible to verify whether Michelangelo was copying a verse from Bembo, Accolti, or Cecco Angiolieri (see p. 191) than to certify that he copied, let us say, the attitude of the *Madonna della Febbre* from Jacopo del Sellaio's *Pietà.* No such hesitation is called for in presenting plagiarisms uniting the *Rime* of Michelangelo and the spiritual effusions of Vittoria Colonna. The two friends read each others' rhymes assiduously. The first is the powerful imprecation to God, "Vorrei voler, Signor, quel ch'io non voglio," in which Michelangelo expresses the need for the greater certainty which will be necessary for his salvation. His outcry,

> Squarcia 'l vel tu, Signor! Rompi quel muro
> Che con la sua durezza ne ritarda
> Il sol della tua luce al mondo spenta!
>
> (For translation see p. 225.)

is echoed by the troubled pleas of the Marchioness of Pescara:

> Deh squarci omai la man piagata il velo,
> Che 'n questo cieco error gia quattro lustri
> Fra varie tempre ancor mi tiene involta?[23]
>
> Squarcia 'l vel tu, Signor! Rompi quel muro
> Ch'ancor gli copre; e di quell'ombre antiche
> Del vecchio Adamo freddo, empio, nemiche
> Al divin raggio tuo caldo e securo.[24]

Unfortunately for the unhappy Marchioness, her doubts were to prove more costly than Michelangelo's.

There is a considerable amount of common imagery in the verse of Michelangelo and the learned Vittoria. The sonnet on the death of her husband, borrowing a line of Petrarch "Piagner l'aere e la terra e 'l mar dovrebbe," adopts the basic theme found also in one of the fifty epitaphs for Cecchino;

> Lo mostro al mondo e presto sel ritolse. (G 213)
> Che sol ne mostrò il ciel, poi se 'l ritolse[25]

After Vittoria's death Michelangelo returns to the same theme: "Iddio/ Dal mondo poco achorto/Se l'a ripresa e tolta agli ochi nostri" (G 265).

The theme of the eye dazzled like the bestiary eagle by brilliance is common to each:

> Mira' tante bellezze uniche e sole,
> Fermar gli ochi com' aquila nel sole . . . (G 80)
> Nel mio bel sol la vostra aquila altera
> Fermando gli occhi, alla piu alta meta
> Sarebbe giunta[26]

Indeed, the image of the sun runs rampant in both Vittoria's *Rime* and the epitaphs to the adolescent Cecchino:

> Com'occhio offeso da chi troppo splende (G 149)
> Qual occhio fu da troppa luce offeso[27]

There is no more solemn and awesome tribute to the Crucified Christ than the three-planed baroque sonnet which, as we have stated, consoles us for the fact that, notwithstanding the juvenile wooden *Crocifisso* of Santo Spirito, Michelangelo never left us in paint, marble, or bronze the awesome spectacle of Christ nailed on the Cross. As one editor says of this piece, "With the powerful fancy which intuited the tragic *terribilità* of the *Giudizio universale*, Michelangelo in this sonnet unfolds the mystery of redemption in a setting structured on three planes."[28] The Christ in this sonnet is not however the *Christus Iudex* but rather the suffering Christ who populated the canvasses of Bellini, Mantegna, and so many others of varying talents that Da Vinci penned in his notebooks the protest, "What, Christ crucified again!" Since this piece is by common consent dated at the end of Michelangelo's life, the Christ shared by the artist and Vittoria Colonna (see immediately below) is rather the pitiful Christ of the Rondanini or Palestrina Pietàs:

> Non fur men lieti che turbati e tristi
> Che tu patissi, e non gia lor, la morte,
> Gli spirti eletti, onde le chiuse porte
> Del ciel di terra al huom col sangue apristi:
> Lieti, poiche creato, il redimisti
> Dal primo error di suo misera sorte;
> Tristi, a sentir ch'a la pena aspra e forte,
> Seruo de serui in croce diuenisti.
> Onde e chi fusti, il ciel ne die tal segno,
> Che scurò gli ochi suoi, la terra aperse,
> Tremorno i monti, e torbide fur l'acque.
> Tolse i gran padri al tenebroso regno,

Gli angeli brutti in piu doglia sommerse:
Gode sol l'huom, ch'al battesmo rinacque. (G 298)

(For translation see p. 132.)

It was when he was working on the *Giudizio* (1536) that Michelangelo met the Marchioness of Pescara. An important collection of her *Rime* was published in Venice in 1540, the year before the *Giudizio* was completed. In this collection we find a poem which no one has hitherto connected with Michelangelo, but which must be juxtaposed in Italian with the sonnet above:

> Gli angeli eletti e quel bene infinito
> Braman hoggi soffrir penosa morte;
> Poi che nell'alta gloriosa corte
> Non fia piu il servo del Signor gradito.
> Piange la nostra madre il giusto ardito
> Ch' a' figli suoi del Ciel chiuse le porte;
> E che la man piagate hor sieno scorte
> Per riducri al camin da lei smarrito.
> Ascondo il Sol la sua fulgente chioma
> Spezzanti i sassi vivi, apronsi i monti,
> Trema la terra ancor, turbansi l'acque.
> Piangon i spirti a nostri danni pronti
> De le catene loro l'aggiunta somma,
> L'uomo non piange, e pur piangendo nacque.[29]

If the sonnet of Michelangelo, whose final six lines coincide so closely with these concluding tercets, is penned as late as commonly agreed, then we have here a clear case of plagiarism on his part—a plagiarism, however, from a dearest friend. It is one of those rare cases where the borrowed piece even surpasses the original, disproving the poet's remark about those who follow others never outdoing them—just as Du Bellay's "A un vanneur de blé" overshadows the original of Navagero. Vittoria Colonna, suspect for her sympathies with the Reformation and a close correspondent of such "liberals" as Marguerite d'Angoulême, touches upon two sensitive subjects: the elect (predestination) and salvation through Christ's blood. Michelangelo follows suit. If he borrowed from her in this instance, he made up for it "in kind" by giving her two drawings on this pious theme, a *Deposizione* and a *Crocifissione*. In any case, the borrowings from Vittoria Colonna are probably the most interesting of all those listed in this chapter, and perhaps the most revealing.

Only one other borrowing is as symptomatic: the poem on milady's garland and girdle which he took from Poliziano, for in it the artist is not, as his contemporaries were so willing to do, warming over the passions of Anacreon, Ovid, Catullus, or Petrarch in order to sing the praises of a real mistress. We must conclude that he is taking a word portrait by Poliziano, devoid of plastic quality, and "sculpturing" in words the clothed figure of Simonetta-Aphrodite. He decided to express in verse a thought which obsessed him as artist: clothing has no more meaning than the *soverchio* of a statue, the excess material which encases true form and must be cleared away.

In conclusion, a survey of Michelangelo's borrowings show verifiable plagiarisms only from the few poets who held a profoundly personal meaning for him: Dante, Petrarch, Poliziano, Lorenzo de' Medici, Vittoria Colonna, and possibly Accolti. For the rest, he remained both as poet and artist one of the most autonomous creative geniuses of the Renaissance.

NOTES

1 Giuseppe Calero, *Michelangelo poeta, ed. cit.*, p. 129.
2 G. Vasari, *Le vite, ed. cit.*, VII, 280.
3 These lines of 1533 are actually set into a context of love rather than art.
4 See Mariani, *La poesia di Michelangelo, ed. cit.*, p. 100.
5 Armenini, *De veri precetti* (Ravenna, 1586), p. 66.
6 Arturo Farinelli, "Michelangelo poeta," *loc. cit.*, p. 311.
7 Benedetto Varchi, *Due lezzioni,* quoted in the Guasti edition of the *Rime*, p. xcii.
8 Benedetto Varchi, "Della maggioranza delle arti," in *Trattati d'arte del Cinquecento*, ed. Paola Barocchi (Bari, 1960–62), I, 57.
9 Enrico Bevilacqua, *op. cit.*, p. 649. Consult on this subject Ettore Fattore, *Michelangelo e Dante* (Florence, 1875).
10 John E. Taylor, *Michelangelo Considered as a Philosophic Poet, ed. cit.*, p. 28.
11 Vincenzo Pascale, *op. cit.*, p. 79.
12 Vasari, *Le vite, ed. cit.*, VII, 221.
13 Condivi is referring to *Purg.* XXVII, 100–05 and *Para.* XXVIII, 118 ff.
14 L. Goldscheider, *The Drawings of Michelangelo, ed. cit.*, p. 50.
15 *Rime*, ed. Girardi, p. 479. Mentioned also by Condivi.
16 *Ibid.*, p. 475.
17 D. Giannotti, *Dialogi, ed. cit.*, p. 68.
18 *Rime*, ed. Girardi, p. 301.
19 Vincenzo Pascale, *op. cit.*, p. 163.
20 Pierre de Bouchaud, *op. cit.*, p. 101.
21 *Rime inedite del '500* (Bologna, 1918), p. 36.
22 See Insinga, *op. cit.*, p. 45 for numbering and pagination of these parallel verses.
23 *Le Rime di Vittoria Colonna* (Rome, 1840), p. 347.
24 *Ibid.*, p. 214.
25 *Ibid.*, p. 58.
26 *Ibid.*, p. 12.
27 *Ibid.*, p. 11. These last two *rapprochements* were found by my student Miss Vicki Mistacco.
28 *Rime*, ed. Ceriello, p. 276.
29 Vittoria Colonna, *Rime* (Venice, 1540), p. 36.

20

VALUES AND FAME AS POET

WILLING TO ACKNOWLEDGE that he "sculptured divine things" (G 282), Michelangelo made no such glorious claims for his writings, as we have shown. Yet he was not unaware of the kudos to be gained from poetising. Three tributes reveal this. A sonnet to Dante acknowledges that the Florentine Trecentist had attained a stature beyond compare: "Simil uom ne maggior non naqque mai" (G 250). He felt that Vittoria's 215 sonnets, so close in spirit to his own, would never perish:

> Ne mecter puo in oblio,
> Ben che 'l corpo sie morto.
> I suo dolci, leggiadri e sacri inchiostri. (G 265)

(For translation see p. 281.)

Art's power of conferring immortality, which he acknowledges in more than one poem, is attributed as well to such poetry as that of his friend Berni:

> Et dice, che la uita de suo marmi
> Non basta a far il uostro nom' eterno,
> Come lui fanno i diuin uostri carmi. (G 85)

(For translation see p. 264.)

Prose such as that of Vasari is no less a vessel of glory (G 277).

These passages permit us to suppose, as we stated earlier, that Michelangelo did not view poetry merely as a pastime or a refuge but as yet another means to demonstrate his talent and virtuosity. Certainly his "editors" Giannotti and Riccio, prodding him to write, urging revisions, and editing his autographs to give them Latinate spellings, may well have dwelt upon his ability to gain fame through his "inchiostri."

The fame which he came to covet or expect was slow in arriving. In Chapter I we traced the development of his reputation as poet during his lifetime. Let us, in this final section, follow his posthumous fame down to the present, when at last the recognition he timidly hoped for has been fully won. We shall proceed by examining in turn the growth of Michelangelo's poetic fame in Italy; the difficulties inherent in making him an international poet, including those of translation; the slow, sure spread of his fame abroad; a summary of the critical reactions to the *Rime*; and finally, a reappraisal of his poetic values which seem most valid.

The fame and accurate appreciation of the *Rime* within Italy, as we have shown, was handicapped by the lack of a correct and complete edition of the corpus lying in wait for a "dotta mano" in Rome and Florence. The defective and bowdlerised edition of 1623 was still being used in 1726, when the printer Manni in Florence republished the *Rime*. It was not until the early nineteenth century, at the time when the Romanticists were rediscovering the Middle Ages and the Renaissance, that the flood of more accurate editions spread over Italy. Editions after the Roman printing of 1808 followed in 1817 (the first to include the Vatican codices), 1821 (in Paris and Milan), 1842, 1858, 1860, 1863, 1872 (in Bremen), 1880, and finally the Frey edition of 1897. Including the present century, as our Bibliography will show, twenty-seven different editions (including the little-known 1943 printing by Viau in Buenos Aires) attest to the increasing acceptance of Michelangelo as a major figure in the history of Italian poetry. Textbooks, anthologies, and school curricula now include Michelangelo between Ariosto and Tasso. The chronology of editions listed above would seem to justify Ugo Foscolo's complaint in his essay of 1826 that his countrymen had neglected Michelangelo as poet—that Tiraboschi had typically made a passing mention of the artist as poet "carelessly."[1] The few serious monographs and essays on the *Rime* in Italy came very late indeed, considering that as early as 1817 a corpus for serious study was available. The earliest essays on the *Rime* in Italy were brief, thin, and repetitious. Large blocks of the poetry (those to Cecchino/many on the fine arts) were neglected entirely, while the more Petrarchistic and Platonistic received almost exclusive attention. Most of the essayists were too dazzled by Michelangelo's sovereignty in the arts to approach his poetry judiciously. Almost nothing was done in the Ottocento to find sources of the *Rime*, to order them accurately, to exploit other veins than the religious or philosophical, to isolate themes, or to find the subtle but inevitable identity of thought between the *Rime* and the art. Even in the present century dilettantism has prevailed over study of the *Rime* in Italy. Essays are numerous, but studies are rare. As late as 1943 Giuseppe Calero wrote a book, *Michelangelo poeta*, dwelling on amoristic and religious elements in the *Rime*, utterly without originality, without interest in variants, without concern for chronologies or sources. Other examples of this superficial approach are the works of Pierre de Bouchaud, Natale de Sanctis,

Ottone Degregorio, Riccardo Tartuffi, and Vincenzo Italo Pascale. Only a few of the items in our Bibliography represent original thinking and serious study of the *Rime*; those of Amico-Mantia, Enrico Bevilacqua, Giuseppe Guido Ferrero, Enzo Girardi, Arturo Insinga, Valerio Mariani, F. Rizzi, and of course Papini, the scholarly antischolar. It may be safely said that the various editors of the *Rime* in Italy have understood the artist as poet much better than have the essayists. Later in this chapter we shall return to the matter of the currents of critical reaction to the *Rime*.

Despite the fact that Michelangelo's art was known to all of Europe before his late death, with artists copying him as far away as Flanders, his fame as artist did not carry over to his literary activities. It could hardly have been otherwise. The lack of a printed collection on which translations could be based and the difficulty of translating the few poems which had arrived abroad prevented his poetic fame from spreading as had that of Ariosto and Tasso. The difficulties of translating Michelangelo have discouraged many a good poet. They stalled Rilke, who never finished his projected complete translation. Grimm gave up before achieving a full translation, declaring himself unable to render into German the "sublime grandeur" of the thought and expression. The fact that Michelangelo requires paraphrase for the Italians themselves (which many editors have supplied) would explain why translators of the *Rime* have been tempted to *explain* rather than *translate*, a weaker type of "imitation" approved in the Renaissance but hardly considered satisfactory today. The explicative process carries the translation one further remove from the original, as does —of necessity—the attempt to retain the original rhyme pattern. Almost all translators of Michelangelo into the several European languages have felt the necessity of keeping the rhyme scheme, even though to Michelangelo himself rhyme often seemed a secondary "finishing process." Creighton Gilbert's translations into English assonance are an attempt at a happy compromise. It is typical that when Michelangelo himself abandons an attempt at perfect rhyming the translators try to improve upon him. Thus, when Michelangelo unconcernedly rhymes *tolse* twice with itself, the repetitions are "corrected" in a recent American translation to become "eyes/sunrise/prize." Inevitably the translation is forced away from the original Italian. One recalls Valéry's *mot* to the effect that translations are like women, the more beautiful, the less faithful—and vice versa.

Many of the translations from the *Rime* were executed by established poets (see Bibliography). These translators have been tempted to leave a cachet and quality of their own and to shrug off the charge "traduttore traditore." The corrective impulses of modern translators have too often led them to make of the rough and unfinished artist in verse a finished and polished poet.

Rilke expressed the goal of the ideal translator. He asserted that his own translations from the *Rime* were so "genaue und reine" that there was no room for himself in them. As an independent poet he even complained of this literalness in a letter to Ellen Dulp: "Nein, natürlich spreche ich nicht Meiniges in ihnen aus, wenn ich sie meiner Sprache zu fassen gebe . . . nicht von meinen Verhängnissen handeln sie."[2] Yet even Rilke retains the rhyme scheme while occasionally adding "something of his own." Perhaps the worst offenders were the Victorian poets. It is sometimes possible to confront two Victorian translations of the same Michelangelo poem and be uncertain whether they are of the same original.

The scarcity of good translations of the *Rime*, with or without rhyme, has been noted by Insinga. "To render into verse or carry over into a foreign language the poems of Michelangelo is a real hardship, and translations of them are most rare."[3]

One last footnote concerning translations of the *Rime* in Italy: like Petrarch deciding to give Boccaccio stature by translating into Latin the *novella* on Griselda, Antonio Gigante in 1595 put into Latin Michelangelo's sonnet "S'auien che spesso il gran desir promecta" (G 296) as "Et spes annis nondum contenta peractis."[4]

Germany, which pioneered the study of Michelangelo's life and art, was typical in appreciating the poetry early. Back in 1822, four years before Foscolo's essays, Karl Foerster discussed the *Rime* in *Die Muse* of Leipzig, and translated nine of them into German. Even before such major German contributions as Frey's editions of the *Rime* (1897) and the *Vite* of Condivi and Vasari (1882, 1887), the *Rime* had appeared in Germany in Italian (Bremen, 1872) and in German (Berlin, 1842; Leipzig, 1875; Berlin, 1896). Very popular and accessible were the translations included in Hermann Grimm's biography of Michelangelo, called by Rilke "das schönste grundlegende Buch, das sein Leben erzählt." Preceding the magistral edition of Carl Frey by one year, Walter Robert-Tornov published German translations of the Guasti corpus, as had Sophie Hasenclever in 1875; he broke away from Guasti's generic arrangement of the poems and disposed them in biographical order, as Frey and Girardi were to do. The leading twentieth-century translators into German have been R. Guardini, Heinrich Nelson, Henry Thode, Rainer Maria Rilke, Max Kemmerell, and Edwin Redslob. The German students of Michelangelo's life and art, from Frey and Grimm and Thode to the present, have been very conscious of the importance of Michelangelo's poetry in approaching his thoughts and aesthetics. Among the German translators, my own preference continues to be Rilke, and it is to be regretted that during the many years he devoted to his *Dichtungen des Michelangelo* (ca. 1914–23), he was unable to translate the whole corpus available to him in the Frey edition which he utilised.[5] We have shown elsewhere that Rilke made subtle use of the *Rime* as he composed his *Geschichten vom lieben Gott*.[6]

Notable musical settings for the *Rime* were composed by Hugo Wolf (*Drei Gedichte von Michelangelo*, 1897), for bass voice; by Richard Strauss (*Fünf Lieder*, 1895); by Theodore Streicher (*Michelangelo, zwölf Lieder*, 1922); by Hans Pfitzner (*Das dunkle Reich*, ca. 1930) and by the Liechtensteiner Joseph Rheinberger (*Gesänge altitalienischer Dichter*, 1912). Perhaps one might add here the Dutch composer Matty Niel (*Drei Liederen*, Amsterdam, 1961), a work called to my attention by my friend and student Richard Fabrizio.

The roster of poets in England and America who have translated from the *Rime* includes many great names and many Italophiles, those "devils incarnate." The first Englishing of a poem by Michelangelo, as Melchiori has shown in his *Michelangelo nel Settecento inglese*, was of "Caro m'è 'l sonno e piu l'esser di sasso" (G 247), in Christopher Hervey's *Letters* of 1760–61, published in 1785. William Roscoe's lives of Lorenzo de' Medici and of Leo X (1785, 1805) praised Michelangelo as poet. In 1796 Thomas James Mathias showed that by then Michelangelo's poetry was known to some Englishmen:

> Michael, in full Pierian pow'rs erect,
> The sculptor, painter, poet, architect,
> Michael to Britain dear[7]

Melchiori shows that individual poems of Michelangelo were presented to the English by Giuseppe Baretti (1755), Leonardo Nardini and Serafino Bonaiuti (1769–98), and Thomas Mathias (1802, 1808). Capel Lofft at this time published three sonnets of Michelangelo and hailed him as one of the greatest Italian lyricists. Meanwhile Michelangelo was attracting the attention of the more important poets. William Wordsworth and Robert Southey contributed sonnets to Richard Duppa, who was writing his popular *Life of Michelangelo Buonarroti, with his Poetry and Letters*, published in 1806 but reprinted many times. In the pantheon of outstanding English and American poets of the nineteenth century who translated Michelangelo we find not only Wordsworth and Southey, but Henry Wadsworth Longfellow, Ralph Waldo Emerson, Charles Eliot Norton, George Santayana, and (later) Robert Bridges, many of whom are represented in our book *Michelangelo: A Self-Portrait*. The Platonism of the *Rime* found a compatible reception in Transcendentalist New England of the late nineteenth century, Emerson's reading lists include Michelangelo's *Sonnets* from 1834 on, and Michelangelo's spiritual sonnets were taken to heart by a generation which turned its back on all the other *Rime* which did not conform to this spirituality. The mid- and late-century taste for Michelangelo is clarified in John E. Taylor's *Michelangelo Considered as a Philosophic Poet* (London, 1852).

With interest more or less limited to the spiritual or Neo-Platonic and easily associated pieces ("Caro m' è l' sonno," etc.) it was inevitable that these would receive multiple translation while others were neglected. Thus, we have discovered no fewer than eight different nineteenth-century versions of the sonnet on Dante ("Quante dirne si de' non si puo dire") (G 250) including variants by Ednah Dow Cheney, Lorna de' Lucchi, Grinnell-Milne, Charles Eliot Norton, Robert Southey, and Longfellow. Longfellow, a thorough scholar of Michelangelo, as attested by his drama on the artist, usually succeeds in keeping closest to the original Italian.

It was the reflective poems which interested the musicians also; "Veggio co be uostr' ochi" (G 89) was set to music by both William Platt (1895?) and Benjamin Britten (*Seven Sonnets of Michelangelo,* 1940).

Despite this dilettantish interest in individual poems of the artist, until recently no complete Englishing of the *Rime* had been undertaken. For decades the standard collection in English was John Addington Symonds's *The Sonnets of Michael Angelo and Thomas Campanella* (London, 1878, with many subsequent editions). As he limited himself in Victorian fashion to the spiritual sonnets, Symonds's choice offered only a limited idea of the range of the artist's muse. Retaining the rhyme scheme, Symonds frequently departed from the original Italian text. The principal twentieth-century translators into English are S. Elizabeth Hall, George Santayana, Nesca Robb, Cecil Clifford Palmer, Creighton Gilbert, and Joseph Tusiani. In 1945 and 1947 Creighton Gilbert published in *Italica* bibliographies of English translations of the *Rime*.

No important study of the *Rime* has as yet appeared in England or America. Ugo Foscolo wrote two essays of a general nature praising the *Rime* and fitting them into Dantean and Petrarchan traditions. His essay on the poetry in the *Retrospective Review* (1826) has more historic than critical importance, however. In 1873 appeared Walter Pater's celebrated *The Renaissance*, made up of nine essays on literature and art. It was this book which founded the Anglo-Saxon cult of the *Mona Lisa,* for its effusive and purple prose on the Gioconda's "mysterious" smile showed the extent to which the English public of the time was receptive to "aesthetic" criticism. The same volume contained a chapter on "The Poetry of Michelangelo," full more of enthusiasm and divagation than clarity or information. Although this thin volume launched the fortunes of one of Leonardo's lesser works, it did not similarly launch the fortunes of Michelangelo's *Rime*. It was John Addington Symonds's biography of the artist, popular in England and America and enriched by his many translations, which first made the English-speaking world aware of the unity of Michelangelo the artist, man, and poet. Despite an occasional scholar like John E. Taylor or W. P. Ker, the Anglo-Saxon world which reveres Michelangelo as artist has nurtured few students of the *Rime*.

It may be safely asserted that Michelangelo's *Rime* were unknown to that Renaissance France whose monarch Francis I invited him in vain to accept a commission—that France which also managed to lose several of his important works. The only occurrence of a translation is one which I have pointed out in an earlier volume, a translation of the famous quatrain, "Non ha l'ottimo artista alcun concetto" (G 151). Philippe Desportes rendered it as follows:

> Le sculpteur excellent desseignant pour ouvrage
> Une plante, un lion, un homme, un élément,
> Si la main obeyt et suit l'entendement,
> Trouve en un marbre seul toute sorte d'image.[8]

In Chapter VII we have proposed that some unknown French poet apparently translated a lost poem of the artist's on the bronze *David*. Although a florilegium of the *Rime* with critical notes was published by M. A. Vercollier in 1826, the first complete translation into French dates from the 1860 edition of Auguste Lannau-Roland, an attempt dismissed by Insinga, with reason, as "lacrimevole."[9] Much better are the subsequent translations by Boyer d'Agen and Paul Hazard. As our Bibliography will attest, French scholarship has not concerned itself particularly with the *Rime*, the longest study, that of Pierre de Bouchaud, being not only superficial but based apparently on incomplete editions. (He claims, for example, that after "long years of study," he can find no poems written to Febo di Poggio or Gherardo Perini, and seems ignorant of the epitaphs to Cecchino.) As of this date, I know of at least two French composers, Jeanne Leleu (see Bibliography) and Jacques Benoit-Méchin (in the *Revue musicale* of 1931) who have set poems by Michelangelo to music.

Despite the frequent mentions of Michelangelo in Spanish Siglo de Oro poetry,[10] and the cult of the artist initiated by Francisco de Hollanda, the *Rime* were unknown to the Spanish Renaissance. However, the quatrain launched by Varchi in a reading before the Florentine Academy and known to the France of Desportes's generation managed to precede the rest into Spain. In the elaborate allegory praising the arts which occurs near the opening of Saavedra Fajardo's *República literária* I find this curious vision: "En lo mas alto de este frontispicio estaba representada la Arquitectura en una doncella de mármol, levantando el brazo derecho con un compás y el izquierdo estribando en una planta del edificio, y a sus pies, por el plano del pedestal, corrían estos dos versos de Miguel Angel:

> Non ha l'ottimo artista alcun concetto,
> Ch'un marmo solo in se non circoscriva.[11]

It has been reported to me that a Spanish translation of the *Rime* has recently made them available to Spain and Spanish America, but in three recent trips to Spain I have been unable to locate it, finding only the Viau selection published in Buenos Aires (in modernised Italian). If Spanish scholarship on Michelangelo as poet is not to be found, two excellent essays exploit the poetry in creditable fashion. The interesting if brief *Comedia del alma de Miguel Ángel*, by Angela Mariutti de Sánchez Rivero (Madrid, Espasa Calpe, 1943) exhibits a number of the poems in order to elucidate the artist's personality and his love for Vittoria Colonna. I cannot praise too highly Juan Ramón Masoliver's pioneer exploitation of the *Rime* to approach Michelangelo's ideas on sculpture. This brief article ("De las ideas estéticas de Miguel Ángel y de sus poesías de esculptor"), which might well have been expanded, appeared in *Escorial*.[12]

The *Rime* seem little known in other countries, although one of the best books on the *Rime* is *Michelangiolo Poet* of the Franco-Romanian scholar, N. Façon (Bucharest, 1939). Gyorgy Vermei translated a selection of the *Rime* into Hungarian, published in Budapest in the same year, 1939. Translations and studies involving other languages have not at this date appeared in the libraries of Italy, England, and America utilised for the present volume. (However, see Bibliography.)

A study of the dates of the items in our Bibliography makes plain that Michelangelo's poetry is becoming available at an accelerated rate, and that it is at last being studied with greater accuracy and in its totality. Thus it seems that his poetry, like his works of art, will thrive, as he phrased it in his madrigal, "Sol d'una pietra uiua": ". . . al par degli anni" (G 240).

No one has summarised the evolution of the critical reception to Michelangelo's *Rime* after the manner of Pietro Mazzamuto's useful *Rassegna Bibliografico-Critica della letteratura italiana*. The nearest anyone has come to this is the few pages of Riccardo M. Sati, "Interpretazioni della Poesia di Michelangelo."[13] This very condensed essay finds the first critical reaction typically Romantic; the second, Crocean, stressing the prosaic expression of the *Rime*; the third view, typified by Stefano Bottari, sees the *Rime* as a "diario poetico"; and the fourth phase, popularised by Mariani, accepts the pieces as sculptured verse. The essay of Bottari to which Sati refers is his "Il diario poetico di Michelangelo," which appeared in *La critica figurativa e l'estetica moderna*[14] and which held the *Rime* to be "una ideale biografia dell'anima," a view which many had held before him, however. Into this tentative sequence one could insert the Victorian or limitative group of critics (Bouchaud, Thomas, Taylor), who confined their interest to the religious, Platonic, and metaphysical content of the *Rime*. One should add a classification for the "aesthetic" approach of Pater and his followers. Certainly a special category beyond these six should be advanced to include

Erwin Panofsky (*Studies in Iconology*), Edgar Wind, Helmut Hatzfeld, Charles de Tolnay, Ludwig Goldscheider (*Drawings of Michelangelo*), and others of what might be called the Princeton–Warburg Institute school. These scholars, none of whom has devoted a book specifically to the *Rime*, have held the intransigent view that all of Michelangelo's various productions have an essential unity. They exploit the *Rime* constantly to demonstrate this and constantly seek new meanings and interpretations to his works, which—if acceptable—make Michelangelo more deeply grounded than hitherto supposed in classical and humanistic literature, in iconography, and in formal and textual philosophy.

The weakness of the Victorian approach was of course that it could not cope with the minority of poems in which the Bernesque or realistic or ironic or comic vein of Michelangelo came to the fore. The limitations (or special character) of this school are illustrated by Taylor's genteel book on Michelangelo as a "philosophic poet." (To state that Vittoria Colonna died, he writes: ". . . when her lofty and gentle spirit had forsaken its earthly tenement.")

Much critical opinion of the *Rime* has centered on the question of the artist's style. We have devoted space to this matter in Chapter II and shall not return thereto except to note that Croce's denial of lyrical or poetic qualities to the *Rime* unleashed a debate on the question of whether Michelangelo was a poet at all. It is unfortunately the Italians who have permitted themselves to indulge in this futile pastime, perhaps demonstrating again that the influence of the historian Croce was not always felicitous when he dealt with literature. Typical is Enrico Bevilacqua, who in the *Revista d'Italia* questions whether Michelangelo deserves the name of poet: "I should not hesitate or blush to propose the counteraffirmation: Michelangelo's best poetry is truly not worth his most neglected and roughest piece of carved marble, his most careless sketch on paper or canvas."[15]

Stephen Spender somewhere defined literary criticism as the "substitute muse of the universities." We are less in need of evaluations of Michelangelo's poetry than clarifications of it. The trouble has been that those who denied him the name of poet or overpraised him as poet have served little the exegetical function. While debate has continued concerning his value as poet, the poetry has increased in influence. In addition to composers we have mentioned, major writers have reflected it: Leopardi, D'Annunzio, Rilke, among others.

Censures of Michelangelo's several arts are common and of long standing. As a sculptor he was accused of departing from nature (Annibale Caracci tried to deflate his reputation as sculptor by observing that it was interesting to see how bodies had looked in the days of Buonarroti),[16] of disregarding the finishing process, and of limiting himself to *uniche vedute*. As an architect he was accused of sacrificing constructive principles for aesthetic ones (one modern historian holds him responsible for the "decay of Renaissance architecture").[17] As painter he was accused of trying to reduce this art to mere line and relief.

Criticisms of Michelangelo's three major arts may be vehement, and they may even be valid in their limited way, without detracting from his eventual greatness. The same may be alleged of criticisms of his poetry. It was precisely because Michelangelo broke with the poetic practices of his day that he was a poet worthy of our attention. As he broke from tradition, poetry came to be a new battle to be won. The critics quoted in Chapter II are correct in repeating that Michelangelo viewed poetry as a struggle of thought and with form. This was precisely how he viewed art—a struggle to match the *concetto* with the material. Once the contest had been won—as we noted in Chapter II—the finishing process held less interest for him. This was true of Michelangelo as sculptor but even more true of him as poet, when he was writing for private communication or for personal release—unconcerned with the approval of critics—least of all critics of the twentieth century. In this context thought came to matter as much as form. The translation of feeling, the relief of confession, and often the release from passion or bitterness, these were what counted, even as he struggled to wed content and form. Thus, some appropriate indices by which to evaluate his poetry are sincerity, power, variety, originality, and emotional charge. By these standards his *Rime* stand with the finest of the Renaissance. As for the *canto* (lyricism) which Croce, Sapegno, and others find missing from his poems, we need only repeat that Jacob Archadelt, Bartolomeo Tromboncino, Costanzo Festa, Jean de Conseil, and Luigi Porta found challenging lyrical qualities in some of them. Surely, such sonnets as "S'un casto amor" and "Veggio co be uostr' ochi" can be judged by any criteria whatsoever and remain at the pinnacle of Renaissance lyrical poetry.

In this volume we have avoided joining another current debate, especially keen among the late New Critics of the Anglo-Saxon countries: the inherent value of a work of art independent of its maker. The *Iliad* has indisputable values as history or allegory whether or not it was written by Homer—indeed, whether Homer was one man or seven men. In the case of the *Rime*, this issue is utterly irrelevant. The value of the *Rime* is not an autonomous one. Beyond the many inherent values which we have attributed to them, their value lies not only in their being identified closely with one of the world's greatest creative spirits, but also in their magnificent potential for explaining that enigmatic man and his work. We cannot let formal, stylistic, or even lyrical qualities distract us from the principal claim we made at the outset: without understanding Michelangelo's *Rime*, we simply cannot claim to understand his art.

NOTES

[1] Ugo Foscolo, *Opere*, Edizione Nazionale (Florence, 1953), X, 450.
[2] R. M. Rilke, *Briefe* (Wiesbaden, 1950), II, 292.
[3] Arturo Insinga, *op. cit.*, p. 27.
[4] See *Rime*, ed. Guasti, p. lxxxi.
[5] R. J. Clements, *The Peregrine Muse* (Chapel Hill, 1959), p. 29.
[6] *Ibid.*, pp. 27–42.
[7] Giorgio Melchiori, *Michelangelo nel Settecento inglese* (Rome, 1950), p. 74.
[8] See above, Chap. IV, n. 16.
[9] Insinga, *op. cit.*, p. 27.
[10] See Miguel Herrero García, *Contribución de la literatura a la historia del arte* (Madrid, 1943), which contains 29 Siglo de Oro references to Michelangelo.
[11] Saavedra Fajardo, *República literaria* (Madrid: Libreria Fernando Fe, n.d.), p. 40.
[12] *Escorial*, XIX (1942), 233–58.
[13] *Il Vasari*, 1941, pp. 36–42.
[14] *La critica figurativa* . . . (Bari: Laterza, 1935), pp. 109–60.
[15] Enrico Bevilacqua, *loc. cit.*, p. 637.
[16] M. de Chantelou, *Journal de voyage du Cavalier Bernin* (Paris, 1885), p. 40.
[17] W. J. Anderson, *Architecture of the Renaissance in Italy* (London, 1896), p. 128.

BIBLIOGRAPHY

EDITIONS OF THE POETRY

Rime di Michelagnolo Buonarroti, raccolte da Michelagnolo suo nipote. Florence: i Giunti, 1623.

Rime di Michelagnolo Buonarroti il Vecchio, con una lezione de Benedetto Varchi e due di Mario Guiducci. Florence: Manni, 1726. (Based on edition of 1623.)

Le Rime di Michelagnolo Buonarroti. Rome: Desideri, 1808.

Le Rime di Michelagnolo Buonarroti, con Rime inedite tolte da un codico del Vaticano. Rome, 1817. (Anonymous editor was Alessandro Maggiori.)

Le Rime di Michelagnolo Buonarroti il Vecchio, col commento di G. Biagiolo. Paris, 1821.

Rime e prose di Michelagnolo Buonarroti. Milan: Silvestri, 1821.

Rime e prose di Michelagnolo Buonarroti. Naples: Aldo Manuzio, 1842. 2 vols.

Rime e lettere di Michelagnolo Buonarroti. Florence: Barbera, 1858, 1860, 1880, 1903, 1908, 1914.

Le Rime di Michelagnolo Buonarroti, cavate dagli autografi e pubblicate da Cesare Guasti, Accademico della Crusca. Florence: Le Monnier, 1863.

Le Rime di Michelagnolo Buonarroti, Nachdichtungen von Hans Grasberger. Bremen, 1872.

Die Dichtungen des Michelagniolo Buonarroti, herausgegeben und mit kritischem Apparte versehen von Karl Frey. Berlin, 1897.

Liriche di Michelangiolo Buonarroti, con prefazione di G. L. Passerini. Venice, 1908.

Le Rime, con prefazione di A. Castaldo. Rome: Garroni, 1910.

Le poesie di Michelangelo, con prefazione di Giovanni Amendola. Lanciano, 1911 and 1931.

Le Rime, con prefazione e note da Aldo Foratti. Milan: Caddeo, 1921.

Le Rime di Michelangelo, con prefazione di Ausonio Dobelli. Milan, 1933.

Le poesie ("Una scelta di poesie di Michel Agniolo da lui stesso destinata alla stampa"). Montagnola di Lugano, 1923.

Michelagnolo poeta, scelta di rime commentate da F. Rizzi. Milan: Treves, 1924.

Lettere e Rime. Turin: Società Editrice Internazionale, 1925.

Dalle lettere e dalle Rime, a cura di F. Rizzi. Florence: "La Voce," 1925.
Le Rime di Michelangelo Buonarroti, con prefazione di Giovanni Papini. Florence: Rinascimento del Libro, 1927.
Le Rime, introduzione e note di Valentino Piccoli. Turin, 1930.
Michelangelo (vol. I, *Vita* e *Opere*). Milan: Rietti, 1932.
Michelangelo Buonarroti. *Le Rime*. Buenos Aires: Viau, 1943.
Le Rime di Michelangelo. Milan: Rizzoli, 1954.
Michelangiolo Buonarroti, *Rime*, edizione di Enzo Noè Girardi. Bari: Laterza, 1960.
Michelangelo, *Rime e Lettere*. Milan: Istituto ed. Italiano, n.d.

TRANSLATIONS OF THE *RIME*

LATIN

Hetruscum Michaelis Angeli Bonarotae Latime redditum, in *Carmina Antonii Gigantis Forosemproniensis*. Bologna, 1595. (Translation of sonnet "S'auien che spesso il gran desir promecta.")

GERMAN

Karl Foerster, in *Die Muse* (Leipzig, 1822), pp. 95–127. (Nine translations.)
Michel Angelo Buonarroti's sämmtliche Gedichte, mit Anmerhungen von Gottlob Regis. Berlin, 1842.
Saemmtliche Gedichte Michelangelo's in Guasti's Text, herausgegeben von Sophie Hasenclever, Leipzig, 1875.
Die Gedichte des Michelangelo Buonarroti, übersetzt und biographisch geordnet von Walter Robert-Tornov. Berlin, 1896.
Michelangelo, *Gedichte und Briefe*, ed. R. Guardini, herausgegeben von Pan-Verlag (Berlin, 1907).
Michelangelo Buonarroti Dichtungen, übertragen von Heinrich Nelson. Iena, 1909 and 1922.
Michelangelo's Gedichte in deutscher Übersetzung, von Henry Thode. Berlin, 1914.
Dichtungen des Michelangelo, übertragen von Rainer Maria Rilke. Wiesbaden, 1923.
Michelangelos Dichtungen, deutsch von Max Kemmerell. Frankfurt am Main, 1931.
Sonette, übertragen von Edwin Redslob. Berlin, 1948.

FRENCH

Les Poésies de Michel-Ange, traduites de l'italien. Notes littéraires et historiques par M. A. Vercollier. Paris, 1826. See also *Six sonnets de Michel-Ange* (versions françaises de Vercollier) *mis en musique par Jeanne Leleu*. Paris, 1925.
Michel-Ange poète, première traduction complète de ses poésies, par Auguste Lannau-Roland. Paris: Didier, 1860.
L'œuvre littéraire de Michel-Ange d'après les Archives Buonarroti, introduction par Boyer d'Agen. Paris: Delagrave, 1911.
Poésies de *Michel-Ange* traduites en français intégralement pour la premiere fois, by Marie Dormoy.
Poésies de Michel-Ange traduites en vers, by Count A. de Montesquieu (Meulan de Masson, 1875).
Sonnets de Michel-Ange Buonarroti, traduits par Paul Hazard. Dijon, 1928.

ENGLISH

Life of Michel Angelo, with Translations of Many of His Poems and Letters, by Richard Duppa. London, 1806.

The Sonnets of Michel Angelo and Thomas Campanella, translated by John Addington Symonds. London, 1878, and many successive editions.

Selected Poems of Michelangelo, translated by Ednah Dow Cheney. Boston, 1885.

Sonnets of Michel Angelo, translated by S. Elizabeth Hall. London, 1905.

Michel Angelo, *Poems,* put into English by Cecil Clifford Palmer. Zurich: Johannespresse, 1941.

The Complete Poems of Michelangelo, translated by Joseph Tusiani. New York, 1960.

Complete Poems and Selected Letters of Michelangelo, translated by Creighton Gilbert. New York, 1963.

Michelangelo: A Self-Portrait, edited by Robert J. Clements. New York: Prentice-Hall, 1963.

HUNGARIAN

Michelangelo versei, translated by Gyorgy Ronay. Budapest, 1939.

POLISH TRANSLATIONS

Poezye Michiala-Aniola Buonarrotega, by Lucyana Siemenskiego (Krakowie, 1861)

Michal Aniol Buonnaroti, *Poezye,* tr. by Leopold Staff (Warsaw, 1922).

CROATIAN TRANSLATION

A single translation appeared in *Nove Europe* of Zagreb in 1926.

BOOKS AND ESSAYS ON MICHELANGELO'S *RIME*

Amico-Mantia, Antonio. *L'amore e le Rime di Michelangelo.* Trapani, 1899.

Andreucci, Ottavio. *La filosofia del Concetto nelle opere di Michelangelo* (lecture). Florence, 1875.

Baldacci, L., "Lineamenti della poesia di Michelangelo," *Paragone,* VI (Dec., 1955), 27 ff.

Beall, Chandler B., "The Literary Figure of Michelangelo," *Italica,* Sept., 1964, pp. 235–51.

Berseviczy, Alberto. "Les sonnets de Michel-Ange et de Shakespeare" (offprint). Budapest, 1914.

Bevilacqua, Enrico. "Michelangelo scrittore" (fasc.). Milan-Rome, 1926.

Bizzicari, Alvaro. "L'idea della bellezza nelle poesie di Michelangelo," *Italica,* Sept., 1964, pp. 252–65.

Borinski, K. *Die Rätsel Michelangelos: Michelangelo und Dante.* Munich, 1908.

Bosco, Umberto. *Il Rinascimento e la lirica di Michelangelo.* Rome, 1960–61 (dispensa).

Bottari, Stefano. "Il Diario poetico di Michelangelo," in *La critica figurativa e l'estetica moderna* (Bari: Laterza, 1935), pp. 109–60.

Bouchaud, Pierre de. *Les Poésies de Michel-Ange et de Vittoria Colonna.* Paris, 1912.

Calero, Giuseppe, *Michelangelo poeta.* Turin, 1943.

Cambon, Glauco. "Sculptural Forms as Metaphysical Conceits in Michelangelo's Verse," *Sewanee Review,* LXX (1962), 155–65.

Chaleschi, Cattaneo B. *Le Rime di Michelangelo*. Prato, 1900.

Clements, Robert J. "Eye, Mind, and Hand in Michelangelo's Poetry," *Publications of the Modern Language Association*. New York, 1958, pp. 324–36.

Clements, Robert J. "Michelangelo as a Baroque Poet," *Publications of the Modern Language Association*. New York, 1961, pp. 182–92.

Clements, Robert J. "Another Muse for the Master," *Saturday Review*, July 6, 1963, pp. 33–34.

Clements, Robert J. "Berni and Michelangelo's Letters," *Italica*, Sept., 1964, pp. 266–80.

Clements, Robert J. "Il concetto del tempo nelle *Rime* di Michelangelo," *Acta* of Fourth Centenary Convegno of Michelangelo Studies, 1965.

Clements, Robert J. "Prayer and Confession in Michelangelo's Poetry," *Studies in Philology*, April, 1965.

Contini, G. "Il senso delle cose nella poesia di Michelangelo," *Rivista Rosminiana*, 1937.

Croce, Benedetto. *Poesia popolare e poesia d'arte*. Bari, 1946.

De Santis, Natale. *La lirica amorosa di Michelangelo Buonarroti*. Palermo, 1898.

Desplaces, Auguste. "Michel-Ange poète," *Revue de Paris*, XVIII (1840), 129–40.

Di Pino, G. "Le Rime di Michelangelo," *Umanità e stile* (Florence, 1957), pp. 101 ff.

Façon, N., *Michelangiolo Poet*. Bucharest, 1939.

Farinelli, Arturo. *Michelangelo e Dante, ed altri saggi*. Turin, 1918.

Farinelli, Arturo, "Michelangelo poeta," in *Raccolta di studi critici dedicata ad A. D'Ancona*. Florence, 1901.

Fattore, Ettore. *Michelangelo e Dante*. Florence, 1875.

Ferrero, Giuseppe Guido. *Il Petrarchismo del Bembo e le Rime di Michelangelo*. Turin, 1935.

Foerster, Karl. "Über Michelangelo als Dichter," *Die Muse*, IV (1822), 95–127.

Foscolo, Ugo. "Poems of Michel Angelo," *Retrospective Review*, XII (May, 1826). Reprinted in the *Edizione nazionale delle opere di Ugo Foscolo*, X (Florence, 1953) 468–91.

Galassi, G. "Plasticità di Michelangelo poeta," in *Michelangelo Buonarroti*. Florence, 1943, pp. 146 ff.

Gasparini, E. "La poesia di Michelangelo," *La cultura*, X, vii (1931).

Gengaro, M. L. "La 'poetica' di Michelangelo," *Acme* (Milan: Università statale), VI, fasc. 1 (1953), 3 ff.

Giannotti, Donato. *Dialogi de' giorni che Dante consumò nel cercare l'Inferno e 'l Purgatorio*. Florence, 1939.

Girardi, Enzo Noè, "Per l'edizione delle *Rime* di Michelangelo," *Rinascimento*, VI (June, 1955), 75 ff.

Girardi, Enzo Noè. "Due sestine ignote di Michelangelo," *Lettere italiane*, LI, 10 (1959), 333–38.

Girardi, Enzo Noè. "Michelangelo Buonarroti," offprint from *Letteratura italiana* (*I Minori*) Milan, 1961, pp. 841–71.

Girardi, Enzo Noè. *Studi sulle Rime di Michelangiolo*. Milan: Eroica, 1964.

Guasti, Cesare. *Alcune critiche tedesche sulla nuova edizione delle Rime di Michelangelo* (offprint). Rome, 1868.

Guerrisi, Michele. "La poesia e l'arte di Michelangelo," *Il Vasari*, XII (1941), 36–42.
Harrys, Herman. *Michelangelo's und Raffael's Gedichte*. Halle, 1906.
Insinga, Arturo. *Michelangelo poeta*. Palermo, 1919.
José, Alessandro. "Interpretazioni della poesia di Michelangelo," *Brutium*, 1958.
Ker, W. P. "The Poems of Michael Angelo," *Edinburgh Review* (1888), pp. 1–34.
Lang, Wilhelm. *Michelangelo als Dichter*. Stuttgart, 1861.
Lang, Wilhelm. *Die echte Gedichte Michelangelos*. Florence, 1863.
Lang, Wilhelm. *Michelangelos Gedichte*. Berlin, 1868.
Lang, Wilhelm. "Die Gedichte Michelangelos," *Preussische Jahrbücher*. Berlin, 1892.
Levi, David. *La mente di Michelangelo*. Milan, 1883.
Mann, Thomas. "La concezione dell'amore nella poesia di Michelangelo," *Lettere moderne*, I, 4 (Dec., 1950), 427–34.
Mariani, Valerio. *La poesia di Michelangelo*. Rome, 1941.
Mariani, Valerio. "Parole e creazione plastica in Michelangelo," *Acta* of Fourth Centenary Convegno of Michelangelo Studies (1965).
Misciatelli, Piero. *Vicino all'anima di Michelangelo*. 1911.
Nardini, B. "Poesia di Michelangelo," in *Dialoghi*, I (May–June, 1953), no. 2.
Oberdorfer, A. *Saggio su Michelangelo*. Palermo, 1913.
Orelli, Johann Kaspar. "Michelangelo Buonarroti als Dichter" (10 pp.). Zurich, 1810.
Orvieto, Angiolo. "Valutazioni della poesia di Michelangelo," *Il Marzocco*, May 17, 1931.
Papini, Giovanni. *La vita di Michelangiolo nella vita del suo tempo*. Milan, 1949.
Pascale, Vincenzo Italo. *Michelangelo Buonarroti poeta, studio letterario, storico, filosofico*. Naples, 1902.
Pater, Walter. "The Poetry of Michelangelo," in *The Renaissance*. London, 1873.
Sati, Riccardo M. "Interpretazioni della poesia di Michelangelo," *Il Vasari* (1941), pp. 36–42.
Saviotti, Gino. *La vita e le Rime di Michelangelo Buonarroti*. Livorno, 1916.
Scrivano, R. *Il manierismo nella letteratura del Cinquecento*. Padua, 1959.
Sturdza, Alexandru. *Michel-Ange poète et épistolier*. Paris, 1906.
Taruffi, Riccardo. *Michelangelo poeta* (lecture). Florence, 1875.
Taylor, John E. *Michelangelo Considered as a Philosophic Poet*. London, 1852.
Thomas, Gabriel. *Michel-Ange poète: Étude sur l'expression de l'amour platonique*. Paris-Nancy, 1892.
Tolnay, Charles de. *The Art and Thought of Michelangelo*. New York, 1964.
Trollope, Thomas A. *The Homes and Haunts of the Italian Poets: Michael Angelo*. London, 1878.
Varchi, Benedetto. *Due lezzioni, nella prima delle quali si dichiara un sonetto di M. Michelangelo Buonarroti*. Florence, 1549.
Varchi, Benedetto. *Orazione funerale nell'essequie di Michelagnolo*. Florence, 1564.

INDEX OF NAMES

Accolti, Bernardo, 8, 327–28, 331
Aeschylus, 25, 282
Aesop, 62
Alamanni, Luigi, 204–205, 283, 326
Alberti, Leon Battista, 8, 30, 77, 170, 228, 247, 278
Alciati, Andrea, 170–71
Aldovrandi, Giovan Francesco, 7, 317, 326
Ambrosius, Saint, 26, 314
Amendola, Giovanni, 18, 26, 84, 101, 177
Amico-Mantia, Antonio, 35, 196, 314, 322–23, 334
Ammannati, Bartolommeo, 206, 255
Anacreon, 22, 114, 330
Angiolieri, Cecco, 191, 266, 328
Angiolini, Bartolommeo, 60
Anguissola, Sofonisba, 206, 216
Apollonius of Athens, 12
Archadelt, Jacob, 4, 254, 308, 341
Archilochus, 205
Aretino, Pietro, 6, 8, 12, 30, 144–46, 161, 201, 208, 211–13, 227, 251, 259–60, 265
Ariosto, Ludovico, 8, 315, 333–34
Aristophanes, 189
Aristotle, 23, 65, 77, 95, 229, 306, 313
Armenini, Giovan Battista, 36, 76, 171
Atanagi, Dionigi, 5
Attavanti, Faustina Lucia Mancini, 14, 56, 73–74, 253, 290

Baldi, Accursio, 16
Bandinelli, Baccio, 99, 240, 243, 307
Bayazid, Sultan, 129–30, 138, 238, 244
Beccadelli, Lodovico, 4, 85–86, 182, 252, 256–58, 285, 319
Begarelli, Antonio, 68, 92
Bellori, Giovanni Battista, 64–65
Bembo, Pietro, xv, 8, 78, 228, 231, 261, 269, 314–15, 328
Berni, Francesco, xv, 4, 8–9, 12, 15, 22, 25–26, 30, 60, 68, 76, 92, 129–30, 229, 259–70, 278, 280–82, 290, 302, 315, 327, 332
Bernini, Lorenzo, 45, 91, 123, 163
Bertoldo Di Giovanni, 7, 66
Bevilacqua, Enrico, 4, 11, 26, 30, 98, 101–102, 187, 262, 296, 316, 334, 340
Bible, The, 26, 43, 104, 106, 109, 132, 160, 308–309, 314
Boccaccio, Giovanni, 192, 235, 260, 317, 324–25, 335
Boiardo, Matteo Maria, 111, 315
Bologna, Giovanni, 70
Bosch, Hieronymus, 56
Botticelli, Sandro, 7, 164, 170, 205
Bouchaud, Pierre de, 12, 23, 177, 325, 333, 338–39
Bramante, Donato, 91, 253, 314
Bridges, Robert, 336
Britten, Benjamin, 4, 337
Brueghel, Peter, 56
Brutus, Marcus Junius, 162, 243, 304, 316
Bunnett, Fanny Elizabeth, 65, 70, 103, 187, 297
Buonarroti, Buonarroto, 10, 14, 67, 182–83, 292, 301

Buonarroti, Filippo, 239
Buonarroti, Giovan Simone, 84, 95, 123, 222, 292, 299
Buonarroti, Gismondo, 123, 222
Buonarroti, Lionardo (brother), 53, 84, 303
Buonarroti, Lionardo (nephew), 16, 41, 67, 122, 182, 186, 258
Buonarroti, Lodovico, 7, 14, 23, 28, 47, 75, 94, 97, 134, 143, 183, 291, 300, 306
Buonarroti, Michelangelo Il Giovane, 16–18, 23–24, 35, 42, 56, 79, 90, 128, 130, 149–50, 159, 167, 293, 308 and *passim*
Burchiello, Domenico, 328
Burckhardt, Jacob, 60, 238
Buscaroli, Rezio, 120

Calderón de la Barca, Pedro, 39, 53, 143
Calero, Giuseppe, 203, 242, 313, 315, 333
Calvin, Jean, 42, 124, 294
Camelli, Antonio, 8, 129–30, 179
Caracci, The, 39, 340
Carnesecchi, Pietro, 56, 263–64
Caro, Annibale, 8, 73, 144, 253
Cartarus, 162
Castiglione, Baldassare, 4, 181, 201
Cato the Censor, Marcus Porcius, 7
Catullus, 136, 330
Cavalieri, Tommaso, 4, 9, 13, 22, 28, 45, 56, 62, 81, 103, 109–11, 113–15, 118–19, 122–23, 134, 141, 144–45, 179, 182, 185–88, 191, 197, 201, 204, 206–11, and *passim*
Cecchino dei Bracci, 6, 9, 14, 16–17, 20, 24, 28, 39, 49, 53, 55–56, 65–66, 74–75, 81–82, 96–97, 111, 121, 134–53, 185, 199, 206–207, 212–13, and *passim*
Cellini, Benvenuto, 39, 99, 131, 177, 240, 275, 307
Ceriello, G. R., vii, 29, 43, 76, 103, 142, 213, 241, 297, 329
Cervantes, Miguel de, vii, 53, 337
Cesis, Cardinal De, 212
Charles V, 238, 298
Cheney, Ednah Dow, 82, 291, 292
Chesneau, Henri, 154–57, 159
Christ, 11, 13, 26, 41–44, 49, 56, 62–63, 73, 84, 104, 109, 120, 122, 124–33, and *passim*
Cicero, Marcus Tullius, 8, 12, 171, 299
Clement VII, 56, 96, 108, 251–52, 260, 263–64
Colonna, Vittoria, 4, 11–13, 20, 33, 42, 45, 47, 60–61, 64–65, 67–68, 72–73, 83, 86, 94, 103, 107, 111, 115–16, 124, 132, 134, 141–42, 179, 182, 184–86, 188, 194–202, 206 and *passim*
Condivi, Ascanio, 8, 18, 80, 91, 107, 135, 141, 151, 185, 196, 209, 254, 263, 335
Conseil, Jean de, 3, 341
Crashaw, Richard, 44, 51, 55–56, 58
Croce, Benedetto, ix, 35, 339–41
Cuilich, Lucilla, 31–32

Dante Alighieri, 5, 7–8, 12, 14, 17, 25–26, 36, 43–44, 64, 67, 99, 101, 105, 121, 125, 127, 132, 134, 161–63, 184, 193, 197, 206, 232, 234, 315–19 and *passim*
Danti, Vincenzo, 64
d'Aubigné, Agrippa, 43, 54
Desportes, Philippe, 64, 338
de Tolnay, Charles, 18, 97, 112, 162, 178, 187, 242–43, 276, 279, 314, 340
Dolce, Lodovico, 30, 161, 259, 313
Donatello, 38, 66, 159
Doni, Anton Francesco, 98, 279
Donne, John, 285
Dossi, Dosso, 95
du Bellay, Joachim, 29, 129, 156, 233, 246, 330
du Bos, Abbé, 77
du Cerceau, Jacques Androuet, 155–57, 159
Dürer, Albrecht, 78
Dwight, J. S., 225

Eliot, T. S., 56
Ellis, Havelock, 144
Emerson, Ralph Waldo, vii, ix, 98, 190, 336
Equicola, Mario, 117

Fabriano, Gilio da, 227
Fabrizio, Richard, 336
Façon, N., 201, 314, 339
Farinelli, Arturo, 11, 23, 26, 36, 161, 249, 315, 319, 325
Fattucci, Giovan Francesco, 3–4, 26, 200, 211–12, 252, 260, 290
Febo di Poggio, 20, 28, 45, 56, 62, 103, 111, 115, 118–19, 134, 144–45, 179,

182, 185, 206–208, 210, 212–15, 229, 254, 256, 321
Ferrero, Giuseppe, 35, 314, 334
Festa, Constanzo, 3, 341
Ficino, Marsilio, 7–8, 64, 76, 78–79, 184, 187, 191, 228, 232, 234, 236, 262, 314
Figiovanni, Giovanbattista, 10, 108, 223
Filicaia, Vincenzo da, 100
Foerster, Karl, 335
Foscolo, Ugo, 17, 25, 64, 101, 196, 278, 315, 333, 335, 337
Francis I, 62, 138, 238, 243–44, 251, 253, 260, 338
Freud, Sigmund, 144, 146
Frey, Carl, viii, 6, 12, 18–19, 23, 29–30, 35, 52, 62, 74, 90–91, 99, 104, 139, 141–42, 148, 213, 232, 241, 251, 253, 279 and *passim*

Galilei, Galileo, 64
Galli, Jacopo, 14
Gautier, Théophile, 25, 64
Ghiberti, Lorenzo, 66
Ghirlandaio, Domenico, 7, 66, 159, 202, 282
Giannotti, Donato, 4–9, 11–12, 15–16, 31, 33, 35, 72, 96, 99, 106, 134–36, 139, 146–47, 171, 180, 182, 187, 198, 207, 223 and *passim*
Gié, Maréchal de, 95, 105, 155, 238
Gigante, Antonio, 335
Gilbert, Creighton, vii, 152, 334, 337
Giotto di Bondone, 118, 282, 313, 320
Giovanni di Benedetto da Pistoia, 12, 23, 92, 128, 130, 246, 252–53, 268–69, 318
Girardi, Enzo, viii, 6–7, 9–10, 12, 16–20, 29, 33–35, 62, 67, 70, 83, 91, 99, 108, 111, 128, 150, 168, 213, 215, 241, 254, 260 and *passim*
Goethe, Wolfgang von, 112–13, 193
Goldscheider, Ludwig, 110, 118–19, 215, 278, 314, 317, 340
Góngora, Luis de, 53
Goya, Francisco de, 184
Greco, El, 38–39, 44
Grésy, Eugène, 154, 156
Grimm, Hermann, 18, 30, 98, 135, 144, 202, 213, 334–35
Grinnell-Milne, G., 68, 337
Guarini, Battista, 282, 283
Guasti, Cesare, 17–19, 29, 46, 74, 90, 128, 137, 150–51, 166, 213, 221, 239, 241, 323
Guicciardini, Francesco, 26, 314
Guinizelli, Guido, 195
Guittone D'Arezzo, 205

Hall, S. Elizabeth, ix, 66, 72, 90, 92, 102, 104, 108, 126–27, 187, 203, 246, 255, 257, 286, 337
Hatzfeld, Helmut, 40, 53, 340
Hervey, Christopher, 100, 336
Hollanda, Francisco de, 25, 36, 43, 63, 65, 76–77, 95, 109, 128, 182, 244, 261, 282, 338
Homer, 8, 177, 299, 314–15, 341
Horace, 8, 22, 25, 71, 101, 180, 205, 207, 267, 281, 313, 321
Horapollo, 162, 170
Hutton, James, 98

Insinga, Arturo, 7, 142, 164, 184, 244, 282, 314, 327–28, 334–35

Jacopone da Todi, 131
Julius II, 11, 13, 28, 42, 52, 56, 73, 75, 90–91, 105–108, 128, 162, 171, 182, 202, 239, 245, 252–53, 286, 290, 298, 302

Ker, W. P., 338

Landino, Cristoforo, 117, 316
Leo the Jew, 234, 314
Leonardo da Vinci, 27, 38, 61, 77, 151, 172, 184, 196, 201, 247, 278, 315, 329, 337
Leoni, Leone, 160
Leopardi, Giacomo, 340
Lomazzo, Giovan Paolo, 30, 64, 87, 181, 262, 275, 298
Longfellow, Henry W., vii, 64, 85, 200, 217, 273, 296, 336–37
Loyola, Ignatius, 40, 51, 226, 261
Lucian, 117
Lucretius Carus, Titus, 8, 118, 314
Lungo, Isidoro del, 26
Luther, Martin, 42, 124, 261, 263, 298

Maccius, Paulus, 171

Machiavelli, Niccolò, 8, 102–103, 106, 135, 238
Maggiori, Alessandro, 18
Mantegna, Andrea, 91, 329
Marco da Siena, 275
Marguerite de Navarre, 44, 330
Mariani, Valerio, 26, 80, 104, 108, 142, 160, 198, 204, 339
Marino, Giambattista, 51, 102, 157, 282
Marot, Clément, 29
Martelli, Niccolò, 62
Masaccio, 118, 282, 313
Medici, Allessandro dei, 96, 99, 111, 238, 240, 304
Medici, Cosimo dei (Duke), 85, 99, 138, 240, 307
Medici, Cosimo dei (The Elder), 228
Medici, Giuliano dei (Duke), 96–97
Medici, Ippolito dei, 263–64
Medici, Lorenzino dei, 96, 99, 243, 259, 304
Medici, Lorenzo dei (Il Magnifico), 7–8, 15, 76, 95, 101, 168, 179, 184, 206, 228–29, 234, 238–39, 252, 269, 282, 284, 292, 325–27, 331
Melchiori, Giorgio, 100, 336
Metastasio, Pietro, 114
Milanesi, Gaetano, 147–48, 251
Milton, John, 43
Mini, Antonio, 70, 77
Molière, 10, 181, 189
Momigliano, Attilio, 36
Montaiglon, Anatole de, 157
Montaigne, Michel de, 102, 200, 288
Morgan, Charles, 104
Mourgues, Odette de, 40

Navagero, Andrea, 330
Norton, Charles Eliot, vii, 135, 336

Ovid, 8, 26, 118–19, 190, 314, 330

Pacioli, Luca, 78
Palladio, Andrea, 8
Panofsky, Erwin, 61, 170, 236, 280, 349
Papini, Giovanni, 5, 18, 23, 42, 135, 138, 142, 144, 152, 182, 199, 202, 206, 212, 252–53, 267, 292, 334
Pascale, Vincenzo, 12, 28, 36, 135, 202, 242, 266, 315, 317, 323, 325, 334
Pater, Walter, 196, 337, 339
Paul III, 26, 77, 227, 251
Perini, Gherardo, 45, 102, 110–12, 118, 144–45, 206–208, 211–12, 215, 253, 321
Perugino, Il, 184
Petrarch, Francis, 5, 7–8, 17, 24, 26, 32, 36, 46–47, 51, 56, 83, 102, 104, 110, 112, 118, 128, 136, 139, 141, 149, 170, 184, 188, 200, 206, 234, 319–24, and *passim*
Petrarchism, 23, 27–28, 35–36, 45–46, 74, 142, 206, 319–24
Petreo, Antonio, 96, 100, 106, 240
Piccoli, Valentino, 24–25
Pico della Mirandola, 7, 78, 117, 210, 228, 234
Pike, Warburton, 86, 98
Pindar, 22, 72, 280, 313
Pino, Paolo, 30, 36, 247
Pio da Carpi, Ridolfo, 294
Planudean Anthology, 8
Plato, 8, 26, 34, 63–65, 67, 73, 184, 228–37, 268
Platonism, 13, 24–26, 28, 34–35, 42, 45, 53, 63–65, 73, 76–79, 86, 119, 144, 150, 152, 162, 179, 185, 189 and *passim*
Pliny, 8
Plotinus, 8, 78, 228, 230, 314
Plutarch, 8
Pole, Reginald, 256
Polidori, F.-L., 150
Politian, 7–8, 26, 93, 111–12, 164, 194, 204, 206, 228, 235, 282–83, 285, 315, 321, 325–26, 331
Pontanus, Jovianus, 129
Pontormo, Jacopo da, 110
Porrino, Gandolfo, 73–74, 252–53
Praz, Mario, 40, 46
Priscianese, Francesco, 7, 31, 106, 149
Procacci, Ugo, 151
Pythagoras, 8, 247

Quevedo, Francisco de, 44, 46

Rabelais, François, 165
Raffaello da Urbino, 13, 36, 73, 90–91, 161, 170, 181, 184, 253, 264, 267
Ramsden, E. H., 3, 148, 153, 212, 292
Redig de Campos, 18
Rembrandt van Rijn, 53, 184

Remstein, Donald, 112, 120, 194
Reynolds, Joshua, 25
Riccio, Luigi del, 3–4, 6, 9, 11–16, 19, 28, 31, 33–35, 69, 74, 84, 91, 93, 96, 99, 106, 134–41, 144, 146–50, 178, 182–83, 189–90, and *passim*
Rilke, Rainer Maria, vii, 30, 60, 334–35, 340
Ripa, Cesare, 162, 164, 166, 170–72
Robb, Nesca, ix, 26, 69, 145, 228, 231, 233, 236, 337
Robertet, Florimond de, 154, 158
Rodin, Auguste, 178
Rolland, Romain, 135, 182, 187
Ronsard, Pierre de, 17, 25, 154–57, 159
Roscoe, Mrs. Henry, 61
Rosselli, Piero, 92

Saavedra Faxardo, 64, 339
Saavedra, Venegas de, 157
Sadoletus, Jacopus, 8, 156
Sanborn, Franklin, 101
Sangallo, Antonio, 100, 165
Sangallo, Francesco, 38
Sangallo, Giuliano, 38
Sannazaro, Jacopo, 8, 26, 286, 314
Santayana, George, vii, ix, 208, 211, 232, 336–37
Sapegno, Natalino, 36, 341
Sappho, 8, 80, 194
Sasso, Pamfilo, 111, 314
Saviotti, Gino, 23, 101–102, 268–69
Savonarola, Girolamo, 13, 26, 28, 42–43, 56, 61, 78, 95, 104, 122, 129, 198, 238–39, 261, 288, 290, 314
Scaliger, Julius-Caesar, 29
Schoenberg, Arnold, 289
Schongauer, Martin, 282, 313
Sebastiano del Piombo, 2, 4, 9, 22, 76, 92, 108–109, 177, 206–207, 252, 260–65, 283, 290, 301
Serafino d'Aquila, 71, 111, 314–15, 328
Shakespeare, William, 6, 93, 101, 187, 199, 206, 231, 308, 314
Sidney, Philip, 101
Signorelli, Luca, 282, 317
Silla, Emperor, 243
Solari, Cristoforo, 33
Southey, Robert, vii, 316, 336–37
Speroni, Sperone, 29
Spitzer, Leo, 52
Stampa, Gaspara, 35
Steinmann, Ernst, 38
Strauss, Richard, 4, 336
Strozzi, Filippo, 243
Strozzi, Giovanni, 4–5, 23, 64, 96, 98–99, 156, 240
Swift, Jonathan, 167
Symonds, John Addington, 74, 110, 144, 148, 198, 210, 213, 224, 272–73, 288, 337

Tasso, Torquato, 53, 282, 335
Taylor, John E., ix, 199, 233, 317, 336–37, 339, 340
Tebaldeo, Antonio, 71, 314–15, 328
Tennyson, Alfred, 202
Teresa, Saint, 44–46, 51, 56, 58, 275
Tesauro, Emmanuele, 98
Theocritus, 286
Thode, Henry, 18, 335
Tintoretto, Il, 39
Titian, Vecelli, 73, 184, 267
Tolstoy, Leo, 227, 260
Tommaso di Celano, 26, 41, 52, 120, 124, 131, 314
Torrigiani, Pietro, 179
Tromboncino, Bartolommeo, 3–4, 20, 341

Urbano, Piero [also Pietro], 17, 252
Urbino (Francesco Amadori), 14, 16, 33, 47, 81, 134, 138, 140, 143, 206, 257–58, 290–91
Urbino, Duke of, 147, 261, 292

Valdés, Juan de, 41, 123–24, 201, 225
Valeriano, Piero, 171
Varchi, Benedetto, xv, 5–6, 8, 12, 20, 26, 64, 77–78, 134–35, 148, 150, 211, 229, 232, 243, 261, 263, 301, 315
Vasari, Giorgio, 4–5, 9, 12, 14, 18, 72, 76, 78, 85–86, 91–92, 102, 107, 118, 123, 131, 134–35, 141, 145, 169, 171, 182, 209, 242, 246, and *passim*
Velásquez, Diego de, 73
Venturi, Adolfo, 12
Vergil, 8, 118, 232, 314
Veronese, Paolo, 43, 197
Verrocchio, Andrea del, 159
Villani, Giovanni, 8, 26, 314
Visconti, Gasparo, 70

Vitruvius Pollio, Marcus, 8, 38, 76, 78, 251
Vives, Luis, 39
Voltaire, 167
Volterra, Daniele da, 17, 60

Weisbach, Werner, 40
Wilson, Heath, 148
Wittkower, Rudolf, 18, 38
Wolf, Hugo, 4, 336
Wölfflin, Heinrich, 40
Wordsworth, William, vii, 81, 125, 181, 190, 200, 222, 227, 248, 282, 284, 296, 336

Zeuxis, 199

INDEX OF MICHELANGELO'S WORKS OF ART

SCULPTURE

Bacchus 57, 89, 282, 325
Brutus 13, 99, 178, 240, 243, 317
Cecchino dei Bracci (Tomb) 72, 74, 81, 96, 137–38, 158, 178, 253
Centauromachia 7, 282, 325
Christ, The Risen 17, 127
Crucifixion of Santo Spirito 43, 329
David (bronze) 10, 32, 56, 95, 129, 155–60, 167, 238, 277, 279, 338
David (marble) 158, 166–67, 178, 203, 242, 277
Deposition (Florence) 57, 113, 124, 131–33, 178, 223
Disciples for Sta. Maria del Fiore 7
Giuliano, Duke 14, 24, 53, 73, 95, 113, 151, 161, 178, 204, 279, 304
John, Saint 43, 107
Julius II (bronze) 20, 71, 73, 90–91, 128, 182, 301
Leah 278, 317
Lorenzo, Duke 73, 113, 151, 161, 178, 204, 279
Madonna della Febbre (Pietà) 102, 158, 161, 279, 329
Matthew, Saint 8, 39, 43, 64
Moses 55, 107, 162, 178
Nicodemus 43, 56, 113, 131–32, 178, 223
Night (Notte) 11, 14, 24, 64, 90, 98–104, 145, 162, 172, 241, 279
Night and Day 53, 56, 68, 93–97, 101, 158, 304
Palestrina Pietà 66, 89, 329
Paul, Saint 107
Piccolomini Altar 178

Pitti tondo 215
Proculus, Saint 43, 178
Rachel 317
Rondanini Pietà 66, 89, 329
Self-Portraits 178
Slave "Atlante," The 64, 307
Slaves 106–108, 307
Times of Day 14, 24, 90, 93–97
Victory (Victor) 108–10, 178, 211

PAINTING

Adam (Creation of Man) 57, 167–68, 303
Ancestors of Christ 155, 186, 278
Bartholomew, Saint 15, 39, 43, 48, 57, 89, 113, 143, 178
Battle of Cascina 8, 129, 215, 282
Brazen Serpent Spandrel 271
Christus Judex 11, 28, 45, 57, 124–30, 178, 210, 226–27, 242, 245, 294, 307, 309, 329
Conversion of Paul 234
Creation of Sun and Moon 90, 93–97, 234
Crucifixion of Peter 178
Cumaean Sibyl 39, 55
Damned Souls (Dannati) 75, 169, 298
David and Goliath Spandrel 159, 167
Doni Madonna 145, 282
Esther 162, 186, 241
Expulsion and Fall of Man 116, 271, 282
Eve, Creation of 282
Haman 38, 116, 186, 227
Holophernes 178, 186
Jeremiah 104–106, 178, 308–309
Jonah 282
Judith 162, 178, 186, 241
Last Judgement 11, 17, 39, 41–43, 45, 48–49, 52, 56–57, 89, 92, 94, 113, 120–24, 131, 161, 169, 210–11, 226–27, 249, 253, 261, 271, 288, 307, 317, 330
Leda and the Swan 109, 186, 243
Noah Triptych 75, 276, 282
Nude Youths (Ignudi) 75, 145, 280, 282
Pauline Chapel 282
Self-Portraits 178
Separation of Light and Darkness 90, 93–97, 276
Sibyls 168
Sistine Ceiling vii, 3, 14–15, 38–39, 57, 75, 91–92, 94, 102, 113, 130, 140, 145, 156, 162, 196, 233, 241, 268, 278

DRAWINGS

Annunciation (British Museum) 190, 192
Archers and Herm (Arcieri, Saettatori) 56, 112–18, 145, 178, 186, 218, 277, 305
Baccanalia dei Putti 56, 118
Crow 55
Crucifixion for Vittoria Colonna 227, 278, 330
Dream of Human Life 39, 53, 57, 234, 303, 306
Ganymede 118–19, 186
Lazarus 108–109, 234, 261
Madonna Nursing Son 168
Madonna, Christ Child, and Saint Ann 27, 320
Male Nude, two Putti, Leg Study 215
Noli Me Tangere 110, 243
Phaeton 119–20, 161, 168, 186, 214, 234, 282, 314
Putto Urinating 212, 260
Resurrection of Christ 234
Running Satyr 186
Sacrifice of Isaac 234
Samson and Delilah 185
Skeleton 287
Study of Lady (British Museum) 204
Tityus 118–19, 168, 186, 234, 314
Venus, Mars, and Cupid 110–12, 185, 305
Venus with Cupid 110–12
Woman with Sagging Breasts, *Fica* Gesture, and Coifed Male Head 89, 172, 178, 201

ARCHITECTURE

Capitoline Stairs 234
Fortifications of Florence 239–40
Julius II, Tomb of 42, 107–108, 135, 141, 147, 260
Laurentian Library 194
Laurentian Library Stairs 10, 234, 255
Medici Chapel 95–97, 101, 108, 228
St. Peters, Floor plans of 223
San Lorenzo, Façade of 3, 62, 290

INDEX OF THE *RIME*

(*Note:* Spellings correspond to those in index of Girardi edition; a poem's number in Girardi edition precedes first line below; pages following line refer to pages in present volume.)

98	A che più debb'i' omai l'intensa voglia	56, 110, 150, 211
156	A l'alta tuo lucente dïadema	34, 197
215	A la terra la terra e l'alma al cielo	48, 75, 139
97	Al cor di zolfo, a la carne di stoppa,	62, 77, 80, 271
A 5	Al dolce mormorar d'un fiumicello	283
299	Al zucchero, a la mula, a le candele,	10, 249, 255
158	Amor, la morte a forza	47, 49, 51, 55, 216
49	Amor, la tuo beltà non è mortale:	24, 192, 232
262	Amor, se tu se' dio,	35, 217
86	Ancor che 'l cor già mi premesse tanto	23, 47, 75, 94, 97, 183, 292, 306
118	Ancor che 'l cor già molte volte sia	51–52, 54, 216
193	A pena prima aperti gli vidd'io	74, 137–39, 147, 150, 188
281	Arder sole' nel freddo ghiaccio il foco	50, 219, 272
134	Beati voi che su nel ciel godete	216, 305
45	Ben doverrieno al sospirar mie tanto	47, 94, 247
100	Ben fu, temprando il ciel tuo vivo raggio,	120, 214, 277
99	Ben mi dove' con sì felice sorte,	56, 115, 120, 277
166	Ben posson gli occhi mie presso e lontano	57, 65, 191, 230–31
69	Ben provvide natura, né conviene	83
259	Ben può talor col mie 'rdente desio	82, 209
292	Ben sarien dolce le preghiere mie	222, 294
120	Ben tempo saria omai	52, 115, 301
114	Ben vinci ogni durezza	83, 192

293 Carico d'anni e di peccati pieno 54, 119, 126, 294
247 Caro m'è 'l sonno, e più l'esser di sasso, 5, 14, 24, 56, 98, 127, 244, 336–37
A 10 . . . che Febo alle . . . nora 215
22 Che fie di me? che vo' tu far di nuovo 50, 113–14
226 Che l'alma viva, i' che qui morto sono 49, 143, 306
A 26 Che mal si può amar ben chi non si vede 232
A 39 Che posso o debbo o vuoi ch'io pruovi ancora, 192
53 Chi di notte cavalca, el dì conviene 51, 190, 304
7 Chi è quel che per forza a te mi mena, 54, 116, 192
278 Chi non vuol delle foglie 152, 190, 308
199 Chi qui morto mi piange indarno spera, 49, 55, 139–40
21 Chiunche nasce a morte arriva 27, 29, 289
224 Chiusi ha qui gli occhi, e 'l corpo e l'alma sciolta 139
218 Col sol de' Bracci il sol della natura, 29, 139
104 Colui che fece, e non di cosa alcuna, 94, 102–103
9 Colui che 'l tutto fe', fece ogni parte 63, 80, 322
12 Com'arò dunche ardire 3, 20, 48, 54, 107, 192, 327
48 Come fiamma più cresce più contesa 275, 308, 318
264 Come portato ho già più tempo in seno 46
8 Come può esser ch'io non sia più mio? 32, 54, 117, 191, 327
239 Com'esser, donna, può quel c'alcun vede 48, 63, 65, 71–72, 280
85 Com'io ebbi la vostra, signor mio, 9, 56, 60, 106, 263–66, 280–81, 302, 332
133 Condotto da molt'anni all'ultim'ore, 47, 51, 86, 226, 296–97, 306
148 Con più certa salute 190, 195, 197, 303
282 Con tanta servitù, con tanto tedio 54, 61, 280
172 Costei pur si delibra, 10, 20, 44, 68, 71–72, 84, 163, 179, 205, 278
142 Credo, perc'ancor forse 113, 217–18
17 Crudele, acerbo e dispietato core, 51, 93, 188, 301, 305
70 Crudele stella, anzi crudele arbitrio 303

275 Dagli alti monti e d'una gran ruina, 65–66
30 Dagli occhi del mie ben si parte e vola 191
248 Dal ciel discese, e col mortal suo, poi 43, 105, 245–46, 301, 304, 316
206 Dal ciel fu la beltà mia diva e 'ntera, 139–40
78 Dal dolce pianto al doloroso riso, 188
119 Dal primo pianto all'ultimo sospiro, 192, 197
94 D'altrui pietoso e sol di sé spietato 48
129 Da maggior luce e da più chiara stella 104, 197, 199

A 3 Davitte colla fromba e io coll'arco 158
203 De' Bracci nacqui, e dopo 'l primo pianto, 139, 189
147 Deh dimmi, Amor, se l'alma di costei 4, 222, 308
274 Deh, fammiti vedere in ogni loco! 291
39 Del fiero colpo e del pungente strale 51, 113, 193
220 Deposto ha qui Cecchin sì nobil salma 139
A 9 Deus in nomine tuo salvum me fac 221
287 Di giorno in giorno insin da' mie prim'anni, 224
42 Dimmi ni grazia, Amor, se gli occhi mei 79, 198, 230
295 Di morte certo, ma non già dell'ora, 49, 104, 294
301 Di più cose s'attristan gli occhi mei, 105, 124, 126, 294, 309
271 Di te con teco, Amor molt'anni sono 233
15 Di te me veggo e di lontan mi chiamo 190, 300
A 7 . . . dolce stanza nell'inferno 106, 301
254 Donn', a me vecchio e grave, 57, 188, 191, 318
16 D'un oggetto leggiadro e pellegrino, 52

75 Egli è pur troppo a rimirarsi intorno 278
35 El ciglio col color non fere el volto 76–77
14 El Dì e la Notte parlano, e dicono: 14, 24, 56, 68, 96, 304
214 Era la vita vostra il suo splendore: 74, 139
113 Esser non può già ma' che gli occhi santi 192, 194

A 16 Febbre, fianchi, dolor, morbi, occhi e denti 179, 259
79 Felice spirto, che con zelo ardente, 60
66 Forse perché d'altrui pietà mi vegna, 47, 54, 223–24
27 Fuggite, amanti, amor, fuggite 'l foco; 112, 216, 324

285 Giunto è già 'l corso della vita mia, 44, 47, 85, 106, 116, 120–21, 141, 219, 277, 296
286 Gl'infiniti pensier mie d'error pieni, 225
107 Gli occhi mie vaghi delle cose belle 231–32
146 Gli sguardi che tu strazi 192–94
196 Gran ventura qui morto esser mi veggio: 139
3 Grato e felice, a' tuo feroci mali 9, 113, 192, 277

24 I' fe' degli occhi porta al mie veneno, 114, 277
223 I' fu' Cecchin mortale e or son divo: 139–40, 150
225 I' fu' de' Bracci, e qui dell'alma privo 139
202 I' fu' de' Bracci, e se ritratto e privo 139, 241, 280

23	I' fu', già son molt'anni, mille volte	114, 116, 277, 300
5	I' ho già fatto un gozzo in questo stento,	15, 28, 48, 91–92, 158, 246, 259, 268, 277
71	I' l'ho, vostra mercè, per ricevuto	162, 246, 252, 268
112	Il mio refugio e 'l mio ultimo scampo	50, 231
80	I' mi credetti, il primo giorno ch'io	50, 314, 329
90	I' mi son caro assai più ch'i' non soglio;	70–71, 109, 115, 190
108	Indarno spera, come 'l vulgo dice,	277
37	In me la morte, in te la vita mia;	10, 225
177	In noi vive e qui giace la divina	56
139	In più leggiadra e men pietosa spoglia	193
65	In quel medesmo tempo ch'io v'adoro,	117
A 36	In tal misero stato, il vostro viso	214
54	Io crederrei, se tu fussi di sasso,	15, 45, 51, 65, 71, 107, 191, 203, 235, 259, 268–69, 274, 305, 308
110	Io dico a voi, c'al mondo avete dato	288
147	Io dico che fra noi, potenti dei	4, 241
74	I' piango, i' ardo, i' mi consumo, e 'l core	114–15, 307
267	I sto rinchiuso come la midolla	15, 27, 43, 47, 49–50, 53–54, 65, 85, 106–107, 179, 181, 219, 234, 239, 249, 266–68
201	I' temo più, fuor degli anni e dell'ore	140, 143
55	I' t'ho comprato, ancor che molto caro,	255–56
183	La beltà che qui giace al mondo vinse	82, 139
197	La carne terra e qui l'ossa mie, prive	46, 48, 143, 147
13	La fama tiene gli epitaffi a giacere;	97, 279
279	La forza d'un bel viso a che mi sprona?	42, 190, 200
136	L'alma, che sparge e versa	180, 193, 226, 308
187	L'alma di dentro di fuor non vedea,	139
280	L'alma inquieta e confusa in sé non truova	44, 132, 224
A 17	La m'arde e lega e temmi e parm'un zucchero	10, 326
167	La morte, Amor, del mie medesmo loco,	117, 306
A 1	La morte è 'l fin d'una prigione scura	320
178	La nuova alta beltà che 'n ciel terrei	41, 47, 55, 74, 254
263	La nuova beltà d'una	122, 218
43	La ragion meco si lamenta e dole,	189, 225, 242, 276, 301, 322
A 13	L'ardente nodo ov'io fui d'ora in ora,	320
A 15	Laudate parvoli	221
34	La vita del mie amor non è 'l cor mio,	195, 230
288	Le favole del mondo m'hanno tolto	86, 141, 256, 293

155 Le grazie tua e la fortuna mia 35, 189
115 Lezi, vezzi, carezze, or, feste e perle, 55

A 41 Mal fa chi tanta fé sì tosto oblia 320
44 Mentre c'alla beltà ch'i' vidi in prima 79, 186, 230, 305
135 Mentre c'al tempo la mie vita fugge, 191, 193, 226, 303
132 Mentre che 'l mie passato m'è presente, 86, 97, 226, 287, 296, 306
73 Mentre del foco son scacciata e priva, 180, 308
255 Mentre i begli occhi giri, 186, 306
294 Mentre m'attrista e duol, parte m'è caro 5, 41, 44, 122, 133, 294
176 Mestier non era all'alma tuo beltate 107, 117
18 Mille rimedi invan l'anima tenta: 162, 189
1 Molti anni fassi qual felice, in una 8
237 Molto diletta al gusto intero e sano 67–68, 82

19 Natura ogni valore 52, 54
241 Negli anni molti e nelle molte pruove, 65, 69
251 Nel dolce d'una immensa cortesia, 149, 183
171 Nella memoria delle cose belle 272
169 Nel mie 'rdente desio, 192
232 Non altrimenti contro a sé cammina 48, 50, 189, 218
A 24 Non altrimenti Dedal si riscosse, 120, 234, 276, 281
238 Non è non degna l'alma, che n'attende 249
289 Non è più bassa o vil cosa terrena 41, 44, 121, 132, 293–94
231 Non è più tempo, Amor, che 'l cor m'infiammi, 192, 216, 219
260 Non è sempre di colpa aspra e mortale 53, 144–45, 235
130 Non è senza periglio 47, 192, 305
298 Non fur men lieti che turbati e tristi 22, 43–44, 132, 202, 226, 329–30
149 Non ha l'abito intero 69
151 Non ha l'ottimo artista alcun concetto 5, 14, 26, 64, 135, 338
150 Non men gran grazia, donna, che gran doglia 304
116 Non mi posso tener, né voglio, Amore, 303
302 Non più per altro da me stesso togli 44, 124, 126, 132, 219, 294
82 Non posso altra figura immaginarmi 48
149 Non posso non mancar d'ingegno e d'arte 197, 329
186 Non può per morte già chi qui mi serra 49, 82, 121–22, 139
283 Non può, Signor mie car, la fresca e verde 54
153 Non pur d'argento o d'oro 52, 66, 274
127 Non pur la morte, ma 'l timor di quella 51, 216, 288, 306
109 Non sempre a tutti è sì pregiato e caro 180, 188
76 Non so se s'è la desïata luce 50–51, 211–12, 236

105 Non vider gli occhi miei cosa mortale 81, 119, 185, 233
A 40 Non vi si pensa quanto sangue costa 163, 318
182 Non volse morte non ancider senza 33, 82, 139
175 No' salda, Amor, de' tuo dorati strali 115–16, 218, 239, 277
67 Nuovo piacere e di maggiore stima 15, 27, 75, 163–66, 169–72, 181, 221, 239, 248, 283–85

229 Occhi mie, siate certi 199
81 Ogni cosa ch'i' veggio mi consiglia 35, 189
29 Ogn'ira, ogni miseria e ogni forza, 191
103 Ogni van chiuso, ogni coperto loco, 102
243 Ognor che l'idol mio si rappresenta 52, 194
51 Oilmè, oilmè, ch'i' son tradito 47–48, 86, 121, 163, 278, 290, 322
36 Oltre qui fu, dove 'l mie amor mi tolse, 194, 321–22
102 O notte, o dolce tempo, benché nero, 100–101
162 Ora in sul destro, ora in sul manco piede 50, 197
269 Or d'un fier ghiaccio, or d'un ardente foco, 52, 55, 105, 217, 278, 301

276 Passa per gli occhi al core in un momento 27, 208, 318
144 Passo inanzi a me stesso 47, 94
291 Penso e ben so c'alcuna colpa preme, 224
141 Perc'all'alta mie speme è breve e corta, 190, 304
212 Perc'all'altru' ferir non have pari 139
91 Perc'all'estremo ardore 192
101 Perché Febo non torce e non distende 103–104
268 Perché l'età ne 'nvola 47, 217
168 Perché 'l mezzo di me che dal ciel viene 50, 61, 232
181 Perché ne' volti offesi non entrasti 139
28 Perché pur d'ora in ora mi lusinga 27, 189
257 Perché sì tardi e perché non più spesso 52, 95, 103, 216
252 Perch'è troppo molesta, 186, 193
230 Perché tuo gran bellezze al mondo sieno 236
300 Per croce e grazia e per diverse pene 180, 257, 291
159 Per esser manco, alta signora, indegno 86–87, 197
164 Per fido esemplo alla mia vocazione 65, 80, 146, 208
249 Per molti, donna, anzi per mille amanti 14, 56, 96, 99, 162, 240–41
265 Per non s'avere a ripigliar da tanti 199, 281, 329, 332
161 Per qual mordace lima 41, 44, 47, 49, 55, 125, 198
174 Per quel che di vo,' donna, di fuor veggio, 35, 192–93
106 Per ritornar là donde venne fora, 35, 46, 62, 75, 81, 146, 208, 233

207	Per sempre a morte, e prima a voi fu' dato	139–40
157	Pietosa e dolce aita	6, 189, 305
204	Più che vivo non ero, morto sono	29, 139, 304
138	Porgo umilmente all'aspro giogo il collo,	46, 108
266	Qual maraviglia è, se prossim'al foco	55, 277, 327
40	Quand'amor lieto al ciel levarmi è volto	189
26	Quand'avvien c'alcun legno non difenda	191
47	Quand'el ministro de' sospir mie tanti	32–33, 200, 280–81
25	Quand'il servo il signor d'aspra catena,	108, 217, 239, 267, 307
38	Quanta dolcezza al cor per gli occhi porta	82, 192
250	Quante dirne si de' non si può dire,	105, 245, 302, 316–17, 337
163	Quante più fuggo e odio ognor me stesso,	198–99, 300
123	Quante più par che 'l mie mal maggior senta	83
143	Quant'ognor fugge il giorno che mi resta	47, 52, 218, 273, 308
11	Quanto sare' men doglia il morir presto	193, 215
4	Quanto si gode, lieta e ben contesta	10, 112, 202–205, 326
92	Quantunche 'l tempo ne costringa e sproni	45, 218
258	Quantunche sie che la beltà divina	95, 305
10	Qua si fa elmi di calici e spade,	20, 49, 127–30, 239, 245, 264, 279
124	Questa mie donna è sì pronta e ardita,	51, 106, 193, 301
208	Qui chiuso è 'l sol di c'ancor piangi e ardi:	106, 302
221	Qui giace il Braccio, e men non si desia	139
216	Qui serro il Braccio e suo beltà divina,	139
209	Qui sol per tempo convien posi e dorma	75, 143
189	Qui son chiusi i begli occhi, che aperti	139
184	Qui son de' Bracci, deboli a l'impresa	56, 144
190	Qui son morto creduto; e per conforto	139, 147
185	Qui son sepulto, e poco innanzi nato	139
222	Qui stese il Braccio e colse acerbo il frutto	56, 139, 144, 322
194	Qui vuol mie sorte c'anzi tempo i' dorma,	139, 188
A 11	Raccoglietele al piè del tristo cesto	318
95	Rendete agli occhi mei, o fonte o fiume,	27, 285–86
227	Ripreso ha 'l divin Braccio il suo bel velo:	55, 121
A 4	Rott'è l'alta colonna e 'l verde lauro	56, 239, 279, 319

256 S'alcuna parte in donna è che sie bella, 35, 83, 305
160 S'alcun legato è pur dal piacer molto, 239, 307
52 S'alcun se stesso al mondo ancider lice, 24, 51, 107, 276, 293, 324
284 S'a tuo nome ho concetto alcuno imago, 72, 288
296 S'avvien che spesso il gran desir prometta 35, 51, 287, 294, 301, 335
217 S'avvien come fenice mai rinnuovi 276
290 Scarco d'un'importuna e greve salma, 5, 44–45, 123, 125, 132, 151, 226–27, 294
236 Se ben concetto ha la divina parte 34, 65, 70
A 37 Se ben talor tuo gran pietà m'assale, 193, 216
277 Se con lo stile o coi colori avete 254, 332
145 Se costei gode, e tu solo, Amor, vivi 9, 53, 304
173 Se dal cor lieto divien bello il volto, 63, 80, 178, 280
188 Se dalla morte è vinta la natura 50, 139
233 Se da' prim'anni aperto un lento e poco 9, 52, 271–72
198 Se fussin, perch'i' viva un'altra volta, 140
117 S'egli è che 'l buon desio 54, 299–300, 324
242 S'egli è ch n' dura pietra alcun somigli 70, 178, 299
111 S'egli è, donna, che puoi 299
210 Se gli occhi aperti mie fur vita e pace 139
140 Se l'alma al fin ritorna 43, 49, 122, 193, 226, 307
126 Se l'alma è ver, dal suo corpo disciolta, 235
191 Se l'alma vive del suo corpo fora, 139
165 Se 'il commodo degli occhi alcun constringe 32, 300
244 Se 'l duol fa pur, com'alcun dice, bello, 194, 299–300
122 Se 'l foco al tutto nuoce, 180, 275
77 Se 'l foco fusse alla bellezza equale 273
64 Se 'l foco il sasso rompe e 'l ferro squaglia, 50, 274
58 Se l'immortal desio, c'alza e corregge 209
46 Se 'l mie rozzo martello i duri sassi 50, 63, 67
228 Se 'l mondo il corpo e l'alma il ciel ne presta 139–40
128 Se 'l timor della morte 51, 216
261 Se 'l troppo indugio ha più grazia e ventura 287
297 Se lungo spazio del trist'uso e folle 218
245 Se 'l volto di ch'i' parlo, di costei, 45
205 Se morte ha di virtù qui 'l primo fiore 306
72 Se nel volto per gli occhi il cor si vede, 95, 123, 125, 127, 210, 247, 322
88 Sento d'un foco un freddo aspetto acceso 35, 57, 191, 247
137 Se per gioir pur brami affanni e pianti, 29, 113, 300

213	Sepulto è qui quel Braccio, che Dio volse	72, 328
195	Se qui cent'anni t'han tolto due ore,	96–97, 139
179	Se qui son chiusi i begli occhi e sepolti	50, 136, 139
273	Se sempre è solo e un quel che sol muove	41, 65, 123
192	S'è ver, com'è, che dopo il corpo viva,	5, 31, 75, 139, 143, 299
211	Se, vivo al mondo, d'alcun vita fui	139–40
63	Sì amico al freddo sasso è 'l foco interno	52, 273
61	S'i' avessi creduto al primo sguardo	54, 276–77, 325
84	Sì come nella penna e nell'inchiostro	22, 65–66, 72, 230
152	Sì come per levar, donna, si pone	49, 61, 64, 274
96	Sì come secco legno in foco ardente	210
253	S'i' fussi stato ne' prim'anni accorto	10, 182, 218, 278
200	S'i' fu' già vivo, tu sol, pietra, il sai,	39, 53, 139, 143, 306
A 31	Signore, io fallo e veggio el mio fallire,	320–21
6	Signor, se vero è alcun proverbio antico,	13, 42, 52, 56, 90, 106–107, 162, 182, 253, 299, 302
57	S'i' vivo più di chi più m'arde e cuoce,	51, 193
240	Sol d'una pietra viva	68, 339
2	Sol io ardendo all'ombra mi rimango	8, 182, 193, 215
	Sol perchè tuo' bellezze al mondo sieno	79, 82
62	Sol pur col foco il fabbro il ferro stende	47–48, 52, 71, 230, 272–73
131	Sotto duo belle ciglia	57, 158, 277, 305
170	Spargendo gran bellezza ardente foco	52, 273
93	Spargendo il senso il troppo ardor cocente	4
41	Spirto ben nato, in cu 'si specchia e vede	79, 323
59	S'un casto amor, s'una pietà superna,	50, 119, 186–87, 233, 322, 341
125	Tanto di sé promette	216
234	Tanto non è, quante da te non viene,	41, 200, 278
154	Tanto sopra me stesso	197
246	Te sola del mie mal contenta veggio,	23, 214
272	Tornami al tempo, allor che lenta e sciolta	116, 217, 277, 306
20	Tu ha' 'l viso più dolce che la sapa,	15, 28, 43, 76, 81, 92, 179, 203, 206, 235, 269, 277, 327
270	Tu mi da' di quel c'ognor t'avanza	195
60	Tu sa' ch'i' so, signor mie, che tu sai	28, 207, 301
A 33	un'altra sera, ché stasera piove,	254
68	Un gigante v'è ancor, d'altezza tanta	56, 105, 166–69, 247, 302

235	Un uomo in una donna, anzi un dio	45, 196, 198
A 22	Valle locus clausa toto mihi nullus in orbe	212, 282, 319
89	Veggio co' be' vostr'occhi un dolce lume	52, 187, 232–33, 337, 341
83	Veggio nel tuo bel viso, signor mio,	48, 76, 78, 145, 207, 230–31, 309
32	Vivo al peccato, a me morendo vivo;	42, 50–51, 107, 119, 151, 169, 225, 309
56	Vivo della mie morte, e se ben guardo,	193
87	Vorrei voler, Signor, quel ch'io non voglio:	9, 28, 41, 45, 52, 54, 57, 123, 165, 225, 295, 328

I. *Michelangelo: Pen sketch of woman with sagging breasts, fica gesture, and coiffed head of the artist.*

(*Archivio Buonarroti, folio 40 B vo.*)

(*See pp.* 89, 172, 178, 201.)

II. *Michelangelo: Autograph of extendea sonnet, "I' o gia facto un gozo in questo stento," with "Self-Portrait."*

(*Archivio Buonarroti, XIII, folio 6a.*)

(*See pp.* 15, 28, 48, 91-92, 158, 246, 259, 268, 277.)

Giunto e gial corso della uita mia
per tempestoso mar cō fragil barca
al comũ porto oua render si uarca
~~cahon~~
Conto eragio dognio pra falsa eria
ō de laffectuosa fātasia
chebbe larte peridole monarca
Conosco or bē quantera derror carca
e quel cognuō cōtral suo bē desia

I pēsier mie gia demie dammi lieti
che fienor ca duo morte mauicino
luna me certa e laltra mi minaccia

Ne pinger ne scolpir fie piu che quieti
lanima uolta aquellamor diuino
Caperse ī Croce ce aprendo noi le braccia

III. *Copy of Michelangelo's sonnet, "Giunto è gia 'l corso della uita mia."*
(*Vatican, latino* 3211, *folio* 24*a*.)
(*See pp.* 44, 47, 85, 106, 120-21, 141, 219, 277, 296.)